A History of
Modern Psychology

Second Edition

A History of Modern Psychology

Second Edition

Duane Schultz
American University

Academic Press   *New York   San Francisco   London*
A Subsidiary of Harcourt Brace Jovanovich, Publishers

6/22/75

ACADEMIC PRESS, INC.
111 Fifth Avenue, New York, New York 10003

United Kingdom Edition published by
ACADEMIC PRESS, INC. (LONDON) LTD.
24/28 Oval Road, London NW1

Library of Congress Cataloging in Publication Data

Schultz, Duane P
     A history of modern psychology.

     Includes bibliographies.
     1.   Psychology–History.   I.   Title.   [DNLM: 1.   Psy-
chology–History.   BF95 S387h]
BF95.S35 1975   150'.19   74-10197
ISBN 0–12–633042–5

PRINTED IN THE UNITED STATES OF AMERICA

To My Parents

Contents

Preface   **xv**

1 The Study of the History of Psychology   **1**

Introduction   1
The Physiological Influence   3
The Relevance of the Past for the Present   3
Where Does the History of Psychology Begin?   6
The Development of Schools of Thought in Psychology   7
Conceptions of Scientific History:
Personalistic and Naturalistic   10

2 Direct Philosophical Influences on Psychology   **15**

The Spirit of Mechanism: The Universe as a Machine   15
The Beginnings of Modern Science: Descartes (1596–1650)   17

*The Life of Descartes   The Contributions
of Descartes*

British Empiricism and Associationism   23

*John Locke (1632–1704)   George Berkeley
(1685–1753)   David Hume (1711–1776)
David Hartley (1705–1757)   James Mill
(1773–1836)*

Contributions of Empiricism to Psychology   34

3   Physiological Influences on Psychology   37

Developments in Early Physiology: An Overview   37

The Beginnings of Experimental Psychology   40

*Why Germany?   Hermann von Helmholtz
(1821–1894)   Ernst Weber (1795–1878)
Gustav Theodor Fechner (1801–1887)*

The Formal Founding of the New Science   52

A Note on "Founding"   53

**4   The New Psychology:
Structuralism and Its Early Opponents   55**

An Overview of Structuralism   55

Wilhelm Wundt (1832–1920)   56

*The Life of Wundt   The Wundtian System
The Research Topics of the Leipzig Laboratory
In Retrospect*

Other Early European Psychologists   68

*Hermann Ebbinghaus (1850–1909)   George
Elias Müller (1850–1934)   Franz Brentano
(1838–1917)   Carl Stumpf (1848–1936)   Oswald
Külpe (1862–1915)*

Comment   80

5   Structuralism: Final Form   83

Edward Bradford Titchener (1867–1927)   83

*The Life of Titchener   Titchener's
Systematic Position*

Original Source Material on Structuralism:
From *A Text-Book of Psychology* by E. B. Titchener   91

The Fate of Structuralism   102

*Criticisms of Structuralism   Contributions
of Structuralism*

6   Functionalism: Antecedent Influences   107

What Is Functionalism?   107

Historical Overview of Functionalism   108

The Evolution Revolution: Charles Darwin (1809–1882)   109

*The Life of Darwin   The Works of Darwin
The Influence of Darwin upon Psychology*

Individual Differences: Sir Francis Galton (1822–1911)   115

*The Life of Galton   The Works of Galton
Comment*

Animal Psychology   124

A Final Note   125

7   Functionalism: American Pioneers   127

"Only in America"   127

Anticipator of Functional Psychology:
William James (1842–1910)   128

*The Life of James   The Contributions of James
Comment*

G. Stanley Hall (1844–1924)   139

The Life of Hall   The Works of Hall   Comment

James McKeen Cattell (1860–1944)   144

*The Life of Cattell   The Works of Cattell
Comment*

Ganz Amerikanisch   149

8   Functionalism: Formal Development   153

The Founding of Functionalism   153

The Chicago School   154

*John Dewey (1859–1952)   James Rowland
Angell (1869–1949)   Harvey A. Carr (1873–1954)*

Original Source Material on Functionalism:
From *Psychology* by H. A. Carr   161

Functionalism at Columbia:
Robert Sessions Woodworth (1869–1962)   168

Criticisms of Functionalism   170

Contributions of Functionalism   172

9   Behaviorism: Antecedent Influences   **175**

Introduction   175

Animal Psychology   178

Edward Lee Thorndike (1874–1949)   179
   *The Life of Thorndike   Thorndike's
   Connectionism   Comment*

Ivan Petrovitch Pavlov (1849–1936)   183
   The Life of Pavlov   Pavlov's Research   Comment

Vladimir M. Bekhterev (1857–1927)   189

Comment   190

Functionalism   191

10   Behaviorism: The Beginning   **195**

Introduction: John B. Watson (1878–1958)   195

Original Source Material on Behaviorism:
From "Psychology as the Behaviorist Views
It" by J. B. Watson   199
   Comment

The Methods of Behaviorism   207

The Subject Matter of Behaviorism   210

Specific Views and Concepts   211
   Instinct   Learning   Emotion   Thought

Watson's Popular Appeal   216

A Final Note   218

Criticisms of Watsonian Behaviorism   218

Contributions of Watsonian Behaviorism   221

11   Behaviorism: After the Founding   223

Early Behaviorists   223
> *Edwin B. Holt (1873–1946)   Albert P. Weiss*
> *(1879–1931)   Karl Lashley (1890–1958)*

The Influence of Operationism   227

More Recent Behaviorists   229
> *Edward Chace Tolman (1886–1959)   Edwin Ray*
> *Guthrie (1886–1959)   Clark Leonard Hull*
> *(1884–1952)   Burrhus Frederick Skinner (1904–   )*

Concluding Commentary on Behaviorism   256

12   Gestalt Psychology   259

Introduction   259

Antecedent Influences   262

The Founding of Gestalt Psychology   265
> *Max Wertheimer (1880–1943)   Kurt Koffka*
> *(1886–1941)   Wolfgang Köhler (1887–1967)*

The Nature of the Gestalt Revolt   269

Original Source Material on Gestalt Psychology:
From "Gestalt Theory" by Max Wertheimer   271

Wertheimer's Principles of Organization   277

Gestalt Principles of Learning   278
> *The Mentality of Apes: Köhler   Productive*
> *Thinking: Wertheimer*

The Principle of Isomorphism   282

The Reaction in America   283

Post-Founding Developments   284

*The Spread of Gestalt Psychology after the
Founding   Field Theory: Kurt Lewin (1890–1947)
Lewin and Social Psychology*

Criticisms of Gestalt Psychology   290

Contributions of Gestalt Psychology   291

13   Psychoanalysis: The Beginnings   **295**

Introduction   295

Historical Antecedents   296

*Early Theories of the Unconscious   The Influence
from Psychopathology   Other Sources
of Influence*

Sigmund Freud (1856–1939) and the
Development of Psychoanalysis   302

Psychoanalysis as a Method of Treatment   310

Freud's Method of Research   312

Psychoanalysis as a System of Personality   313

*The Unconscious and Conscious Aspects of
Personality   Instincts   Anxiety   Stages of
Personality Development*

Mechanism and Determinism in Freud's System   318

Early Conflicts between Psychology and Psychoanalysis   319

Criticisms of Psychoanalysis   321

Contributions of Psychoanalysis   323

14   Psychoanalysis: After the Founding   **327**

Carl Gustav Jung (1875–1961)   327

*The Life of Jung   Jung's System: Analytical
Psychology   The Structure of Personality
Personality Development   Introversion–
Extraversion   Word Association   Comment*

Social–Psychological Theories in
Psychoanalysis: The *Zeitgeist* Strikes Again   334

Alfred Adler (1870–1937): Individual
Psychology   335
>   *The Life of Adler   Adler's Systematic Position
>   Striving for Superiority   Inferiority Feelings and
>   Compensation   Style of Life   The Creative
>   Self   Order of Birth   Comment*

Karen Horney (1885–1952)   341
>   *Horney's System   Horney's Theory of Neurosis
>   Comment*

Erich Fromm (1900–   )   344
>   *Comment*

Critique of the Social–Psychological Theories   347

The Mainstream after Freud   348

15   Epilogue: More Recent Developments   **353**

The Dissolution of the Schools   354

Contemporary American Psychology   356
>   *Methods   Major Research Areas
>   Professionalization*

Contemporary Psychology in Other Countries   367
>   *Germany   England   Soviet Union   Japan
>   Other Countries*

The Future: Humanistic Psychology?   370

References   377

Index   387

Preface

This new edition retains the same format, scope, and focus as the earlier one. There are four basic premises that continue to underlie and characterize its approach.

First, our discussion of the history of psychology concentrates on the last century of development in the field. It does not attempt to cover earlier philosophical thought, except where such thought relates directly to the establishment of psychology as a separate discipline—as is the case, for example, with the British empiricists.

In short, the book is a history of modern psychology, not of both psychology and all the work in philosophy that preceded it.

The second premise is defined by one of the most striking and consistent characteristics of the century-old history of modern psychology: the continuous development and decline of different systematic positions or schools of thought. A definite continuity of development can be seen from each of these schools of thought to the one that subsequently replaced it. This orderly and meaningful developmental pattern is, I believe, the most useful framework within which to understand the history of psychology.

Our discussion will demonstrate how each system began as a revolt against the existing order, and how each, in turn, inspired a revolution that opposed and eventually replaced (or at least supplemented) the older system. Specific individuals are discussed within the context of the systematic position they helped to formulate, advance, or destroy.

Each of the systematic positions is discussed in terms of three stages or levels of development: (1) its historical antecedents or precursors, (2) the formal founding and development, and (3) later influence of the school.

Contemporary influences on the various systems are discussed in order to demonstrate the continuity of development from the old to the new, i.e., how psychology as we know it today evolved from these earlier points of view.

Discussion of each school concludes with both criticisms and contributions of the position so that students can see the weaknesses of each system as well as their points of influence on psychology's later development.

The third premise is concerned with the important—indeed, determining—influence of the *Zeitgeist* on each school of thought. The development and decline of each systematic position are discussed in terms of the general intellectual and social climate of the era or region in which it occurred.

Using this approach, the student is able to see that changes in psychological thinking were influenced and augmented by broader changes in man's attitudes toward himself and the world around him.

The final premise has to do with the general style of writing and level of difficulty of the book. It is written expressly for the undergraduate student's initial exposure to the history of his discipline, and not for the instructor teaching the course. Too many undergraduate textbooks are written in the style of an article for the *Psychological Bulletin* or *Psychological Review*, intended for one's peers. As a result, they appear dull, uninspiring, and pedantic to the beginning undergraduate.

Without sacrificing content, I have tried to tell the story of psychology's development and progress in interesting—and perhaps even entertaining—fashion, rather than reporting a catalog or encyclopedia of dates, names, articles, and events. I have tried to present the history of psychology as I do in the classroom.

Having the opportunity to revise the book has been a stimulating, enjoyable, and rewarding task. Aside from the opportunity to correct errors and rephrase difficult concepts, such a revision allows the chance to incorporate the results of additional years of study in the field and to reflect feedback from the instructors and students who used the first edition. The changes range from the insertion of a single (hopefully clarifying) word to the addition of entire new sections.

Major changes include the following: a greater emphasis on the spirit of mechanism as it influenced the beginnings of the new psychology; the continuing influence of mechanism through the century of systems covered; new material on the lives and work of many individuals; and (perhaps reflecting the *Zeitgeist*) a greatly expanded discussion of B. F. Skinner, more attention to psychology in other countries, and expanded coverage of the so-called Third Force movement.

The chapter dealing with associationism has been elmiinated because it now seems clear to me that it was not a movement of protest and opposition comparable to, say, behaviorism or Gestalt psychology. Rather, it is a topic of study like perception or motivation. I do not believe there were any flag-waving members of a "school" of associationism, as there were structuralists or psychoanalysts.

Thorndike and Pavlov, the two primary figures in the chapter formerly dealing with associationism, are now discussed, more appropriately, as antecedents of behaviorism where their influence on the work of J. B. Watson is clearly seen.

Three of the four original source materials are new to this edition—Titchener, Carr, and Wertheimer. Watson's classic article remains. I believe the addition of such articles by psychology's "great men" in the contexts of the discussions of their positions is of value to the student. It provides the opportunity to read an individual's systematic position in the great man's own words, and presents what students of psychology were reading in an earlier time.

The new source materials were written at a level more appropriate for undergraduate students, selected from introductory textbooks rather than journal articles.

Finally, I have tried to relate each school of thought not only to its past as well as contemporaneous developments, but also to place each one in the total context of evolving ideas in psychology and to show temporal and geographical relationships among them.

I am grateful to my colleague, Professor George Windholz, who read and reread every chapter and offered the benefit of his rigorous scholarship and passion for precision. The book owes a great debt to his energetic exclamations, questions, and criticisms which mark the margins of my rough draft.

My greatest debt remains to my wife, Sydney Ellen, for her cogent criticisms, enthusiasm, patience, and expert handling of the myriad details that miraculously turn a messy sheaf of handwritten pages into a finished book.

D.S.

The application of the experimental method to the problem of mind is the great outstanding event in the history of the study of the mind, an event to which no other is comparable.

E. G. Boring

1

The Study of
the History of Psychology

Introduction

The antecedents of modern psychology can be traced to the earliest
of inquiring minds. Man seems always to have been fascinated by his
own behavior, and ruminations on human nature and conduct fill many
philosophical and theological volumes. Broadly speaking, the same kinds
of questions now asked about the nature of man were asked centuries
ago. The important difference between modern psychology and its intellectual precursors is not so much the kinds of questions asked as the
methods used to seek the answers.

Until the last quarter of the nineteenth century, man attempted to
study himself by speculation, intuition, and generalization from his own
experiences. The major change or breakthrough occurred when man
tried to answer his questions about human nature by using the tools
and methods of science, which had already been demonstrated successful
in answering questions in the natural sciences. When man tried to use
carefully controlled observation and experimentation to study human
nature, then and only then did psychology begin to attain some independence from its philosophical antecedents.

In order to break away from philosophy, psychology had to develop
a more precise and objective way of dealing with its problems than

1

its forebears had used. Much of the history of psychology after its break with philosophy involves, as we shall see, the continuing refinement of its tools, techniques, and methods of study in order to achieve increased precision and objectivity in both its answers and questions.

The first sign of a distinct field of inquiry known as psychology, then, was the adoption, in the last quarter of the nineteenth century, of the scientific method as the means for attempting to solve its problems. During that period there were several formal indications that psychology was beginning to flourish. In 1879[1] in Leipzig, Germany, Wilhelm Wundt established what is generally considered to be the first psychological laboratory in the world. Wundt also established, in 1881, a journal, *Philosophische Studien*, considered to be the first journal of psychology containing experimental reports. In 1888, the University of Pennsylvania appointed James McKeen Cattell as Professor of Psychology, the first professorship in psychology in the world. Prior to that time, psychologists received appointments in departments of philosophy. With Cattell's appointment, however, psychology received formal recognition in academic circles of its independence from philosophy. In 1887, G. Stanley Hall established the *American Journal of Psychology*, the first American psychology journal.

Between 1880 and 1895, dramatic and sweeping changes took place in psychology in the United States. During that time, 24 psychological laboratories and 3 psychology journals were established. In 1892, the first scientific organization of psychologists, the American Psychological Association, was founded (its membership now exceeds 35,000).

In 1908, psychology was defined by William McDougall as the "science of behavior," apparently for the first time. Thus, by the early part of the twentieth century, psychology had succeeded in gaining its independence from philosophy, developing laboratories in which to use the methods of science, establishing its own scientific organization, and giving itself a formal definition as a science—the science of behavior.

---

[1] There is some dispute as to whether 1875 or 1879 was the founding year for the first experimental laboratory. Boring (1963) noted that Wundt was given space for experimental demonstrations in 1875, but it was not until 1879 that the space was used for independent research. R. I. Watson (1971) accorded the honor to 1875, while other sources (Chaplin & Krawiec, 1968; Flugel & West, 1964; Miller & Buckhout, 1973; Murphy & Kovach, 1972; Peters, 1965) agreed on 1879. James McKeen Cattell (1928), who studied under Wundt, noted that the 50th anniversary of the founding of the laboratory was celebrated in Leipzig in 1926! Boring and Watson noted (as did other sources) that 1875 also saw William James equipping a small laboratory at Harvard. The significance of the event, however, is far more important than the precise date on which it occurred.

The Physiological Influence

Much of psychology's heritage comes from philosophy. However, while early philosophers were preparing the way for an experimental attack on the functioning of the mind, another group of scholars was independently approaching some of the same problems from an entirely different direction. Early physiologists were making great strides toward understanding the bodily mechanisms underlying the mental processes. Obviously, the methods of study of the physiologists differed markedly from those of the philosophers. The eventual union of these disparate disciplines produced a field of study in which, at least in the more formative years, an attempt was made to preserve the conflicting traditions and beliefs of both. Fortunately, psychology eventually succeeded in attaining an identity and stature of its own.

During the period just prior to the emergence of psychology as an experimental science (from 1800 through the 1870s), physiologists were working on problems of great relevance to psychology. In Chapter 3 we will examine the work of some of these physiological precursors to psychology and the research techniques they developed which were to be used by the new science.

The Relevance of the Past for the Present

This section might aptly be entitled, "Why study the history of psychology?" This is a legitimate question to ask when beginning any new course of study. How will your knowledge of and competence in psychology be enhanced by a study of the history of the field? The methods of present-day psychology certainly bear little formal resemblance to those used in the early psychological laboratories and even less resemblance to the prescientific philosophical approach. Indeed, the development of psychology has been so dynamic that psychology of only 25 years ago seems remote. Will knowledge of the history of the field produce a better understanding of today's psychology? Considering the vast amount of material to be studied in psychology, is it worth the effort to know what happened 50 or 100 years ago?

We consider, first, evidence of psychologists' own interest in the history of their field, on the assumption that this reflects their feelings about the importance of the study of the history of psychology. One such point of evidence is that your psychology department offers the course you are now taking. Most psychology departments give such a course, and some think it important enough to require it for undergraduate and graduate degrees (Nance, 1962). Most other science departments do not offer courses in the history of their fields. A general course in the history of science is sometimes offered by the humanities division of a university, but it is seldom taught by a scientist. Psychologists feel that the history of psychology is a useful addition to their curriculum.

In 1958, a committee of the American Psychological Association reported on a survey of graduate departments in psychology in American universities. The survey sought to determine which courses composed an ideal undergraduate curriculum for prospective graduate students. The results revealed that History of Psychology and Schools and Systems were rated among the top 10 ideal courses for preparing prospective graduate students in psychology (American Psychological Association, 1958a). In 1971, a survey of graduate psychology departments in the United States and Canada revealed that *A History of Experimental Psychology* by the master historian of psychology, the late E. G. Boring, was one of a few books recommended consistently since 1953 (Solso, 1971).

At the professional level there are definite signs of growing interest among psychologists in the history of psychology. In 1965, the multi-area journal, the *Journal of the History of the Behavioral Sciences,* under the editorship of a psychologist, was begun. Also in 1965, the Archives of the History of American Psychology was established, at the University of Akron (Ohio), to serve the needs of scholars by collecting and preserving source materials of the history of psychology. The Division of the History of Psychology (Division 26) was formed in the American Psychological Association in 1966, and in 1969 the International Society for the History of the Behavioral and Social Sciences was established. Graduate work in the history of psychology is being offered at the University of New Hampshire under the directorship of Robert Watson. Textbooks such as this one, and professional monographs dealing with aspects of psychology's history, appear frequently, reflecting the importance that psychologists attribute to the study of the history of psychology.

Why is psychology unique among the sciences in its expression of interest in its own background? It has been suggested that of all the sciences, psychology is unique in that it has attracted man's attention and interest for centuries. From the beginnings of recorded time, man has attempted to study and understand his own behavior and has reached many respectable insights and conclusions. Of course, a number of inaccuracies and myths about human nature have also survived from man's early attempts to understand himself. Because of man's extreme complexity, many questions asked about human nature centuries ago are still asked, in one form or another. There is, then, a continuity of problems and questions (if not of methods) in psychology that is not found in the other sciences. Thus, there exists a more immediately visible and tangible link with the past in psychology, a connection that many psychologists find interesting to explore.

Does the knowledge of psychology's past contribute to an understanding of psychology's present? Boring has said that without a degree of historical sophistication in his field, the psychologist

> sees the present in distorted perspective, . . . mistakes old facts and old views for new, and . . . remains unable to evaluate the significance of new movements and methods. In this matter I can hardly state my faith too strongly. A psychological sophistication that contains no component of historical orientation seems to me to be no sophistication at all [1950, p. ix].[2]

Since scientific facts or data are most meaningful when considered in the light of earlier related facts or data, modern psychology is most meaningful when related to its past developments.

The scientist must also be concerned with the history of his field in order to avoid repeating the past. As we shall see, the history of science contains instances of supposedly new discoveries and insights that, as it turned out, had been anticipated years earlier—the new discovery being made in ignorance of the earlier work.

Knowledge of the past might help predict the future. Boring took issue with this idea, noting that, "The past is not a crystal ball [1963, p. 5]"in which one may foresee the future. Esper (1964), however, argued strongly for the position that the past is the only basis on which one may intelligently plan for the future. Since one purpose of the study of the history of a science is to better understand the present, Esper asked what the functional significance of this understanding would be if not to provide some preparation for the future.

Rollo May (1967) suggested that only through the study of history can we see how cultural and social forces have molded the attitudes that have gone into framing psychology as we know it today. Our methods, our theories, and, indeed, our selves are the products of forces and traditions evolving over time. If we are not aware of these forces, "we shall have cut ourselves off from our very roots. To cut off history is to sever our arterial link with humanity [p. 55]."

Wertheimer (1970) suggested two additional reasons for the study of the history of psychology. First, the complexity and vastness of contemporary psychology may tend to confuse students in their attempts to relate the various concepts, areas, and approaches to one another. An

[2] This and all subsequent quotations credited to Boring, 1950 are from Edward G. Boring, *A History of Experimental Psychology*, 2nd ed., © 1950. Reprinted by permission of Prentice-Hall, Inc., Englewood Cliffs, New Jersey.

understanding of the history of psychology can help one to integrate the many areas and subareas that compose modern psychology and to recognize the existence of interrelationships between the various facts and theories. A reaction often reported by students at the end of the course is an awareness of how all the different, seemingly unrelated, topics in psychology tie together. They are inextricably related to one another through the pattern of their historical development.

Wertheimer's second reason, probably the best of all those cited, is sheer intellectual curiosity. The study of history, he suggested, really needs no defense or attempt at justification. The fascination of the story is reward enough. The chapters that follow contain much in the way of human drama, revolutionary ideas and movements, and despair-filled defeats of individuals and their ideas.

Upon completing this course, you will hopefully have gained some appreciation of the great progress that has been made in knowledge and methodology in the comparatively short time since psychology became an independent discipline. There were false starts and mistakes, but over-all there is a thread of continuity moving toward increasing precision and objectivity in subject matter and techniques, a goal toward which psychology as a science has always striven, strengthened by its past mistakes and victories alike.

Where Does the History of Psychology Begin?

A second question to be answered in starting a course in the history of psychology is where to begin the coverage. We could, as do some history of psychology textbooks, begin with the Greek philosophers—Hippocrates, Plato, Aristotle, among others—five centuries before the birth of Christ.

As was noted earlier, man has always inquired into his own nature, and we could spend the entire semester (or, just as easily, the academic year) probing these early philosophical inquiries into the nature of man. But to do so would, in our opinion, be of limited help in understanding the complex issues that define and divide psychology today. And that understanding is the ultimate purpose of this course.

In light of this goal, then, the proper starting point for the history of psychology is that time, roughly a century ago, when psychology became a truly independent discipline with its own unique methods of inquiry and theoretical rationale.

There is no denying that the prescientific scholars speculated on problems concerning the nature of man. Certainly they did, but their influence on the later development of psychology as a separate and primarily experimental science is quite limited.

Psychology is truly a product of the nineteenth and twentieth centuries, for only in the last 100 years have psychologists defined the subject matter and established its foundation, thus asserting psychology's independence from philosophy. While the early philosophers concerned themselves with problems that are of general and current interest, they approached these problems in a vastly different manner. They were not psychologists, at least not as we define the term today, and we will cover their ideas only where they relate directly to the establishment of psychology as a separate discipline.

However, our discussion of the history of psychology does include the more immediate philosophical context. Psychology became a distinct and experimental science at a time when European thought was imbued with the spirit of positivism, empiricism, and materialism. The idea that the methods of science could be applied to mental phenomena is inherited from philosophical notions of the seventeenth to nineteenth centuries, and that exciting era is the starting point for our discussion of the history of modern psychology.

The Development of Schools of Thought in Psychology

Psychology evolved as a separate scientific discipline in the last quarter of the nineteenth century. In the initial years, the direction of the new psychology was influenced profoundly by one man, Wilhelm Wundt, who had very definite ideas as to what form this new science (*his* new science) should take. He alone determined the subject matter, proper method of research, topics on which research should be performed, and goals of the new science. He was guided, or at least strongly influenced, of course, by the spirit of the times in which he lived and the then current thinking in philosophy and physiology. Nevertheless, it was Wundt in his role as agent of the times who drew together various lines of thought and, through the force of his personality and his intensive and exacting writing and research, fashioned the new psychology. He was a compelling and forceful agent of the inevitable. And so, for a time, psychology was molded in his image.

In a few years, however, the situation in psychology changed radically, and a great deal of controversy and cleavage developed among the growing number of psychologists. The spirit of the times was changing, as it always is, and new ideas were forming in other sciences as well as in the general culture. Reflecting these new currents of thought, some psychologists took issue with Wundt's version of psychology and proposed their own views. As a result, by the turn of the century, several different systematic positions or schools of thought were in existence.

The term "school" refers to a group of psychologists who became associated ideologically, and sometimes geographically, with the leader of a movement. For the most part, the members of a school worked on common problems and shared a common theoretical or systematic orientation.

The emergence of different schools of thought and their subsequent decline is one of the most striking characteristics of the history of psychology. The phenomenon is not unique to psychology, however, for all the sciences experienced a similar period early in their respective histories when competing schools of thought divided the field of study (Kuhn, 1970).

Each of these schools was a movement of protest, indeed a rebellion, against the prevailing systematic position. Each pointed out what it saw as the shortcomings and failures of the older point of view and each presented new definitions, concepts, and research strategies designed to correct the perceived weaknesses. When a new school of thought captured the scientific community's attention, it resulted in the rejection of the once honored position. These intellectual combats between incompatible positions (the old and the new) were fought with feverish tenacity on both sides.

Very often, the leaders of the older school were never wholly converted to the new school of thought. Usually older in years, these leaders were too deeply committed to their position, intellectually as well as emotionally, to change. Many of their adherents, particularly the younger, hence less committed, became converts to the new position, while others continued to cling to the old traditions, working in increasing isolation and loneliness. As Boring (1950) commented:

> What would happen to science if its great men did not eventually die, no one can guess. What does happen is that a new man takes up the work of an older man without the constraint of inertia from his past, that he thinks, works and writes more simply and directly, and that thus from the old he creates something new that gradually itself accumulates inertia [p. 399].

In a blunter statement, the physicist, Max Planck, wrote: "New scientific truth does not triumph by convincing its opponents and making them see the light, but rather because its opponents eventually die [1949, p. 33]."

Thus, several different schools of thought developed in the early years of psychology, each one an effective protest against what had gone before. Each new school used its older opponent as a base from which to push to gain momentum. Each position proclaimed proudly and loudly what it was not, that is, how it differed from the older theoretical system. As the new system developed and grew in numbers and influence, it served to inspire opposition and the whole combative process began anew. What was once a pioneering, aggressive revolution became, with success, the older, less flexible, tradition, which then succumbed to the vigorous force of a new youthful movement.

Their success killed them as movements. A movement feeds on opposition, and when it has destroyed its opposition, the passion and ardor of the once new movement die.

Even though the dominance of at least some of these schools was only temporary in nature, each played a vital role in the development of psychology. Their influence can be seen in contemporary psychology even though the psychology of today bears little similarity to the earlier systems (for new doctrines again have replaced the old). Heidbreder (1933) compared the role of the schools of psychological thought to that of the scaffolding used in erecting a tall structure. Without the scaffolding from which to work, the building could not be erected. And yet, the scaffolding does not remain—it is torn down when it is no longer needed. In analogous fashion, the structure of today's psychology has been built within the general framework and guidelines established by the schools.

We cannot look on any of the schools as complete accounts of scientific fact; they are not finished products in any sense. Rather, they provided the tools, methods, and conceptual schemes that psychology has used to accumulate and organize a body of scientific fact. This is not meant to imply that the psychology of today is in a finished form. New guidelines have replaced the schools but nothing guarantees their permanence in the evolutionary process of science-building. The schools of psychology, therefore, were temporary but very necessary stages in the development of psychology.

It is in terms of the historical development of these systems—these revolutions—that the exciting advance of psychology can best be understood. Individuals stand out as having made pioneering pronouncements and contributions, but their full significance is most notable when considered in the context of the ideas that preceded theirs (on which they often built) and the work that followed them.

After a detailed look at the beginnings of experimental psychology (Chapters 2 and 3), we will consider each of the major psychological schools at three different levels: (*1*) the prescientific development of the position, including the work of earlier scholars who developed their insights without the use of the experimental method; (*2*) the early attempts to attack particular problems using the methods of science; and (*3*) the formal establishment of each school and its influence on the contemporary psychological scene.

A schematic representation of the historical development of the various psychological systems, in terms of selected great men, is given in Table 1.1. The table serves to indicate the noteworthy figures in each school and the relative periods of their contributions. The order of the schools in the table does not represent any sort of ranking in terms of importance.

Conceptions of Scientific History: Personalistic and Naturalistic

There are two approaches that can be taken to a study of scientific history: the personalistic or "great man" theory and the naturalistic theory. The great man conception of scientific history derives from the standpoint of the massive achievements and contributions of certain individuals. According to this point of view, all progress and change are directly attributable to the will and force of unique "great men" who alone charted and changed the course of history. A Napoleon, a Hitler, or, in science, a Darwin were, so this theory goes, the prime movers and shapers of great events. The theory implies that the great events might not have happened had it not been for the appearance of the great men. The theory says in effect: The man makes the times.

At first glance, it appears obvious that science is indeed the work of extremely creative and intelligent people who alone determined its direction. We often define an era by the name of the great man whose discoveries marked the period; we talk about physics "after Einstein," psychology "before Watson," and so on.

It is readily apparent, both in science and in the general culture, that individuals have produced dramatic, sometimes traumatic, changes that have altered the course of history. We have only to think of Hitler or Freud to see the truth of that.

So the great man theory is not wrong, but is it sufficient to fully explain the development of societies or of science? No. There have been too many instances when a would-be great man has failed to change the times; when, as the expression goes, he has been "ahead of his time."

The phrase seems to imply that the "times" may determine whether what the great man is saying will be heeded or ignored, praised or for-

Table 1.1

Historical Development of the Psychological Schools

	1650	1700	1750	1800	1850	1900	1930	1970
Structuralism						Wundt Titchener Brentano Stumpf Külpe		
Functionalism					Darwin Galton	James Dewey Hall Cattell	Angell Carr Woodworth	
Behaviorism	Descartes			Comte	Romanes	Morgan Thorndike Loeb Pavlov	Watson Tolman Holt Lashley	Guthrie Hull Skinner
Gestalt				Kant	Mach	von Ehrenfels	Wertheimer Koffka Köhler	Lewin
Psychoanalysis		Leibnitz		Herbart		Charcot Freud Janet	Adler Jung	Horney Fromm

gotten. The history of science is replete with instances of lack of acceptance of new discoveries or insights at given points in time. Even the greatest of minds (perhaps especially the greatest of minds) have often been constrained by what has been called the *Zeitgeist*—the spirit or intellectual climate of the times. The acceptance and use of a discovery, therefore, may be limited by the dominant patterns of thought in a given culture, region, or era. Thus, an idea that is too novel or too preposterous to gain acceptance in one period of civilization may be accepted readily and easily a generation or perhaps a century later. Slow change seems to be the rule for scientific progress.

Perhaps, then, the notion that the man makes the times is not entirely correct. Perhaps, as the second approach, the naturalistic theory of history, would have it: "The times make the man," or at least make possible the acceptance of what he has to say. Unless the *Zeitgeist* is ready for what the great man has to say, he may not be heard (or he may be laughed at, or burned at the stake—this too may depend on the *Zeitgeist*).

The inhibiting or delaying capacity of the *Zeitgeist* is operative not only at the level of the general culture but within science itself, and its effects are perhaps even more pronounced at this "local" level. There are, in the history of science, many instances of early discoveries that remained dormant for long periods before being recognized and accepted. The concept of conditioning of responses, for example, was first suggested by Robert Whytt in 1763. It was well over 100 years later that Ivan Pavlov expanded these early observations into the basis for a new system of psychology. Mendel's work on genetics was ignored for about 35 years (possibly because of its publication in an obscure journal), before making its impact. A discovery, then, must await its time.

Instances of simultaneous discovery also support the naturalistic theory of history. For example, there have been highly similar discoveries by individuals working far apart geographically and often in complete ignorance of one another's work. Postman (1962) noted that in 1900 three different investigators, working independently (indeed unknown to one another), rediscovered Mendel's work. "If one scientist won't do it, then another will; or if one scientist does it at the wrong time, three others will do it at the right time [Postman, 1962, p. 26]!"

Existing theoretical positions in a field of science can often exert a negative influence by standing in the way of further progress. An existing theory may so thoroughly dominate a discipline that investigation (or even consideration) of a new field of inquiry is inhibited. Existing theories can also influence, indeed determine, the way in which the phenomena or data pertaining to a problem are categorized. This, of course, may prevent the scientist from looking at the data in a new way.

This inhibiting effect of the *Zeitgeist* within science can operate with methods and techniques of investigation as well as with theoretical formulations. And it can also operate with regard to what is considered to be the proper subject matter for investigation. We shall see in later chapters the tendency to focus on consciousness and subjective aspects of man in the early years of scientific psychology. Even as the methods of study began to be more objective and precise, the focus of study continued for a long time to be subjective in nature. Psychology had to wait until the second decade of this century before it finally lost its mind!

The truth probably lies somewhere between the two extremes of the personalistic and naturalistic theories of history. The intellectual climate of the times certainly has played a vital role in facilitating or inhibiting new points of view. Herrnstein and Boring (1965) suggested that modern historical analysis has served to reduce the role of the great man in scientific progress. Virtually every major step forward in science turns out, on historical investigation, to have been anticipated by past discoveries. The new discovery is assigned to the great man whose name it bears because the *Zeitgeist* had prepared the way for its acceptance in his time (rather than earlier), and/or because the great man's demonstrations were more thoroughly convincing than those of his predecessors.

The great men, as Boring (1963) has suggested, have become eponyms, that is, their names have been given to systematic positions or laws, and this process has fostered the belief that the discovery was the result of a sudden insight by these great men. In point of historical fact, the development of the discovery has usually been much more gradual. Eponymy may thus serve to distort history by not taking proper account of the *Zeitgeist* and earlier neglected contributions.

A history of a science such as this one must, it seems, be eponymous, for it chooses representative great men to exemplify the development of the science. What would the history of psychology be like if the names of all the great men were left out? It would still exist, but the historian would be forced to find other labels with which to designate eras, schools of thought, and the like. Also, an eponymous account of the growth of psychology need not distort historical development as long as we remember that the thinking of the great man and the acceptance of what he had to say were strongly influenced by the spirit of the times in which he lived.

It should be clear by now that a history of psychology, to be discussed adequately, must be considered in terms of both theories of history. There are great men—of that history leaves no room for doubt—but there are also great events, and the two intertwine, each influencing the other.

It seems, however, that the *Zeitgeist* plays the major role, for no matter how great is the man, if he is too far out of phase with the climate of the times, he and his insights will die in obscurity.

The great man "grows out of his time and land, and is the product and symbol of events as well as their agent and voice; without some situation requiring a new response his new ideas would be untimely and impracticable [Durant & Durant, 1968, p. 34]."

SUGGESTED FURTHER READINGS

The readings listed at the end of each chapter are recommended for the student who wishes to investigate further a particular issue or individual.

Boring, E. G. *Psychologist at large: An autobiography and selected essays.* New York: Basic Books, 1961.

Boring, E. G. *History, psychology, and science.* New York: Wiley, 1963.

Crutchfield, R. S., & Krech, D. Some guides to the understanding of the history of psychology. In L. Postman (Ed.), *Psychology in the making: Histories of selected research problems.* New York: Knopf, 1962. Pp. 3–27.

Kuhn, T. S. *The structure of scientific revolutions.* (2nd ed.) Chicago, Illinois: Univ. of Chicago Press, 1970.

2

Direct Philosophical
Influences on Psychology

The Spirit of Mechanism:
The Universe as a Machine

In the royal gardens of Europe in the seventeenth century there appeared a whimsical form of amusement among the many marvels of
a truly exciting age. Water, running through underground pipes, operated
mechanical figures that performed a variety of movements, played musical
instruments, and even produced word-like sounds.

These amusements of the aristocracy were reflecting and reinforcing
seventeenth century man's fascination and wonder over the miracle of
the machine. All manner of machines were invented, perfected, and improved for science, industry, and entertainment. Mechanical clocks with
an accuracy never thought possible, pumps, levers, pulleys, and cranes
were developed to serve man; and there seemed to be no limit to the
kinds of machines that could be devised, or the uses to which they could
be put.

You may wonder what this has to do with the history of modern
psychology. It is, after all, a time 200 years prior to the establishment
of psychology as a science, and focuses on technology and physics, disciplines seemingly far removed from the study of man.

The relationship, however, is direct and compelling, for those mechanical figures of the seventeenth century, and the guiding principle they embodied, dictated the direction and form the new psychology, once begun, had to take.

We are dealing with the *Zeitgeist* of the seventeenth to nineteenth centuries, which provided the intellectual soil to nourish the new psychology. The basic idea of the seventeenth century, the philosophy that would nurture the new psychology, was the spirit of *mechanism*—an image of the universe as the "great machine."

This idea originated in physics (or "natural philosophy," as it was then known) as a result of the work of Galileo and, later, Newton. The nature of all that existed in the universe was held to be nothing more than particles of matter in motion. Matter, according to Galileo, was composed of discrete corpuscles or atoms that affected each other by direct contact, as billiard balls do.[1]

If the universe consists simply of atoms in motion, then every physical effect (the movement of each atom) followed from a direct cause (the movement of the atom that struck it), and so should be subject to laws of measurement and calculation, and hence prediction.

This "game of billiards," then, the physical universe, was orderly, lawful, and predictable—like a clock or any other good machine. The physical universe was designed by God with absolute perfection (in the seventeenth century it was still possible to attribute cause and perfection to God, even for scientists), and once one knew the laws by which it worked, it was possible to know how it would behave in the future.

The methods and findings of science were growing apace with technology during this time and the two meshed very effectively. *Observation* and *experimentation* came to be the hallmarks of science and were followed closely by *measurement.*

It began to appear that every function or phenomenon could be defined or described by a number—a characteristic certainly vital to the study of the universe as a machine. The thermometer, barometer, slide rule, micrometer, pendulum clock, and other measuring devices were developed and perfected in this age of the machine, and served to further reinforce the notion that it was possible to measure all aspects of the mechanical universe.

What did the idea of mechanism and the methods of science imply, indeed dictate, for the study of man? Simply stated, it is this: If all

---

[1] Isaac Newton later improved upon the Galilean version of mechanism by positing that movement was communicated not by physical contact, but by attracting and repelling forces. This idea, while vastly important in physics, did not radically change the basic idea of mechanism and the use to which it was put in the new psychology.

the universe is like a machine—orderly, predictable, observable, measurable—why cannot man be considered in the same light?

It was thought then that the nature of man was also mechanical and clocklike. Consequently, the same experimental and quantitative methods which were so successful in exploring the secrets of the physical universe could be applied to the exploration of man.

"Let us then conclude boldly," said the French philosopher de la Mettrie, in 1748, "that man is a machine [1912, pp. 148–149]." This theme became a driving force of the *Zeitgeist,* not only in philosophy, but in all aspects of life, and drastically changed man's image of himself.

And so we see during the seventeenth to nineteenth centuries the growing image of man as a machine, as well as the method by which his nature could be investigated—the *scientific method.* Human beings became machines, the modern world became dominated by the scientific outlook, and all aspects of mankind were seen as subject to mechanical laws.

The Beginnings of Modern Science: Descartes (1596–1650)

As mentioned, the seventeenth century saw far-ranging developments in science. Prior to that time, man looked to the past for his answers, to the works of Aristotle and other ancient scholars, and to the *Bible.* The ruling forces of inquiry were dogma and authority.

In the seventeenth century, however, a new force became dominant—*empiricism*—the observation of nature itself. There had developed a suspicion of knowledge handed down from the past, and of philosophical and theological dogma.

It was, as we have noted, a truly golden era, illuminated by the discoveries and insights of many great men who successfully created (or reflected) a changing atmosphere in which scientific inquiry flourished. They are, therefore, of great importance in the history of science in general, but, for the most part, they were not *directly* related to the evolution of psychology.

One scholar, however, did contribute directly to the history of modern psychology; more than anyone else, he freed inquiry from the rigid theological and traditional dogmas that had dominated it for centuries. "Not since Aristotle had a philosopher constructed a new and influential system of thought that took into account the sum of knowledge, which in two thousand years had grown so significantly [Herrnstein & Boring, 1965, p. 581]." This great man, who symbolizes a transition from the Renaissance to the modern period of science, and who, many feel, represents the beginnings of modern psychology, was René Descartes.

The Life of Descartes

Descartes was born in March 1596, at La Haye in Touraine, France. His father was a councilor at the parliament of Brittany and from him Descartes inherited enough money to support his life of study and travel. That Descartes, unlike others in similar circumstances, did not lead a life of dilettantism was apparently attributable to his sheer genius, curiosity and hunger for knowledge, indifference to dogmatic authority, and constant desire for evidence and proof.

From 1604 to 1612 he was a student at the Jesuit College at La Flèche, where he was educated in the humanities and mathematics and displayed considerable talent, particularly in the latter discipline. Because Descartes' health was frail, the rector, Father Charlet, excused him from the morning religious duties and allowed him to lie in bed, a habit he retained all his life. It was during these mornings abed that he studied his lessons and did his most creative thinking.

After his formal education, he sampled the pleasures of Paris for awhile and then, finding this existence tiresome, went into seclusion to study mathematics. In 1617 he became a gentleman volunteer in the army of Prince Maurice of Nassau (Holland), a seemingly strange thing for one of such a contemplative existence to do.

In November 1619, while still serving in the army, Descartes had a series of dreams which were to radically change his life. As he told it, he spent the day of November 10th alone in a stove-heated room, thinking about certain mathematical and scientific ideas. He fell asleep and in his dreams was, as he interpreted it, rebuked for the idleness of his past life, and visited by the "Spirit of Truth," which took possession of his mind.

This profound experience convinced him that he should devote his life to the notion that mathematics could be applied to all the sciences and thus produce certainty of knowledge. He resolved that no ties of any kind, neither marriage nor friendship, would prevent him from pursuing these insights.

Returning to Paris in 1623, Descartes once again pursued his favorite study of mathematics but found Parisian life too distracting and moved to Holland in 1628. So great was his need for solitude and seclusion that, during the next 20 years in Holland, he lived in 13 different towns and 24 different houses, always keeping his address unknown to all but his most intimate friends, with whom he corresponded voluminously.

His only other apparent requirements, in addition to seclusion, were proximity to a Roman Catholic church and a university.

Most of his important works were written during the years in Holland, where freedom of thought was characteristic during the seventeenth century. His freedom was slightly marred by some degree of attempted religious persecution. At one time, booksellers were forbidden to sell his works, and he was brought before the magistrates to answer charges brought by the theologians of Utrecht and Leyden that he was an atheist and a profligate—serious charges for a devout Catholic. White (1965) noted that Descartes "was condemned by Catholics and Protestants alike. Since Roger Bacon, perhaps, no great thinker had been so completely abased and thwarted by theological oppression [p. 80]."

Descartes' growing fame led to an invitation from Queen Christina of Sweden to instruct her in philosophy. Reluctant though he was to give up his freedom and seclusion, he nonetheless had a great respect for royal prerogative and went to Sweden on the warship sent for him. Apparently the Queen was not a very good student and, to make matters worse, insisted on having her lessons 3 times a week at 5 A.M. in her cold library during an unusually bitter winter. One can imagine Descartes' chagrin at having to be up so early in the morning, much less to have to instruct a not very bright pupil. He withstood the early rising and extreme cold for 4 months before dying of pneumonia on February 11, 1650.

The Contributions of Descartes

Descartes' most important work, from the standpoint of the future development of psychology, is his attempt to resolve the mind–body problem, which had been a controversial issue for centuries. Scholars throughout the ages have argued about how the mind, or purely mental qualities, could be distinguished from the body and all other physical qualities.

The basic and deceptively simple question is this: Are mind and body—the mental world and the material world—two totally different essences or natures?

Ever since the time of Plato, most scholars had taken the so-called *dualistic* position—that mind and body were of different natures. However, the acceptance of that position raises another question: What is the nature of the relationship between mind and body? Does one influence the other, or are they independent of each other?

The position held prior to Descartes' work was that of an essentially one-way interaction. Mind, it was said, could exert an enormous effect on the body, but the body had very little effect on the mind.

As Lowry (1971) suggested, the mind and body were related to one another in the same way as a puppeteer and his puppet are joined together. In this early view, the mind was clearly the puppeteer pulling the strings of the body.

Descartes accepted the dualistic position. Mind and body were indeed different, as he viewed them, but where he deviated from the past was in his definition of the nature of the relationship between the mind and the body.

It is true, Descartes said, that the mind does influence the body. However, he argued, the body can exert a much greater influence on the mind than had been previously supposed; the relationship is one of mutual interaction—a radical idea in the seventeenth century, and fraught with important implications.

The mind (or soul or spirit) was no longer the master of the two entities, no longer the puppeteer functioning almost independently of the body. The body, the material side of man, was viewed in a new and more central manner. What this meant was that certain functions previously attributed to the mind were now considered to be functions of the body.

For example, in the Middle Ages, the mind was held responsible not only for thought and reason, but also for reproduction, perception, and locomotion. Descartes argued that the mind had only one function—thought. All the other processes were functions of the body.

Descartes was the first to offer an approach to the mind–body problem that focused attention on a strictly physical-*psychological* dualism. In so doing, he turned attention away from the study of the soul, in its abstract sense, to the study of the mind and the mental operations it performs. Methods of inquiry changed as a result from metaphysical analysis and deduction to induction and objective observation. Where the soul could only be speculated upon, the mind and its operations could be *observed*.

Mind and body, according to Descartes, then, are two distinct entities. There is no qualitative similarity between the body, or the world of the physical, and the mind. Matter and the body are extended substances that operate by, and can be explained in terms of, mechanical principles. The soul or mind is unextended, free, and insubstantial, or lacking in substance. But the most important point, the idea that was radical and new, was that mind and body, though totally separate and distinct, are capable of interacting in the human organism. The mind can influence the body and the body can influence the mind—the so-called mind–body theory of interactionism.

Let us take a more detailed look at Descartes' conception of the body.

Since the body is made up of physical matter, it must share those characteristics common to all matter: extension in space and capability of movement. If the body is matter, then the laws of physics and mechanics that account for movement and action in the physical world must also be applicable to the body.

The body, when it is considered apart from the mind (and it can be so considered since the two are separate entities), is like a machine, the operation of which can be adequately explained by the mechanical laws of the movement of objects in space. With this line of reasoning, Descartes developed his "physics of physiology [Boring, 1950, p. 162]." Descartes was very strongly influenced by the mechanistic spirit of the age. He saw the mechanically operated figures in the gardens of the day and found a resemblance between them and the operation of the human body. The statues and figures were caused to move in the absence of voluntary action on their part, and this was reflected in Descartes' observation that movements of the body frequently occurred without conscious intention on the part of the individual. From this line of analogizing, he arrived at the idea of the *undulatio reflexa*, a movement not supervised or determined by a will to move. Because he formulated this notion, he is often called the author of the theory of reflex action.

Additional support for the mechanical interpretation of the workings of the human body—one with which Descartes was very familiar—came from the exciting new advances in physiology.

In 1628, Harvey had discovered the gross facts about the circulation of the blood, and much was being discovered about the process of digestion. It was also known that the muscles of the body work in opposing pairs, and that sensation and movement are somehow dependent upon the nerves. Physiological research had taken great strides in understanding the human body, though far from completely. The nerves, for instance, were considered to be hollow tubes through which animal spirits flow. The point of importance, however, is not the accuracy or completeness of the knowledge of human physiology, but rather that it was consonant with a mechanical, physical interpretation of the body. The body was therefore considered to operate like a machine. Since animals did not possess souls, they were considered to be automata, or machines that move themselves. Thus, the difference between man and animals so important to Christian religion was preserved. These views were part of an overall trend toward the notion that the behavior of man is predictable. The mechanical body will move and behave in predictable ways so long as the inputs are known. Animals, being completely machinelike, belong entirely in the area of physical phenomena. Hence, animals have no immortality, are not capable of thought, and have no freedom of will (since they have no will). Descartes made some minor adjustments in his thinking on animals in later years, but he never changed his basic conviction that animal behavior can be explained mechanistically.

The nonmaterial mind, according to Descartes, has the capacities of thought and of consciousness, and consequently provides us with knowledge of the external world. It has none of the properties of matter. The most important characteristic of the mind is its capacity to think; this sets it apart from the physical world of matter. This "thinking thing" is free, immaterial, and unextended.

Since the mind perceives and wills, it must somehow influence, and be influenced by, the body. Descartes recognized that when the mind "decides" to move from one point to another, for example, this decision is carried out somehow by the nerves and muscles of the body. Similarly, when the body is stimulated in some fashion, as by light or heat, the mind recognizes and interprets these sensory data and makes a decision as to the appropriate response.

Thus, Descartes was led to formulate what is perhaps the most important part of his theory: the interaction of these two totally different entities. He had to find a point of interaction where the mind and the body could engage in their mutual influence. Several considerations were involved in the search for this place of interaction. First, Descartes conceived of the soul as being unitary, which meant that it must interact with only one part of the body. Descartes was also convinced that the point of interaction must be somewhere within the brain, for research was demonstrating ever more clearly that sensations travel to the brain and that movement originates within the brain. Clearly, then, the brain had to be the focal point for the mind's functions. Since the only structure of the brain that is single and unitary (that is, not divided and duplicated in both hemispheres) is the pineal gland or conarium, Descartes considered it the only logical choice for a point of interaction.

The manner in which this interaction between mind and body takes place is treated in mechanistic terms by Descartes. Movement of the animal spirits in the nerve tubes produces an impression on the conarium, and from this impression the mind produces a sensation. What occurs is that a quantity of motion (the flow of animal spirits) produces a purely mental quality (a sensation). The reverse also occurs, in that the mind can somehow make an impression on the conarium (in a manner never made clear), which in turn, by inclining to one direction or another, influences the direction of flow of the animal spirits to the muscles, which results in a movement. Thus, a purely mental quality can influence motion, a property of the body.

It is important to remember that Descartes did not maintain that the soul is confined or contained in the conarium. The conarium is simply the point of interaction and nothing more. Descartes believed that the soul is united with all parts of the body and thus the entire body becomes the "seat of the soul."

Because of its profound influence on the subsequent development of psychology, another of Descartes' formulations—his doctrine of ideas—deserves mention. Descartes believed that the mind gives rise to two different kinds of ideas: derived and innate. Derived ideas are those produced by the direct application of an external stimulus, such as the sound of a bell or the sight of a tree. These derived ideas, then, are products of the experiences of the senses.

Of far more importance is the notion of innate ideas, which are not derived from sensory experience. These ideas are not produced by objects in the external world impinging on the senses. The label "innate" describes their source: They develop out of the mind or consciousness alone. Their innate tendency or potential existence is independent of sense experience, though they may be realized or actualized in the presence of appropriate sense experience. Some of these innate ideas, according to Descartes, are the ideas of self, God, the geometric axioms, perfection, and infinity.

This notion of innate ideas is discussed again in later chapters, for it eventually culminates in the nativistic theory of perception and the Gestalt school. We also will see its influence in terms of the spirited opposition it inspired among the early English empiricists and associationists and among the more modern empiricists, such as Helmholtz and Wundt.

The work of Descartes served as a most important catalyst for many trends later prominent in psychology. His most important systematic conceptions are his mechanistic conception of the body, his mind–body theory of interactionism, the localization of the mind's functions in the brain, and the doctrine of innate ideas.

With Descartes we see the doctrine of mechanism applied to man—at least to his body. So pervasive was the mechanistic philosophy, however, that it was only a matter of time before the mind of man would also be reduced to nothing more than a machine. And it is that far-reaching event to which we now turn.

British Empiricism and Associationism

After Descartes, the development of modern science in general and of psychology in particular was most rapid and prolific. By the middle of the nineteenth century, the long period of what has been called prescientific psychology came to an end. During this time European philosophical thought became infused with a new spirit: positivism. The term and the concept are the work of Auguste Comte, who was working on a systematic survey of all knowledge—an ambitious project indeed! To make the project more manageable, Comte wanted to limit his work strictly to facts the truth of which was beyond question, that is, those facts determined through the methods of science.

Positivism, then, refers to a system based exclusively on facts that are immediately observable and undebatable. All else of a speculative or inferential nature is rejected as illusory. A positivistic philosophy deals with only those things that can be known through the senses.

Other ideas quite supportive of antimetaphysical positivism were also extant in philosophy. The materialists strongly believed that all things could be described in physical terms and understood in the light of the physical properties of matter and energy. They further believed that consciousness could be explained in the terms of physics and chemistry. In discussions of mental phenomena, they tended to focus on their physical aspect, the anatomical and physiological structure of the brain.

A third group of philosophers, the empiricists, were also quite active, particularly in England. They were concerned with how the mind acquires knowledge, and argued that the only valid source of knowledge is sensory experience.

Man's conception of himself and the world around him was rapidly changing. Positivism, empiricism, and materialism were to become the philosophical foundations of the new psychology. Discussion of psychological phenomena were beginning to be conducted within a framework made up of factual, observational, and quantitative evidence based on sensory experience. More focus was being placed on the physiological processes involved in mental functioning (see Chapter 3). Of the three new traditions or orientations, empiricism played the major role in shaping the early development of the new science of psychology.

Empiricism provided the new psychology with both a method and a theory. The method of the empiricists is observation, and, to some extent, experimentation. In contrast to the older, rational and speculative methods of inquiry, the empirical method relies completely on objective observation.

The theoretical aspect of empiricism relates to the growth of the mind—how it acquires knowledge. The empiricistic view is that the mind grows through the progressive accumulation of sensory experiences. This attitude is in distinct opposition to the nativistic viewpoint, as exemplified by Descartes, which says that some ideas are present at birth (are innate). We will now consider some of the major British empiricists.

John Locke (1632–1704)

The son of an attorney, Locke studied at Westminster and Oxford, receiving his bachelor's degree in 1656 and his master's degree soon after that. He remained at Oxford for several years, tutoring in Greek, rhetoric, and philosophy, and then took up the practice of medicine. He had also developed an interest in political matters while at Oxford, and in 1667 went to London, where he became secretary to the Earl of Shaftesbury and, in time, the confidant and friend of this controversial statesman.

Shaftesbury's political stature and influence declined, and in 1681, after his participation in a plot against Charles II, he fled to Holland. Though Locke was not involved in the plot, his close relationship with Shaftesbury brought him under suspicion and he, too, fled to Holland. In 1689, he was able to return to England, where he took the post of Commissioner of Appeals and began writing a series of works on education, religion, and economics. He was particularly concerned with religious freedom and the right of men to govern themselves. Locke's writings brought him much fame and influence and he was heralded throughout Europe and England as a champion of liberalism in government.

Locke's major work of importance to psychology is *An Essay Concerning Human Understanding*, which appeared in 1690 and was the culmination of some 20 years of study and thought. This classic, which had gone through four editions by 1700, and was translated into French and Latin, marked the formal beginning of English empiricism.

Locke was concerned primarily with the question of how the mind acquires knowledge. In attacking this question he first denied the existence of innate ideas, arguing that man is not equipped at birth with any knowledge whatever. He admitted that certain ideas may appear to be innate to an adult because he has been constantly taught them (such as the idea of God) from childhood and cannot remember any time when he was not aware of them. Therefore, the adult comes to believe that he must have had the ideas since birth. Thus, apparent innateness of ideas is explained by Locke in terms of learning and habit.

How, then, does the mind acquire knowledge? To Locke, the answer was, emphatically, through experience: All knowledge is empirically derived.

In an often quoted passage from his *Essay*, Locke noted:

> Let us then suppose the mind to be, as we say, white paper, void of all characters, without any ideas:—How comes it to be furnished? Whence comes it by that vast store which the busy and boundless fancy of man has painted on it with an almost endless variety? Whence

has it all the *materials* of reason and knowledge? To this I answer, in one word, from EXPERIENCE. In that all our knowledge is founded; and from that it ultimately derives itself [Book II, Chapter 1].

Locke recognized two different kinds of experience, one deriving directly from sensation and the other from reflection. Some ideas arise from direct sensory input from physical objects in the environment. They are simple sense impressions. In addition to the operation of sensations upon the mind, however, the operation of the mind itself—reflection—can give rise to ideas. It is important to remember that the mental function of reflection as a source of ideas is also dependent on sensory experience. The ideas produced by reflection are based on those already experienced sensorially.

In the development of the individual, sensation comes first. It is a necessary precursor to reflection, for there must exist a reservoir of sense impressions in order for the mind to be able to reflect. In reflection, the individual remembers past sensory impressions and combines them in various new ways to form abstractions and other higher-level ideas. All ideas, then, no matter how abstract and complex, arise from these two sources, but the overall origin remains sense impressions or experience.

Locke also made the distinction between simple and complex ideas. Simple ideas can arise from both sources (sensation or reflection), are received passively by the mind, and are elemental or unanalyzable (that is, they cannot be further reduced to simpler ideas). As we have seen, the mind, through the process of reflection, can actively create new ideas through combinations of other ideas. These derived ideas are what Locke called the complex ideas, and they arise from simple ideas of both sensation and reflection. Thus, complex ideas are compounded or "built up" out of simple ideas, and hence are capable of being analyzed or resolved into simple ideas.

This notion of a mental combination or compounding of ideas (and their analysis) marks the beginning of the so-called mental chemistry that characterizes the notion of association. The decomposition of mental life into elements (simple ideas), and the compounding of these elements to form complex ideas subsequently formed the core of the new scientific psychology.

In essence, Locke treated the mind as though it behaved in accordance with the laws of the physical universe. The basic particles (or corpuscles or atoms) of the mental world were the *simple ideas*, conceptually analogous to the material atoms in the Galilean–Newtonian mechanistic scheme.

As Lowry (1971) noted, "it is possible to see the whole of Locke's psychology as a kind of Newtonian cosmos in miniature [p. 21]." The basic elements of the mind—the simple ideas—are indivisible. They cannot be broken down into anything simpler and, like their counterparts in the material world, they can join in various ways to form more complex structures. It was a significant step in the direction of considering the mind—like the body—as a machine.

Another Lockean doctrine of considerable interest to psychology is his notion of primary and secondary qualities as they apply to simple ideas of sense. Primary qualities exist in the object whether we perceive them or not. For instance, the size and shape of a building are primary qualities, whereas the color of the building is not inherent in the object, but is dependent on the experiencing person.

The secondary qualities, such as colors, odors, sounds, and tastes are not in the object; rather, they exist in one's perception of the object. The tickle of a feather is not in the feather itself but in one's reaction to the feather. The pain inflicted by a knife is not in the knife itself but in one's experience in relation to the knife.

A simple experiment to illustrate this doctrine is as follows. Take three containers of water—one cold, one lukewarm, one hot. Place one hand in cold water and the other in hot water, then place both hands in the pan of lukewarm water. One hand perceives this water as warm while the other hand perceives it as cold. The water, of course, is one temperature. It is not both warm and cold at the same time. Therefore, the qualities or experience of heat and cold must exist only in our perception and not in the object—the water—itself.

These secondary qualities exist, then, only in the act of perception. If you did not bite into a peach, the taste would not exist. The primary qualities, such as the shape of the peach, exist in the object whether we perceive them or not.

This was not the first time such a distinction between primary and secondary qualities had been suggested. Galileo had made essentially the same point: "I think that if ears, tongues, and noses were removed, shapes and numbers and motions [primary qualities] would remain, but not odors nor tastes nor sounds. The latter, I believe, are nothing more than names when separated from living beings [Boas, 1962, p. 262]."

The position is necessarily congruent with the spirit of mechanism. Indeed, Locke admitted as much when he noted that the distinction resulted from "a little excursion into natural philosophy."

The mechanical view of the universe held that matter in motion constituted the only objective reality in the world. Since matter is all that exists objectively, it must follow that perception of anything else—colors, odors, or tastes—is subjective in nature. Hence, the primary qualities are all that can exist independently of the perceiver.

Locke, in making this distinction, recognized the subjectivity of much of our perception of the world. The secondary qualities were introduced in an attempt to explain the fact that there is not always an exact correspondence between the physical world and an individual's perception of it.

Once having accepted this distinction between primary and secondary qualities—some existing in reality and others existing only in man's perception—it was inevitable that someone would ask if there was, after all, any difference between primary and secondary qualities. Perhaps all perception is in terms of secondary qualities; that is, subjective and dependent on the observer. The man who did ask (and answer) this question was George Berkeley.

George Berkeley (1685–1753)

Locke's immediate successor in British empirical philosophy, Berkeley was born and educated in Ireland. He was a deeply religious man and at the age of 24 was ordained a deacon in the Anglican Church. Shortly thereafter he published two important philosophical works that were to exert an influence on psychology: *An Essay Towards a New Theory of Vision* (1709) and *A Treatise Concerning the Principles of Human Knowledge* (1710).

With these two books, his contribution to psychology ended. Thereafter he traveled extensively in Europe and returned to Ireland to hold a number of posts, including teaching at Trinity College. He became financially independent through the gift of a large amount of money from a woman whom he had apparently met only once at a dinner. He traveled in the United States, spent 3 years at Newport, Rhode Island, and gave his house and library to Yale University when he left. The last years of his life were spent as Bishop of Cloyne in Ireland.

Berkeley's fame (or at least name) lingers in America today. In the mid-nineteenth century, a clergyman from Yale, the Reverend Henry Durant, established an academy in California. He named it Berkeley (Morgan, 1969, p. 115), in honor of the good bishop, perhaps in recognition of Berkeley's poem (*On the Prospect of Planting Arts and Learning in America*), which includes the line: "Westward the course of empire takes its way."

Berkeley agreed with Locke that all knowledge of the external world comes from experience but disagreed with Locke's doctrine of primary and secondary qualities by arguing that there are no primary qualities at all. There are only what Locke called secondary qualities for, to Berkeley, all knowledge is a function of the experiencing or perceiving person. The name given to this position some years later was "mentalism," to denote Berkeley's emphasis on purely mental phenomena.

Berkeley argued that perception is the *only* reality of which we can be sure. We cannot know with absolute certainty the nature of physical objects in the experiential world. All we can know for sure is how we perceive these objects and, since our perception is within ourselves and thus individually subjective, we do not mirror the external world directly in our perception. Thus, to Berkeley, a physical object would have been nothing more than an accumulation of sensations that we have experienced together, so that force of habit renders them associated in our minds. The experiential world is the summation of our sensations.

There is, then, no material substance of which we can be certain, for if we take away the perception, the quality disappears. There can be no color, for instance, without the perception of color. Things exist only in being perceived.

Berkeley was not saying that real objects exist in the material world only when they are perceived. He argued, rather, that since all experience is within ourselves, relative to our own perception, we can never know with certainty the nature of real objects. We know only our own perception of them.

However, he did recognize a certain degree of independence, consistency, and stability of objects in the real world and he had to find some way of accounting for this. He did so by invoking God. (He was, after all, a bishop.) God functioned as a kind of Permanent Perceiver over all objects in the universe. Thus, a tree in an isolated forest exists and has certain characteristics, even when no man is there to perceive it, because God is always perceiving it.

Berkeley invoked the theory of association to explain our knowledge of objects in the real world. This knowledge is essentially a construction or compounding of simple ideas (the mental elements) held together by the mortar of association.

Complex ideas are formed, then, by the joining together of simple ideas from the various senses, as seen in this paragraph from Berkeley's *An Essay Towards a New Theory of Vision.*

> Sitting in my study I hear a coach drive along the street; I look through the casement and see it; I walk out and enter into it. Thus, common speech would incline one to think, I heard, saw, and touched the same thing, to wit, the coach. It is nevertheless certain the ideas intromitted by each sense are widely different, and distinct from each other; but, having been observed constantly to go together, they are spoken of as one and the same thing.

Thus the mind constructs complex ideas by fitting together the basic building blocks of the mind—the simple ideas. The mechanical analogy in the use of the words "construct" and "building blocks" is not coincidental.

Berkeley also used this notion of association to explain depth perception. In his *An Essay Towards a New Theory of Vision*, he attacked the problem of how we perceive the third dimension of depth with a retina of only two dimensions. His answer was that we perceive the third dimension of depth as a result of experience—as a result of the recurring association of visual impressions with sensations of touch and movement that occur in ocular adjustments in looking at objects at different distances, or in bodily movements in moving toward or away from seen objects. In other words, the continuing sensory experiences of walking toward or reaching for objects and the sensations from the eye muscles become associated to produce the perception of depth. For example, when an object is brought closer to the eyes, the pupils will move inward toward one another or converge. This convergence diminishes when the object moves away at a greater distance. Thus, depth perception is not a simple sensory experience, but rather an association of ideas that must be learned.

Perhaps for the first time, a purely psychological process was explained in terms of association of sensations. Berkeley thus continued the growing associationistic tradition in empiricism. His explanation rather accurately anticipated the modern view of depth perception in that he discussed the important influences of the physiological cues of accommodation and convergence.

David Hume (1711–1776)

A philosopher and historian, Hume studied law at the University of Edinburgh but was not graduated. He tried the world of business but found this not to his liking, so he lived on his small income during 3 years of self-study in philosophy in France. After returning to England, he published *A Treatise of Human Nature*, his most important work for psychology, in 1739.

Other books followed, and he gained much fame as a writer while also working as a tutor, companion, secretary, librarian, and judge–advocate in a military expedition. He was very well received in Europe and England and held several posts in government.

Hume reemphasized Locke's notion of the compounding of simple ideas into complex ideas, developing and making more explicit the notion of association. He agreed with Berkeley on the nonexistence of the material world except when it is perceived, but took yet another step. He abolished mind as a substance and said that the mind is a secondary quality like matter! It, too, is observable only through perception. Hume believed that mind is nothing more than the flow of ideas, sensations, memories, and so on.

Of greater importance to psychology, however, is the clear distinction he drew between the two kinds of mental contents: impressions and ideas. Impressions are the basic elements of mental life and are akin to "sensation" and "perception" in today's terminology. An idea is the mental experience we have in the absence of any stimulating object; the modern equivalent is "image."

Hume did not define these two mental contents either in physiological terms or in reference to any external stimulating object. He was quite careful not to assign any ultimate causes to impressions. These two mental contents differ not in terms of their source or point of origin, but in terms of their relative strength or vivacity: Impressions are strong and vivid, whereas ideas are weaker by comparison.

Furthering his notion of difference between ideas and impressions, Hume said that ideas are weak copies of impressions. Both of these mental contents may be simple or complex, with a simple idea resembling its simple impression. Complex ideas, however, do not necessarily resemble any simple idea, since the complex idea evolves from a combination of several simple ideas in some new and novel pattern.

Complex ideas are compounded from simple ideas by association and Hume's two ultimate laws of association are resemblance or similarity, and contiguity in time or place. The more similar and contiguous are two ideas, the more readily they will be associated.

Hume's work fits into the continuing development of empiricism and associationism within the framework of the mechanistic spirit. He argued that just as astronomers had determined the laws and forces by which the heavenly bodies function, so it is possible to determine the laws of the mental universe.

Hume believed that the law of association of ideas was the mental counterpart of the law of gravity in the physical world; that is, a universal principle of the operation of the mind. Once again we have the mechanical notion of complex ideas being constructed by an amalgamation of simple ideas.

David Hartley (1705–1757)

Hartley, the son of a minister, was preparing for a career in the church himself, but because of doctrinal difficulties, turned to medicine instead. He led a quiet and uneventful life, practicing medicine and studying philosophy. In 1749 he published *Observations on Man. His Frame, His Duty, and His Expectations*, his single most important work, often considered the first systematic discourse on associationism.

Hartley is considered important, not so much for the originality of his work on associationism, but for the great clarity and precision of his organization and systematization of previous work. The basic premises of this doctrine are certainly not new with Hartley, but he served the very important function of bringing together the earlier threads of thought, and is often acknowledged as the founder of associationism as a formal doctrine.

Hartley's fundamental law of association is contiguity, by which he attempted to explain memory, reasoning, emotion, and both voluntary and involuntary action. Those ideas or sensations that recur together, either simultaneously or successively, become associated, so that future occurrences of one result in a repetition of the other. Thus, repetition, in addition to contiguity, is necessary for the formation of associations.

Hartley agreed fully with Locke that all ideas and knowledge are derived from sensory experience; there are no associations present at birth. As the child grows and accumulates a variety of sensory experiences, connections and trains of association of greater and greater complexity are established. In this fashion, higher systems of thought are developed by the time adulthood is reached. Thus, higher order mental life is capable of analysis or reduction to the elements or atoms from which it was formed through the mental compounding of associations. Hartley became the first to use the doctrine of association to explain all types of mental activity.

Hartley, like others before him, saw the world of the mind in mechanical terms. In one respect, however, he went beyond the aims of the earlier English empiricists and associationists. Not only did he explain the psychological processes in mechanical terms, he also tried to explain the underlying physiological processes within the same sort of framework.

Newton had said that impulses in the physical world are vibratory in nature; Hartley used this principle to explain the operation of the brain and nervous system. Vibrations in the nerves (which he considered solid, not hollow tubes as Descartes thought) transmit impulses from one part of the body to another. The vibrations in the nerves "set up" or give rise to smaller vibrations in the brain, which he considered to be the physiological counterparts of ideas.

The importance of this notion for our purposes is not in the details of its operation, but in the fact that it was yet another attempt to use the principles of the mechanical universe as a model for understanding the nature of man.

James Mill (1773–1836)

Educated at Edinburgh, James Mill was for a short time a clergyman, but left the Church of Scotland to earn his livelihood as a writer. His writings were many and varied, and his most famous literary work is the *History of British India,* a book that took 11 years to write. His most important contribution to psychology is *Analysis of the Phenomena of the Human Mind,* which appeared in 1829.

Mill applied the notion of mechanism to the human mind with a directness and comprehensiveness not shown by his predecessors. His intention was to destroy the idea of subjective, psychical activities and to show that the mind of man was nothing more than a machine. Mill felt that others, in arguing that the mind was like a machine or machine-like in its operations, had not gone far enough. The mind was a machine—it functioned in the same mechanical way as a clock functioned—set in operation by external physical forces and run by internal physical forces.

In Mill's view, the mind is totally passive; it is acted upon by external stimuli. The individual simply responds to these stimuli (in clockwork fashion) and is not capable of acting spontaneously. Obviously, then, there is no such thing as freedom of the will. This point of view persists in the forms of psychology that have derived from the mechanistic spirit, most notably contemporary behaviorism.

As the title of his major work suggests, Mill believed that the mind must be studied through its reduction or analysis into basic elementary components. This is, as we have seen, a strong tenet of the mechanistic spirit. To understand complex phenomena, it is necessary to break them down into the smallest component parts. Mill wrote: "a distinct knowledge of the elements is indispensable to an accurate conception of that which is compounded of them [1829, Vol. 1, p. 1]."

He held that sensations and ideas are the only two kinds of mental elements. In the by now familiar empiricist–associationist tradition, all knowledge begins with sensations, from which are derived the higher level complexes of ideas through the process of association. Association is a matter of contiguity or concurrence alone and may be either synchronous or successive.

Mill believed that the mind has no creative function because he felt that association was a purely passive process. In other words, sensations that have occurred together in a certain order are mechanically reproduced as ideas, and these resulting ideas occur in the same order as their corresponding sensations. Association was thus treated in very mechanistic terms, with the resulting ideas being merely the accumulation or sum of the individual elements.

Contributions of Empiricism to Psychology

With the development of empiricism, philosophy was turning away from its older tradition of rationalism and dogmatism. It was still concerned with many of the same problems, but its method of attacking these problems had become empirical, atomistic, and mechanistic.

Consider again the emphases of empiricism: the primary role of the processes of sensation; analysis of conscious experience into elements; the synthesis of elements to form more complex mental experiences through the mechanism of association; and emphasis on conscious processes. The major role empiricism played in influencing the new scientific psychology will be evident, for we will see that these areas stressed by empiricism form the basis of the subject matter of psychology.

By the mid-nineteenth century, when psychology was on the verge of becoming a science, its philosophical anticipators had become empirical in both subject matter and method. Philosophy had done all it could; the theoretical rationale for a natural science of man had been established. What was needed to translate the theory into actuality was an experimental attack on the subject matter. And that was soon to develop, as we shall see in the next chapter.

SUGGESTED FURTHER READINGS

Mind–Body Problem

Feigl, H. Mind–body, *not* a pseudo problem. In S. Hook (Ed.), *Dimensions of mind*. New York: New York Univ. Press, 1960. Pp. 24–36.

McDougall, W. *Body and mind*. New York: Macmillan, 1911 (paperback edition, Boston, Massachusetts: Beacon Press, 1961).

Reeves, W. *Body and mind in Western thought*. Glasgow: Penguin, 1958.

Scher, J. M. (Ed.) *Theories of the mind*. New York: Free Press, 1962.

Descartes

Balz, A. G. A. *Descartes and the modern mind*. New Haven, Connecticut: Yale Univ. Press, 1952.

Pirenne, M. H. Descartes and the body–mind problem in physiology. *British Journal of the Philosophy of Science*, 1950, **1**, 43–59.

The Development of Science

Butterfield, H. *The origins of modern science: 1300–1800*. New York: Macmillan, 1959.

Hall, A. R. *The scientific revolution: 1500–1800*. Boston, Massachusetts: Beacon Press, 1956.

Sarton, G. *Six wings: Men of science in the Renaissance.* Bloomington, Indiana: Indiana Univ. Press, 1957.

Whitehead, A. N. *Science and the modern world.* New York: Macmillan, 1925.

The Mechanistic Philosophy

Hall, A. R. *From Galileo to Newton: 1630–1720.* London: Collins, 1963.

Lowry, R. *The evolution of psychological theory: 1650 to the present.* Chicago: Aldine-Atherton, 1971. [Chapters 1–4]

Matson, F. W. *The broken image.* New York: George Braziller, 1964. [Chapters 1–3]

Toulmin, S., & Goodfield, J. *The architecture of matter.* New York: Harper, 1962.

Locke

Aaron, R. I. *John Locke.* (2nd ed.) Oxford: Clarendon Press, 1955.

Berkeley

Luce, A. A. *The life of George Berkeley, Bishop of Cloyne.* London: Melson, 1949.

3

Physiological Influences
on Psychology

As we have seen, the precursors of a separate discipline of psychology had become empirical in nature; the next step was to become experimental. That great step was facilitated by the influence of experimental physiology, which provided the kinds of experimentation that laid the foundation for the new psychology.

Developments in Early Physiology:
An Overview

The physiological research that directly stimulated and guided the new psychology was a product of the late nineteenth century. As with all endeavors, however, it too had its antecedents, and it is instructive to consider briefly some of the earlier work in physiology.

Physiology became an experimentally oriented discipline during the 1830s, primarily under the influence of Johannes Müller (1801–1858), who strongly advocated the application of the experimental method to physiology. Müller wrote a *Handbook of Physiology* (appearing in several revisions between 1833 and 1840), which summarized the physiological research of the period and contained a large body of knowledge.

The almost immediate publication of revisions, citing much new work, indicates how prolific research in experimental physiology had become. The need for such a book was reflected in the rapid translation into English of the first volume in 1838 and the second in 1842.

Müller is also of great importance in both physiology and psychology for his doctrine of the specific energies of nerves. The doctrine states that the arousal or stimulation of a given nerve always gives rise to a characteristic sensation because each sensory nerve has its own specific energy. This idea stimulated a great deal of research that sought to localize functions within the nervous system and to delimit sensory receiving mechanisms on the periphery of the organism.

Several early physiologists made substantial contributions to the study of brain functions. Their work is of importance to psychology because of their discoveries of specialized areas of the brain and their development of research methods that became widely used in later physiological psychology.

A pioneer in the investigation of reflex behavior was Marshall Hall (1790–1857), who observed that decapitated animals continued to move for some time if subjected to appropriate forms of stimulation. Hall concluded that various levels of behavior depend on different parts of the brain and nervous system. Specifically, he postulated that voluntary movement depends on the cerebrum, reflex movement depends on the spinal cord, involuntary movement depends on direct stimulation of the musculature, and respiratory movement depends on the medulla.

Pierre Flourens (1794–1867), in extending Hall's research, systematically destroyed various parts of the brain and spinal cord and observed the resulting changes in animal behavior. He concluded that the cerebrum controls the higher mental processes, parts of the midbrain control visual and auditory reflexes, the cerebellum controls coordination, while the medulla governs heartbeat, respiration, and certain other vital functions.

The findings of Hall and Flourens, though still generally valid, are second in importance, for our purposes, to their introduction of the method of extirpation. This technique essentially consists of investigating the function of a given part of the brain by removing or destroying it and observing the resulting changes in the animal's behavior.

In the middle of the nineteenth century, two experimental approaches to the study of the brain were introduced. The clinical method was developed in 1861 by Paul Broca when performing an autopsy on a man who had been unable to speak intelligibly for many years. The autopsy revealed a lesion in the third frontal convolution of the cerebral cortex; Broca labeled this section of the brain the speech center (since called, appropriately enough, Broca's area).

The clinical method has since become a very useful supplement to study by extirpation, since it is somewhat difficult to secure human subjects who will agree to removal of part of the brain. As a sort of posthumous extirpation, the clinical method provides the opportunity of finding the damaged brain area assumed to be responsible for a behavioral condition that existed before the patient died.

The other new experimental approach to brain study was that of electrical stimulation, introduced by G. Fritsch and E. Hitzig in 1870. As its name suggests, the method involves the exploration of the cerebral cortex with weak electric currents. Fritsch and Hitzig found that stimulating certain cortical areas resulted in motor responses. With the development of more sophisticated and precise electronic equipment, the method of electrical stimulation has probably become the single most productive technique for studying the functions of the brain.

Much was being learned, then, of the structure and function of the human brain. Considerable research was also conducted on the structure of the nervous system and the nature of neural activity.

As we have seen, there were two earlier theories of how nervous activity was transmitted in the body—the nerve tube theory embraced by Descartes, and Hartley's theory of vibrations.

Toward the end of the eighteenth century, the Italian, Galvani, had suggested that the nature of nerve impulses was electrical. Research in this area proceeded so rapidly and convincingly that before the middle of the nineteenth century it was accepted as fact. It was thought that the nervous system was essentially a conductor of electrical impulses and that the central nervous system functioned much like a switching station, shunting the impulses onto either sensory or motor nerve fibers.

Though this position was far advanced over the models of Descartes and Hartley, it was conceptually very similar, as Lowry (1971) points out. Both the newer and older points of view were reflexive in nature. Something from the external world (a stimulus) impinged on a sense organ and excited a nervous impulse that travelled to the appropriate place in the brain or central nervous system. There, in response to the impulse, a new impulse was generated and transmitted via the motor nerves to effect some response on the part of the organism.

The anatomical structure of the nervous system was also being defined during the nineteenth century. It came to be understood that the nerve fibers were actually composed of separate structures—neurons—somehow joined together at synapses.

Such findings were congruent with a mechanistic and materialistic image of man. It was believed that the nervous system, like the mind, was composed of atomistic structures which, when combined, produced a more complex product.

The spirit of mechanism was just as dominant in the physiology of the nineteenth century as it was in the philosophy of that time. Nowhere was this more pronounced than in Germany. In the 1840s, a group of scientists, many of them former students of Johannes Müller, formed the Berlin Physical Society. The scientists, all in their twenties, were committed to one overriding proposition: the belief that all phenomena, including that which pertained to living matter, could be accounted for in physical terms. What they hoped to do was to relate or connect physiology with physics; a physiology consonant with the spirit of mechanism was their goal.

In a dramatic gesture, four of the young scientists (including Helmholtz, whom we will meet shortly) made a solemn oath—signing it with their own blood, according to legend—stating that the only forces active within the organism are the common physical–chemical ones.

Materialism, mechanism, empiricism, experimentation, measurement—all formed the central core of physiology by the mid-nineteenth century.

The developments in early physiology indicate the kinds of research techniques and discoveries that were supportive of a scientific approach to the psychological investigation of the mind. We have pointed out how the direction of research in physiology influenced the newly emerging psychology. The major point is that, while philosophy was paving the way for an experimental attack on the mind, physiology was experimentally investigating the physiological mechanisms underlying mental phenomena. The next step was to apply the experimental method to the mind itself.

The British empiricists had argued that sensation is the only source of all man's knowledge. Physiologists had defined the structure and function of the senses. It was time to experiment with and quantify this "doorway to the mind," the subjective, mentalistic experience of sensation. Techniques were available to investigate the body; now they were being developed to explore the mind. Experimental psychology was ready to begin.

The Beginnings of Experimental Psychology

Four men are directly responsible for the initial applications of the experimental method to the subject matter of psychology: Hermann von Helmholtz, Ernst Weber, Gustav Fechner, Wilhelm Wundt. All four were German, well trained in physiology, and aware of the impressive developments in physiology, and science in general, in the middle of the nineteenth century.

Why Germany?

Scientific thought was developing in most of the countries of Western Europe in the nineteenth century, particularly in England, France, and Germany. No one country held a monopoly on the enthusiasm, conscientiousness, or optimism with which it viewed and used the tools of science. Why then did experimental psychology begin in Germany and not in France or England? Were there some unique characteristics that made science in Germany a more fertile breeding ground for the new psychology?

Although generalizations may be suspect and exceptions to the rule frequently found, it can nonetheless be suggested that the times favored Germany as the place of origin for the new psychology. For a century, German intellectual history had paved the way for an experimental science of psychology. Experimental physiology was firmly established there and received a degree of recognition not yet achieved in France and England. There were very good reasons for this. The so-called German temperament was better suited to careful and minute taxonomic description and classification than that of France or England. While these other countries favored the deductive and mathematical approach to science, Germany, with its emphasis on conscientious, thorough, and careful collection of observational fact, favored the classificatory or inductive approach.

Since biological and physiological science does not lend itself well to grand generalizations from which facts can be deduced, France and England were slow to accept biology into their scientific community. Germany, however, with its interest and faith in description and classification, welcomed biology to its family of sciences.

Further, the Germans construed science in a very broad sense. While French and British science limited itself to physics and chemistry (which could be approached quantitatively), the Germans included a variety of areas—phonetics, philology, history, archeology, aesthetics, logic, even the critical analysis of literature.

Others were skeptical about using science to study something as complex as the mind of man. Not so the Germans, and they plunged ahead, unconstrained by prejudgments, to explore and measure the mind with the tools of science.

Hermann von Helmholtz (1821–1894)

One of the greatest scientists of the nineteenth century, Helmholtz was a prolific researcher in physics and physiology. Psychology was actually in third place among his areas of scientific contributions, yet, together with Fechner and Wundt, his work was instrumental in beginning the new psychology.

The Life of Helmholtz

Born in Potsdam, Germany, where his father taught in the gymnasium, Helmholtz was tutored at home initially because of his delicate health. At the age of 17, he entered a Berlin medical institute where no tuition was charged to those who agreed to serve as surgeons in the army after graduation. Helmholtz served for 7 years, during which time he continued his studies in mathematics and physics, published several articles, and presented a paper on the indestructibility of energy in which he gave mathematical formulation to the law of conservation of energy. After leaving the army, Helmholtz accepted a position as Associate Professor of Physiology at Königsberg. Over the next 30 years he held academic appointments in physiology at Bonn and Heidelberg, and in physics at Berlin.

Possessed of tremendous energy, Helmholtz published in several different areas. In the course of his work in physiological optics he invented the ophthalmoscope. His three-volume work *Physiological Optics* (1856–1866) was so influential that it was translated into English 60 years later. His research on acoustical problems resulted in the publication of *On the Sensations of Tone* in 1863, summarizing his own research as well as the entire available literature. He also published in such diverse areas as afterimages, color blindness, the Arabian–Persian musical scale, the form of the horopter, human eye movements, the regulation of ice, geometrical axioms, and hay fever! In later years he contributed indirectly to the founding of wireless telegraphy and radio. In the fall of 1893, while returning from the Chicago World's Fair and visits to other parts of the United States, Helmholtz suffered a severe fall aboard ship. He never fully recovered his health and died 11 months later.

The Contributions of Helmholtz

Of interest in the history of psychology are Helmholtz's investigations of the speed of the neural impulse, audition, and vision.

The speed of the neural impulse was instantaneous, or at least was too fast to be measured. Helmholtz provided the first empirical measurement of the rate of conduction by stimulating a motor nerve and the attached muscle from the leg of a frog (the nerve–muscle preparation), which was so arranged that the precise moment of stimulation, as well as the resulting movement, could be recorded. Working with different lengths of nerve, he recorded the delay between stimulation of the nerve near the muscle and the muscle's reaction, and then did the same for stimulation farther from the muscle. These measurements gave him the time taken for conductance. His results yielded the modest rate of 90 feet per second.

He also experimented with the reaction time for sensory nerves with human subjects, studying the complete circuit from stimulation of a sense organ to the resulting motor response. His findings showed such enormous differences between individuals and from one trial to the next with the same subject that he abandoned the research altogether.

Helmholtz's demonstrations that the speed of conduction was not instantaneous suggested that thought and movement follow one another at a measurable interval and do not occur simultaneously, as had previously been thought. Helmholtz, however, was interested only in the sheer speed of the nerve impulse and not in its psychological significance. Later, the psychological implications of his research were recognized by others who went on to make reaction-time experiments a fruitful line of research in the new psychology. Helmholtz's research was one of the first demonstrations that it was possible to experiment upon and measure a psychophysiological process.

Helmholtz's work on vision has had a profound influence. Besides working on the external eye muscles and the mechanism by which the lenses are focused by the internal eye muscles, Helmholtz extended a theory of color vision originally published in 1802 by Thomas Young, which has since become known as the Young–Helmholtz theory of color vision. No less important was his work on audition, including perception of combination tones and individual tones, the nature of harmony and discord, and his resonance theory of hearing. The lasting influence of his theories of vision and hearing is attested to by their continued inclusion in modern textbooks of psychology.

Comment

Helmholtz was not a psychologist, nor were psychological problems his main interest, but he contributed a large and important body of knowledge to sensory psychology and helped to greatly strengthen the newly developing experimental approach to the study of psychological problems. He considered psychology a separate discipline, allied to metaphysics. The psychology of the senses was an exception, as far as Helmholtz was concerned, because of its close association with physiology. He was not really involved (or concerned) with the establishment of psychology as an independent science, yet his influence was of such magnitude that he must be included among the direct contributors to the new science.

Ernst Weber (1795–1878)

Weber was born in Wittenberg, Germany, the son of a theology professor. He received his doctorate at Leipzig in 1815, and taught anatomy and physiology there from 1817 until his retirement in 1871. His primary research interest was the physiology of the sense organs, an area in which he made outstanding and lasting contributions.

Previous research on the sense organs had been confined almost exclusively to the higher senses of vision and audition. Weber's work consisted largely of exploring new fields, notably cutaneous and muscular sensations. He is particularly noteworthy for his brilliant application of the experimental methods of physiology to problems of a psychological nature. In particular, his experiments on the sense of touch mark a fundamental shift in the status of the subject matter of psychology. The ties with philosophy were, if not severed, at least severely weakened. Weber allied psychology with the natural sciences and helped to pave the way for the use of experimental investigation in the study of the mind.

Two-Point Threshold

Specifically, Weber made two major contributions to the new psychology. One involves his experimental determination of the accuracy of the two-point discrimination of the skin—the distance necessary between two points before the subject reports two distinct sensations. Without the use of vision, a subject is asked to report whether he feels one or two points touching the skin. When the two points of stimulation are close, the subject reports a clear sensation of being touched at only one point. As the distance between the two sources of stimulation is increased, using an apparatus resembling a drawing compass, the subject reports uncertainty as to whether he feels one or two sensations. Finally, a distance is reached where the subject reports two distinct points of stimulation. Thus, a threshold is demonstrated at which the two points can be discriminated as such—the two-point threshold. Weber's research marks the first systematic, experimental demonstration of the concept of threshold; a concept widely used in the new psychology from its beginnings to the present day.

In further research, Weber demonstrated that this two-point threshold varies both in different parts of the body of the same subject, and from one subject to another for a given region of the body. His attempt to account for these findings by hypothesizing "sensory circles" (areas in which doubleness is not perceived) has diminished in importance, but his experimental method remains of permanent significance.

The Just Noticeable Difference

Weber's second and more significant contribution eventually led to the statement of the first truly quantitative law in psychology. He wanted to determine the smallest difference between weights—the just noticeable difference—that could be discriminated. To do so, he had a subject lift two weights, a standard and a comparison weight, and report whether one felt heavier than the other. Small differences between the weights resulted in judgments of sameness, while large differences resulted in judgments of disparity between the weights. As his research progressed, Weber found that the just noticeable difference between two weights is a constant ratio, 1:40, of the standard weight. For example, a weight of 41 grams is reported as just noticeably different from a standard weight of 40 grams, an 82-gram weight just noticeably different from a standard weight of 80 grams.

Weber then undertook to investigate the contributions of muscular sensations in the discrimination of weights of differing magnitudes. He found that a subject could discriminate much more accurately if the weights to be judged were lifted by the subject rather than simply placed in the subject's hand. In lifting the weights, both tactual and muscular sensations are operative, whereas when the weight is placed in the hand, only tactual sensations are experienced.

Since smaller differences in weight could be discriminated when the weights were lifted (a ratio of 1:40, as already noted) as compared to when the weights were simply placed in the hand (a ratio of 1:30 being necessary), Weber concluded that this demonstrates the influence of the internal muscle sense on discrimination.

From these experiments, Weber found that discrimination seems to depend not on the absolute magnitude of the difference between two weights, but rather on the relative difference or the ratio of one to another. The just noticeable difference between two stimuli can then be stated as a fraction that is constant for a given sense modality. Weber conducted experiments involving visual discrimination and found that the fraction was smaller than it was with the muscle sense experiments. From this he suggested that there exists a constant fraction for just noticeable differences for each of the senses.

This provided an experimental demonstration that there is not a direct one-to-one correspondence between the physical stimulus and the perception of it. Weber, however, like Helmholtz, was concerned with physiological processes and so he did not appreciate the significance of his work for psychology. What his research revealed was a way of investigating the relationship between body and mind, between the stimulus and the resulting sensation. This was indeed a major breakthrough; all that was necessary was for someone to realize its significance.

Weber's research was experimental in the strictest sense of the term. Under well-controlled conditions, he systematically varied the stimuli and recorded the differential effects on the reported experience of the subject. His experiments stimulated a great deal of research and served to focus the attention of subsequent physiologists on the validity and importance of experimentally approaching strictly psychological problems. Weber's work on threshold measurement was to be of paramount importance in the new psychology, and his demonstration that sensations can be measured has influenced virtually every aspect of psychology to the present day.

Gustav Theodor Fechner (1801–1887)

Fechner was a remarkably diverse scholar whose intellectual pursuits ranged over an active career of more than 70 years. Consider the scope of this man, who was a physiologist for 7 years, a physicist for 15, an invalid for 12, a psychophysicist for 14, an experimental estheticist for 11, and a philosopher for about 40 years throughout this period (Boring, 1950, p. 283). Of all these endeavors, it is the work on psychophysics that brought him his greatest fame, even though he did not wish his name to go down in posterity as a psychophysicist. "The world, however, chose for him; it seized upon the psychophysical experiments, which Fechner meant merely as contributory to his philosophy, and made them into an experimental psychology [Boring, 1950, p. 276].

The Life of Fechner

Fechner was born in a small village in southeastern Germany where his father was the minister. He began medical studies at the University of Leipzig in 1817 at the age of 16, and remained at Leipzig for the rest of his life.

Even before graduating from medical school, a humanistic side of Fechner showed signs of rebellion against the prevailing materialism of his scientific training. Under the pen name "Dr. Mises" he wrote satirical essays lampooning medicine and science, a practice that he continued over the next 25 years, suggesting the continuing conflict between these two sides of his personality: a love of science and of the metaphysical. His first such essay, *Proof that the Moon is Made of Iodine*,[1] attacked the then current medical fad of the use of iodine as a panacea. He was troubled by materialism and strove to establish his "day view," that the universe can be regarded from the point of view of consciousness, in opposition to what he called the "night view," which held the universe, including consciousness, to be inert matter.

Upon completion of his medical studies, Fechner began a second career in physics and mathematics at Leipzig, during which time he translated French handbooks of physics and chemistry into German. By 1830 he had translated more than a dozen volumes, which served to gain him some recognition as a physicist. In 1824 he had begun lecturing in physics at Leipzig and undertaking research of his own. By the late 1830s he developed an interest in sensation and seriously injured his eyes by looking at the sun through colored glasses while studying afterimages.

The combination of overwork and the eye disorder was too much for him and he became, in the language of that era, a nervous invalid with neurotic depression, hypochondriacal tendencies, and thoughts of suicide. Having resigned his chair of physics in 1840, he was cut off from everyone except his wife for 3 years. In 1844 he was given a small pension from the university and thus officially established as an invalid. Yet, not 1 of the next 44 years of his life went by without a serious contribution from him.

The Contributions of Fechner

1. QUANTITATIVE RELATION BETWEEN MIND AND BODY. The many hours spent in meditation and reflection during these years deepened Fechner's religious awareness and his concern over the problem of the soul. He turned to philosophy and began to direct the full force of his genius toward the question of the relationship between the mind and the body.

---

[1] Several texts claim that this essay is entitled *Proof that* Man *is Made of Iodine*. The original title in German is *Beweis dass der Mond aus Iodine bestehe*.

He decided that the two are identical; both are aspects of the same fundamental unity. They are related to one another as the inside of a circle is related to the outside. The apparent difference between the two, Fechner said, is merely the result of the way in which they are viewed. Fechner's fame, however, comes from his psychophysics, not his philosophy; his attempt to verify his philosophical views empirically is a milestone in the history of psychology.

On the morning of October 22, 1850—an important date in the history of psychology—Fechner had an insight that the law of the connection between the mind and body can be found in a statement of quantitative relation between mental sensation and material stimulus. An increase in the intensity of a stimulus, he said, does not produce a one-to-one increase in the intensity of the sensation. Rather, a geometric series characterizes the stimulus, while an arithmetic series characterizes the sensation. For instance, adding the sound of 1 bell to that of an already ringing bell produces a greater increase in sensation than adding 1 bell to 10 others already ringing. Thus, the effects of stimulus intensities are not absolute, but are relative to the amount of sensation already existing at the time.

What this simple, yet brilliant, revelation pointed out was that the amount of sensation (the mental quality) depends on the amount of stimulation (the physical quality). Thus, to measure the change or increase in sensation one must measure the change or increase in stimulation, for the former depends on the latter. Therefore, it is possible to relate the two worlds—mental and material—quantitatively. Fechner thus crossed the barrier between mind and body, or at least caused it to disappear, by being able to empirically relate one to the other.

The concept is simple and clear, but how was it to be translated into actuality? To do so would mean measuring precisely both intensities, the subjective and the objective, the mental and the physical. To measure the physical intensity, the stimulus, is, of course, quite easy. But how does one measure a sensation—the experience of consciousness a subject reports when he responds to a stimulus?

Fechner believed there were two ways to measure sensations. First, he said, we can determine whether a stimulus is present or absent, sensed or not sensed. We can then measure the stimulus intensity at which a subject reports the first appearance of a sensation. What is being measured in this case is the *absolute threshold* of sensitivity; that is, that point (in stimulus intensity) below which no sensation is reported, and above which the subject does experience a sensation.[2]

---

[2] It should be noted that this is not the first use of the concept of threshold. Weber, as noted, used it, and earlier in the century the German philosopher Herbart also discussed the concept (see Chapter 13).

This measurement, while useful, is limited. It is possible to determine only one sensation value (its lowest level). If we are to relate both intensities, we must be able to specify the full range of stimulus values and their resulting sensation values.

To accomplish this, Fechner proposed the use of the *differential threshold* of sensitivity—the least amount of change in a stimulus that will give rise to a change in sensation. For example, how much must a weight be increased in heaviness before the subject will sense the change; that is, report a just noticeable difference in sensation?

To measure how heavy a particular weight appears to a subject—how heavy it "feels"—we cannot use the physical measurement of the weight of the object. We can, however, use that physical measurement as a basis for measuring the psychological intensity of the sensation, by first measuring how much the weight must be decreased in intensity before the subject is barely able to discriminate the difference. Then the weight of the object is changed to this new lower value and the size of the difference threshold is again measured. Since both weight changes are just barely noticeable, Fechner assumed that they must be subjectively equal. This process can be repeated until the object is barely felt by the subject. Since every decrement in weight is subjectively equal to every other decrement, the number of times the weight has to be decreased, that is, the number of just noticeable differences, can then be used as an objective measure of the subjective magnitude of the sensation. In this way, we are measuring the stimulus values necessary to give rise to a difference between two sensations.

Fechner suggested that for each sense modality there is a certain relative increase in the stimulus that always produces an observable change in the intensity of the sensation. Thus, the sensation (the mind quality) as well as the exciting stimulus (the body or material quality) can be measured and the relation between the two can be stated in the form of an equation: $S = K \log R$, in which S is the magnitude of the sensation, K is a constant, and R is the magnitude of the stimulus. The relationship is logarithmic, since one series increases arithmetically and the other geometrically.

Fechner said that this notion was not suggested by a knowledge of Weber's work (with which it is consonant), even though Weber was also at Leipzig and had written about this matter only 4 years earlier. Heidbreder (1933) noted that Fechner did not discover Weber's work until after he had begun the series of experiments designed to test his own hypothesis. Fechner then realized that his principle was essentially what Weber's results demonstrated, and he gave mathematical form to the relationship.

2. METHODS OF PSYCHOPHYSICS. The immediate result of Fechner's insight was the development of a program of research on what he later called psychophysics. (The word defines itself: psycho-physics—the relationship between the mind and the material world.) In the course of this research, with its classic experiments on lifted weights, visual brightness, and tactual and visual distances, Fechner developed one, and systematized two, of the three fundamental methods of psychophysics that are still basic today: the method of average error, the method of constant stimuli, and the method of limits.

Fechner developed the method of average error in cooperation with A. W. Volkmann. It consists in having a subject adjust a variable stimulus until he perceives it to be equal to a constant standard stimulus. Over a number of trials, the mean value of the differences between the standard stimulus and the subject's setting of the variable stimulus represents his error of observation. The method assumes that our sense organs are subject to variability so as to prevent the obtaining of a "true" measure. Accordingly, we obtain a large number of approximate measures, the mean of which represents the best single approximation that can be made of the true value. The technique is useful in measuring reaction time, visual and auditory discriminations, and the extent of illusions. In an extended form it is basic to much current psychological research. Every time we calculate a mean we are, in essence, using the method of average error.

The method of constant stimuli, first called the method of right and wrong cases, was originated by Vierordt in 1852 but developed as a tool by Fechner. It was used for his very elaborate work with lifted weights, which involved over 67,000 comparisons. The technique involves two constant stimuli, the aim being to measure the difference between the stimuli that is required to produce a given proportion of "right" judgments. For example, a subject first lifts the standard weight of 100 grams and then lifts a comparison weight of, say, 88, 92, 96, 104, or 108 grams. He judges whether the second weight is heavier, lighter, or equal to the first. The procedure is continued until a certain number of judgments have been made for each comparison. For the heavier weights, subjects almost always report a judgment of "heavier," while the lightest weights almost always are reported as "lighter." From these data, the stimulus difference (standard versus comparison weights) is determined for that point at which the subject correctly reports "heavier" 75% of the time. A number of variations of the basic procedure render the technique useful in a wide range of measurement problems in the determination of sensory thresholds and in aptitude measurement.

The third of Fechner's psychophysical methods was originally known as the method of just noticeable differences, and later came to be called the method of limits. The technique has been traced back to 1700, and was formalized by Delezenne in 1827. Weber also used the method of just noticeable differences, as we have seen, but the method was given more formal development by Fechner in connection with his work on vision and temperature sensations. The method consists in presenting two stimuli and increasing or diminishing one of them until the subject reports that he detects a difference. Fechner recommended starting the variable stimulus at an intensity clearly higher than the standard stimulus at one time, and clearly lower than the standard the next time. Data from a number of such trials are obtained and the just noticeable differences are averaged to determine the differential threshold. A variation using a single stimulus presented in the ascending and descending approaches is used to determine the absolute threshold.

Comment

Fechner carried on his research for 7 years, publishing part of it for the first time in two short papers in 1858 and 1859. In 1860, the formal and complete exposition of his work appeared in the *Elemente der Psychophysik*, a text of the exact science "of the functionally dependent relations . . . of the material and the mental, of the physical and psychological worlds [1966, p. 7]." The book is considered to be one of the outstanding original contributions to the development of the science of psychology.

Fechner failed in his attempt to found a philosophy on exact science, and his research findings have not withstood later criticism. At the time, however, Fechner's statement of the quantitative relationship between stimulus intensity and sensation was considered comparable to Galileo's discovery of the laws of the lever and of falling bodies (Müller–Freienfels, 1935). Fechner's efforts made it possible for the first time to measure the impalpable mind—a truly remarkable breakthrough.

At the beginning of the nineteenth century, the German philosopher Immanuel Kant insisted that psychology would never become a science because it was impossible to experiment with or measure psychological phenomena and processes. Due to Fechner's work, such an assertion could no longer be regarded seriously.

It was in large measure attributable to Fechner's psychophysical research that Wundt conceived the plan of his experimental psychology. More important, Fechner's methods have proven applicable to a wider range of psychological problems than Fechner ever dreamed of, and, with only minor modifications, these methods are still in use in psychological research. Boring (1950) commented that without Fechner there would have been

> little of the breath of science in the experimental body, for we hardly recognize a subject as scientific if measurement is not one of its tools. Fechner, because of what he did and the time at which he did it, set experimental quantitative psychology off upon the course which it has followed [pp. 294–295].

Although Weber's work preceded Fechner's, accolades have been heaped upon the latter. Fechner seems to have used Weber's work and built upon it, but he did much more than just extend Weber's research. Weber's aims were rather limited; he was a physiologist working on just noticeable differences. The larger significance of this work escaped him. As R. I. Watson (1971) noted, Weber was an "eventful" man, whereas Fechner was an "event-making" man. Fechner sought a mathematical statement of the relation of the physical to the spiritual world. His brilliant and independent insights about measuring sensations and relating them to their stimulus measures were necessary before the implications and consequences of Weber's earlier work could be recognized and applied to make psychology an exact science.

The Formal Founding of the New Science

By the mid-nineteenth century the methods of natural science were being applied to purely mental phenomena. Techniques and methods of investigation had been developed, apparatus devised, important books written, and a widespread interest aroused. British empiricism emphasized the importance of the senses, and the Germans described how the senses worked. The positivistic spirit of the times encouraged the convergence of these two lines of thought. Still lacking, however, was someone to bring them together—in a word, to "found." This final touch was provided by Wilhelm Wundt.

Wundt is the "founder" of psychology as a formal academic discipline, the first man in the history of psychology to be designated properly and unreservedly as a *psychologist*. Moreover, the Wundtian approach constituted psychology's first school of thought—structuralism.

As the first experimental psychologist, Wundt founded the first laboratory, edited the first journal, and began experimental psychology as a science. The areas Wundt investigated, including sensation and perception, attention, feeling, reaction, and association, became basic chapters in textbooks that were yet to be written. That so much of the history of psychology following Wundt consisted of opposition to his view of psychology does not detract from his achievements and contributions.

A Note on "Founding"

Why have the honors for founding the new psychology fallen to Wundt and not to Fechner? Fechner's *Elements of Psychophysics* was published in 1860, at least 15 years before Wundt is said to have begun psychology. Wundt himself said that Fechner's work represented the "first conquest" in experimental psychology (Wundt, 1888, p. 471). All historians seem to agree on Fechner's monumental importance; some even question whether psychology could have begun when it did were it not for Fechner's work.

Why then does history not record that Fechner founded psychology since his work was so vital and preceded that of Wundt? The answer lies in the nature of the process of founding.

Founding is a deliberate, intentional act involving certain abilities or characteristics that go beyond those required for brilliant scientific achievement. It requires the organization and integration of a great deal of work that has gone on before, and then publication and promotion of the newly organized material.

Boring (1950) described founding in these terms: "When the central ideas are all born, some promoter takes them in hand, organizes them, adding whatever else seems to him essential, publishes and advertises them, insists upon them, and in short 'founds' a school [p. 194]."

Founding is quite different from originating, though we need not make that distinction a disparaging one. Both originators and founders are vital to the continued growth of science, as vital as both the architect and the builder in constructing a house.

With this distinction in mind, we can see why Fechner is not called the founder of psychology; he was simply not trying to found a new science. His quest was to understand the nature of the relation between the material and spiritual worlds. He sought to demonstrate a unified concept of mind and body that, although starting from mystical speculation, had a scientific basis.

Wundt, however, set out quite deliberately to found a new science. In the preface to the first edition of his *Principles of Physiological Psychology*, published in 1874, Wundt wrote: "The work I here present to the public is an attempt to mark out a new domain of science." Thus,

Wundt was greatly interested in promoting the idea of psychology as an independent science. Nevertheless, it bears repeating that although Wundt is considered to have founded psychology, he did not originate it. It has emerged from a long line of creative efforts.

During the last half of the nineteenth century the *Zeitgeist* was ready for the development and application of the experimental approach to problems of mind. Wundt was a particularly vigorous agent and promoter—of the inevitable.

SUGGESTED FURTHER READINGS

Early Experimental Physiology

Brazier, M. A. B. The historical development of neurophysiology. In J. Field (Ed.), *Handbook of physiology*, Vol. I. Baltimore, Maryland: Williams & Wilkins, 1959. Pp. 1–58.

Fearing, F. *Reflex action: A study in the history of physiological psychology.* Baltimore, Maryland: Williams & Wilkins, 1930.

Lachman, S. J. *History and methods of physiological psychology: A brief overview.* Detroit, Michigan: Hamilton, 1963.

Ladd, G. T., & Woodworth, R. S. *Physiological psychology.* (Rev. ed.) New York: Charles Scribner's Sons, 1911.

Fechner

Boring, E. G. Fechner: Inadvertent founder of psychophysics. *Psychometrika*, 1961, **26**, 3–8.

Fechner, G. *Elements of psychophysics*, Vol. I. Translated by H. E. Adler. New York: Holt, 1966. First published in 1860.

Stevens, S. S. To honor Fechner and repeal his law. *Science*, 1961, **133**, 80–86.

Helmholtz

Koenigsberger, L. *Hermann von Helmholtz.* New York: Dover, 1965.

Warren, R. M., & Warren, R. P. *Helmholtz on perception: Its physiology and development.* New York: Wiley, 1968.

4

The New Psychology:
Structuralism and Its Early Opponents

An Overview of Structuralism

Wundt's founding of the new experimental science of psychology marked the beginning of the first systematic position or school of thought in psychology, structuralism. In America, it has become customary to consider Wundt the forerunner of structural psychology and to accord the honors for more formally developing the school to the English psychologist, E. B. Titchener, who worked in this country. Wundt, however, is certainly more than a mere antecedent of the structuralist position for, as we shall see, Titchener's position is very similar to that of Wundt. Wundt mapped out the entire field of structural psychology, though at the time there was no reason to call it anything other than "psychology." It remained for Titchener to coin the term "structural psychology" in 1898, for reasons we will discuss in the next chapter.

What is structuralism and why did it develop as the first systematic position in psychology? The subject matter of the new psychology, conscious experience, as well as the task, the experimental investigation of the structure of consciousness, were determined by the *Zeitgeist*. The influence of British empiricism and German experimental physiology were evident. The new psychology absorbed the experimental methods and basic approach of the older natural sciences. It adapted the scientific methods of investigation for its own use and proceeded to study its subject matter in the same way the natural sciences were studying theirs. Thus, the spirit of the times helped to shape both the subject matter and the methods of investigation of the new psychology.

The task of the early structuralists was to discover the nature of elementary conscious experiences, that is, to analyze consciousness into separate parts, and by so doing to discover the structure of consciousness. We shall see how they succeeded in their task and, more important, how this initial systematic position influenced the later development of psychology.

Wilhelm Wundt (1832–1920)

The Life of Wundt

Wundt's early education was undertaken by a Lutheran vicar, presumably the assistant of Wundt's pastor–father. Apparently there was a much closer emotional attachment to this mentor than to Wundt's own parents. When the vicar was transferred to a neighboring village, Wundt became so dejected that he was allowed to live with the vicar to continue his private education. He entered the gymnasium[1] at age 13, and though he did rather poorly (having to repeat 1 year), he was ready for the university at 19. Boring (1950) commented:

> Certainly this was a sober childhood and a serious youth, unrelieved by fun and jollity, which prepared the young Wundt for the endless writing of the ponderous tomes which eventually did so much to give him his place in history. He never learned to play. He had no friends in childhood and only intellectual companions in adolescence. He failed to find parental love and affection, substituting for the more happy relationship this deep attachment for his vicar–mentor. One can see the future man being formed—the humorless, indefatigable, aggressive Wundt [p. 317].

In order to earn a living and study science at the same time, Wundt decided to become a physician. His medical studies took him for 1 year to the University of Tübingen and for the next $3\frac{1}{2}$ years to Heidelberg, where he studied anatomy, physiology, physics, chemistry, and medicine. He slowly came to realize that the practice of medicine was not for him, so he shifted to physiology in order to satisfy a lifelong quest for scholarship.

[1] In Europe, a high school–junior college preparatory to the university.

After a semester of study in Berlin with the great physiologist Johannes Müller, Wundt returned to Heidelberg to take his doctorate in 1856. He held an appointment as *Dozent* (lecturer) in physiology at Heidelberg from 1857 to 1864. In 1858 he was appointed assistant to Helmholtz, but found his work of drilling new students in their laboratory fundamentals a dreary task and resigned after a few years of this routine. In 1864 he was made Associate Professor and continued at Heidelberg until 1874.

While doing research in physiology at Heidelberg, Wundt's conception of psychology as an independent and experimental science was beginning to emerge. His initial proposal for a new science of psychology appeared in the book entitled *Beiträge zur Theorie der Sinneswahrnehmung* (*Contributions to the Theory of Sensory Perception*), various sections of which were published between 1858 and 1862. In addition to reporting his own original experiments, he expressed his views on the methods of the new psychology. In this book Wundt spoke of "experimental psychology" for the very first time. Along with Fechner's *Elemente* (1860), this work is often considered to mark the literary birth of the new science.

The *Beiträge* was followed in 1863 by another and perhaps even more important book, *Vorlesungen über die Menschen- und Thierseele* (*Lectures on the Minds of Men and Animals*). An indication of its importance was its revision almost 30 years later with an English translation and repeated reprintings until after Wundt's death in 1920. It contains many problems that were to occupy the attention of experimental psychologists for a number of years.

Beginning in 1867, Wundt gave a course on physiological psychology at Heidelberg; this was the very first formal offering of such a course. Out of this work came what is often considered the most important book in the history of psychology, *Grundzüge der physiologischen Psychologie* (*Principles of Physiological Psychology*), which was published in two parts in 1873 and 1874, and went through six editions in 37 years, the last appearing in 1911. Undoubtedly Wundt's masterpiece, this book firmly established psychology as a laboratory science with its own problems and methods of experimentation. For many years the *Grundzüge* served experimental psychologists as a storehouse of information and a record of the progress of the new psychology. It was in the preface of this book that Wundt noted his goal of attempting "to mark out a new domain of science." That this book uses "physiological psychology" in its title is of great significance. Wundt intended that his psychology use the methods of research developed in physiology.

Wundt began the longest and most important phase of his career in

1875 when he became Professor of Philosophy at Leipzig, where he worked as prodigiously as ever for 45 years. He established his laboratory at Leipzig shortly after his arrival there, and in 1881 began the journal *Philosophische Studien* (*Philosophical Studies*), the official organ of the new laboratory and the new science. With Wundt's handbook, laboratory, and scholarly journal, the new psychology was well under way.

His spreading fame and the laboratory drew a large number of students to Leipzig to work with Wundt. Among these students were many subsequent contributors to psychology, including several Americans, most of whom returned to the United States to begin laboratories of their own. Through these students, the Leipzig Laboratory exercised an immense influence on the development of psychology. It served as the model for the many new laboratories that were developed in the latter part of the nineteenth century. The many students who flocked to Leipzig, united as they were in point of view and common purpose, at least initially, constituted a school of thought in psychology.

Wundt's lectures at Leipzig were very popular and extremely well attended. His classroom manner has been described by Titchener as follows:

> Wundt would appear at exactly the correct minute—punctuality was essential—dressed all in black and carrying a small sheaf of lecture notes. He clattered up the side aisle to the platform with an awkward shuffle and a sound as if his soles were made of wood. On the platform was a long desk where demonstrations were performed. He made a few gestures—a forefinger across his forehead, a rearrangement of his chalk—then faced the audience and placed his elbows on the bookrest. His voice was weak at first, then gained in strength and emphasis. As he talked his arms and hands moved up and down, pointing and waving, in some mysterious way illustrative. His head and body were rigid, and only the hands played back and forth. He seldom referred to the few jotted notes. As the clock struck the end of the hour he stopped and, stooping a little, clattered out as he had clattered in [Miller & Buckhout, 1973, p. 29].

At the first conference with each new group of graduate students, Wundt appeared with a list of research topics, which he proceeded to assign to the students in the order in which they stood. (There was, apparently, no question of their sitting down in his presence.) Research on those assigned topics was most thoroughly supervised and Wundt held absolute power of acceptance or rejection on completion of the thesis. The spirit of German scientific dogmatism flourished openly at the Leipzig Laboratory.

In his personal life, Wundt was quiet and unassuming, his days following a carefully and totally regulated pattern. In the morning he worked on a current book or article, read student theses, and edited his journal. In the afternoon he attended examinations or visited the laboratory. Cattell (1928) remarked that Wundt's laboratory visits were limited to no more than 5 or 10 minutes. Apparently, despite his great faith in laboratory research, "he was not himself a laboratory worker [p. 545]." After this, he walked while thinking about his lecture for the afternoon, always given at 4 P.M. In view of his rigorous and regulated life of scholarship, it is perhaps surprising to find that many of his evenings were occupied by his interests in music and current affairs.

A laboratory and a journal established, an immense amount of research under direction, Wundt turned his tremendous energy to philosophy in the years 1880–1891, writing on ethics, logic, and systematic philosophy. In addition to these efforts, he published the second edition of *Physiological Psychology* in 1880 and the third edition in 1887, all the while contributing articles to the *Studien*.

Yet another field on which Wundt focused his considerable talent was a task he had outlined in the *Beiträge* in 1862: the creation of a social psychology. Toward the end of the nineteenth century, he returned to this project, which culminated in the 10 volumes of his *Völkerpsychologie (Folk Psychology)*, published between 1900 and 1920. Folk psychology was concerned with the investigation of the various stages of mental development in mankind as manifested in language, art, myths, social customs, law, and morals. The implications of this work for psychology are of far greater significance than its content, for it served to divide the new science of psychology into two parts, the experimental and the social. The simpler mental functions, such as sensation and perception, can and must be studied by laboratory investigation, Wundt believed. But he argued that scientific experimentation is impossible when it comes to the study of the higher mental processes, since they are so thoroughly conditioned by linguistic habits and other aspects of one's cultural training. Thus, according to Wundt, the higher thought processes could be studied effectively only by the nonexperimental approaches of sociology, anthropology, and social psychology. This contention that social forces play a major role in the development of the complicated higher mental processes is both true and important. However, Wundt's conclusion—that the higher mental processes cannot be studied experimentally—was negated by later research efforts.

Wundt's enormous productivity continued, without a break, for 63 years until his death in 1920. Consistent with his lifelong systematic habits, he died shortly after completing his psychological reminiscences. Boring

(1950) noted that Wundt wrote 53,735 pages in all, an output of 2.2 pages a day from 1853 to 1920! To read his works would take nearly 2½ years at the rate of 60 pages a day. Few men have accomplished so much, at such a high level of competence, in such a short period of time.

The Wundtian System

The Subject Matter of Psychology

Wundt stated that the subject matter of psychology is immediate experience as opposed to mediate experience. Mediate experience provides us with information or knowledge about something other than the experience itself. This is the usual form in which we use experience to acquire knowledge about our experiential world. If we look at a flower and say, "The flower is red," the statement implies that our primary interest is in the flower and not in the fact that we are experiencing red. According to Wundt, the immediate experience in looking at this flower is not in the object itself (the flower), but rather in the experience of red. Thus, immediate experience, for Wundt, is experience per se, free and unbiased by any higher-level interpretations (as in describing this experience of red as a flower). If we describe the various experiences we "feel" when we have a toothache, our concern is with immediate experience. If, however, we say "I have a toothache," we are concerned with mediate experience.

To Wundt, it was the basic experiences such as red (the experience of red) that formed the basic states of consciousness or elements of the mind. Wundt wanted to analyze or break down the mind or consciousness into its most elemental components, just as the natural scientists were breaking down their subject matter, the material universe.

The Method of Study

Since, according to Wundt, psychology is the science of experience, the method of psychology must therefore involve observation of experience. Since no one can observe an experience except the person having it, the method must involve self-observation or introspection. The use of introspection was not new with Wundt, for even a cursory review can trace its use back to Socrates. What was an important innovation was Wundt's application of precise experimental control over the conditions of introspection.

The use of introspection in psychology was derived from physics, where introspection had been used to study light and sound, and physiology, where it had been used to study the sense organs. To obtain information on the operations of the sense organs, for example, the investigator would apply a stimulus to a sense organ and ask the subject to report on the sensation produced.

Wundt set forth quite explicit rules for the proper use of introspection in his laboratory: (1) the observer must be able to determine when the process is to be introduced; (2) he must be in a state of readiness or "strained attention"; (3) it must be possible to repeat the observation several times; and (4) the experimental conditions must be capable of variation in terms of controlled manipulation of stimuli. The last condition invokes the essence of the experimental method—varying the conditions of the stimulus situation and observing the resulting changes in the experiences of the subject.

Introspection, as practiced at Leipzig, was a skill acquired by Wundt's students only after a very long period of rigorous apprenticeship. To be able to report on the basic elements of an experience required arduous training.

For example, Boring (1953) reports that observers in Wundt's reaction-time experiments had to perform approximately 10,000 introspective observations before they were considered skilled enough to provide valid data.

The Goals of Psychology

Having defined psychology's subject matter and method, Wundt then considered its threefold goal or problem: (1) to analyze the conscious processes into their basic elements; (2) to discover how these elements are connected; and (3) to determine their laws of connection.

The Elements of Experience

Wundt considered sensations—aroused whenever a sense organ is stimulated and the resulting impulse reaches the brain—as one of the elementary forms of experience. He classified sensations according to either their modality (vision, hearing, and so on), intensity, or duration. Wundt saw no fundamental difference between sensations and images, for images are also associated with cortical excitation. In keeping with his physiological orientation, Wundt assumed the existence of a direct correspondence between the excitation of the cerebral cortex and the corresponding sensory experience. He regarded the mind and body as parallel, but not interacting, systems. Thus, the mind did not depend on the body and could be studied effectively by itself.

Feelings were the other elementary form of experience. Wundt thought that both sensations and feelings are simultaneous aspects of immediate experience. Feelings are the subjective complements of sensations but they do not come directly from any sense organ. Sensations are accompanied by certain feeling qualities, and when sensations combine to form a more complex state, a feeling quality will result from this combination of sensations.

Wundt developed his famous, and highly controversial, tridimensional theory of feeling from his own introspective observations. Working with a metronome (which produces audible clicks at regular intervals), Wundt reported that at the end of a row of clicks, some rhythmic patterns appeared to be more pleasant or more agreeable than others. He concluded that part of the experience of any such pattern is a subjective feeling of pleasure or displeasure. (Note that this subjective feeling is a simultaneous aspect of the sensation of the clicks.)

He then suggested that this feeling state can be placed at a point along a continuum ranging from agreeable to disagreeable. A second kind of feeling was also detected while listening to the clicks. Wundt reported the feeling of a slight tension while waiting for each successive click, followed by a feeling of relief after the occurrence of the anticipated click. From this he concluded that, in addition to a pleasure–displeasure continuum, his feelings seemed to have a tension–relief dimension. Moreover, he reported a mildly excited feeling when the click rate was increased, and a more quiet feeling when the rate was reduced.

Through this laborious procedure of patiently varying the speed of the metronome and meticulously noting his experiences (his sensations and feelings), Wundt arrived at three independent and distinct dimensions of feeling: (1) pleasure–displeasure; (2) tension–relaxation; (3) excitement–depression. Every feeling, he stated, can be located somewhere in this three-dimensional space, presented in Figure 4.1.

Wundt felt that emotions are complex compounds of these elementary feelings, and that each of the elementary feelings could be effectively described by defining its position on each of the three dimensions. Emotions are thus reduced to conscious contents of the mind. His theory of feelings stimulated a great deal of research in his own and other laboratories, but did not withstand the test of time.

The Doctrine of Apperception

Wundt recognized that when we look at the real world we see a unity of perceptions. For example, we see a tree as a unity; we do not "see" the many and varied sensations of brightness, hue, shape, and so on, that his observers reported in the laboratory. Our visual experience

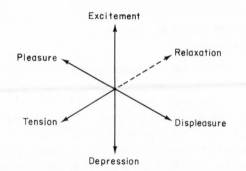

Figure 4.1. Wundt's tridimensional theory of feeling. (From p. 21, *Psychology* by G. A. Miller with slight modification. Copyright 1962 by G. A. Miller. Reprinted by permission of Harper & Row.)

"comprehends" the tree as a unity and not as each of the numerous elementary sensations and feelings that might constitute the tree.

How is this totality of conscious experience compounded or built up from elementary component parts? Wundt postulated his doctrine of apperception to account for our unified conscious experiences. He designated the actual process of relating or combining the various elements into a unity as the principle of *creative synthesis* or *law of psychic resultants.* The many elementary experiences are organized into a whole by this process of creative synthesis, which says, in essence, that the combination of elements creates new properties. As Wundt stated it, "Every psychic compound has characteristics which are by no means the mere sum of the characteristics of the elements [1896, p. 375]." Thus, something new is created out of the synthesis of the elemental parts of experience. Perhaps we might say, as the Gestalt psychologists said repeatedly, beginning in 1912, that the whole is more than the sum of its parts.

This notion of a creative synthesis has a counterpart in chemistry: The combination of chemical elements produces resultants containing new properties that are not properties of the original elements. Apperception, therefore, is an active process—it is not merely acted upon by the experienced elements; rather it acts upon them in the creative synthesis of the parts to make up the whole.

Wundt gave the larger share of his attention to the opposite of creative synthesis: the analysis of mind, the reduction of conscious experience to its elementary component parts. The notion of a creative synthesis of these parts was relatively neglected by him. Yet the fact that he did make synthesis a feature of his formal system is historically significant because the notion was to have important repercussions.

The Research Topics of the
Leipzig Laboratory

Wundt himself defined the problems for experimental psychology during the early years of the Leipzig Laboratory. The great man assigned to his students research topics that coincided with his own aims. For a number of years the problems with which the new experimental psychology concerned itself were defined by the work done at the Leipzig Laboratory. Even more important, the extensive research performed there demonstrated that an experimentally based science of psychology was possible.

Since the methods and subject matter of the Leipzig Laboratory formed the foundation for the new science, it is important to understand the nature of the work during the early years. Wundt believed that his new science should initially be concerned with research problems that had already been investigated and reduced to some kind of empirical and quantitative form. For the most part, he did not occupy himself with new areas of research, concerning himself chiefly with the extension and more formal development of existing research problems.

Almost all the work emerging from the Laboratory was published in the *Studien*. Very little research was published in this journal that had not been done either at Leipzig or by Wundt's students so soon after leaving Leipzig that it still bore the imprint of the master. Over 100 studies were performed in the first 20 years of the Laboratory's existence.

The first series of studies involved the psychological and physiological aspects of vision and hearing and, to some extent, the so-called lower senses. Typical problems investigated in the area of visual sensation and perception included the psychophysics of color, color contrast, peripheral vision, negative afterimages, visual contrast, color blindness, visual size, and optical illusions. Psychophysical methods were used to investigate auditory sensations. Tactual sensations were studied as well as the time-sense, that is, the perception or estimation of intervals of varying lengths of time.

A topic that also claimed a great amount of attention in the Laboratory was reaction time. The speed of a reaction had been a topic of investigation since the end of the eighteenth century and had been studied by Helmholtz and by J. C. Donders, a Dutch physiologist. Wundt believed that he could demonstrate experimentally the three stages that he thought were present in a person's response to a stimulus—perception, apperception, and will.

On presentation of a stimulus, the subject first perceives it, then apperceives it, and finally wills to react (from which muscular movement results). Wundt hoped to develop a "chronometry of the mind" by being able to measure the times for the various mental processes such as cognition, discrimination, will, and so on. The promise of the method was not to be realized, for in practiced subjects the three stages were not clearly apparent, and the times for the separate processes were neither constant from person to person nor from study to study.

Studies on reaction time were replaced by research on attention and feeling. Wundt considered attention to be the most vivid perception of only a small portion of the entire content of consciousness at any one time. The reference is to what is commonly called the focus of attention. Those stimuli in this focus are the most clearly perceived and are quite distinct and separate from the rest of the visual field. A simple example is constituted by the words you are now reading relative to the rest of this page and other objects in the surrounding environment that are perceived less clearly. In addition to studying the range and the fluctuation of attention in the Leipzig Laboratory, one of Wundt's students, James McKeen Cattell, performed a classic study of attention span, finding that four, five, or six units could be perceived in one short exposure.

Studies of feeling were undertaken in the 1890s to attempt to support the tridimensional theory. Wundt used the method of paired comparisons, which requires the comparison of stimuli in terms of the subjective feeling aroused. Other studies attempted to relate bodily changes, such as pulse rate, breathing, and so on, to corresponding feeling states.

Another area of investigation was the analysis of verbal associations, work begun by the Englishman, Sir Francis Galton (see Chapter 6), in which subjects are asked to respond with a single word upon the presentation of the stimulus word. Wundt proceeded to classify the types of word association discovered when single-word stimuli were presented, in order to determine the nature of all verbal association.

The experimental areas of the psychophysiology of the senses, reaction time, psychophysics, and association constituted more than half of all the work published in the first few years of the *Studien*. Wundt manifested some slight concern with child psychology and animal psychology, but apparently undertook no experimentation in these areas, believing that the conditions of study could not be adequately controlled.

In Retrospect

Wolman (1960) suggested that the act of establishing the first psychological laboratory at Leipzig required a great deal of courage. To do so at that time required a man well versed in both contemporary physiology and philosophy, and capable of combining these disciplines effectively. In order to accomplish his goal of establishing a new science, Wundt had to get rid of the nonscientific past and cut the ties between the new scientific psychology and the old mental philosophy. —

By postulating that the subject matter of psychology was experience and that psychology was a science based on experience, Wundt was able to avoid discussions of the nature of the immortal soul and its relationship to the mortal body. He said simply, though emphatically, that psychology does not deal with this issue. At that time, this assertion was a great and significant step forward.

One cannot help but marvel at Wundt's outstanding creative energy and endurance for a period of more than 60 years. His creation of a scientific experimental psychology commands immense respect and is the source of his greatest influence. He began (as he had announced his intention of doing) a new domain of science, and conducted purely psychological research in a laboratory he designed exclusively for that purpose. He published the results in his own journal and tried to develop a systematic theory of the human mind. His thoroughly trained students founded additional laboratories, and continued experimenting on the problems and with the techniques set forth by the great man. Thus, Wundt provided psychology with all the accouterments of a modern science.

Murphy (1949) noted, "Before Wundt published his *Physiological Psychology* and established his laboratory, psychology was little more than a waif knocking now at the door of physiology, now at the door of ethics, now at the door of epistemology. In 1879, it set itself up as an experimental science with a local habitation and a name [p. 159]." The times were, of course, ready for the Wundtian movement, which was the natural outcome of the development of the physiological sciences, particularly in the German universities. That Wundt was the culmination of the movement and not its originator in the strictest sense of the word does not diminish his stature. It did, after all, require the stroke of a kind of genius, and a firm sense of dedication, courage, and vigor, to bring such a movement to its fulfillment. The results of his efforts represent an achievement of such overwhelming importance that Wundt is accorded a unique position among psychologists of the more modern period.

Like any great man, Wundt was subject to criticism with regard to many points of his systematic position and his experimental technique of introspection. With respect to the method he chose for the new science, it is very hard to verify his research findings. If a different person's introspection gives different results, how can we decide who is right?

Experiments using introspection, unlike more objective experimentation, do not insure agreement among experimenters, since introspective observation is a strictly private affair. As such, disagreements cannot be settled by repeated observations. However, given the subject matter—conscious experience—introspection was the only tool available at the time, and it was thought that with more training and experience the method could be improved. We will discuss further criticisms of structuralism at the end of the next chapter.

During Wundt's lifetime, it was difficult to criticize his total system, primarily because he wrote so much and so fast: By the time a critic had prepared an attack on a particular point, Wundt had changed his argument in a new edition or was writing on an entirely new and different topic. A critic, in a word, would be outwritten and buried under volumes of highly detailed and complex writings.

Further, since his theories were more like classificatory schemes, they tended to be somewhat loosely knit and almost impossible to verify. There was no vital center to his program where a critic might damage him with a single stroke. As William James noted: "Cut him up like a worm, and each fragment crawls; there is no *nœud vital* in his mental medulla oblongata, so that you can't kill him all at once [Perry, 1935, p. 68]."

The Wundtian position, as boldly and forcefully advanced by his student Titchener (Chapter 5), has not withstood the test of time. Structuralism is no longer an active issue in contemporary psychology and has not been for many years. Contemporary psychologists have voiced complaints about what they now see as the narrowness of Wundt's position. However, as we shall see in the following chapters:

> Almost all the new schools have been founded as a protest against some one or other characteristic of Wundt's psychology, but we may welcome the schools without condoning the complaint. At any one time a science is simply what its researches yield, and the researches are nothing more than those problems for which effective methods have been found and for which the times are ready [Boring, 1950, p. 343].

Wundt's achievements, however, are not diminished by the fact that much of the history of psychology after him consisted of rebellion against some of the limitations he had placed on the field. Indeed, that fact enhances his achievements. Forward movement must have something to push against and Wilhelm Wundt provided a compelling and magnificent beginning to modern experimental psychology.

Other Early European Psychologists

Wundt held his monopoly on the new psychology for only a short time. At other laboratories in Germany the science was also beginning to flourish. Although he was obviously the most important organizer and systematizer in the early days of psychology, there were others who also began to influence the new science. Some of these early psychologists disagreed with Wundt on a number of points but all shared his belief that introspection was the only proper method to be used in psychology. Some of them, rather paradoxically, came to influence structural psychology by their opposition to it rather than by any direct positive contributions to the position. Even though these early non-Wundtian psychologists had different points of view, all were engaged in the common enterprise of developing the new psychology. Their endeavors made Germany the undisputed center of the new movement.

However, while Germany was the focal point of the new science of psychology, there were simultaneous developments in England which were to give psychology an entirely new theme and direction. Charles Darwin proposed his theory of evolution and Sir Francis Galton began work on the psychology of individual differences. These influences were to direct the development of American psychology at least as much as the work of Wundt, and perhaps more so.

In addition, early American psychologists (most of whom studied at Leipzig) returned home and made of the Wundtian psychology they had studied something uniquely American in form and temperament.

But more of these developments later. The important point for now is that very shortly after its founding, psychology became divided into differing directions. Although Wundt had developed "the" psychology, it shortly became only one of several distinct varieties.

We now turn to a discussion of Wundt's contemporaries in Germany.

Hermann Ebbinghaus (1850–1909)

Just a few years after Wundt stated that it was not possible to experiment upon the higher mental processes, a then unknown psychologist who worked alone, isolated from any center of psychology, began successfully to experiment upon these processes.

Hermann Ebbinghaus became the first psychologist to experimentally investigate learning and memory. In doing so, he not only challenged Wundt, but he changed quite radically the way in which association or learning could be dealt with.

Prior to Ebbinghaus, most notably in the work of the British empiricists and associationists, the customary way to study association was to deal with those associations already formed. The investigator would, in a sense, "work backward," that is, attempt to determine how the associations had been formed. Ebbinghaus began at a different starting point: the development of associations. In this way, it was possible to control the conditions under which the associations were formed and thus to make the study of learning considerably more objective.

Accepted as one of the truly great manifestations of original genius in experimental psychology, Ebbinghaus' investigation of learning and forgetting was the first venture into a truly *psychological* problem area, one that was not simply a part of physiology, as was the case with so much of Wundt's research. As a result, experimental psychology was considerably widened in scope.

Born near Bonn in 1850, Ebbinghaus undertook his university studies first at Bonn in history and philology and then at Halle and Berlin. In the course of his academic training his interests shifted to philosophy, in which he received his degree in 1873, following military service during the Franco–Prussian War. The next 7 years were devoted to independent study in Berlin, England, and France, where his interests shifted toward science. About 1876, Ebbinghaus bought a secondhand copy of Fechner's *Elemente der Psychophysik* at a bookstall in Paris. This chance encounter profoundly influenced him, and shortly, the new psychology. Fechner's mathematical approach to psychological phenomena was an exciting disclosure to the young Ebbinghaus, and he resolved to do for the study of memory what Fechner had done for psychophysics, through rigid systematic measurements. He wanted to apply the experimental methods to the higher mental processes and decided, probably as a result of the influence of the English associationists, to make the attempt in the field of memory.

Consider the scope of Ebbinghaus' course of action in the light of the status of the problem he chose and his own personal situation. Learning and memory had never been studied experimentally; only a few years before, the eminent Wundt had stated that they could not be. [Boring (1950) notes that Ebbinghaus must surely have known of this work.] Further, he had no academic appointment, no university setting in which to conduct his work, no teacher, and no laboratory. Nevertheless, he carried out alone, over a period of 5 years, a long series of carefully controlled and thorough studies, using himself as the only subject.

For the basic measure of learning he adapted a technique from the English associationists, who had gradually been emphasizing the principle of frequency of associations as a condition of recall. He reasoned that the difficulty of learning material could be measured by simply counting the number of repetitions needed to learn the material to a criterion of one perfect reproduction.

In addition to using similar (though not identical) materials to be learned, Ebbinghaus repeated the same task over and over again so as to be assured of the accuracy of his results. In this way he could cancel out variable errors from trial to trial. Then he was able to take an average measure. So systematic was Ebbinghaus in his experimentation that he even regulated his own personal habits, keeping them as constant as possible and following the same rigid daily pattern, always learning the material at exactly the same time each day.

For the subject matter of his research—the material to be learned—Ebbinghaus invented the nonsense syllable. He recognized an inherent difficulty in using prose or poetry: Meanings or associations are already attached to words by those who know the language. These already formed associations can facilitate the learning of material and, since they exist at the time of experimentation, cannot be meaningfully controlled. Ebbinghaus therefore sought material that would be uniformly unassociated, completely homogeneous, and equally unfamiliar, material with which there could not be any past associations. Nonsense syllables, formed of two consonants with a vowel in between, as in *lef, bok,* or *yat,* satisfied these criteria. He put all possible combinations of consonants and vowels on separate cards, giving him a supply of 2300 syllables from which to draw at random those to be learned.

Ebbinghaus designed a number of experiments to determine the influence of various conditions on both learning and retention. One of these studies investigated the difference between his speed in memorizing lists of nonsense syllables and in memorizing meaningful materials. To determine this difference, he memorized stanzas of Byron's *Don Juan,* each stanza having 80 syllables. He found that it required about nine readings to memorize one stanza. He then memorized a list of 80 nonsense syllables and found that this task required almost 80 repetitions. He concluded that meaningless material is approximately nine times as hard to learn as meaningful material.

He also investigated the effect of the length of the material to be learned on the number of repetitions necessary for a perfect reproduction, and found that longer material required more repetitions and, consequently, more time to learn. He found, further, that the average time per syllable was markedly increased by lengthening the number of syllables to be learned. These results, of course, are predictable enough in a general way; the more we have to learn, the longer it will take us. The great significance of the work is in his very careful control of conditions, his quantitative analysis of the data, and the finding that both total learning time and time per syllable increase with longer lists.

Ebbinghaus went on to investigate a number of other variables thought to influence learning and retention, such as the effect of overlearning (repeating the lists more times than necessary for one perfect reproduction), near and remote associations within lists, effect of repeated learning or review, and influence of the passage of time between learning and recall.

His research on the influence of the passage of time produced the famous Ebbinghaus curve of forgetting. This curve, as every psychology student knows, demonstrates that material is forgotten very rapidly in the first few hours after learning, and more and more slowly thereafter.

In 1880, Ebbinghaus received an academic appointment at the University of Berlin, where he continued his research on memory, repeating and verifying his earlier studies. He published the results of all of his research in the important *Über das Gedächtnis (On Memory)* in 1885. "It was epoch-making, not merely because of its scope and style, although these features must have helped, but because it was seen at once to be a breach by experimental psychology in the barrier about the 'higher mental processes.' Ebbinghaus had opened up a new field . . . [Boring, 1950, p. 388]."

This book represents what is perhaps the most brilliant single investigation in the history of experimental psychology. In addition to beginning a whole new field of study (which is still vital today), it provided a striking example of great technical skill, perseverance, and ingenuity. It is not possible to find, in the entire history of psychology, any other single investigator working alone who subjected himself to such a rigid regime of experimentation. His research was so exacting, thorough, and systematic that it is still cited in modern textbooks.

Ebbinghaus did not continue research on memory but instead let others develop the field and extend and refine the methodology. Actually, he published relatively little in any area after 1885. In 1886, he was promoted to assistant professor at Berlin. He founded a laboratory and a journal (the latter with Arthur König), the *Zeitschrift für Psychologie und Physiologie der Sinnesorgane (Journal of Psychology and Physiology of the Sense Organs)* in 1890. A new journal was needed in Germany because Wundt's *Studien*, as the exclusive organ of the Leipzig Laboratory, could not present all the research being conducted at that time. The need for a new journal, just 9 years after Wundt had begun his, is significant testimony to the phenomenal growth, in both size and diversity, of the new psychology.

Apparently because of his lack of publications, Ebbinghaus was not promoted again at Berlin and in 1894, he moved to a lesser post in the university hierarchy at Breslau, where he remained until 1905. There he developed a sentence completion test, apparently the first successful test of the so-called higher mental capacities, a modified form of which is used in many modern-day tests of general intelligence.

In 1902, Ebbinghaus published in complete form his highly successful general text, *Die Grundzüge der Psychologie (The Principles of Psychology)*, and in 1908 there appeared an even more popular text, *Abriss der Psychologie (A Summary of Psychology)*. Both books went through several editions and were revised several times by others after Ebbinghaus' death. Ebbinghaus left Breslau for Halle in 1905, and died suddenly of pneumonia 4 years later at the age of 59.

Ebbinghaus did not make any theoretical or systematic contributions to psychology; indeed, he had no formal system, no disciples of importance to psychology. He did not found a school, nor did he seem to want to. Yet, he is of great importance not only to the study of learning and memory, which he began, but also to experimental psychology as a whole. Boring commented that he was influential "because he helped to make articulate and effective the spirit of the times that called for an emancipation of psychology from philosophy [1950, p. 392]."

One measure of the overall historical worth of a scientist is how well his position and research findings stand up to the test of time. By that standard, one might suggest that Ebbinghaus was more important than Wundt. His research brought objectivity, quantification, and experimentation to the study of association or learning, a topic that has become a central one in contemporary psychology. It is due to Ebbinghaus that the concept of association changed from mere speculation about its attributes, to its investigation with the aid of the scientific method. Further, many of his findings on learning and memory remain valid today, a century later. There are few psychologists in the history of the field about whom this can be said.

George Elias Müller (1850–1934)

A physiologist and philosopher by training, Müller also had a strong interest in psychology, which he expressed in a 40-year career at Göttingen. From 1881 until 1921 his well equipped laboratory rivalled that at Leipzig and attracted many students from Europe and America.

Müller's research contributions were so substantial that Titchener delayed for 2 years the second volume of his *Experimental Psychology* so that he could incorporate material from Müller's new book.

Müller did considerable work on color vision, and extensively criticized and elaborated on Fechner's work in psychophysics. He was one of the first to work in the area begun by Ebbinghaus—the experimental study of learning and memory. His careful research verified and extended many of Ebbinghaus' findings. Ebbinghaus' approach had been strictly objective; that is, he had not recorded any introspections about his mental processes while engaged in his learning tasks. Müller felt that Ebbinghaus' reports tended to make learning appear as too much of a mechanical or automatic process. He believed that the mind is more actively involved in the learning process, and so, while he used the objective methods of Ebbinghaus, Müller added introspective report. His results indicated that the learning of his subjects was not proceeding mechanically, that the subjects were quite actively involved in learning. They seemed to be consciously organizing and grouping the material, and even finding meanings in the nonsense syllables.

On the basis of this research, Müller concluded that association by contiguity alone cannot adequately account for learning because the subjects seemed to be actively searching for relations among the stimuli to be learned. He suggested that there is a set of mental phenomena, such as readiness, hesitation, and doubt (the so-called "conscious attitudes"), that actively influence learning. Similar findings soon followed from the work of the Würzburg laboratory.

One final contribution to the study of learning deserves mention. Along with Friedrich Schumann, Müller developed the memory drum, a revolving drum that makes possible the uniform presentation of material to be learned. By now a familiar piece of laboratory equipment, this apparatus is significant because it increased the precision and objectivity of learning research.

Franz Brentano (1838–1917)

At about age 16, Brentano began his training for the priesthood, studying at Berlin, Munich, and Tübingen, where he received his degree in philosophy in 1864. He was ordained the same year, and 2 years later began teaching philosophy at Würzburg, writing and lecturing on Aristotle.

In 1870, the Vatican Council accepted the doctrine of papal infallibility, with which Brentano could not agree. He resigned his professorship (to which he had been appointed as a priest) and left the Church. His most famous work, *Psychologie vom empirischen Standpunkte* (*Psychology from an Empirical Standpoint*), was published in 1874, the year in which the second part of the first edition of Wundt's *Principles of Physiological*

Psychology was published. Brentano's book was in direct opposition to the Wundtian view, attesting to the dissent apparent in the new psychology from the outset.

Also in 1874, Brentano was appointed Professor of Philosophy at the University of Vienna, where he remained for 20 years, during which time his influence grew considerably. He was a popular lecturer and among his students were several men who gained their own places of prominence in the history of psychology: Carl Stumpf, Christian von Ehrenfels, and Sigmund Freud. In 1894, Brentano retired and spent his remaining years in Italy and Switzerland, engaged in study and writing.

Brentano was one of the more important non-Wundtians because of his diverse influences within psychology. (We will see, in Chapter 12, that he is one of the intellectual precursors of the school of Gestalt psychology.)

Despite their vastly different approaches, Brentano shared with Wundt the goal of making psychology a science. However, whereas Wundt's psychology was plainly experimental, Brentano's was empirical. The primary method of psychology for Brentano was observation, not experimentation, though he did not reject the utility of the experimental method. An empirical approach generally is broader in scope in that it obtains its data from observation and individual experience as well as experimentation.

Brentano opposed one of Wundt's fundamental points—that psychology should study the content of conscious experience. Instead, Brentano argued that the proper subject matter of psychology is mental activity; the mental act of seeing, for example, as opposed to the study of mental content (that which is seen).

Brentano's so-called act psychology thus countered the Wundtian view that the psychic processes are contents. He argued that the distinction must be drawn between experience as a structure and experience as an activity. The sensory content of red is quite different from the activity of sensing red. Brentano urged that this act of experiencing is the true subject matter for psychology.

He argued that a color is not a mental but strictly a physical quality. The act of seeing the color, however, is mental. Of course, the act always involves an object, that is, a content is always present because the act of seeing is meaningless unless something is seen. This different subject matter also necessitated a different method of study, for acts (unlike sensory contents) are not accessible through the analytical introspection of the Leipzig Laboratory.

To study mental acts requires observation on a larger scale than that practiced by orthodox introspectionists. As a result, act psychology, as we have seen, is more empirical than experimental in its methodology. This is not to imply that Brentano's psychology was a return to speculative philosophy; though not experimental in nature, it did rely on careful observation.

Brentano's position had its loyal adherents, but the Wundtian psychology of content still maintained the place of prominence in the new psychology. Since Wundt wrote much more than Brentano, his position was better known. Also, it was easier to study sensations or contents with the new methods of psychophysics than to study the more elusive acts.

Carl Stumpf (1848–1936)

The son of a medical family, Stumpf came into contact with science at an early age but developed a greater interest in music. At the age of 7 he began studying the violin, and by age 10 was composing music. As a student at Würzburg, he was captivated by Brentano and began to study philosophy and science. At Brentano's suggestion, he went to Göttingen, where he received his doctorate in 1868. He held a number of academic appointments over the following years, during which time he turned seriously toward psychology.

In 1894, he received the most prized professorship in German psychology—at the University of Berlin. (Wundt, who at that time was the dean of German psychologists, would have seemed the logical choice for the position. It has been suggested that the influential Helmholtz opposed the appointment of Wundt.) The years at Berlin were extremely productive and the original laboratory of three small rooms grew into a large and important institute. Though his laboratory never rivaled Wundt's in scope or intensity of research, Stumpf is often considered Wundt's major direct competitor.

Stumpf's first psychological writings are concerned with space perception, but his most influential work is *Tonpsychologie* (*Psychology of Tone*), which appeared in two volumes in 1883 and 1890. This work and his other studies of music earned him a place second only to Helmholtz in the field of acoustics and were a pioneer effort in the psychological study of music.

The strong influence of Brentano was probably a reason for Stumpf's acceptance of a less rigorous form of introspection than that considered necessary at Leipzig. Stumpf argued that the primary data of psychology are phenomena. Phenomenology, the kind of introspection he favored, refers to the examination of unbiased experience—experience just as it occurs. He did not agree with Wundt on breaking experience down into elements,' for to do so, he argued, is to render the experience artificial and abstract—no longer "natural." (It was a student of Stumpf's, Edmund Husserl, who later developed the important philosophy of phenomenology.) The phenomenological movement in Germany was a precursor to other forms of psychology, notably Gestalt psychology, as will be discussed later.

A bitter controversy raged between Wundt and Stumpf in a series of publications on introspection of tones, which was started by Stumpf on a theoretical level but was made more personal by Wundt. In essence, the issue involved the question of which introspectionist's reports were the more credible. When dealing with tones, should one accept the results of highly trained introspectionists (Wundt) or of expert musicians (Stumpf)? Stumpf would not accept the results obtained at Wundt's laboratory on this problem.

Continuing to write on music and acoustics, Stumpf also began a center for the collection of recordings of primitive music from all over the world, founded the Berlin Association for Child Psychology, and published a theory of feeling in which he attempted to reduce feeling to sensation. Stumpf became one of a number of Germans who maintained their independence from Wundt and so strove to enlarge the boundaries of psychology.

Oswald Külpe (1862–1915)

Initially a student, disciple, and follower of Wundt, Külpe, in the course of his career, led a group of students in a movement to break away from what he considered the limitations of the master's work. Though Külpe's movement was not a revolution, it was a declaration of freedom against the narrowness of some of Wundt's views. Külpe worked on a number of problems that Wundt's brand of structuralism had disregarded.

After an apparently uneventful childhood, Külpe began his university training at the age of 19 at Leipzig. His original intention was to study history, but under the influence of Wundt he changed, for a while at least, to philosophy and experimental psychology, which at that time (1881) was still very much in its infancy. History still held a strong attraction for Külpe, however, because after 1 year with Wundt he went to Berlin to study it again for a semester. Two further academic forays into psychology and history followed before he finally (1886) returned to Wundt and Leipzig for 8 years. After receiving his degree at Leipzig, he stayed on as *Dozent* and assistant to Wundt, carried on research in the Laboratory, and wrote a psychology textbook, *Grundriss der Psychologie* (*Outline of Psychology*). This text, published in 1893 and dedicated to Wundt, defined psychology as the science of the facts of experience as dependent on the experiencing individual.

In 1894, Külpe became a professor at Würzburg, where 2 years later he established a laboratory that before long became almost as important as the Leipzig Laboratory. Among the students attracted to Würzburg were several Americans, one of whom, James Rowland Angell, was an important figure in the development of functionalism (Chapter 8). Strangely enough, Külpe was apparently more concerned with philosophy and esthetics than with psychology during his laboratory's early years. While his own writings are philosophical in nature, a great deal of research performed under his direction in his laboratory was published. Külpe served not only as the inspiration for his students' research, but also as observer in most of the laborious and routine introspective experiments.

In the *Grundriss*, Külpe did not discuss the higher mental process of thought at all. In this respect his position was congruent with that of Wundt, in whose shadow he still operated. By the turn of the century, however, Külpe was convinced that the thought processes could be studied experimentally. Memory, another higher mental process, had already been studied experimentally by Hermann Ebbinghaus in 1885, as we have seen. If memory could be studied in the laboratory, why not thought? For the first time, experimentation was consistently applied to the higher mental processes. Posing this question put Külpe into direct opposition to his former mentor, for Wundt had said most emphatically that the higher mental processes could not be studied experimentally.

A second point of difference between the Würzburg school (as it came to be called) and Wundt's system related to the method of introspection. For Wundt, introspection involved having an experience and then describing it. Külpe developed a new method, called "systematic experimental introspection," involving the performance of a complex task, such as the establishment of logical connections between concepts, after which the subject was required to render a retrospective report of his experiences during the task. In other words, the subject had to perform some mental process, such as thinking or judging, and then examine how he thought or judged. The method is systematic in that the whole experience is described quite precisely by fractionating it into time periods. Similar tasks were repeated many times so that the introspective accounts could be corrected, corroborated, and amplified. Also, introspective reports were often supplemented by questioning to direct the subject's attention to particular points.

— The two forms of introspection also differed in that Külpe's subjects did not know in advance what they were to observe, whereas Wundt's subjects did. Thus, there were vast differences in both subject matter and method between the two laboratories.

Külpe did not reject, however, Wundt's focus on conscious experience, his research tool of introspection, nor even his fundamental task of analyzing consciousness into its basic structure. The Würzburg school did not so much revolt against the master as attempt to expand his concept of psychology's subject matter to include the higher mental processes, and to refine the method of introspection.

What were the results of this attempted expansion and refinement? Wundt's point of view, as we have seen, stressed that conscious experience can be reduced to its component sensory or imaginal elements: All experience, Wundt had said, is composed of sensations or images. Külpe's program of direct introspection of thought processes found evidence supporting just the opposite point of view: that thinking can occur without any sensory or imaginal content! This finding came to be identified as "imageless thought," to represent the notion of meanings in thought that do not seem to involve any specific images. A nonsensory form or aspect of consciousness was thus identified.

The first important contribution from this school was a study by Karl Marbe on the comparative judgment of weights. Marbe found that although sensations and images are indeed present during the task, they seem to play no part in the process of judgment itself. The subject really does not know how the judgments (of lighter or heavier) come into his mind. This finding contradicted the belief about thought that had been held for centuries. It had been supposed that in making a judgment of this kind, the subject retained a mental image of the first object and compared it with the sensory impression of the second object. Marbe's experiment demonstrated that there is no such comparison of image and impression, and that the process of judgment is much more elusive than had been supposed.

These and related experiments conducted at Würzburg demonstrated that, though the conscious elements usually considered necessary for thought are not essential for thought, there are apparently other conscious states present that had not been previously suspected. These "new" states, such as hesitation, doubt, confidence, searching, or waiting for an answer, were considered to be neither sensations, images, nor feelings, and were initially called "conscious attitudes." In a subsequent work, J. Orth suggested that Wundt's feelings of strain–relaxation and excitement–calm can be reduced to these same intangible and obscure conscious attitudes.

The Würzburg group also dealt with association and will. A classic study by Henry Watt demonstrated that in an associative task (for example, asking a subject to find a subordinate or superordinate of a particular word), the subject has little relevant information to report as regards his conscious process of judgment. This finding provided a further demonstration of conscious experience that could not be reduced to Wundt's sensations and images. Watt found that his subjects were able to respond correctly without being consciously aware of intending to do so during the time of response. He concluded that the conscious work was done prior to the performance of the task, at the time when the instructions were given and understood. Upon receipt of the instructions, the subject, according to Watt, determined to react in the manner required. Upon presentation of the stimulus word, the subject carried out the instructions without any further conscious effort. Through the instructions the subject had apparently established an unconscious set or "determining tendency" to respond in the way the instructions directed. Once the task had been understood and this determining tendency adopted, the actual task was performed with little, if any, conscious effort. What the Würzburgers suggested is that predispositions outside of consciousness are somehow able to control conscious activities.

A new period in the Würzburg school began in 1907 with the work of Karl Bühler, whose method involves presenting to the subject a question that requires some thought before it can be answered. The subject then gives as complete an account as possible of the steps involved in reaching the answer, with the experimenter interjecting questions about the process. Bühler's importance lies in his careful demonstration of the existence of nonsensory thought processes. This notion had already been uncovered, as we have seen, but it had been only an aspect, and not a major focus, of the previous Würzburg work. Bühler, more than any of the other Würzburgers, stressed the notion of elements of experience that are not sensory in nature. He asserted quite explicitly that these new types of structural elements, these thought elements, are vitally important in the process of thought and must be given serious consideration.

Not unexpectedly, Külpe's refinement of Wundt's method of introspection and the attempt to add to the list of elements evoked strong criticism from the more orthodox Wundtian structuralists. It came in the form of vigorous and scathing attacks from Wundt and his pupil, Titchener. Wundt called the Würzburgers' form of introspection "mock" experiments and said that their method did not really involve experimentation or introspection. Through it all, Külpe maintained the highest regard for both of his critics.

In a way it is strange that the Wundtians so strongly opposed the Würzburgers' notion of nonsensory mental life, for Külpe, after all, proceeded along paths that Wundt had opened. And had not Wundt himself thought along not too dissimilar lines? Was not his notion of feelings a recognition of nonsensory elements of conscious experience? It was certainly no accident that Külpe, a product of Wundtian training, had instigated this movement.

Are there really fundamental points of difference between the Würz-burgers and the Wundtians? In terms of basic emphasis, goals, and methods, probably not. Külpe and his followers were still, after all, trying to find the elements of conscious experience through introspective report. They were, like Wundt, analytical in their approach and structuralists in their basic orientation.

The 15 years that Külpe remained at Würzburg were his most influential in the history of psychology. In 1909 he went to Bonn, where he founded a laboratory, and in 1913 he moved to Munich. His interest in philosophical problems, particularly esthetics, came to the fore in his post-Würzburg years. Külpe wrote very little concerning his students' work at Würzburg, and his planned description of the nature of the thought processes was never written. Boring commented that Külpe "did not in his life-time convince his critics. At the dramatic moment in this work he died, too early, at the age of 53, without having yet convincingly demonstrated to the world that Wundt was wrong, or that Wundt was right, when he said that one can not experiment upon thought [1950, p. 409]." Whether the world was so convinced or not, the notions developed by the Würzburgers were, to some degree, influential for the later Gestalt psychologists.

A major contribution to modern psychology is the Würzburgers' emphasis on the topic of motivation. Their key concept of determining tendency or set certainly has a bearing on motivation as treated in today's psychology. Also, their demonstration that experience depended not only on conscious elements, but also on the unconscious determining tendencies, suggests the role of unconscious determinants of behavior, which forms a major part of Freud's systematic position (Chapter 13).

Comment

We see, then, division and controversy enveloping psychology almost as soon as it was founded. But it must be emphasized that over all their differences these early psychologists shared a unity of theme and purpose.

Wundt, Ebbinghaus, Brentano, Stumpf, and others had irrevocably changed the study of man. Due to their efforts, the new psychology was no longer

> a study of the soul, certainly not an inquiry by rational analysis into its simplicity, substantiality and immortality. It was a study, by observation and experiment, of certain reactions of the human organism not included in the subject matter of any other science.

The German psychologists, in spite of their many differences, were to this extent engaged in a common enterprise; and their ability, their industry, and the common direction of their labors all made the developments in the German universities the center of the new movement in psychology [Heidbreder, 1933, p. 105].[2]

One should not conclude that the more traditional orthodox Wundtian structuralism was dead by the end of the nineteenth century. This was decidedly not the case, as we shall see from our discussion of Wundt's stalwart standard-bearer, E. B. Titchener.

SUGGESTED FURTHER READINGS

Wundt

Boring, E. G. On the subjectivity of important historical dates: Leipzig 1879. *Journal of the History of the Behavioral Sciences*, 1965, **1**, 5–9.

Cattell, J. McK. The psychological laboratory at Leipzig. *Mind*, 1888, **13**, 37–51.

Titchener, E. B. Wilhelm Wundt. *American Journal of Psychology*, 1921, **32**, 161–178.

Brentano

Puglisi, M. Brentano: A biographical sketch. *American Journal of Psychology*, 1924, **35**, 414–419.

Rancurello, A. C. *A study of Franz Brentano*. New York: Academic Press, 1968.

Titchener, E. B. Brentano and Wundt: empirical and experimental psychology. *American Journal of Psychology*, 1921, **32**, 108–120.

Stumpf

Langfeld, H. S. Carl Stumpf: 1848–1936. *American Journal of Psychology*, 1937, **49**, 316–320.

Külpe and the Würzburg School

Ogden, R. M. Oswald Külpe and the Würzburg School. *American Journal of Psychology*, 1951, **64**, 4–19.

Ebbinghaus

Shakow, D. Hermann Ebbinghaus. *American Journal of Psychology*, 1930, **42**, 505–518.

Müller

Boring, E. G. Georg Elias Müller, 1850–1934. *American Journal of Psychology*, 1935, **47**, 344–348.

[2] This and all subsequent quotations credited to Heidbreder, 1933 are from Edna Heidbreder, *Seven Psychologies*, © 1933, Renewed 1961. Reprinted by permission of Prentice-Hall, Inc., Englewood Cliffs, New Jersey.

5

Structuralism:
Final Form

~ The orthodox Wundtian brand of the new psychology was transplanted to the United States by Wundt's most devoted pupil, E. B. Titchener, and underwent its fullest development at his hands. A knowledge of Wundt's psychology provides a reasonably accurate picture of Titchener's system, though the two positions are not identical. The pupil differed on some points with the teacher, nonetheless the Titchenerian system is unmistakably Wundtian in methods, content, and spirit. ~

Edward Bradford Titchener (1867–1927)

The Life of Titchener

Titchener, a fascinating man, was English by birth, German in his professional and personal temperament, and spent his most productive years at Cornell University in the United States. For Titchener, who is often pictured clad in the academic gown he invariably wore to class, every lecture was a dramatic production. The staging was carefully prepared by assistants (under Titchener's watchful eye); his staff and junior faculty (who attended all his lectures) entered through one door to take front-row seats, and the professor came through another that led directly to the lecture platform. Afterwards, the lecture was solemnly discussed by the faculty and graduate students.

As Titchener put it, the wearing of his Oxford gown gave him the right to be dogmatic. Although he spent only 2 years with Wundt, Titchener resembled his mentor in many respects, including his autocratic nature, his very formal lectures, and even his bearded appearance.

Born in Chichester, England, of an old family that had little money, Titchener relied on his considerable intellectual abilities to win scholarships to further his education. He initially attended Malvern College and then Oxford, where he studied philosophy and the classics for 4 years and became a research assistant in physiology for the fifth year.

While there, Titchener became interested in Wundt's new psychology, an interest that was neither shared nor encouraged by anyone at Oxford. Quite naturally, then, he journeyed to Leipzig, the mecca for scientific pilgrims, to study under Wundt for 2 years, receiving his degree in 1892. There seems no doubt that Wundt made a lifelong impression on the young student, though Titchener apparently saw little of him (Wundt was 35 years older and somewhat aloof). The 2 years at Leipzig determined Titchener's future in psychology, that of his many future students, and to a certain extent, the course of American psychology for a number of years. Titchener became a most zealous disciple of Wundt's, with all the ardor and narrowness of view that characterize a new convert to any faith. As Arthur Koestler so perceptively noted:

> Disciples tend to be more fanatical than their masters; they have committed themselves to his system, invested years of labour and staked their reputation on it; they fought the opposition and cannot tolerate the idea that the system might be at fault. [This is] as common among scientists devoted to their theory as it is among politicians or theologians devoted to a doctrine [1971, p. 33].

Such faithful and fanatical stewardship on the part of Titchener was both his greatest strength and his ultimate undoing.

After receiving his degree, Titchener wanted to become the pioneer of the new experimental psychology in England. The British, however, were skeptical of a scientific approach to one of their favorite philosophical subjects. Therefore, after a few months as an extension lecturer in biology at Oxford, Titchener went to the United States to teach psychology and direct the laboratory at the new Cornell University. He was then 25 years old, and he remained at Cornell for the rest of his life.

The years 1893–1900 were spent in developing his laboratory, acquiring equipment, conducting research, and writing some 62 articles. As more and more students were attracted to Cornell, Titchener relinquished the time-consuming task of participating personally in every study and, in later years, his research was conducted almost entirely by his students.

It was through direction of his students' research that his systematic position reached fruition. Titchener gave over 50 doctorates in psychology in 35 years and most of these dissertations bear the stamp of his personal thought. He exercised great authority in the selection of his students' research problems, assigning topics that were relevant to the issue with which he was concerned at the time. In this way, Titchener built a unified systematic position, with all graduate students at a given time expected to work collectively on the problem that then occupied Titchener's attention. As Roback (1952) noted, "Titchener thus erected an ivory tower in which he was to sit aloft and direct the course of what he considered to be the only scientific psychology worthy of the name [p. 184]."

This is not to imply that Titchener's own publications were few. His bibliography lists 216 articles and notes and a number of books. Quite naturally, Titchener translated the master; when he had completed the third edition of Wundt's *Principles of Physiological Psychology*, he found that Wundt had finished a new edition. Titchener then translated this fourth edition, only to learn that the tireless Wundt had published a fifth edition!

Titchener wrote *An Outline of Psychology* in 1896, *Primer of Psychology* in 1898, and the four-volume *Experimental Psychology* in 1901–1905. Külpe is said to have described the latter work as "the most erudite psychological work in the English language [Boring, 1950, p. 413]." These textbooks enjoyed wide popularity in this and other countries, and some were translated into Russian, Italian, German, Spanish, and French.

Titchener engaged in several hobbies or avocations that tended to divert time and energy from psychology. He became so proficient in music that he conducted a small ensemble at his home every Sunday evening, and at one time substituted for a music professor at Cornell. His avid interest in coin collecting led him, with typical thoroughness, to learn such remote and difficult languages as Chinese and Arabic, in order to master the characters on the coins. In addition to his knowledge of classical languages, he was conversant with a half-dozen modern languages, including Russian. Throughout his career, he maintained a voluminous correspondence with a number of colleagues. The majority of these letters were typewritten by Titchener with added hand-written material.

As he grew older, he withdrew more and more from social and university life. He had become a living legend at Cornell, though a number of faculty members had never met him. He did a great deal of his work at home and spent relatively little time at the university. Indeed, after 1909, he lectured only on Monday evenings of the Spring semester of each year. He was well protected in his study at home from any intrusions from the outside world. His wife screened all callers and it was well understood that no student would telephone him except in a matter of extreme emergency.

Though tending to be rather autocratic (in the mold of the German professor), he was also very kind and helpful to students and colleagues, as long as they paid him the deference and respect he felt was his due. Stories are told of his junior faculty members and students washing his car and putting up his window screens in the summer, not on command, but out of respect and admiration.

Dallenbach (1967), a former student, quotes Titchener as saying, "A man could not hope to become a psychologist until after he had learned to smoke." Accordingly, most of his students took to cigars, at least in his presence.

Titchener's concern for his students did not end when they left Cornell, nor did his impact upon their lives. Dallenbach, on receiving his Ph.D., intended to go to medical school, but Titchener had obtained a teaching position for him at the University of Oregon. Dallenbach (1967) thought Titchener would approve of his going to medical school, "but he did not. I had to go to Oregon, as he did not intend to have his training and work with me wasted [p. 91]."

His relations with psychologists outside his own group were never very close. Elected to the American Psychological Association by the charter members in 1892, he resigned shortly thereafter because the association would not expel a member he accused of plagiarism. It is said that a friend paid Titchener's dues for a number of years so that his name might be listed.

In 1904, a group of psychologists called the "Titchener experimentalists" was formed and met regularly to compare research notes. As might be suspected, Titchener selected both the topics and the guests, and generally dominated these meetings.

Around 1910, Titchener began work on what was intended to be a thorough exposition of his systematic point of view. Unfortunately, it was never completed, though a few sections were published in a journal and reprinted posthumously in a book in 1929. His productivity diminished in the last 10–15 years of his life and he died of a brain tumor at age 60.

Titchener's Systematic Position

Subject Matter

The subject matter for psychology, according to Titchener, is experience. Of course, as he noted, all sciences share the same subject matter—some aspect of the world of human experience—but each deals with a different aspect. The subject matter of psychology, as distinct from the subject matter of the other sciences, is experience as it is dependent on the experiencing person. This kind of experience is vastly different from that studied by a physicist. For example, light and sound may be studied by both a physicist and a psychologist, but the physicist looks at the phenomena from the viewpoint of the physical processes involved, while the psychologist views them in terms of how they are experienced by a human observer.

The other sciences, Titchener said, are independent of experiencing persons. The temperature in a room may be 85° whether anyone experiences the level of heat or not. If an observer stands in a room and reports that he feels uncomfortable, however, this feeling is experienced by, and is dependent on, the experiencing individual. And it is this experience, and only this experience, that is the subject matter for psychology.

Titchener cautioned that in the study of experiencing one must not commit what he called the "stimulus error," that is, confusing the mental process with the object being observed. For instance, an observer seeing an apple and reporting it as an apple, instead of describing the hues, brightnesses, and spatial characteristics he is experiencing, is committing the stimulus error. The object of observation is not to be described in terms of everyday language but rather in terms of the conscious content of the experience.

When an observer focuses on the stimulus object instead of the conscious process, he fails to distinguish what he knows about the object (for example, that it is called "apple") from his own immediate experience. The only things an observer really knows about an object are its color, brightness, and spatial pattern (for example, that the object is red, shiny, and round). If he describes anything other than these characteristics, he is interpreting the object, not observing it.

Titchener defined consciousness as the sum total of a person's experiences as they exist at a given point in time. Mind is defined as the sum of a person's experiences accumulating during his lifetime. Mind and consciousness are thus generally the same, except that consciousness involves mental processes occurring at the moment rather than the total accumulation of processes.

Titchener argued that psychology must study the generalized human mind, not individual minds, and certainly not individual differences among minds. The purpose of this study is solely that of understanding the mind. Titchener agreed wholeheartedly with Wundt that psychology has no concern with attempting to influence, modify, or even improve the mind.

Titchener's psychology was thus a pure science, having no applied or utilitarian concerns. Psychology was not, he said, in the business of curing "sick minds" or reforming individuals or society. Its only legitimate concern is to discover the facts of the mind.

He believed that the scientist has to remain completely free of any concern for the practical worth of his work. He opposed child psychology, animal psychology, indeed any area of the science that did not fit in with his introspective experimental psychology of the content of consciousness.

Methods of Psychology

Psychology, like all sciences, depends on observation, but it depends on observation of conscious experience, or introspection. Titchener's form of introspection was even more highly developed and formalized than Wundt's. Titchener felt that introspection could be performed only by very well-trained observers and was strongly opposed to the use of untrained observers. He realized that everyone learns to describe experience in terms of the stimulus, and that in everyday life this is beneficial and necessary. In the laboratory, however, this habit had to be unlearned through intensive training; his trained introspectors had to relearn how to perceive so as to describe the conscious state, not the stimulus. (The difficulties in specifying precisely what observers learned to do are discussed in a later section, "Criticisms of Structuralism.")

The influence of the mechanistic spirit is evident in the image structuralism developed of the human subjects who supplied its data. In the journal articles of the day, subjects were frequently called "reagents." Note the parallel with chemistry.

A reagent is a substance which, because it has a capacity for certain reactions, is used to detect, examine, or measure other substances. A reagent, then, is rather much a passive agent, one that is simply applied to something from which it elicits certain reactions.

Applying this to the human subject in Titchener's laboratory, we see that subjects were used as recording instruments, objectively noting the characteristics of the object being observed. The human subject was, then, nothing more than an objective and detached observing machine, a view noted by Titchener who spoke of trained observation becoming mechanized or habitual; that is, no longer a conscious process.

If human subjects are machines, how easy it is to think that all men are machines. The point deserves mention for it shows the continuing impact of the Galilean–Newtonian mechanical view of the universe—an influence that did not cease with the demise of structuralism. We shall see, as the history of psychology continues to unfold, that this image of man-the-machine still characterizes experimental psychology today.

Titchener believed that observation in psychology must be not only introspective in nature, but also experimental. Thus, he diligently observed the rigid rules of scientific experimentation, noting that:

> An experiment is an observation that can be repeated, isolated and varied. The more frequently you can *repeat* an observation, the more likely are you to see clearly what is there and to describe accurately what you have seen. The more strictly you can *isolate* an observation, the easier does your task of observation become, and the less danger is there of your being led astray by irrelevant circumstances, or of placing emphasis on the wrong point. The more widely you can *vary* an observation, the more clearly will the uniformity of experience stand out, and the better is your chance of discovering laws. All experimental appliances, all laboratories and instruments, are provided and devised with this one end in view: that the student shall be able to repeat, isolate and vary his observations [1909–1910, p. 20].

Aim of Psychology

Titchener's three problems or aims of psychology are very similar to those of Wundt. The psychologist seeks (*1*) to reduce conscious processes to their simplest, most basic components; (*2*) to determine how these elements are combined and their laws of combination; and (*3*) to bring the elements into connection with their physiological conditions. Thus, the aims of psychology coincide with those of the natural sciences. After a scientist decides what part of the natural world to study, he proceeds to discover its elements, to demonstrate how they are compounded into more complex phenomena, and to formulate the laws governing the phenomena.

Views on Particular Problems

We have seen that one of psychology's goals, to Titchener, is that of reducing consciousness to its component elements. How do we know if a given conscious process is elemental, that is, cannot be broken down into anything simpler? Titchener's answer is that if the process remains unchanged in the face of rigorous and persistent introspection, it is a true element. In essence, his test of the irreducibility of elements into anything simpler is analogous to the chemist's criterion for establishing chemical elements.

Titchener believed that there are three elementary states of consciousness: sensations, images, and affective states. Sensations, he said, are the basic elements of perception and occur in the sounds, sights, smells, and other experiences occasioned by physical objects actually present in the environment. Images are the elements of ideas and are found in the process that pictures or reflects experiences not actually present at the moment, such as a memory of a past experience. It is not totally clear from Titchener's writings that he considered sensations and images as belonging in mutually exclusive categories. In fact, he emphasized the similarity between the two while nevertheless arguing that they could be distinguished. Affections are the elements of emotion and are found in experiences such as love, hate, or sadness.

In *An Outline of Psychology* (1896), Titchener presented a list of his discovered elements of sensation; it comprised more than 44,000 sensation qualities, the majority of which were visual (32,820) and auditory (11,600). Each single element was believed to be conscious and distinct from all others, and each could be blended or combined with others to form perceptions and ideas.

Although basic and irreducible, these elements could still be classified, just as chemical elements are grouped into various classes. Despite their simplicity, elements have characteristics that enable us to distinguish among them. To the Wundtian attributes of quality and intensity, Titchener added duration and clearness. He considered these four attributes basic characteristics of all sensations that are present to some degree in all experience.

Quality is the characteristic that clearly distinguishes each element from every other, such as cold or red. Intensity refers to the strength or weakness, loudness or brightness, of a sensation. Duration refers to the course of a sensation over time, and clearness refers to the role of attention in conscious experience. That which is in the focus of attention is more dominant than that toward which attention is not directed.

It is noted that sensations and images possess all four of these attributes, but that affection has only three—it lacks clearness. Titchener felt that it was not possible to focus attention directly on the quality of pleasantness, for example. When we try to do so, the affective quality disappears.

Some sensory processes, particularly vision and touch, also possess the attribute of extensity, in that they spread out in space.

Thus, all conscious processes are reducible to one of these elements. The findings of the Würzburg school did not cause Titchener to modify his position. He recognized that obscure and ill-defined qualities may occur during thought but he held that they were still sensory or imaginal elements. The subjects in the Würzburg laboratory had, Titchener said, succumbed to the stimulus error because they paid more attention to the object than to their conscious processes.

A good deal of research on affection or feeling was carried out in the Cornell laboratory and resulted in rejection of Wundt's tridimensional theory. As noted earlier, affection has only three attributes, quality, intensity, and duration. Thus, sensations and affections are processes of the same general type sharing these three attributes in common. They differ in that affection lacks the attribute of clearness. Titchener felt that affection had only one dimension, pleasure–displeasure, denying Wundt's other two dimensions of tension–relaxation and excitement–depression.

Original Source Material on Structuralism:
From *A Text-Book of Psychology* by E. B. Titchener

The following material is reprinted from Titchener's very popular *A Text-Book of Psychology*, published in 1909–1910.[1] It describes the structuralist view of the subject matter and methodology of the new science of psychology.

This material supplements the earlier discussion of Titchener and provides an example of the style of exposition, both of the man and the times, that psychology students were studying more than a half century ago.

All human knowledge is derived from human experience; there is no other source of knowledge. But human experience, as we have seen, may be considered from different points of view. Suppose that we take two points of view, as far as possible apart, and discover for ourselves what experience looks like in the two cases. First, we will regard experience as altogether independent of any particular person; we will assume that it goes on whether

[1] Reprinted with permission of Macmillan Publishing Co., Inc. from *A Text-Book of Psychology* by E. B. Titchener (pp. 6–9, 15–25, 36–41). Copyright 1909 by Macmillan Publishing Co., Inc. Revised 1937 by Sophia K. Titchener. (Footnotes omitted.)

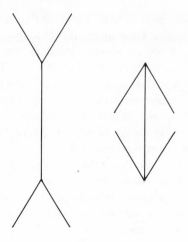

Figure 5.1.

or not anyone is there to have it. Secondly, we will regard experience as altogether dependent upon the particular person; we will assume that it goes on only when someone is there to have it. We shall hardly find standpoints more diverse. What are the differences in experience, as viewed from them?

Take, to begin with, the three things that you first learn about in physics: space, time and mass. Physical space, which is the space of geometry and astronomy and geology, is constant, always and everywhere the same. Its unit is 1 cm., and the cm. has precisely the same value wherever and whenever it is applied. Physical time is similarly constant; and its constant unit is the 1 sec. Physical mass is constant; its unit, the 1 gr., is always and everywhere the same. Here we have experience of space, time and mass considered as independent of the person who experiences them. Change, then, to the point of view which brings the experiencing person into account. The two vertical lines in Fig. 1 [Figure 5.1, this volume] are physically equal; they measure alike in units of 1 cm. To you, who see them, they are not equal. The hour that you spend in the waiting-room of a village station and the hour that you spend in watching an amusing play are physically equal; they measure alike in units of 1 sec. To you, the one hour goes slowly, the other quickly; they are not equal. Take two circular cardboard boxes of different diameter (say, 2 cm. and 8 cm.), and pour sand into them until they both weigh, say, 50 gr. The two masses are physically equal; placed on the pans of a balance, they will hold the beam level. To you, as you lift them in your two hands, or raise them in turn by the same hand, the box of smaller diameter is considerably the heavier. Here we have experience of space, time and mass considered as dependent upon the experiencing person. It is the same experience that we were discussing just now. But our first point of view gives us facts and laws of physics; our second gives us facts and laws of psychology.

Now take three other topics that are discussed in the physical text-books: heat, sound and light. Heat proper, the physicists tell us, is the energy of molecular motion; that is to say, heat is a form of energy due to a movement of the particles of a body among themselves. Radiant heat belongs, with light, to what is called radiant energy,—energy that is propagated by wave-movements of the luminiferous ether with which space is filled. Sound is a form of energy due to the vibratory movements of bodies, and is propagated by wave-movements of some elastic medium, solid, liquid or gaseous. In brief, heat is a dance of molecules; light is a wave-motion of the ether; sound is a wave-motion of the air. The world of physics, in which these types of experience are considered as independent of the experiencing person, is neither warm nor cold, neither dark nor light, neither silent nor noisy. It is only when the experiences are considered as dependent upon some person that we have warmth and cold, blacks and whites and colours and greys, tones and hisses and thuds. And these things are subject-matter of psychology.

We find, then, a great difference in the aspect of experience, according as it is viewed from the one or the other of our different standpoints. It is the same experience all through; physics and psychology deal with the same stuff, the same material; the sciences are separated simply—and sufficiently—by their point of view. From the standpoint of physics, we get such sciences as physics (in the narrower sense), chemistry, geology, astronomy, meteorology. From the standpoint of psychology we get, in the same way, a special group of sciences. . . .

It must be clearly understood that we are not here attempting to give a strict definition of the subject-matter of psychology. We assume that everybody knows, at first hand, what human experience is, and we then seek to mark off the two aspects of this experience which are dealt with respectively by physics and psychology. Any further definition of the subject-matter of psychology is impossible. Unless one knows, by experience itself, what experience is, one can no more give a meaning to the term "mind" than a stone can give a meaning to the term "matter." . . .

Mental Process, Consciousness and Mind. The most striking fact about the world of human experience is the fact of change. Nothing stands still; everything goes on. The sun will someday lose its heat; the eternal hills are, little by little, breaking up and wearing away. Whatever we observe, and from whatever standpoint we observe it, we find process, occurrence; nowhere is there permanence or stability. Mankind, it is true, has sought to arrest this flux, and to give stability to the world of experience, by assuming two permanent substances, matter and mind: the occurrences of the physical world are then supposed to be manifestations of matter, and the occurrences of the mental world to be manifestations of mind. Such an hypothesis may be of value at a certain stage of human thought; but every hypothesis that does not accord with the facts must, sooner or later, be given up. Physicists are therefore giving up the hypothesis of an unchanging, substantial matter, and psychologists are giving up the hypothesis of an unchanging, substantial mind. Stable objects and substantial things belong, not to the world of science, physical or psychological, but only to the world of common sense.

We have defined mind as the sum-total of human experience considered as dependent upon the experiencing person. We have said, further, that the phrase "experiencing person" means the living body, the organised individual; and we have hinted that, for psychological purposes, the living body may be reduced to the nervous system and its attachments. Mind thus becomes the sum-total of human experience considered as dependent upon a nervous system. And since human experience is always process, occurrence, and the dependent aspect of human experience is its mental aspect, we may say, more shortly, that mind is the sum-total of mental processes. All these words are significant. "Sum-total" implies that we are concerned with the whole world of experience, not with a limited portion of it; "mental" implies that we are concerned with experience under its dependent aspect, as conditioned by a nervous system; and "processes" implies that our subject-matter is a stream, a perpetual flux, and not a collection of unchanging objects.

It is not easy, even with the best will possible, to shift from the common-sense to the scientific view of mind; the change cannot be made all in a moment. We are to regard mind as a stream of processes? But mind is personal, my mind; and my personality continues throughout my life. The experiencing person is only the bodily organism? But, again, experience is personal, the experience of a permanent self. Mind is spatial, just as matter is? But mind is invisible, intangible; it is not here or there, square or round.

These objections cannot be finally met until we have gone some distance into psychology, and can see how the scientific view of mind works out. Even now, however, they will weaken as you look at them. Face that question of personality. Is your life, as a matter of fact, always personal? Do you not, time and again, forget yourself, lose yourself, disregard yourself, neglect yourself, contradict yourself, in a very literal sense? Surely, the mental life is only intermittently personal. And is your personality, when it is realised, unchanging? Are you the same self in childhood and manhood, in your working and in your playing moods, when you are on your best behaviour and when you are freed from restraint? Surely, the self-experience is not only intermittent, but also composed, at different times, of very different factors. As to the other question: mind is, of course, invisible, because sight is mind; and mind is intangible, because touch is mind. Sight-experience and touch-experience are dependent upon the experiencing person. But common sense itself bears witness, against its own belief, to the fact that mind is spatial: we speak, and speak correctly, of an idea in our head, a pain in our foot. And if the idea is the idea of a circle seen in the mind's eye, it is round; and if it is the visual idea of a square, it is square.

Consciousness, as reference to any dictionary will show, is a term that has many meanings. Here it is, perhaps, enough to distinguish two principal uses of the word.

In its first sense, consciousness means the mind's awareness of its own processes. Just as, from the commonsense point of view, mind is that inner self which thinks, remembers, chooses, reasons, directs the movements of the body, so is consciousness the inner knowledge of this thought and government. You are conscious of the correctness of your answer to an examination question, of the awkwardness of your movements, of the purity of your motives. Consciousness is thus something more than mind; it is "the perception of what passes in a man's own mind"; it is "the immediate knowledge which the mind has of its sensations and thoughts."

In its second sense, consciousness is identified with mind, and "conscious" with "mental." So long as mental processes are going on, consciousness is present; as soon as mental processes are in abeyance, unconsciousness sets in. "To say I am conscious of a feeling, is merely to say that I feel it. To have a feeling is to be conscious; and to be conscious is to have a feeling. To be conscious of the prick of the pin, is merely to have the sensation. And though I have these various modes of naming my sensation, by saying, I feel the prick of a pin, I feel the pain of a prick, I have the sensation of a prick, I have the feeling of a prick, I am conscious of the feeling; the thing named in all these various ways is one and the same."

The first of these definitions we must reject. It is not only unnecessary, but it is also misleading, to speak of consciousness as the mind's awareness of itself. The usage is unnecessary, because, as we shall see later, this awareness is a matter of observation of the same general kind as observation of the external world; it is misleading, because it suggests that mind is a personal being, instead of a stream of processes. We shall therefore take mind and consciousness to mean the same thing. But as we have the two different words, and it is convenient to make some distinction between them, we shall speak of mind when we mean the sum-total of mental processes occurring in the life-time of an individual, and we shall speak of consciousness when we mean the sum-total of mental processes occurring *now*, at any given "present" time. Consciousness will thus be a section, a division, of the mind-stream. This distinction is, indeed, already made in common speech: when we say that a man has "lost consciousness," we mean that the lapse is temporary, that the mental life will shortly be resumed; when we say that a man has "lost his mind," we mean—not, it is true, that mind has altogether disappeared, but certainly that the derangement is permanent and chronic.

While, therefore, the subject-matter of psychology is mind, the direct object of psychological study is always a consciousness. In strictness, we can never observe the same consciousness twice over; the stream of mind flows on, never to return. Practically, we can observe a particular consciousness as often as we wish, since mental processes group themselves in the same way, show the same pattern of arrangement, whenever the organism is placed under the same circumstances. Yesterday's high tide will never recur, and yesterday's consciousnesses will never recur; but we have a science of psychology, as we have a science of oceanography.

The Method of Psychology. Scientific method may be summed up in the single word "observation"; the only way to work in science is to observe those phenomena which form the subject-matter of science. And observation implies two things: attention to the phenomena, and record of the phenomena; that is, clear and vivid experience, and an account of the experience in words or formulas.

In order to secure clear experience and accurate report, science has recourse to experiment. An experiment is an observation that can be repeated, isolated and varied. The more frequently you can *repeat* an observation, the more likely are you to see clearly what is there and to describe accurately what you have seen. The more strictly you can *isolate* an observation, the easier does your task of observation become, and the less danger is there of your being led astray by irrelevant circumstances, or of placing emphasis on the wrong point. The more widely you can *vary* an observation, the more clearly will the uniformity of experience stand out, and the better is your chance of discovering laws. All experimental appliances, all laboratories and instruments, are provided and devised with this one end in view: that the student shall be able to repeat, isolate and vary his observations.—

The method of psychology, then, is observation. To distinguish it from the observation of physical science, which is inspection, a looking-at, psychological observation has been termed introspection, a looking-within. But this difference of name must not blind us to the essential likeness of the methods. Let us take some typical instances.

We may begin with two very simple cases. (*1*) Suppose that you are shown two paper discs: the one of an uniform violet, the other composed half of red and half of blue. If this second disc is rapidly rotated, the red and blue will mix, as we say, and you will see a certain blue-red, that is, a kind of violet. Your problem is, so to adjust the proportions of red and blue in the second disc that the resulting violet exactly matches the violet of the first disc. You may repeat this set of observations as often as you like; you may isolate the observations by working in a room that is free from other, possibly disturbing colours; you may vary the observations by working to equality of the violets first from a two-colour disc that is distinctly too blue, and secondly from a disc that is distinctly too red. (*2*) Suppose, again, that the chord *c-e-g* is struck, and that you are asked to say how many tones it contains. You may repeat this observation; you may isolate it, by working in a quiet room; you may vary it, by having the chord struck at different parts of the scale, in different octaves.

It is clear that, in these instances, there is practically no difference between introspection and inspection. You are using the same method that you would use for counting the swings of a pendulum, or taking readings from a galvanometer scale, in the physical laboratory. There is a difference in subject-matter: the colours and the tones are dependent, not independent experiences: but the method is essentially the same.

Now let us take some cases in which the material of introspection is more complex. (*1*) Suppose that a word is called out to you, and that you are asked to observe the effect which this stimulus produces upon consciousness: how the word affects you, what ideas it calls up, and so forth. The observation may be repeated; it may be isolated,—you may be seated in a dark and silent room, free from disturbances; and it may be varied,—different words may be called out, the word may be flashed upon a screen instead of spoken, etc. Here, however, there seems to be a difference between introspection and inspection. The observer who is watching the course of a chemical reaction, or the movements of some microscopical creature, can jot down from moment to moment the different phases of the observed phenomenon. But if you try to report the changes in consciousness, while these changes are in progress, you interfere with consciousness; your translation of the mental experience into words introduces new factors into that experience itself. (2) Suppose, again, that you are observing a feeling or an emotion: a feeling of disappointment or annoyance, an emotion of anger or chagrin. Experimental control is still possible; situations may be arranged, in the psychological laboratory, such that these feelings may be repeated, isolated and varied. But your observation of them interferes, even more seriously than before, with the course of consciousness. Cool consideration of an emotion is fatal to its very existence; your anger disappears, your disappointment evaporates, as you examine it.

To overcome this difficulty of the introspective method, students of psychology are usually recommended to delay their observation until the process to be described has run its course, and then to call it back and describe it from memory. Introspection thus becomes retrospection; introspective examination becomes *post mortem* examination. The rule is, no doubt, a good one for the beginner; and there are cases in which even the experienced psychologist will be wise to follow it. But it is by no means universal. For we must remember (*a*) that the observations in question may be repeated. There is, then, no reason why the observer to whom the word is called out, or in whom the emotion is set up, should not report at once upon the first stage of his experience: upon the immediate effect of the word, upon the beginnings of the emotive process. It is true that this report interrupts the observation. But, after the first stage has been accurately described, further observations may be taken, and the second, third and following stages similarly described; so that presently a complete report upon the whole experience is obtained. There is, in theory, some danger that the stages become artificially separated; consciousness is a flow, a process, and if we divide it up we run the risk of missing certain intermediate links. In practice, however, this danger has proved to be very small; and we may always have recourse to retrospection, and compare our partial results with our memory of the unbroken experience. Moreover, (*b*) the practised observer gets into an introspective habit, has the introspective attitude ingrained in his system; so that it is possible for him, not only to take mental notes while the observation is in progress, without interfering with consciousness, but even to jot down written notes, as the histologist does while his eye is still held to the ocular of the microscope.

In principle, then, introspection is very like inspection. The objects of observation are different; they are objects of dependent, not of independent experience; they are likely to be transient, elusive, slippery. Sometimes they refuse to be observed while they are in passage; they must be preserved in memory, as a delicate tissue is preserved in hardening fluid, before they can be examined. And the standpoint of the observer is different; it is the standpoint of human life and of human interest, not of detachment and aloofness. But, in general, the method of psychology is much the same as the method of physics.

It must not be forgotten that, while the method of the physical and the psychological sciences is substantially the same, the subject-matter of these sciences is as different as it can well be. Ultimately, as we have seen, the subject-matter of all the sciences is the world of human experience; but we have also seen that the aspect of experience treated by physics is radically different from the aspect treated by psychology. The likeness of method may tempt us to slip from the one aspect to the other, as when a text-book of physics contains a chapter on vision and the sense of colour, or a text-book of physiology contains paragraphs on delusions of judgment; but this confusion of subject-matter must inevitably lead to confusion of thought. Since all the sciences are concerned with the one world of human experience, it is natural that scientific method, to whatever aspect of experience it is applied, should be in principle the same. On the other hand, when we have decided to examine some particular aspect of experience, it is necessary that we hold fast to that aspect, and do not shift our point of view as the enquiry proceeds. Hence it is a great advantage that we have the two terms, introspection and inspection, to denote observation taken from the different standpoints of psychology and of physics. The use of the word introspection is a constant reminder that we are working in psychology, that we are observing the dependent aspect of the world of experience.

Observation, as we said above, implies two things: attention to the phenomena, and record of the phenomena. The attention must be held at the highest possible degree of concentration; the record must be photographically accurate. Observation is, therefore, both difficult and fatiguing; and introspection is, on the whole, more difficult and more fatiguing than inspection. To secure reliable results, we must be strictly impartial and unprejudiced, facing the facts as they come, ready to accept them as they are, not trying to fit them to any preconceived theory; and we must work only when our general disposition is favourable, when we are fresh and in good health, at ease in our surroundings, free from outside worry and anxiety. If these rules are not followed, no amount of experimenting will help us. The observer in the psychological laboratory is placed under the best possible external conditions; the room in which he works is fitted up and arranged in such a way that the observation may be repeated, that the process to be observed may stand out clearly upon the background of consciousness, and that the factors in the process may be separately varied. But all this care is of no avail, unless the observer himself comes to the work in an even frame of mind, gives it his full attention, and is able adequately to translate his experience into words. . . .

The Problem of Psychology. Science seeks always to answer three questions in regard to its subject-matter, the questions of what, how, and why. What precisely, stripped of all complications and reduced to its lowest terms, is this subject-matter? How, then, does it come to appear as it does; how are its elements combined and arranged? And, finally, why does it appear now in just this particular combination or arrangement? All three questions must be answered, if we are to have a science . . . .

To answer the question "what" is the task of analysis. Physical science, for example, tries by analysis to reduce the world of independent experience to its lowest terms, and so arrives at the various chemical elements. To answer the question "how" is the task of synthesis. Physical science traces the behaviour of the elements in their various combinations, and presently succeeds in formulating the laws of nature. When these two questions have been answered, we have a description of physical phenomena. But science enquires, further, why a given set of phenomena occurs in just this given way, and not otherwise; and it answers the question "why" by laying bare the cause of which the observed phenomena are the effect. There was dew on the ground last night because the surface of the earth was colder than the layer of air above it; dew forms on glass and not on metal because the radiating power of the one is great and of the other is small. When the cause of a physical phenomenon has thus been assigned, the phenomenon is said to be explained.

So far, now, as description is concerned, the problem of psychology closely resembles the problem of physics. The psychologist seeks, first of all, to analyse mental experience into its simplest components. He takes a particular consciousness and works over it again and again, phase by phase and process by process, until his analysis can go no further. He is left with certain mental processes which resist analysis, which are absolutely simple in nature, which cannot be reduced, even in part, to other processes. This work is continued, with other consciousnesses, until he is able to pronounce with some confidence upon the nature and number of the elementary mental processes. Then he proceeds to the task of synthesis. He puts the elements together, under experimental conditions: first, perhaps, two elements of the same kind, then more of that kind, then elementary processes of diverse kinds: and he presently discerns that regularity and uniformity of occurrence which we have seen to be characteristic of all human experience. He thus learns to formulate the laws of connection of the elementary mental processes. If sensations of tone occur together, they blend or fuse; if sensations of colour occur side by side, they enhance one another: and all this takes place in a perfectly regular way, so that we can write out laws of tonal fusion and laws of colour contrast.

If, however, we attempted to work out a merely descriptive psychology, we should find that there was no hope in it of a true science of mind. A descriptive psychology would stand to scientific psychology very much as the old-fashioned natural histories stand to modern text-books of biology, or as the view of the world which a boy gets from his cabinet of physical experiments stands to the trained physicist's view. It would tell us a good deal about mind; it would include a large body of observed facts, which we might classify and, in large measure, bring under general laws. But there would be no unity or coherence in it; it would lack that single guiding principle which biology has, for instance, in the law of evolution, or physics in the law of the conservation of energy. In order to make psychology scientific we must not only describe, we must also explain mind. We must answer the question "why."

But here is a difficulty. It is clear that we cannot regard one mental process as the cause of another mental process, if only for the reason that, with change of our surroundings, entirely new consciousnesses may be set up. When I visit Athens or Rome for the first time, I have experiences which are due, not to past consciousnesses, but to present stimuli. Nor can we, on the other hand, regard nervous processes as the cause of mental processes. The principle of psychophysical parallelism lays it down that the two sets of events, processes in the nervous system and mental processes, run their course side by side, in exact correspondence but without interference: they are, in ultimate fact, two different aspects of the same experience. The one cannot be the cause of the other.

Nevertheless, it is by reference to the body, to the nervous system and the organs attached to it, that we explain mental phenomena. The nervous system does not cause, but it does explain mind. It explains mind as the map of a country explains the fragmentary glimpses of hills and rivers and towns that we catch on our journey through it. In a word, reference to the nervous system introduces into psychology just that unity and coherence which a strictly descriptive psychology cannot achieve.

It is worth while, for the sake of clearness, to dwell on this point in more detail. The physical world, the world of independent experience, just because it is independent of the individual man, is complete and self-contained. All of the processes that make it up are bound together as cause and effect; nowhere is there a gap or break in their connection. Now, among the processes that make up this independent world are the processes of the nervous system. These are linked, as cause and effect, both to one another and also to physical processes, outside the body, which precede and follow them; they have their fixed place in the unbroken chain of physical events; they may themselves be explained, exactly as the occurrence of dew is explained. Mental processes, on the other hand, correspond, not to the whole series of physical events, but only to a small part of them, namely, to certain events within the nervous system. It is natural, then, that mental phenomena should appear scrappy, disconnected, unsystematic. It is also natural that we should seek their explanation in the nervous processes which run parallel to them, and whose causal connection with all the other processes of the independent world ensures the continuity that they so conspicuously lack. Mind lapses every night, and reforms every morning; but the bodily processes go on, in sleep and in waking. An idea drops out of memory, to recur, perhaps quite unexpectedly, many years later; but the bodily processes have been going on without interruption. Reference to the body does not add one iota to the data of psychology, to the sum of introspections. It does furnish us with an explanatory principle for psychology; it does enable us to systematise our introspective data. Indeed, if we refuse to explain mind by body, we must accept the one or the other of two, equally unsatisfactory alternatives: we must either rest content with a simple description of mental experience, or must invent an unconscious mind to give coherence and continuity to the conscious. Both courses have been tried. But, if we take the first, we never arrive at a science of psychology; and if we take the second, we voluntarily leave the sphere of fact for the sphere of fiction.

These are scientific alternatives. Common sense, also, has in its own fashion realised the situation, and has found its own way out. It is precisely because of the incompleteness and disconnectedness of mental experience that common sense constructs a hybrid world, travelling easily from mental to physical and back again, filling up the breaks in the mental by material borrowed from the physical. That way, we may be sure, lies confusion of thought. The truth underlying the confusion is, however, the implicit acknowledgment that the explanatory principle for psychology must be looked for beyond, and not within, the world of dependent experience.—

Physical science, then, explains by assigning a cause; mental science explains by reference to those nervous processes which correspond with the mental processes that are under observation. We may bring these two modes of explanation together, if we define explanation itself as the statement of the proximate circumstances or conditions under which the described phenomenon occurs. Dew is formed under the condition of a difference of temperature between the air and the ground; ideas are formed under the condition of certain processes in the nervous system. Fundamentally, the object and the manner of explanation, in the two cases, are one and the same.

In fine, just as the method of psychology is, on all essential points, the method of the natural sciences, so is the problem of psychology essentially of the same sort as the problem of physics. The psychologist answers the question "what" by analysing mental experience into its elements. He answers the question "how" by formulating the laws of connection of these elements. And he answers the question "why" by explaining mental processes in terms of their parallel processes in the nervous system. His programme need not be carried out in this order: he may get the hint of a law before his analysis is completed, and the discovery of a sense-organ may suggest the occurrence of certain elementary processes before he has found these processes by introspection. The three questions are intimately related, and an answer to any one helps towards the answers to the other two. The measure of our progress in scientific psychology is our ability to return satisfactory answers to all three.

The Fate of Structuralism

Boring (1950) commented that a person often gains prominence in history because he opposed some old thought or position. The situation seems reversed with Titchener, who "stood out in bold relief because every one near him moved away from him. If all movement is relative, then Titchener moved—backwards with respect to his advancing frame of reference [p. 419]." The climate of American and European psychology was changing, but Titchener was not, and some came to look on his efforts as a futile attempt to cling to antiquated principles.

Titchener thought he was establishing the basic pattern for psychology; his work has proved to be but one phase in its history. The era of structuralism collapsed when Titchener died. That it was sustained as long as it was in America is an effective tribute to the commanding personality of the man himself.

Criticisms of Structuralism

The most severe criticisms against structuralism have been leveled at the method of introspection. Introspection, as we have seen, was not new with Wundt and Titchener. Indeed, the method (though in a more broadly defined sense) had been in use for a very long time. The attack on introspection was by no means new either. For example, Kant held that an attempt to introspect changes the conscious experience by virtue of introducing an observing element into the content of this conscious experience. The positivist, Auguste Comte, also attacked the method.

Several decades before Wundt founded the new psychology, Comte wrote this most telling criticism:

> The mind may observe all phenomena but its own. . . . The observing and observed organ are here the same, and its action cannot be pure and natural. In order to observe, your intellect must pause from activity; yet it is this very activity that you want to observe. If you cannot effect that pause, you cannot observe; if you do effect it, there is nothing to observe. The results of such method are in proportion to its absurdity. After two thousand years of psychological pursuit, no one proposition is established to the satisfaction of its followers [1896, Vol. I., p. 9].

Turner (1967, p. 11) lists additional criticisms levelled against introspection by the Englishman, Henry Maudsley, in 1867, a few years *before* the new science of psychology was launched.

(1) There is little agreement among introspectionists.
(2) Where agreement does occur, it can be attributed to the fact that introspectionists must be meticulously trained, and thereby have a bias built into their observations.
(3) A body of knowledge based on introspection cannot be inductive; no discovery is possible from those who are trained specifically on what to observe.
(4) Due to the extent of the pathology of mind, self-report is hardly to be trusted.
(5) Introspective knowledge cannot have the generality we expect of science. It must be restricted to the class of sophisticated, trained adult subjects.
(6) Much of behavior (habit and performance) occurs without conscious correlates.

We see, then, the existence of substantial criticism of introspection before Titchener and Wundt sharpened and modified the method to bring it in line with the requirements of experimentalism. The modifications did not reduce the amount of criticism. As the method was made more specific, so were the attacks against it.

One criticism relates to the definition of introspection. Titchener seems to have had a difficult time defining it with any degree of rigor, and apparently attempted to do so by relating it to the particular experimental conditions. "The course that an observer follows will vary in detail with the nature of the consciousness observed, with the purpose of the experiment, with the instruction given by the experimenter. Introspection is thus a generic term, and covers an indefinitely large group of specific methodological procedures [Titchener, 1912, p. 485]." With so much variation, it is difficult to find similarities among the different uses of the term.

One point mentioned earlier relates to the question of precisely what the structuralist introspectors were trained to do. An observer learning to introspect had to ignore certain classes of words—the so-called "meaning" words—that had become an established part of his vocabulary. The phrase, "I see a table," for example, had no scientific meaning to a structuralist, for the word "table" is a meaning word, based on previously established and generally agreed upon knowledge about the specific conglomeration of sensations we have learned to identify and label as "table." The observation, "I see a table," told the structuralist nothing about the observer's conscious experience. The structuralist was interested not in the aggregate of sensations summarized in a meaning word, but in the specific elementary forms of the experience. An observer who said "table" was committing the stimulus error.

If these everyday, commonly agreed upon words were stricken from the vocabulary, how was the experience to be described? An introspective language or vocabulary had to be developed. Since both Wundt and Titchener emphasized that the external conditions of the experiment must be carefully controlled so that the conscious contents could be precisely determined, then two observers should have the same experience and their results should serve to corroborate one another. Because of these highly similar experiences under controlled conditions, it seemed possible, theoretically at least, to develop a working vocabulary devoid of meaning words. It is, after all, because of commonalities of experience in everyday life that we are able to agree on a conventional meaning for the word "table" (or "house," or whatever).

Although the development of such a vocabulary is perhaps possible in principle, it was never realized in actuality. There was often disagreement among introspectors, even under the most rigidly controlled conditions of observation. Introspectors at different laboratories obtained different results. Even those at the same laboratory often failed to agree. Titchener nevertheless maintained that agreement would be reached eventually, but it never was. It is possible that, had there been sufficient agreement on introspective findings, structuralism might still be a vital force today. —

There were other criticisms of the method of introspection. It was charged that introspection was, in reality, retrospection, because some period of time must elapse between the experience itself and the reporting of it. Since forgetting is particularly rapid immediately after an experience, it seems likely that some of the experience would be lost. The structuralists' answer to this criticism was to specify that the observers work with very short time intervals. The structuralists also postulated the existence of a primary mental image that was alleged to maintain the experience for the observer until it could be reported.

Another difficulty is that the very act of minutely examining the experience in introspective fashion may radically change the experience. Consider the difficulty in introspecting the conscious state of anger. In the process of rationally attending to it and trying to dissect the experience into its elementary components, the anger may subside or disappear completely. Titchener believed, however, that the experienced, well-trained introspector became unconscious of his observational task with continued practice. —

A final criticism of introspection relates to the large and growing body of data that seemed to belong within the province of psychology, but which was decidedly not available to the introspector. Animal psychologists, for example, were rapidly accumulating useful data, obviously without the use of introspection. The psychoanalysts were pointing to the importance of unconscious determinants of behavior, which were not accessible to the introspectionists.

The method of the structuralists was not the only subject of criticism. The movement was accused of artificiality and sterility because of its attempt to analyze conscious processes into elements. Critics agree that the whole of an experience cannot be recovered by any synthesis or compounding of the elemental parts. Experience, they argue, does not come to man in sensory, imaginal, or affective elements, but in unified wholes. Something of the experience must inevitably be lost in what critics consider an artificial breakdown of the conscious experience. The Gestalt school (Chapter 12) made most effective use of this criticism in launching their "new psychology," their revolt against structuralism.

The structuralists' narrow definition of psychology has also come under attack. Psychology was growing in a number of areas and the structuralists, in the person of Titchener, preferred to exclude these newer areas if they were not congruent with the structuralists' definition and method of psychology. Titchener regarded animal and child psychology as not really psychology at all. His conception of psychology was simply too narrow to contain the growing body of data being accumulated by a rapidly increasing number of psychologists. Psychology was moving beyond him, and moving very quickly.

Contributions of Structuralism

There is no denying that structuralism made singularly important contributions to psychology. As Heidbreder (1933) stated, "It is a simple historical fact that it was the kind of psychology which Titchener taught, the enterprise which centered in the German laboratories, that first gained recognition for psychology as a science [p. 148]." For the first time, psychology achieved a formal academic identity and stature clearly separate from philosophy and physiology.

The subject matter of the structuralists—conscious experience—was sharply defined. Their research methods were certainly in the best tradition of science, involving as they did, observation, experimentation, and measurement. Since consciousness was best perceived by the person having the conscious experience, then the best method for that subject matter was self-observation.

While the subject matter and aims of the structuralists are dead issues, introspection, if we define it as simply the giving of a verbal report based on experience, continues to be used in many areas of psychology. Psychophysics, for example, asks a subject whether a second tone sounds louder or softer than the first. Also, verbal reports are rendered by the person describing his experiences in an unusual experimental environment, such as a sensory deprivation cubicle. Clinical reports from a patient and responses on personality tests or attitude scales are introspective in nature. These examples, and many more, involve a verbal report based on experience and are acceptable and legitimate forms of data collecting. Obviously, the current-day usage of introspection is not of the structuralists' sort, as the verbal reports are in the language of behavior, not that of the structuralists.

⏤ The final, and perhaps greatest, contribution of structuralism is its service as a target for criticism. It provided a very strong system of orthodoxy against which the newly developing functional, Gestalt, and behavioristic movements could marshal their forces. These newer schools owed their existence in no small measure to their progressive reformulation of the psychology that the structuralists began. As we noted earlier, forward movement requires something against which to push. With the help of the structuralist position, psychology advanced far beyond its initial boundary.

"Beyond question, the psychology of Titchener played a major role in the development of American psychology, not only as a distinct and lasting achievement, but also as a gallant and enlightening failure [Heidbreder, 1933, p. 151]."

SUGGESTED FURTHER READINGS

Titchener
Boring, E. G. The stimulus-error. *American Journal of Psychology*, 1921, **32**, 449–471.
Boring, E. G. Edward Bradford Titchener: 1867–1927. *American Journal of Psychology*, 1927, **38**, 489–506.

General
Bentley, M. The psychologies called "Structuralism": Historical derivation. In C. Murchison (Ed.), *Psychologies of 1925*. Worcester, Massachusetts: Clark Univ. Press, 1926. Pp. 383–393.
Bentley, M. The work of the structuralists. In C. Murchison (Ed.), *Psychologies of 1925*. Worcester, Massachusetts: Clark Univ. Press, 1926. Pp. 395–404.
Boring, E. G. A psychological function is the relation of successive differentiations of events in the organism. *Psychological Review*, 1937, **44**, 445–461.

Introspection
Bakan, D. A consideration of the problem of introspection. *Psychological Bulletin*, 1954, **51**, 105–118.
Boring, E. G. A history of introspection. *Psychological Bulletin*, 1953, **50**, 169–186.
McKellar, P. The method of introspection. In J. Scher (Ed.), *Theories of the mind*. New York: Free Press, 1962. Pp. 619–644.

6

Functionalism:
Antecedent Influences

What Is Functionalism?

Functional psychology is, as the name suggests, concerned with the mind as it functions or as it is used in the adaptation of the organism to its environment. The movement focused on the very practical and utilitarian question of what the mind or mental processes accomplish. Functionalists studied the mind, not from the standpoint of its composition (that is, a structure of elements), but rather from the point of view of the mind as a conglomerate of activities (functions) which lead to eminently practical consequences in the real world.

The structuralists' study of the mind revealed nothing of the consequences and accomplishments of mental activity. Nor did it want to, of course, for such a goal of practicality was anathema to the pure science approach of Wundt and Titchener.

Functionalism was the first uniquely American system of psychology (we will discuss the interesting reasons for this in Chapter 7). It was a deliberate movement of protest and opposition directed against structuralism, the establishment of the day. The psychology of structure was seen as too narrow, too restrictive—it could not answer the questions the functionalists wished psychology to answer: What does the mind do? How does it do it?

Functionalism was not, however, a protest against the methods and topics of research at Leipzig and Cornell. The functionalists used many of the older school's findings. They did not oppose introspection, nor did they argue against the experimental study of consciousness.

What they did oppose was the structuralists' definition of psychology, a definition that ruled out any consideration of the useful and practical functions of the mind, the ongoing activities or operations of consciousness.

While functionalism was a protest against the existing school of thought, it was not intended that it become as full-fledged a "school" as the one it opposed. The primary reason for this seems to be personal rather than ideological. None of the leaders of the functionalist movement had the ambition to become the new establishment.

Though functionalism did adopt many of the characteristics of a new school of thought, such was not its aim. The leaders seemed content to challenge structuralism and to broaden the base and scope of psychology, which they did with singular success. They modified the existing orthodoxy without feeling the need to totally replace it.

As a result, functionalism was never as rigid or as formally differentiated a systematic position as structuralism; hence, it cannot be described as neatly or precisely as the earlier school. Moreover, there has never existed a single functional psychology, as there was a single structural psychology. There were several functional psychologies, each differing somewhat from the others. All, however, shared an interest in the functions of consciousness. Because of this emphasis on the functioning of an organism in its environment, functionalism was vitally concerned with applied psychology. Thus, that area developed rapidly in America with the supportive attitude of the American functional psychologist.

Historical Overview of Functionalism

Functionalism ranges over a rather long period of history—from the mid-1850s to the present—at least in modified form. Its historical development, unlike that of structuralism, was influenced by a number of intellectual leaders with a variety of interests and backgrounds. It was probably at least partly because of this variegated background that functionalism did not stultify and decline, like structuralism.

This chapter considers the early antecedent influences on the movement, including the works of Charles Darwin, Sir Francis Galton, and early students of animal behavior. Interestingly, although these initial sources of influence were all British, functionalism, as we have already mentioned, formally began and flourished in the United States (see Chapter 7).

It is also important to note the period of time during which these British antecedents of functionalism were developing their ideas; it was before and during the time that structuralism was developing.

Darwin's famous *Origin of Species* was published approximately 20 years before the Leipzig Laboratory was established. Galton's work on individual differences began in 1869 (before Wundt wrote his *Principles of Physiological Psychology*) and was carried through to the end of the century. The early animal psychologists began their work in the 1880s before Titchener had journeyed to Leipzig to come under Wundt's influence.

The point to be remembered is that major work was being done on the functions of consciousness, individual differences, and animal psychology at the time Wundt and Titchener were excluding these areas from the province of psychology.

It remained for the new American psychologists, with their vastly different temperament, to bring function, individual differences, and the white rat to positions of prominence in psychology.

American psychology today is functionalistic in its orientation and attitude. This is evident in psychology's current emphasis on testing, learning, perception, and other such functional processes that aid the organism in its adaptation and adjustment to the environment.

The Evolution Revolution:
Charles Darwin (1809–1882)

On the Origin of Species by Means of Natural Selection, published in 1859, is rightly considered one of the most important books in the history of Western civilization. The theory of evolution presented in this book served to free contemporary intellectuals of restraining traditions and superstitions and ushered in the era of maturity and respectability of the so-called life sciences. Further, there is no denying that the theory of evolution was to have a tremendous impact on contemporary psychology. American psychology today owes its form and substance as much to the influence of evolutionary theory as to any other idea or individual.

The idea that living things change with time, which is the fundamental notion of evolution, was not introduced for the first time by Darwin. Intellectual anticipations of this general idea can be traced as far back as the fifth century B.C., though it was not until the late eighteenth century that the idea began to be investigated systematically. Erasmus Darwin (grandfather of Charles Darwin and Sir Francis Galton) expressed the belief that all warm-blooded animals had evolved from one living filament that had been given animation by the Creator. In 1809,

Chevalier de Lamarck had formulated a behavioral theory of evolution, emphasizing the modification of animal bodily form through the organism's efforts to adapt to its environment—modifications that were inherited by succeeding generations. For instance, the giraffe developed his long neck by generations of reaching up to higher and higher branches for food. In the mid-1800s, Charles Lyell introduced the notion of evolution into geological theory, arguing that the earth had gone through various stages of development in evolving to its present structure.

Why, after so many centuries of acceptance of the Biblical account of creation—"every species after its own kind"—were men driven to seek an alternative explanation? One reason was that man was learning more about the other species which inhabited the earth. Many new kinds and varieties of animal life were reported by explorers investigating new continents. Some thinkers began to ask the not-so-facetious question, "How could Noah have put a pair of each of the animals in his ark?" There were just too many animals to continue to believe in that legend.

Explorers and scientists had found fossils and bones of animals that did not match any existing species. They apparently belonged to animals which had once roamed the earth and then disappeared.

Living forms came to be seen as not constant—not remaining just as they were since creation—but subject to change and modification. Old species became extinct and new species appeared, some of them altered varieties of existing forms. Perhaps, it was speculated, all of nature is a result of, and is still in the process of, continuing change—an evolution.

Not only in the intellectual and scientific realm was the impact of change being observed; it could also be seen in everyday life. Society was being transformed by the forces of the industrial revolution. Values, social relationships, and societal norms which had remained constant for generations were being torn apart as hordes of people migrated from rural areas and small towns to the huge manufacturing centers.

And, overall, there was the continuing (indeed, growing) influence of and faith in science. People were less content to base their knowledge of themselves and their environments on what the *Bible* and other ancient authorities had stated to be true.

Change was very much the *Zeitgeist* of the day. It affected the peasant farmer, whose life now pulsed to the rhythm of the machine he tended instead of to the seasons, as much as the scientist puzzling over a set of ancient bones.

This changing intellectual and social climate rendered the notion of evolution scientifically respectable. There was, however, a great deal of speculating and theorizing, but little in the way of supporting evidence.

On the Origin of Species, with its enormous and well-ordered masses of evidence, provided so much data that the notion of evolution could no longer be ignored. The times demanded such a theory and Charles Darwin became its agent.

The Life of Darwin

Darwin was born in 1809 in England. His father was a physician and his grandfather, Erasmus, was noted as a philosopher, physician, and poet. After 2 years at Edinburgh, Darwin entered Cambridge, receiving his B.A. in 1831. One of his instructors, the noted botanist John Stevens Henslow, promoted Darwin's appointment as a naturalist aboard H.M.S. Beagle, which the British government was then preparing for a scientific voyage around the world. This famous voyage, lasting from 1831 to 1836, began in South American waters and proceeded to Tahiti and New Zealand, to return by way of Ascension Island and the Azores. The trip afforded a unique opportunity to observe and collect a wide variety of plant and animal life, and Darwin returned to England with an immense amount of data.

In 1837, his health forced him to retire to the country, where he was able to work only about 4 hours a day. He was in poor health for the remainder of his life but this did not prevent his writing numerous scientific papers and books.

From the time of his return from the voyage, Darwin was convinced of the validity of the idea of the evolution of species. Why then did he wait 22 years before presenting his theory to the world?

The answer seems to lie in his extremely cautious and conservative attitude, certainly a temperamental requisite for a scientist. He was fully aware of the revolutionary impact his theory would exert, and he wanted to be absolutely certain that it was well buttressed with sufficient supporting data. And so he proceeded with painstaking caution. It was not until 1842 that he felt prepared to write as much as a brief 35-page abstract of the development of his theory. Two years later he expanded this into an essay over 200 pages long. But he was still not satisfied. He continued to keep his idea secret, sharing it with only two people, Joseph Hooker (a botanist) and Lyell.

For 15 more years he pored over his data, checking, elaborating, thinking, making certain that, when he did finally publish it, the theory would be absolutely convincing.

Who knows how much longer Darwin might have worked over his findings if, in June 1858, he had not received a shattering letter from a young acquaintance, Alfred Russel Wallace.

Wallace was a naturalist who, while recovering from an illness in the East Indies, had developed the outline of a theory of evolution amazingly similar to Darwin's.[1]

In his letter, Wallace asked for Darwin's opinion of the theory and for help in getting it published! One can imagine Darwin's feelings, after 22 years of diligent, laborious, and painstaking work; he was certainly in a difficult position. It must be noted, however, that Wallace's theory contained no great wealth of data such as Darwin had collected.

Darwin, though a most competent scientist, possessed another characteristic not unknown among men of science—personal ambition. Even before his explorations on the Beagle, he had written in his diary that he was "ambitious to take a fair place among scientific men [Merton, 1957, p. 647]." Later he wrote, "I wish I could set less value on the bauble fame," and, "I rather hate the idea of writing for priority, yet I certainly should be vexed if any one were to publish my doctrines before me [Merton, 1957, p. 648]."

With an enviable and all-too-rare sense of fair play, Darwin decided, after receiving Wallace's letter, that "It seems hard on me that I should lose my priority of many years' standing, but I cannot feel at all sure that this alters the justice of the case. . . . it would be dishonourable in me now to publish [Merton, 1957, p. 648]."

At this moment of seeming defeat, Darwin's infant daughter died and he was thrown into a greater despair. His friends, Lyell and Hooker, suggested that Darwin read Wallace's paper and portions of his own forthcoming book at a meeting of the Linnean Society on July 1, 1858. The rest is history.

Every one of the 1250 copies of the first printing of *Origin* sold on the day it was published. Excitement and controversy were generated immediately and Darwin, though subjected to much abuse and criticism, nevertheless won "the bauble fame."

The Works of Darwin

The Darwinian theory of evolution is so well known that only an overview of the more fundamental points is presented here. Starting with the obvious fact of variation among individual members of the same species, Darwin reasoned that this spontaneous variability was inheritable. In nature there is a natural selection resulting in the survival of those organisms best fitted for their particular environments, and in the elimination of those that are not fitted. There is, he said, a continuing struggle for survival in nature and those forms that survive are the ones that

---

[1] This is another instance of simultaneous discovery, as discussed in Chapter 1.

have made successful adaptations or adjustments to the environmental difficulties to which they have been exposed; those who cannot successfully adapt do not survive.

Darwin formulated the notion of "struggle for survival" upon reading *Essay on the Principle of Population,* written by Thomas Malthus in 1789. Malthus had argued that the world's food supply increases arithmetically while the human population tends to increase geometrically. The inevitable result, which Malthus described as having "a melancholy hue," is that a large portion of human beings invariably live under near-starvation conditions. Only the most forceful and cunning survive.

Darwin extended this principle to all living organisms and developed the concept of natural selection. Those forms that survive the struggle and reach maturity tend to transmit to their offspring the particular skills or advantages that allowed them to survive. Further, since variation is another general law of heredity, offspring will show variation among themselves, with some possessing the advantageous qualities developed to a higher level than their parents.

These qualities in turn will tend to survive, and in the course of many such generations, great changes in form may develop. Indeed, these changes can be so great as to account for the differences between species as they exist today. Herrnstein and Boring (1965) noted that natural selection was not the only mechanism of evolution for Darwin. He also believed in the Lamarckian doctrine that changes in form brought about by experience during an animal's lifetime can be passed on to subsequent generations.

Many religionists saw the theory as a threat because they thought it inconsistent with the Biblical account of creation. White (1965, p. 93) noted some of the following comments by distinguished clergymen of the time: "an attempt to dethrone God"; "a huge imposture from the beginning"; "If the Darwinian theory is true, Genesis is a lie . . . and the revelation of God to man, as we Christians know it, is a delusion and a snare"; one said succinctly (and perhaps prophetically), "God is dead." The stormy controversy raged for many years.

Within a year of the book's publication, a most exciting debate took place at Oxford between Thomas Henry Huxley, defending Darwin and evolution, and Bishop Wilberforce, defending the Book of Genesis.

> Referring to the ideas of Darwin, [Wilberforce] congratulated himself . . . that he was not descended from a monkey. The reply came from Huxley . . . . "If I had to choose, I would prefer to be a descendant of a humble monkey rather than of a man who employs his knowledge and eloquence in misrepresenting those who are wearing out their lives in the search for truth [White, 1965, p. 92].

The battle is not yet finished. In 1925, the famous Scopes "monkey trial" was held in Dayton, Tennessee, where a high school teacher (John T. Scopes) was prosecuted for teaching evolution. As recently as 1972, a poll showed that 75% of that town's high school students believed the Biblical version of creation. A debate was held there that year between Francis Darwin (great-grandson of Charles) and the local clergy, one of whom said that Darwin's theory "breeds corruption, lust, immorality, greed and such acts of criminal depravity as drug addiction, war and atrocious acts of genocide [*New York Times,* October 1, 1972]."

Also in 1972, the California State Board of Education entered into a heated debate centering on the demand that science textbooks for elementary schools discuss the Biblical account of creation along with the Darwinian theory. The issue was not resolved, but the fact of the debate indicates that science and religion are still at odds over the theory of evolution.

Darwin himself remained aloof from all the controversy of his time and wrote other books of interest to psychology following *Origin.* In 1871, Darwin's second major report on evolution, *The Descent of Man,* appeared. This work marshaled the evidence for the evolution of man from lower forms of life, emphasizing the similarity between the mental processes of animals and those of man, and stressing the importance of sexual selection as a factor in evolution.

Darwin made an intensive study of emotional expression in man and animals and suggested that the changes of gesture and posture that characterize the major emotions could be interpreted in evolutionary terms. This notion was published in 1872 in *The Expression of the Emotions in Man and Animals.* He argued that emotional expressions were remnants of movements that had, at one time, served some practical function.

Beginning in 1840, Darwin kept a diary of his infant son, recording facts of his development, and publishing it in a journal article, *Biographical Sketch of an Infant,* in 1877. This work served as one of the early sources for modern child psychology.

The importance of mental factors in evolution was apparent in Darwin's theory, which frequently cited a number of conscious reactions in man and animals. Because of the role accorded consciousness in evolutionary theory, psychology was compelled to accept an evolutionary point of view.

The Influence of Darwin upon Psychology

As noted earlier, the impact of Darwin on psychology in the last quarter of the nineteenth century probably was as influential as any single factor in shaping psychology as it exists today. The theory raised the intriguing possibility of a basic continuity in mental functioning between animals and man. The Darwinian evidence demonstrating animal–man continuity was largely anatomical in nature, but it strongly suggested similar continuities in the development of behavior as well as mental processes. If the human mind has evolved from more primitive minds, then it follows that there may exist similarities in mentality between animals and man. The discrete gap between animals and man posited by Descartes was thus open to serious question for the first time. Therefore, many scientists turned to the investigation of the mental functioning of animals, introducing a new subject of study into the psychological laboratory. Animal psychology, a field with far-reaching implications for psychology, was the result.

Darwin's influence also brought about a pronounced change in the goal of psychology. The structuralists' focus, as we have seen, was on the analysis of conscious content. Darwin influenced some psychologists, particularly Americans, to consider the functions that consciousness might serve. This seemed to many a more important and basic task than determining the elements of consciousness. Thus, psychology came to be more and more concerned with the adaptation of the organism to its environment and, as a result, the detailed investigation of mental elements began to lose its appeal.

A third great effect of evolution on psychology was a growing focus on the importance of individual differences. The fact of variation among members of the same species was obvious to Darwin as a result of his 5-year observation of so many species and forms. Evolution could not occur at all if each generation were identical with its forebears. Hence, variation was an important ingredient of any evolutionary theory. While the structuralists continued their search for general laws to encompass all minds, other psychologists, influenced by Darwin, began to search for all the many and varied ways in which individual minds could differ from one another. Thus, the study of individual differences began. The psychology of the structuralists had little room for the consideration of animal minds and individual differences. It remained for scientists of a more functionalistic persuasion to pursue these problems.

Individual Differences:
Sir Francis Galton (1822–1911)

Galton effectively brought the spirit of evolution to bear on future psychology in his brilliant work on the problems of mental inheritance and individual differences in human capacity. Prior to Galton's efforts, the phenomenon of individual differences had not been considered a subject for serious study in psychology, certainly a serious omission in the previous history of the field. Only a few isolated efforts existed before the time of Galton, notably those of Weber, Fechner, and Helmholtz, who had reported individual differences in their experiments, but had not investigated them systematically and, as we have seen, Wundt and Titchener did not consider such differences to be a part of psychology.

The Life of Galton

Possessed of a remarkably high degree of intelligence (an estimated IQ of 200) and a wealth of novel ideas, Galton is perhaps without equal in the history of modern psychology. His highly creative curiosity and genius attracted him to a variety of new problems, the details of which he left to be filled in by others. A few of the areas he investigated are fingerprints (which Scotland Yard adopted for identification purposes), fashions, geographical distribution of female beauty, weight lifting, the future of the race, and even an experimental investigation of the efficacy of prayer. There was little that did not interest this versatile and inventive man.

Galton was born in 1822 near Birmingham, England, the last of nine children. His father was a prosperous banker whose wealthy and socially prominent family comprised important persons in all spheres of influence, including Members of Parliament, clergymen, and military leaders. Thus from an early age Galton was acquainted with many influential people through his family connections.

At the age of 16, at his father's insistence, Galton unwillingly began the study of medicine by becoming a house pupil at the Birmingham General Hospital. He worked as an apprentice to the hospital physicians, dispensed pills, studied medical books, set broken bones, amputated fingers, pulled teeth, vaccinated children, and found diversion in reading Horace and Homer. It was, to say the least, not a very pleasant existence and only the continued pressure from his father kept him there.

One amusing incident, reflecting his ever-present curiosity, took place during this medical apprenticeship. Wanting to learn for himself the effects of the various medicines in the pharmacy, he began taking small doses of each one, beginning in systematic fashion with those under the letter "A". This scientific venture ended at the letter "C" when he took a dose of croton oil—a very powerful purgative.

After he completed a year at the hospital, Galton continued his medical education at King's College in London. A year later he changed his plans and enrolled in Trinity College, Cambridge, where, a bust of Newton opposite his fireplace, he specialized in mathematics. Although his studies were interrupted by a severe mental breakdown, he did manage to graduate. He then returned briefly to the study of medicine, but the death of his father released him from this profession, which he had come to dislike intensely.

Travel and exploration claimed Galton's attention next. He traveled in the Sudan in 1845 and in Southwest Africa in 1850. In that same year, he invented a teletype printer. He published accounts of his travels and, in 1854, the Royal Geographic Society awarded him a medal for his exploration of Southwest Africa which was, at the time, a totally unknown land.

In the 1850s he had to stop his travels and exploration because of marriage and poor health, but he served on many committees, wrote a guide for explorers called *The Art of Travel*, organized expeditions for others, and gave lectures on camp life to soldiers as a part of their training for the Crimean War.

His spirited restlessness led him next to meteorology and the design of instruments with which to plot weather data. His meteorological findings were summarized in a book that is considered the first attempt to chart weather patterns on an extensive scale.

When his cousin Darwin published the *Origin of Species*, Galton immediately became vitally interested in the new theory. The biological aspect of evolution interested him at first and he investigated the effects of transfusing blood between rabbits to determine if acquired characteristics could be inherited. Although the genetic side of evolution did not interest him for very long, the social implications of the theory held his attention for quite some time. In the early 1860s, Galton began the work that was destined to have a profound influence on modern psychology.

The Works of Galton

Mental Inheritance

Galton's first important work to influence psychology was *Hereditary Genius*, published in 1869. His purpose was to demonstrate that individual greatness or genius follows family lines with a frequency of occurrence too great to be explained on the basis of environmental influences—hence the thesis that eminent men have eminent sons. For the most part, the biographical studies reported in this book were investigations into the ancestries of famous and influential people—scientists, physicians, etc. Galton's data showed that in each case these men inherited not only genius but specific forms of genius. A great scientist, for example, was born of a family that had attained eminence in science.

Galton's ultimate interest was in encouraging the productivity of the more eminent or fit, and discouraging the birth rate of the unfit. To help achieve this end, he founded the science of eugenics and argued that the human strain, like livestock, could be improved by artificial selection. He believed that if men and women of considerable talents were selected and mated generation after generation, a highly gifted race of people would be the eventual result.

In attempting to verify his eugenic thesis, Galton became very much involved in problems of measurement and statistics. In *Hereditary Genius*, he applied statistical notions to the problems of heredity and ranked the celebrated men in his sample into classes or categories according to the frequency with which their level of ability appeared in the population. He found that eminent men have a higher probability of producing eminent sons than do average men. His main sample consisted of 977 noted men, each so outstanding as to be one in 4000. On a chance basis this group would be expected to have only one prominent relative; instead it had 332. The probability of eminence in certain families was high, but not high enough for Galton to consider seriously any possible influence of superior environment, education, and opportunity open to sons of the outstanding families he studied. Eminence, or the lack of it, was a function of heredity, not of opportunity, he argued.

Galton followed his first book with *English Men of Science* (1874) and *Natural Inheritance* (1889), and between 30 and 40 papers on problems of inheritance. His interest in heredity grew in scope from the individual and the family to the race. He became more and more concerned with the possibility of improving the human race by selective breeding. To this end, in 1883, he formulated proposals for a science of heredity, eugenics, which resulted in the creation of the journal *Biometrika* in 1901, the establishment of the Eugenics Laboratory at University College, London, in 1904, and the founding of an organization for promoting the idea of racial improvement. All of these are still flourishing today.

Statistical Methods

Galton's interest in measurement and statistics has already been noted. Throughout his career, he never seemed fully satisfied with a problem until he had found some means of quantifying the data and statistically analyzing them. In addition to using statistical methods, he developed some of his own.

Adolph Quetelet (1796–1874), a Belgian astronomer, had made the first application of both statistical methods and the normal probability curve to biological and social data. The normal curve had been discovered earlier and used in work on the distribution of measurements and of errors in scientific observation. The principle of normal distribution, however, had never been applied to human variability until Quetelet's demonstration that anthropometric measurements made on unselected samples of people typically yielded a normal curve. For example, he demonstrated that measures of stature of some 10,000 subjects approximated the normal curve of distribution, and he used the phrase *l'homme moyen* (the average man) to express the finding that most individuals tend to cluster toward the average or center of the normal curve, with fewer and fewer cases found as one moves away from the center toward the two extremes.

Impressed by Quetelet's data, Galton assumed that the same results held true for mental as well as physical characteristics. He found, for instance, that the marks given on university examinations followed the same normal curve distribution as had Quetelet's physical measures. Because of the simplicity of this curve and its consistency over a number of traits, Galton proposed that an entire range of measurements could be meaningfully defined and summarized with just two numbers—the average value of the distribution and the dispersion or range of variation around this average value (essentially, the mean and standard deviation, in today's terms). Thus, a large set of measurements or values on human beings could be meaningfully reduced to these two numbers.

Galton's further work in statistics resulted in one of science's most important measures, the correlation. The first report of what he called "co-relations" appeared in 1888. Modern techniques for determining the validity and reliability of tests and the factor analytic methods are direct outgrowths of Galton's discovery of correlation, which resulted from his observation that inherited characteristics tend to regress toward the mean of the distribution of those characteristics. For instance, he noticed that tall men are, on the average, not as tall as their fathers, while the sons of very short men are, on the average, taller than their fathers. He devised the graphic means to represent the basic properties of the correlation coefficient and even developed a formula for its calculation, though it did not remain in use for long.

Galton applied his newfound method to variations in physical measurement, demonstrating a correlation between body height and head length, for example. With Galton's encouragement, his student Karl Pearson developed the presently used mathematical formula for the precise calculation of the correlation coefficient: the Pearson product–moment coefficient of correlation. The traditional symbol for correlation coefficient, *r*, is taken from the first letter of the word "regression," in recognition of its origin in Galton's discovery of the tendency of regression toward mediocrity or averageness in the inheritance of human traits.

The notion of correlation continues to be fundamentally important in the social and behavioral sciences, as well as in engineering and the natural sciences. Many present-day statistical tools and techniques developed in large measure from this pioneering work of Galton's.

Mental Tests

Galton was the first to develop certain specific mental tests; indeed, it may be said that he initiated the whole idea of mental tests (although the term itself came later). He began by assuming that intelligence could be measured in terms of one's level of sensory capacity. Thus, he believed that sensory ability is correlated with intelligence: The higher the intelligence, the higher the level of sensory discrimination.

He had to invent the apparatus from which psychological measurements could be made quickly and accurately on large numbers of people. With characteristic ingenuity and enthusiasm, he devised a number of such instruments measure the senses. To measure the highest frequencies of sound that could be heard, he invented a whistle with which he tested animals as well as people. (He tested animals by walking through the streets and the Zoological Gardens with the whistle fixed to one end of a hollow walking stick that had a rubber bulb at the other end.) This "Galton Whistle," in improved form, became a standard piece of psychological equipment until it was displaced by more sophisticated electronic apparatus in the 1930s.

Other apparatus included: a photometer to measure how precisely a subject could match two spots of color; a calibrated pendulum to measure reaction time to sounds and lights; a series of weights to be arranged in order of heaviness to measure kinesthetic sensitivity; a bar with a variable distance scale to test estimation of visual extension; sets of bottles containing different substances to test olfactory discrimination. Most of his tests were prototypes for standard equipment used in psychological laboratories today.

Armed with his newly devised tests, Galton proceeded to collect data from large numbers of subjects. To accomplish this, he established the Anthropometric Laboratory in 1884 at the International Health Exhibition. Later moved to the South Kensington Museum in London, this laboratory remained active for 6 years, collecting a wide range of data from more than 9000 people. Instruments for taking anthropometric and psychometric measurements were placed on a long table at one end of a narrow room. For a threepence admission fee, a person passed along the table with an attendant who made the successive measurements and filled in the data on a card. Some of the measurements taken included height, weight, breathing power, strength of pull and squeeze, quickness of blow, hearing, seeing, and color sense.

The aim of this large-scale testing program was to determine the range of human capacities for a large number of attributes and abilities. Galton wanted to test the entire population of Great Britain so that the country would know, for the first time, the exact level of the mental resources of its people. Due to his development of mental tests and the establishment of his laboratory, Galton may properly be called the first practitioner of psychology.

Association

Galton worked on two problems of interest in the area of association: the study of the wide diversity of associations of ideas, and the study of the time it takes a person to produce associations.

Following his habit of counting whenever possible, one of Galton's methods for studying the diversity of associations was to walk 450 yards along Pall Mall, the street in London running between Trafalgar Square and St. James Palace. During the walk he focused his attention on an object until it suggested one or two associated ideas to him. The first time he did this, he was amazed at the large number of associations that developed with the nearly 300 objects seen. He found that many of these associations were in the form of recollections of past experiences, including many incidents long forgotten. Repeating the walk a few days later, he found considerable repetition of the associations that had occurred during the first walk. This greatly diminished his interest in this aspect of the study of associations, and he turned to his reaction time experiments, which produced more useful results.

Galton prepared a list of 75 words on individual slips of paper. After a week he exposed them to his view, one at a time, using a chronometer to record the time necessary to produce two associations with each word. Many of the associations were in the form of individual words, but several others appeared not as a single word but as an image or mental picture that required a number of words to describe.

The next task involved the determination of the origin of these associations. He found that a large number of them (about 40%) could be traced back to experiences in his childhood and adolescence. This was one of the very first demonstrations of the influence of early life experiences, particularly those of childhood, on the adult personality.

Of greater importance, however, was the introduction of the experimental study of association. Galton's invention of the word association test marked the first attempt to subject association to laboratory experimentation. Wundt adapted the technique, limited the response to just one word, and used it at Leipzig.

Mental Imagery

Galton's investigation of mental imagery marks the first extensive use of the psychological questionnaire. Subjects were asked to remember a scene, such as their breakfast table of that morning, and to try to elicit images of that scene. They were to indicate whether the images were dim or clear, bright or dark, colored or not colored, and so on.

To Galton's amazement, his first group of subjects, scientific acquaintances, reported no clear imagery at all. Some were not even sure what Galton was talking about when he questioned them about their images. Further investigation, using subjects of more average ability, resulted in the reporting of clear and distinct images that were often full of detail and color. He found the imagery of women and children to be particularly concrete and detailed. As more and more subjects were investigated, it became clear that imagery is more or less normally distributed in the population.

Galton's work began a long line of research on imagery and, generally speaking, his results have been supported. As with most of his research, his interest in imagery was in the attempt to demonstrate hereditary similarities. He found, for example, that similarity in imagery is greater between siblings than between individuals who are not related.

Additional Studies

The areas of research discussed thus far constitute Galton's chief sources of influence on psychology. Since he performed many other studies, however, we will discuss a few of them to indicate further the richness and variety of his talent.

At one time, Galton tried to put himself into the state of mind of the insane by imagining that everything he saw while walking was a spy. As Watson tells it, "By the end of the morning stroll, every horse seemed to be watching him either directly or, what was just as suspicious, they were disguising their espionage by elaborately paying no attention [1971, p. 316]!" He found that it took hours for this state of mind to wear off and that it was all too easy to reestablish.

As noted, the debate between evolution and theology was acute. With great scientific objectivity, Galton investigated the problem and concluded that there was no evidence that religious beliefs are valid just because large numbers of people believe in them intensely. For instance, in one of his books, he discussed the power of prayer to produce results and concluded that it was of no use to physicians as a means of curing patients, or to meteorologists as a method of invoking weather changes, or to clergymen in conducting their worldly affairs!

Galton firmly believed that there is little difference to be found between those who profess a belief in one of the many brands of religion and those who do not, in terms of their dealings with their fellow man or in their own emotional lives. He would have liked to give the world a new set of beliefs, structured in terms of science, as a substitute for religious dogma. He believed that evolutionary development of a finer and nobler race, through eugenics, should be man's goal, instead of heaven.

Galton always seemed to be counting something. He occupied himself at lectures or at the theater by counting the yawns and fidgets of the audience, using the results as a measure of boredom. At one time, he decided to try to count by odors instead of numbers. Training himself to forget what the numbers 1, 2, 3, and so on, mean, he assigned number values for various odors such as camphor and peppermint. He found that he could add or subtract by thinking of odors instead of numbers. Out of this intellectual exercise came a paper entitled *Arithmetic by Smell.*

Comment

Galton spent only 15 years engaged in activities of a psychological nature, yet his efforts during this short period very strongly influenced the direction in which psychology was soon to go. He was not truly a psychologist, any more than he was truly a eugenicist or an anthropologist—he was an extremely gifted amateur whose talent and temperament could not be bound within the confines of any one discipline. Consider the areas that Galton initiated in which psychologists became interested: adaptation; heredity versus environment; comparison of species; studies of children; use of the questionnaire; statistical techniques; the broad question of individual differences; and the field of mental tests. Small wonder Galton is considered such a profound influence on psychology! Flugel and West (1964) commented: "Never again in the history of the science . . . do we meet an investigator so brilliant, so versatile, so wide in his interests and abilities, so little bound by prejudice or preconception. Compared with him, all others (with the one exception perhaps of William James) are apt to appear a little ponderous and pedantic, a little blinkered in their outlook [p. 111]."

Animal Psychology

As mentioned earlier, the evolutionary theory of Darwin provided the impetus for animal psychology. Prior to the Darwinian theory, there was no reason for scientific interest in the animal mind because animals were considered to be soulless automata with no point of similarity to or commonality with man.

Publication of the *Origin of Species* radically changed this notion, for it was made clear that no sharp break existed between the mind of man and that of animals. Instead, a continuity between all aspects of man and animals, mental as well as physical, was posited, since man was believed to be derived from animals by the evolutionary process of continuous change and development. If mind could be demonstrated to exist in animals, and if continuity of the animal mind with the human mind could be shown, such evidence would serve as a defense of Darwin's theory against the man–animal dichotomy espoused by Descartes. A great quest for evidence of mind in animals was begun.

Darwin himself actually undertook the defense of his theory in *Expression of the Emotions in Man and Animals*, in which he argued that emotional behavior in man results from the inheritance of behavior once useful to animals, but no longer of any use to man. One of Darwin's famous examples to demonstrate this point was man's curling of his lips in sneering. He held this to be a remnant of the baring of the canine teeth in rage by animals. Many such examples were cited to demonstrate a continuity between animals and man.

A more systematic and direct approach to the question of mental evolution was made by a friend of Darwin's, George John Romanes (1848–1894). In 1883, Romanes published *Animal Intelligence*, generally considered to be the first book devoted to the field of comparative psychology. Romanes collected a large body of data on the behavior of fish, birds, domestic animals, and monkeys. The method used in collecting these data is referred to in somewhat contemptuous terms as the anecdotal method—the utilization of observational, often rather casual, reports about animal behavior. For example, many of the reports used by Romanes came from uncritical and untrained observers. Such reports were open to the dangers of incorrect observation, careless description, and biased interpretation. These difficulties, together with Romanes' tendency to anthropomorphize, caused his anecdotal method to be discarded by animal psychologists.

Romanes' work fell far short of modern scientific rigor. In fairness, however, it must be noted that he did employ certain rigid criteria for judging the reliability of the reports he used, and he strictly adhered to them. Despite these precautions, however, the line between fact and subjective interpretation in his data is not made clear. Although there are deficiencies in his data and method, Romanes is respected for his pioneer efforts in stimulating the development of comparative psychology and preparing the way for the experimental approach to this area that followed. In many areas of science, reliance on observational data has preceded the development of refined experimental methodology, and it was Romanes who launched the observational stage of comparative psychology.

The weaknesses inherent in the use of the anecdotal method were recognized by C. Lloyd Morgan (1852–1936), who established his "law of parsimony" (often called "Lloyd Morgan's Canon") in an effort to counter the tendency to anthropomorphize. This principle states that an animal's behavior must not be interpreted as the outcome of a higher mental process, if it can be interpreted in terms of lower mental processes.

Morgan also introduced the first large-scale use of the experimental method in animal psychology. His experiments were not conducted under rigid laboratory conditions (as was later the case); rather, they involved careful and detailed observations of the behavior of animals in their natural environments, under special and artificially produced modifications. While not permitting the same degree of control as laboratory experiments, they were nonetheless a great advance over Romanes' anecdotal method.

Though both of these early approaches to comparative psychology were British in origin, leadership in the field rapidly passed to the United States. Part of the reason for this change is attributable to Romanes' early death and Morgan's shift from a career in research to one of administration at the University College of Bristol, a post which left him little time for animals. Characteristically, American psychologists quickly grew to dominate the field.

Comparative psychology was an outgrowth of the excitement and controversy engendered by Darwin's notion of continuity. Perhaps comparative psychology would have begun without the theory of evolution, but most likely it would not have gotten such a sound start, nor would it have begun when it did.

A Final Note

A basic part of Darwin's theory of evolution is the notion of function—and the assertion that as a species evolves, its physical structure is determined by its own requirements for survival. This premise influenced biologists to look on each anatomical structure as a functioning element in a living, adapting, total system. When psychologists began to consider mental processes in the same manner, they created an entirely new movement—functionalism. The following two chapters consider the development of this new movement as it occurred in America.

SUGGESTED FURTHER READINGS

Darwin

Angell, J. R. The influence of Darwin on psychology. *Psychological Review*, 1909, **16**, 152–169.

Boring, E. G. The influence of evolutionary theory upon American psychological thought. In S. Persons (Ed.), *Evolutionary thought in America*. New Haven, Connecticut: Yale Univ. Press, 1950. Pp. 267–298.

Irvine, W. *Apes, angels, and Victorians: Darwin, Huxley, and evolution*. New York: Time, Inc., 1955.

Moorehead, A. *Darwin and the Beagle*. New York: Harper, 1969.

Vorzimmer, P. J. *Charles Darwin, the years of controversy. The* Origin of Species *and its critics, 1859–1882*. Philadelphia, Pennsylvania: Temple Univ. Press, 1970.

Galton

Crovitz, H. *Galton's walk*. New York: Harper, 1970.

Galton, F. *Memories of my life*. London: Methuen, 1908.

Pearson, K. *The life, letters and labors of Francis Galton*. London: Univ. of Cambridge Press, 1914–1924.

Animal Psychology, Romanes, Morgan

Lockard, R. B. Reflections on the fall of comparative psychology. *American Psychologist*, 1971, **26**, 168–179.

Warden, C. J. The historical development of comparative psychology. *Psychological Review*, 1927, **34**, 57–85; 135–168.

7

Functionalism:
American Pioneers

By the turn of the century, psychology in America was assuming a definite character. "It had inherited its physical body from German experimentalism, but it had got its mind from Darwin. American psychology was to deal with mind in use [Boring, 1950, p. 506]." Why did functional psychology develop and thrive in America, rather than in England, where the functional spirit originated? The answer seems to be in what might be called the American temperament—America was ready to accept what the times had for it.

"Only in America"

Until the end of the nineteenth century, the influence of German experimental psychology was very strong in the United States. Americans went to Leipzig in rather large numbers to study under Wundt, and brought back to this country at least the external features of Wundtian psychology. They taught their courses and developed their laboratories on the Wundtian model. Beneath the surface, however, a brand of psychology that resembled Galton's more than Wundt's was developing.

The American *Zeitgeist* radically altered the German psychology, for

America during the latter part of the nineteenth century was still a pioneer country. We were a rough, direct, highly practical, aggressively ambitious, and self-assured people. Land was still freely available to those with the courage, cunning, and ability to take it and wrest a living from it. The principles of natural selection and survival of the fittest were vividly demonstrated in everyday life, where success, and sometimes raw survival, depended on how well one adapted to the demands of the environment.

The historian, Frederick Jackson Turner, described nineteenth century Americans in these terms: "That coarseness and strength combined with acuteness and inquisitiveness; that practical, inventive turn of mind, quick to find expedients; that masterful grasp of material things . . . powerful to effect great ends; that restless, nervous energy; that dominant individualism . . . [1947, p. 235]."

America was oriented toward the practical, the useful, and the functional. American psychology, in its pioneering stages, quite naturally reflected these same qualities. Thus, America was more amenable to evolutionism than Germany or even England. American psychology became a functional psychology because evolutionism and its derived functional spirit were both in keeping with the basic temperament of America.

Anticipator of Functional Psychology:
William James (1842–1910)

In several ways, there is much that is paradoxical about William James and his role and stature in American psychology. On the one hand, he was certainly the leading American precursor of functional psychology. He was also the pioneer of the new scientific psychology in America and America's senior psychologist who, to this day, is considered by many to be this country's greatest psychologist.

On the other hand, there were times when he denied that he was a psychologist or that there was a new psychology. He founded no formal system of psychology and had no disciples in the manner of Wundt.

Although the new psychology he embodied was scientific and experimental, James himself was emphatically not an experimentalist, either in attitude or in deed. Psychology, that "nasty little science," as he once called it, was not his lifelong consuming passion, as it was for Wundt. James remained in it for awhile and then moved on.

Even when he was actively working in psychology, he remained very much himself, refusing to be absorbed by any single ideology, system, or school. Thus, James was neither a follower nor a founder, neither a disciple nor a leader. He was aware of everything that happened in psychology and very much a part of it, but he was able to select from among the various positions only those parts that were congenial with his view of psychology, and reject the rest.

This unique, fascinating man who contributed so greatly to psychology, rather much turned his back on it later in life. He said it consisted of an "elaboration of the obvious" and allowed it to fumble on without his commanding and masterful presence. In spite of that, his place in the history of psychology is both assured and significant.

James did not found functional psychology, but he wrote and thought most clearly and effectively in the functional atmosphere permeating American psychology at that time and, in so doing, he influenced the functional movement through the inspiration he provided to subsequent generations of psychologists.

The Life of James

James was born of a well-known and wealthy family in a New York hotel, the Astor House. (His brother Henry became the eminent novelist.) Their father devoted himself with great enthusiasm to the education of his five children, which alternated between Europe (because of his belief that American schools were too restricted in their outlook) and America (because of his equally strong belief that his children should be educated among their own countrymen). James's early formal education, often interrupted by travel, took place in France, England, Switzerland, Germany, Italy, and the United States. A biography of James contains a chapter dealing with some of this sporadic education and is called, most appropriately, "Zigzag Voyages" (Allen, 1967). The father strongly encouraged intellectual independence among his children, whose family ties remained extremely strong throughout their lives.

The stimulating travel experiences of his youth made James quite literally a man of the world, exposing him to the intellectual and cultural advantages that England and Europe offered a perceptive young man. Frequent trips abroad characterized James's entire life, for his father's unique method of dealing with illness was to send the ailing member to Europe rather than a hospital. Since his health was seldom good, James became something of a commuter between America and Europe.

Although James's father seemed to feel that none of his children would ever need to be concerned with learning a vocation or earning a living, he did nevertheless try to encourage William's early interest in science. When William was 15, he was most excited over a Christmas gift of a microscope. He already had a "Bunsen burner and vials of mysterious liquids which he mixed, heated, and transfused, staining his fingers and clothes, to his mother's annoyance, and sometimes even causing alarming explosions [Allen, 1967, p. 47]."

In spite of this early interest in science, James decided, at the age of 18, that he wanted to be an artist, so the family returned to America. Six months at the studio of William Morris Hunt convinced James that he lacked promise as an artist. In 1861, he enrolled in the Lawrence Scientific School at Harvard. He soon left his first choice, chemistry, apparently because he disdained the painstaking demands of laboratory work, and enrolled in medical school. He was not enthusiastic about the practice of medicine, however, noting that "there is much humbug therein . . . with the exception of surgery, in which something positive is sometimes accomplished, a doctor does more by the moral effect of his presence on the patient and family, than by anything else. He also extracts money from them [Allen, 1967, p. 98]."

James interrupted his medical studies for a year in 1865 to assist the famous zoologist Louis Agassiz during the Thayer Expedition to Brazil. On this trip he sampled another possible career, biology, but found he could not tolerate the precise and orderly collecting and categorizing that this field required. His reaction to chemistry and biology was perhaps prophetic of his subsequent personal distaste for experimentation in psychology.

Although medicine was no more attractive to him after the expedition than when he first studied it, James reluctantly resumed his medical studies since nothing else appealed to him. There was another interruption occasioned by his feeling that he did not have the stamina to continue the hard work, by a host of physical complaints (digestive disorders, insomnia, eye problems, a weak back), and by episodes of deep depression. As Miller and Buckhout (1973) noted:

> It was obvious to everyone that he was suffering from America; Europe was the only cure. In 1867 he went to Dresden and Berlin, where he took baths for his back, read widely in German and other literature, toyed with thoughts of suicide, displayed his loneliness and homesickness by the tremendous volume of his correspondence, and remained just as miserable as he had been at home [pp. 84–85].

He did, however, attend lectures at the University of Berlin on physiology and remarked that it was time for "psychology to begin to be a science [Allen, 1967, p. 140]."

Returning again to the United States, he took his medical degree in 1869, but his depression deepened and his will to live was not very strong. In these dark months, he began to build a philosophy of life, compelled not so much by intellectual curiosity as by sheer desperation.

After reading a number of essays by Charles Renouvier on free will,

James, persuaded of its existence, resolved that his first act of free will would be to believe in free will, and to believe that he could cure himself through belief in the efficacy of the will. He apparently succeeded, at least to some extent, for in 1872 he felt well enough to accept a position at Harvard teaching physiology. After 1 year, he took a year off to travel to Italy, but then returned to teaching.

In 1875–1876, James taught his first course in psychology, called "The Relations Between Physiology and Psychology," the first American offering of the new experimental psychology. (James, by the way, had never received formal classroom instruction in psychology; the first psychology lecture he ever attended was his own.) Also in 1875, the year Wundt established his laboratory at Leipzig, James secured $300 from Harvard to purchase laboratory and demonstrational equipment for the course.

In 1878, two important events occurred. The first was his marriage, which produced five children and a certain amount of much-needed order in his life. Interestingly, it was William's father who first met the 27-year-old school teacher whom William was to marry. He returned from a meeting one night with the announcement that he had just met William's future wife. Shortly after, William verified his father's prophecy.

The second event was the signing of a contract with the publishing house of Henry Holt and Company, which resulted in one of the classic books in psychology. James initially felt that it would take him 2 years to write the book; it actually took 12. It was begun, to the amusement of his friends, on his honeymoon.

In 1880, James was made Assistant Professor of Philosophy, promoted to Professor of Philosophy in 1885, and his title changed to Professor of Psychology in 1889. The work on his book was delayed by travels abroad where he met many European psychologists of the day, including Wundt, who "made a pleasant and personal impression" on him. A few years later he wrote that Wundt "isn't a genius, he is a *professor*—a being whose duty is to know everything, and have his own opinion about everything . . . [Allen, 1967, p. 304]."

The Principles of Psychology finally appeared in two volumes in 1890 and was a tremendous success; it is still considered an extremely important contribution to the field. One indication of the book's popularity is that it is often read by people who are not required to do so. Two years after its publication, James published a condensed version designed to serve as a textbook.

James's reaction to the book on its completion was quite different from the wide public acclaim it was to receive. In a letter to his publisher he described it as "a loathsome, distended, tumefied, bloated, dropsical mass, testifying to nothing but two facts: *1st,* that there is no such thing as a *science* of psychology, and *2nd*, that W. J. is an incapable [Allen, 1967, pp. 314–315]."

With the publication of the *Principles*, James felt that he had said all he knew about psychology, and so he turned to philosophy. No longer wanting to direct the psychological laboratory, James arranged for Hugo Münsterburg, then at the University of Freiburg in Germany, to become director of the Harvard laboratory and to teach courses in psychology. James was thus freed for his work as a philosopher. Münsterberg had been vehemently criticized by Wundt, and this was high praise indeed in James's eyes. Münsterberg, however, never fulfilled James's plan of acquiring a leader in experimental research for Harvard; he worked in a variety of fields, such as psychotherapy, legal psychology, and industrial psychology, and paid little attention to the laboratory after his first few years there.

As for James's attitude toward laboratory work in psychology, we have already mentioned that he was not an experimentalist, although he did begin and equip the laboratory at Harvard. He was never fully convinced of the value of laboratory work and certainly did not like it personally. "I naturally hate experimental work," he had written to Münsterberg. In 1894, he said that the United States had far too many laboratories, and in the *Principles* he commented that the results of laboratory work were not in proportion to the amount of painstaking effort involved. It is hardly surprising, then, that James contributed little of importance in the way of experimental work.

Having made his major contributions to psychology James spent the last 20 years of his life rounding out his philosophical system. In fact, in the 1890s, he became America's leading philosopher.

In 1899, he published *Talks to Teachers*, which developed from a series of public lectures given to teachers, and which helped to apply psychology to the classroom learning situation. *Varieties of Religious Experience* appeared in 1901–1902 and three other important books in philosophy were published in 1907 and 1909.

His health was still poor and he retired from Harvard in 1907. In 1898, while climbing in the Adirondack Mountains, he had been lost for 13 hours and the ordeal aggravated a heart lesion. The condition grew worse and eventually resulted in his death in 1910, 2 days after his return from a final trip to Europe.

The Contributions of James

Since James was neither an experimentalist nor a founder (nor even a psychologist for the last two decades of his life), how did he exercise such a profound influence on psychology? Why is he often considered the greatest American psychologist? Boring (1950) suggested three reasons for his overwhelming stature and influence.

First is his personality, which is reflected to a considerable extent in his written work. He wrote with a brilliance and clarity extremely rare in psychology, or any science, then as well as now. There is great magnetism, spontaneity, and charm throughout his writing.

The second reason for his influence is negative, in the sense in which all movements are negative. He opposed the very foundation of the then current Wundtian psychology; its introspective analysis of consciousness into elements. The third reason is positive: James offered an alternative way of looking at the mind—an approach congruent with the new American functional approach to psychology. The times were ready for the acceptance of what James had to say.

The concept of functionalism is explicit in James's psychology, in which he presented what subsequently became the central tenet of American functionalism: the study of the living person as he adapts to his environment, as opposed to the discovery of elements of experience. The function of consciousness, he said, is to guide the organism to those ends required for survival. Consciousness is thus thought of as an organ, particularly appropriate to the needs of a complex organism in a highly complex environment, without which the process of evolution could not have occurred in man.

The Principles of Psychology

> The publication of *The Principles* was hailed both at home and abroad as an event of the first magnitude in the psychological world. Not only was it a comprehensive survey of a new field of learning, not only was it a new synthesis of the facts of psychology; it was itself a contribution to psychology. From the first, it was recognized as more than a mere book about psychology. Because of its freshness and power, because of its definite attitudes and stimulating suggestions, it was itself an event in the history of psychology [Heidbreder, 1933, p. 197].

A most important characteristic of the book is that it explicitly treats psychology as a natural science; more specifically, as a biological science. Treating psychology as a science was nothing new in 1890, but in James's hands the science of psychology took a different direction from German orthodox psychology. James was concerned with conscious processes as activities of an organism that produced some difference in that organism's life. Mental processes were seen by James as useful *functional* activities to living creatures as they attempt to maintain and adapt themselves in the world of nature.

A related attitude stressed throughout his entire book is James's emphasis on the nonrational aspect of human nature. Man, he noted, is a creature of action and passion as well as thought and reason. Even when discussing purely intellectual processes, he stressed the nonrational influencing factors. For instance, he carefully noted that intellect operates under the physiological influences of the body, that one's beliefs are determined by emotional factors, and that reason and the formation of concepts are influenced by various wants and needs. In short, James did not consider the human being a wholly rational creature by any means.

Let us briefly survey this influential book. The first six chapters of the first volume introduce to the reader certain biological foundations that James believed necessary in order to prepare a base for psychology itself. In them he discusses certain aspects of nervous system activity of importance to mental functioning. He felt that all of mental life is determined in large degree by the tendency of the nervous system to undergo modification by each individual action it makes, so that subsequently the organism will find it easier to perform similar responses. Habit thus becomes a most vital part of all mental life.

James next discusses and criticizes all major philosophical conceptions of the relations between mind and body. He accepted states of consciousness (mind) and brain processes (body) as phenomena in the natural world, and noted a correspondence, term for term, between the succession of conscious states and the succession of brain processes. However, he believed that psychology as a science could accept whatever mind–body relationship(s) it finds, but is under no obligation to explain or account for their existence.

The remainder of the first volume is concerned with the subject matter and methods of investigation for psychology. Here he develops fully his notion of consciousness and its characteristics (discussed later).

The second volume begins with a treatment of sensation, followed by chapters dealing with perception, belief, reasoning, instinct, and volition. The last two chapters, which are almost appendixes, deal with hypnosis and with psychogenesis (the problem of the development of the human species and of the individual). Following are several of James's major points, as expressed in the *Principles*.

SUBJECT MATTER FOR PSYCHOLOGY.   James stated in the opening sentence of the book that "psychology is the Science of Mental Life, both of its phenomena and of their conditions." In terms of subject matter, the key words are "phenomena" and "conditions." Phenomena indicate that the subject matter is to be found in immediate experience; conditions refers to the importance of the body, particularly the brain, in mental life.

The physical substructures of consciousness, then, form an important part of psychology, according to James. He recognized the importance of considering consciousness, which was the focal point of his interest, in its natural setting—the physical human being. This awareness of biology, of the action of the brain on consciousness, is one of the most unique features of James's approach to psychology.

A NEW LOOK AT CONSCIOUSNESS—A REVOLT AGAINST WUNDT.   James rebelled violently against what he considered the artificiality and narrowness of the structuralist position, a revolt which anticipated the more general protest that the functionalists (as well as the Gestalt psychologists) subsequently made. Experiences are simply what they are, he said, not groups or amalgamations of elements. The discovery of discrete elements through introspective analysis does not demonstrate that they exist independently of the observation. He argued that a psychologist reads into an experience what his systematic position in psychology tells him should be there.

A teataster can train himself to discriminate individual elements in a flavor that may not be perceived by the untrained individual. The latter, sipping tea, experiences a fusion of any alleged flavor elements, a total blend or taste not capable of analysis. Similarly, James argued, the fact that one person can analyze his conscious experiences does not mean that the resulting discrete elements are present in the consciousness of anyone else exposed to the same experience. James considered the making of such an assumption the "psychologists' fallacy."

Striking at the heart of Wundtian–Titchenerian psychology, James declared that individual simple sensations (the elements of the structuralists) do not exist in conscious experience. They exist only as a result of a rather tortuous process of inference or abstraction.

In a blunt and characteristically eloquent statement, James wrote: "No one ever had a simple sensation by itself. Consciousness, from our natal day, is of a teeming multiplicity of objects and relations, and what we call simple sensations are results of discriminative attention, pushed often to a very high degree [James, 1890, p. 224]."

In place of the artificial analysis and reduction of conscious experience to alleged elements, James forcefully called for a new positive program for psychology. Mental life is a unity, he argued; a total experience that flows and changes. The basic point of James's conception of consciousness is that it "goes on"—is a stream—and he coined the famous phrase "stream of consciousness" to express this property. Since consciousness is a continuous flow, any attempt to subdivide it into temporally distinct elements or phases can only distort it.

Another characteristic of consciousness is that it is always changing, hence one can never have exactly the same state or thought twice. Objects in the environment can occur again and again, but not the identical sensations or thoughts. It is true, he said, that we may think of an object on more than one occasion, but each time we think of it or experience it, we do so in different fashion because of the effect of intervening experiences. Thus, consciousness is cumulative in nature and not recurrent.

The mind is also sensibly continuous, that is, there are no sharp breaks in the stream of consciousness. There may be gaps in time, as when a person is asleep, for example, but upon awakening the person has no difficulty in making connection with the stream of consciousness that was ongoing prior to the interruption.

Still another characteristic of the mind is its selectivity: It chooses from among the many stimuli to which it is exposed, filtering out some, combining or separating others, selecting or rejecting still others. We can attend to only a part, and a small part at that, of our experiential world, and the criterion of selection, according to James, is relevance. There is a selection of relevant stimuli in order that consciousness may operate in a logical manner and a series of ideas may arrive at a rational end.

Above all, James stressed the purpose of consciousness. He felt that consciousness must have some biological utility to the organism or it would not have survived. The purpose or function of consciousness is to better adapt man to his environment by enabling him to choose. He made a distinction between conscious choice and habit, the latter being involuntary and nonconscious. When the organism faces a new problem and needs a new mode of adjustment, consciousness comes into play. This emphasis on purposiveness clearly reflects the influence of the new evolutionary theory.

THE METHODS OF PSYCHOLOGY.   The foregoing discussion on the subject matter of psychology provides some clues to James's methods of study. Since psychology deals with a highly personal and immediate consciousness, introspection must be a basic tool. James believed that it is eminently possible to investigate states of consciousness by an examination of one's own mind. Since consciousness is not capable of analysis, according to James, his form of introspection could not be of the rigid type practiced by Wundt and Titchener. James considered introspection the exercise of a natural gift, consisting in "catching the very life of a moment as it passed, in a fixing and reporting of the fleeting event as it occurred in its natural setting. It was not the introspection of the laboratory, aided by brass instruments; it was the quick and sure arresting of an impression by a sensitive and acute observer [Heidbreder, 1933, p. 171]."

James was well aware of the difficulties and limitations of introspection and he accepted it as a less than perfect form of observation. He did believe, however, that introspective results could be verified by the use of appropriate checks and through comparison of the findings of different observers. Though not himself a devotee of the experimental method, James did believe in its use as another possible means to psychological knowledge.

Finally, to supplement the experimental and the introspective methods, James urged the use of the comparative method in psychology. By inquiring into the psychological functioning of animals, children, preliterate peoples, and the insane, James felt that variations in mental life could be usefully and meaningfully revealed.

On a higher level, over and above specific methods, James emphasized the value for psychology of pragmatism. The basic tenet of the pragmatic point of view is that the validity of an idea, or of any knowledge, must be tested only by its consequences. In more popular terms, the pragmatic viewpoint is usually stated as "anything is true if it works." The notion of pragmatism had been advanced in the 1870s by Charles S. Peirce, philosopher and lifelong friend of James. Peirce's work, however, remained largely ignored until James wrote his *Pragmatism*, one of his major contributions as a philosopher, in 1907.

EMOTIONS.   James's most famous theoretical contribution, dealing with emotions, illustrates his interest in the nervous system. His theory on emotions, published as an article in 1884 and 6 years later in the *Principles*, completely contradicted the then current way of thinking about emotions. It had previously been assumed that the experience of emotion precedes its physical or bodily expression. For instance, the traditional example— we meet a bear, are frightened, and run—exemplifies the older notion that the emotion (being frightened) precedes the bodily expression (running).

James reversed this and stated that the arousal of the physical response precedes the appearance of the emotion. Thus for James the example would be: We see the bear, run, and are then afraid. In essence, the emotion is nothing but the feeling of the bodily changes as they occur. As for supporting evidence, he appealed to the introspective observation that if these bodily changes, such as increased heartbeat, muscle tension, and so on, are taken away, the emotion also disappears. As another example of simultaneous discovery, the Danish physiologist Carl Lange published an analogous theory in 1885. The similarity between the two led to the designation "James–Lange theory."

James's theory of emotion was the only specific theory to become influential and famous. It led to a great deal of discussion and controversy, stimulated much research, and is considered the starting point for much of modern theory on emotions.

HABIT. The chapter dealing with habit is the most famous one in the *Principles*. In keeping with his awareness of physiological influences, James considered habit to involve the functioning of the nervous system. He posited that repeated actions serve to increase the plasticity of neural matter. As a result, the action becomes easier to perform on subsequent repetitions and, at the same time, requires less attention on the part of the individual. James also felt that habit had enormous social implications, as noted in this oft-quoted passage:

> Habit is thus the enormous fly-wheel of society, its most precious conservative agent. It alone is what keeps us all within the bounds of ordinance, and saves the children of fortune from the envious uprisings of the poor. It alone prevents the hardest and most repulsive walks of life from being deserted by those brought up to tread therein. It keeps the fisherman and the deck-hand at sea through the winter; it holds the miner in his darkness, and nails the country-man to his log-cabin and his lonely farm through all the months of snow; it protects us from invasion by the natives of the desert and the frozen zone. It dooms us all to fight out the battle of life upon the lines of our nurture or our early choice, and to make the best of a pursuit that disagrees, because there is no other for which we are fitted, and it is too late to begin again. It keeps different social strata from mixing. Already at the age of twenty-five you see the professional mannerism settling down on the young commercial traveller, on the young doctor, on the young minister, on the young counsellor-at-law. You see the little lines of cleavage running through the character, the tricks of thought, the prejudices, the ways of the "shop," in a word, from which the man can by-and-by no more escape than his coat-sleeve can suddenly fall into a new set of folds. On the whole, it is best he should not escape. It is well for the world that in most of us, by the age of thirty, the character has set like plaster, and will never soften again [1890, p. 79].[1]

[1] From William James, *Psychology (Briefer Course)*. New York: Collier, 1962. Pp. 158–159. Reprinted by permission of Alexander R. James, Lit. Exec.

Comment

Our coverage of James cannot hope to encompass the scope and brilliance of his form of psychology. The publication of the *Principles* was of major importance and, as mentioned earlier, can legitimately be acclaimed as a great event in the history of psychology.

Perhaps it is easier to admire William James than to attempt to analyze him. His book influenced thousands of students and his position inspired John Dewey and other functional psychologists to move the new science away from the Wundtian view. There is no denying that James is one of the most important psychologists this country has ever produced.

G. Stanley Hall (1844–1924)

Although William James was the first truly great American psychologist, the tremendous growth of psychology in the United States between 1875 and 1900 was hardly the work of James alone. Another remarkable figure in the history of American psychology, and a worthy and influential contemporary of James, was Granville Stanley Hall.

Hall had one of the most interesting and varied careers of any psychologist. He worked in bursts of great energy and enthusiasm in a number of areas, then moved on, leaving the details to be investigated by others. He was not a founder of functionalism, but his contributions to new fields and activities had a pronounced functional flavor.

American psychology owes Hall a great debt because of his outstanding record of "firsts." His was the first American doctorate in psychology, and he was the first American student in the first year of the first psychology laboratory (Wundt's). He began what is often considered the first psychological laboratory in the United States, as well as the first American journal in psychology. He was the first president of Clark University, and the organizer and first president of the American Psychological Association. Also, as Boring (1950) noted, Hall was "forever 'founding' ideas, that is to say, he would . . . bring together certain new ideas that were not original with himself, [and] add to them a supporting mass of other ideas drawn from his omnivorous reading [p. 518]."

The Life of Hall

Born on a farm in Massachusetts, Hall began at an early age to develop a succession of intense interests that became characteristic of him in later life. Also characteristic of him was his personal ambition. At the age of 14, "he vowed to leave the farm and 'do and be something in the world.' . . . His most intense adolescent fear was the fear of mediocrity [Ross, 1972, p. 12]." In 1863, he entered Williams College, where he investigated many fields, including the theory of evolution which impressed him greatly and was to strongly influence his career in psychology. By the time of his graduation, he had won a number of honors and had developed an enthusiasm for philosophy and evolution.

In 1867, he enrolled in the Union Theological Seminary in New York City, without too much in the way of a "call" to prepare for the ministry. His interest in evolution was not exactly to his advantage in the seminary and he was not noted for his religious orthodoxy. The story has often been told that when Hall gave his trial sermon to the faculty and students, the seminary president, whose job it was to criticize such trial sermons, instead knelt and prayed for Hall's soul.

On the advice of the famous preacher Henry Ward Beecher, Hall went to Germany to study. After studying philosophy and theology in Bonn, he went to Berlin, where, in addition to theology and philosophy, he worked in physiology and physics. This phase of his education was supplemented by some romantic interludes and the frequenting of beer gardens and the theater, all quite daring for a young man of strong Puritan background.

He returned home in 1871 with no degree, heavily in debt, and 27 years old. He then took his degree in divinity and preached in a country church for all of 10 weeks. After tutoring in a private family for more than a year, he secured a teaching appointment at Antioch College in Ohio. Besides teaching English literature, French and German language and literature, and philosophy, during his 3 years at Antioch he served as librarian, led the choir, and even preached! In 1874, his interest in the new psychology was aroused on reading Wundt's *Physiological Psychology* and he became uncertain about his future career. Taking a leave of absence from Antioch, he settled in Cambridge, Massachusetts in 1876 and became a tutor in English at Harvard.

In spite of the monotonous and time-consuming work of teaching sophomore English, Hall managed to conduct research at the Medical School. In 1878, he presented his dissertation on the muscular perception of space for his doctorate, the first degree in the new psychology awarded in America. While at Harvard, Hall got to know James very well. The two were close in age, but far apart in background and temperament. Boring (1950) noted that "Hall was a comet, caught for the moment by James's influence, but presently shooting off into space never to return [p. 519]."

Immediately after receiving his degree, Hall left for Europe, first studying physiology at Berlin and then moving to Leipzig, where he became Wundt's first American student. The anticipation of studying with Wundt was apparently greater than the reality. Although he attended Wundt's lectures and dutifully served as a subject in the laboratory, Hall's own research was more along physiological lines. As his career demonstrates, he was little influenced by the great man.

When Hall returned to America in 1880 he had neither a job nor any prospect of one, but he did have a wife—a former student from Antioch whom he had met again and married in Germany. The future must have looked very bleak to the 36-year-old Hall.

Yet, within a short span of 10 years, he was to become a figure of national renown and a leading American psychologist, second only to William James.

The first step in that rise from obscurity to prominence was an invitation from the president of Harvard to give a series of Saturday morning talks on education. These well-received lectures brought Hall much favorable publicity and, in 1881, an invitation to lecture at the Johns Hopkins University (which had begun only 5 years earlier as the first graduate school in America).

His lectures at Johns Hopkins were also successful and he was given a professorship in 1884. During his years there, he began what is usually considered to be the first American psychology laboratory, in 1883, and taught a number of students who later became prominent psychologists, among them Cattell and Dewey. In 1887, Hall began the *American Journal of Psychology*, the very first journal of psychology in America and still an important one today. This journal provided not only a platform for theoretical and experimental contributions, but also a sense of solidarity and independence for the new American psychology. (In a burst of enthusiasm, he had an enormously excessive number of copies of the first issue printed. It took 5 years for both the journal and Hall to pay back those initial printing costs.)

In 1888, Hall accepted the invitation to become the first president of the new Clark University. He aspired to make Clark a graduate university along the lines of Hopkins and the German universities, with primary emphasis on research, not teaching. Unfortunately, the founder, wealthy merchant Jonas Gilman Clark, had different ideas and did not provide as much money as Hall had been led to expect. Upon Clark's death in 1900, the endowment was largely devoted to the founding of an undergraduate college, opposed by Hall, but long advocated by Clark.

Hall was Professor of Psychology as well as president, and continued to teach in the graduate school for a number of years. In spite of what must have been a taxing role as president of a new university, he founded another journal, the *Pedagogical Seminary* (now the *Journal of Genetic Psychology*) in 1891, at his own expense, to serve as an outlet for research in child study and educational psychology.

In 1892, the American Psychological Association was founded mainly through the efforts of Hall. At his invitation a dozen or so psychologists (records are incomplete on the number present) met in his study to plan the organization, and elected him the first president. By 1900, just 8 years later, the organization had grown to 127 members.

Hall continued his interest in religion, founding the *Journal of Religious Psychology* (1904), which ceased publication after a decade. In 1917, he published a book entitled *Jesus the Christ in the Light of Psychology*. His portrayal of Jesus as "a kind of adolescent superman [Ross, 1972, p. 418]" was not very well received by organized religion. In 1915, he founded the currently active *Journal of Applied Psychology*. By this time, there were already 15 other psychology journals in America.

Psychology prospered at Clark under Hall; during his 36 years there, some 81 doctorates were awarded in psychology. Perhaps the best known of these students is Lewis Terman, the American leader in testing and individual differences. At one time it was said that the majority of American psychologists had been associated with Hall, at either Clark or Hopkins, though he was not the primary source of inspiration for them all. Perhaps reflecting the personal influence of Hall is the fact that one third of his doctoral students eventually went into administration, as he had done.

Hall was one of the first Americans to become interested in psychoanalysis, and was in great part responsible for its becoming known in America. To celebrate the twentieth anniversary of Clark University in 1909, Hall invited Freud and Jung to participate in a series of conferences. This was Freud's only visit to the United States and Hall's invitation was a courageous step at that time because of the suspicion with which many American psychologists viewed psychoanalysis.

Hall continued his writing after retiring from Clark in 1920 and died 4 years later, a few months after his election as president of the American Psychological Association for the second time.

The Works of Hall

Hall's intellectual career was characterized by a series of interests, quite unlike Wundt's concentrated devotion to a single focus. A guiding theme, however, pervaded all these intellectual wanderings: evolutionary theory. His work on a wide variety of psychological topics was governed by the conviction that the normal growth of the mind involves a series of evolutionary stages. Hall used the theory of evolution as a framework for all his broad theoretical speculations.

On the whole, Hall contributed more to educational psychology than to experimental psychology. Only the early phases of his productive career involved experimental psychology for, although he was always favorable toward it, he became impatient of its limitations. Laboratory work in the new psychology proved too narrow for Hall's broad goals and efforts.

Hall is often called a genetic psychologist because of his concern with human and animal development, and all the many related problems of adaptation and development.

At Clark, Hall's geneticism led him to the psychological study of the child and, later, of adolescence. In his child studies he made extensive use of questionnaires, a procedure he had learned in Germany. By 1915, Hall and his students had developed and used 194 questionnaires covering a wide variety of topics. So extensive was his use of questionnaires that, for a time, the method came to be associated in America with Hall's name, even though the technique had been used earlier by Galton.

These early studies of the child created great public enthusiasm which led to the so-called child study movement. Although it disappeared in a few years because of poorly executed studies, the movement served to establish the importance of the empirical study of the child and the concept of psychological development.

Hall's most important and influential work is the lengthy (about 1300 pages) two-volume *Adolescence: Its Psychology, and Its Relations to Physiology, Anthropology, Sociology, Sex, Crime, Religion, and Education*, published in 1904. It was not only an encyclopedia of useful material, but also contained the most complete statement of Hall's recapitulation theory of development. He believed that the child in his individual development repeats the life history of the race. When the child plays cowboys and Indians, for example, he is repeating the level of preliterate man. The book contained much material of interest to child psychologists and educators and went through several printings, one 20 years after publication.

As Hall grew older he became interested in a later stage of development—old age. In 1922 he published (appropriately, at the age of 78) the two-volume *Senescence*, the first large-scale geriatric survey of a psychological nature in any language. He also wrote two books of an autobiographical nature in the last few years of his life: *Recreations of a Psychologist* (1920) and *The Life and Confessions of a Psychologist* (1923).

Comment

G. Stanley Hall was once introduced to an audience as "the Darwin of the Mind." It was a characterization that evidently pleased him very much and vividly expressed his aspirations and the basic attitude that flavored his work. Throughout his amazing career he remained extremely versatile and agile in his works. His seemingly limitless enthusiasm was bold, diverse, and nontechnical, and it is perhaps this characteristic that made him so stimulating and spread his influence so far.

In his autobiography he wrote: "All my active conscious life has been made up of a series of fads or crazes, some strong, some weak; some lasting long . . . and others ephemeral [G. S. Hall, 1923, pp. 367–368]." It was a perceptive observation. Mercurial, aggressive, quixotic, often at odds with his colleagues—G. Stanley Hall was never dull. He once noted that Wundt would rather have been commonplace than brilliantly wrong. Perhaps, it has been suggested, Hall would rather have been brilliantly wrong than commonplace.

James McKeen Cattell (1860–1944)

In many ways, the functionalist spirit of American psychology is best represented in the life and works of Cattell, another contemporary of James. He is generally credited with strongly influencing the impressive movement in American psychology in the direction of a very practical test-oriented approach to the study of mental processes. His psychology was concerned with human abilities rather than with conscious content and, in this respect, he comes close to being a functionalist, though, like Hall and James, he was never formally associated with the movement. He did, of course, represent the American functionalistic spirit in his emphasis on mental processes in terms of their utility to the organism.

The Life of Cattell

Born in Easton, Pennsylvania, Cattell received his bachelor's degree in 1880 from Lafayette College, where his father was president. Following the custom of going to Europe for graduate studies, he went to Göttingen and then to Leipzig and Wundt. A paper in philosophy won for him a fellowship at Johns Hopkins at the very time Hall was beginning his laboratory. While at Hopkins, Cattell began research on the time required for different mental activities and this work reinforced his desire to become a psychologist.

His return to Wundt in 1883 is the subject of one of the most famous anecdotes in the history of psychology. Cattell appeared at the Leipzig Laboratory and boldly announced, "Herr Professor, you need an assistant, and I shall be your assistant [Cattell, 1928, p. 545]." Thus, Cattell became Wundt's first assistant! In yet another indication of Cattell's spirit of bold aggressiveness and independence, he made it clear to Wundt that he would choose his own research project, on the psychology of individual differences, a topic hardly a central part of Wundtian psychology. (We have noted earlier that the great man assigned topics of his own choosing to his graduate students—but not to Cattell.) Wundt is said to have characterized both Cattell and his project as *ganz Amerikanisch* (typically or completely American). Wundt's remark was not only justified but prophetic, for the interest in individual differences, a natural outcome of an evolutionary point of view, has since been a feature of American and not German psychology.

There are indications that the relationship between Cattell and Wundt became somewhat strained, though there was certainly never an open break. Apparently, the highly formal Wundt was too rigid and strict for Cattell. There was, for instance, an edict restricting the number of hours a student could spend in the laboratory. If a student wanted to extend the time, the work would have to be carried on at home. Cattell found it difficult to accept such restrictions.

He also firmly believed that the method of Wundtian introspection (fractionating the reaction time into various activities, such as perception or choice), was something he personally could not do. Indeed, he questioned the validity of the method for anyone's use. This attitude did not exactly ingratiate him with Wundt, who did not allow in his laboratory those who were unable to benefit from his method. Consequently, Cattell conducted some of his research in his own room.

In spite of these disagreements, Wundt and Cattell did agree on the value of studying reaction time. Cattell believed it to be especially useful for the study of the time necessary for various mental operations, particularly for research on individual differences. Many of the classic studies on reaction time were carried out by Cattell during his 3 years at Leipzig, and he published over a half-dozen articles on reaction time and individual differences before leaving there.

(Cattell gave Wundt the great man's first typewriter on which most of Wundt's books were written. For this gift, Cattell was criticized in jest for having "done a serious disservice . . . for it had enabled Wundt to write twice as many books as would otherwise have been possible [Cattell, 1928, p. 545].")

After obtaining his degree in 1886, Cattell lectured in psychology at

Bryn Mawr and the University of Pennsylvania for 1 year. He then became lecturer at Cambridge University, where he met Galton and assisted him for a few months at the South Kensington Museum. They shared similar interests and views on individual differences, and Galton, then at the zenith of his fame, served to broaden Cattell's horizons. In addition to admiring Galton's versatility and wide-ranging interests, Cattell seems to have been deeply impressed by his emphasis on measurement and statistics. As a result, Cattell became one of the first American psychologists to stress quantification, ranking, and ratings.

In 1888, Cattell was appointed Professor of Psychology at the University of Pennsylvania. This appointment has great significance because, as the first professorship of psychology anywhere in the world, it represented formal recognition of psychology's separate status. Earlier academic appointments of psychologists had been in departments of philosophy.

Leaving Pennsylvania in 1891, Cattell became Professor of Psychology and head of the department at Columbia University, where he remained for 26 years. Due to his dissatisfaction with Hall's *American Journal of Psychology*, Cattell began a new journal, *The Psychological Review*, in 1894, with another psychologist, J. Mark Baldwin. In 1895 he acquired from Alexander Graham Bell the weekly journal *Science*, which was ceasing publication for lack of funds. Five years later, it became the official journal of the American Association for the Advancement of Science. Cattell began, in 1906, a series of reference works: *American Men of Science, Leaders in Education*, and *The Directory of American Scholars*. He had started *Popular Science Monthly* in 1900; after selling the first name in 1915, he continued to publish the journal as *Scientific Monthly*. Another weekly, *School and Society*, was started in 1915. As can well be imagined, this truly phenomenal organizing and editing record required a great deal of time and, not surprisingly, Cattell's research productivity declined.

During Cattell's career at Columbia, more doctorates in psychology were awarded there than at any other school in the United States. Cattell stressed the importance of independent work and gave his students considerable freedom to do research on their own. He firmly believed that a professor should be equally independent of both the university and students, so long as he was working in his discipline. To emphasize this point and make a reality of it, he lived some 40 miles from the campus, opposite West Point, and even set up a laboratory and editorial office at his home. He came to the university only certain days each week and thus was able to avoid the many inane distractions and interruptions so common to academic life.

This independence was only one of a series of factors that served to strain relations between Cattell and the university administration. He actively urged increased faculty participation in university affairs, arguing that many decisions should be made by faculty and not by administrators. Toward this end, he helped to found the American Association of University Professors and became all the more unpopular with Columbia's administration.

Cattell was not at all tactful or diplomatic in his dealings with the administration. He has been described as "a difficult man to get along with . . . 'ungentlemanly,' 'irretrievably nasty,' and 'lacking in decency' [Gruber, 1972, p. 300]." He did not play by the rules of polite social conduct, preferring slashing satire, ridicule, and irony in his attacks on the administration.

Then, as now, university administrators tend to be intolerant of attacks on their authority, and so Cattell's days at Columbia were numbered. On three occasions, from 1910 to 1917, the trustees considered "retiring" him.

The final blow came during World War I, when Cattell wrote to Congress protesting the practice of sending conscientious objectors into combat. It was a most unpopular position to take at that time but Cattell, with characteristic determination, remained adamant. He was dismissed from Columbia in 1917 on the grounds that he had been disloyal to his country. His reaction was to sue the university for libel, and although he was awarded $40,000, he was not reinstated.

Cattell never returned to academic life. Instead, he devoted himself with even greater zest to his publications, the American Association for the Advancement of Science, and other learned societies. These efforts of a promotional nature, in which he served as a spokesman for psychology to other sciences, tended to give psychology a higher standing in the scientific community.

In 1921, Cattell realized one of his great ambitions—the promotion of the application of psychology. He organized the Psychological Corporation on the basis of stock purchased by members of the American Psychological Association. This corporation, providing psychological services to industry and the public, has grown considerably and is still in operation today.

Cattell remained very active in his roles as editor and spokesman for psychology until his death in 1944. One final aspect of his life that deserves mention is his extremely rapid rise in American psychology. He was a professor at the University of Pennsylvania at 28, chairman of the department at Columbia at 31, president of the American Psychological Association at 35, and the first psychologist elected to the National Academy of Sciences at 40.

The Works of Cattell

We have already mentioned Cattell's early work on reaction time and his interest in the study of individual differences. An indication of the scope of his work was provided in 1914, when a group of his students gathered together his original work, which had been published in numerous short papers. There were five main areas in addition to reaction time: reading and perception, association, psychophysics, the order of merit method, and individual differences.

Without denying the importance of these other works, it seems that Cattell influenced psychology most through his work on individual differences and mental tests. In fact, the central theme of all his research was the problem of individual differences. By the time he went to Columbia in 1891, his interest in the development and promotion of mental tests had become paramount. A few years earlier, while still at Pennsylvania, he had administered a series of tests to students and, in a paper in 1890, had coined the term "mental tests." He continued the testing program at Columbia and collected a large body of data from several entering classes of students.

It is instructive to look at the kinds of tests Cattell used to try to measure the range and variability of human capacity. As distinguished from the later development of intelligence tests, which utilized more complex tasks of mental ability, Cattell's tests (like Galton's) dealt with more elementary bodily or sensory–motor measures. The basic tests he utilized included: dynamometer pressure; rate of movement (how quickly the hand can be moved 50 centimeters); sensation areas using the two-point threshold; pressure causing pain (amount of pressure on the forehead necessary to cause pain); just noticeable differences in weight; reaction time for sound; time for naming colors; bisection of a 50-centimeter line; judgment of a 10-second period of time; and the number of letters that can be remembered after one presentation.

By 1901, enough data had been collected to correlate the test scores with the subjects' academic performance. The correlations proved disappointingly low, as did intercorrelations among individual tests themselves. Similar results using sensory–motor tests had also appeared from Titchener's laboratory, and it seemed that tests of this type were not very valid predictors of intellectual ability.

As every student of psychology knows, in 1905 the French psychologist Alfred Binet, together with V. Henri and T. Simon, developed an intelligence test using much more complex measures of higher mental abilities. This approach provided a much more effective measure of intelligence and marked the beginning of the phenomenal growth of intelligence testing.

Cattell's influence was felt strongly in supporting and promoting the mental test movement. His student, E. L. Thorndike (Chapter 9) was a leader in the psychology of mental tests in America, and Columbia became the leading university in the testing movement for years.

Continuing the tradition of Galton's earlier work, Cattell undertook a series of studies to investigate the nature and origin of scientific ability, using a much improved technique, the method of order of merit, which he developed in 1902. With this method, stimuli ranked by a number of judges are placed in a final rank order by calculating the average rating given to each stimulus item. The method was applied to eminent American scientists by having competent men in each of the scientific fields rank, in order, a number of their outstanding colleagues. The source book *American Men of Science* emerged from this work.

Comment

Cattell's influence on American psychology was exerted not through the development of a system of psychology (he had little patience with theory), nor through an impressive list of publications. Rather, his influence was felt most strongly through his abilities as an organizer, executive, and administrator of psychological science and practice, and as a spokesman for psychology to the scientific community at large. Cattell became something of an "ambassador" of psychology, giving lectures, editing his various journals, and promoting the practical application of psychology.

There was one other way in which he contributed to psychology— through his students. During his 26 years at Columbia he was able to influence the training of more graduate students in psychology than any other single individual in America. A number of these students became leading psychologists in their own right. (Two, E. L. Thorndike and R. S. Woodworth, will be discussed in the following chapters.)

Through his work on mental testing, the measurement of individual differences, and the promotion of applied psychology, Cattell energetically reinforced the movement of functionalism in American psychology.

Ganz Amerikanisch

As we noted at the beginning of this chapter, evolutionary doctrine readily and rapidly took hold in America. And evolution meant, for psychology, an emphasis on individual differences and the techniques with which to measure them. An interest in individual differences began in England but did not flourish there. John Dewey noted, in 1899, that a psychology of individual differences can flourish only in a democracy, as the findings of a psychology of individual differences never support the notion of innate class differences.

A psychology of individual differences tends to be highly practical and we have already noted America's pragmatic spirit and functional orientation. This country wanted a practical shirt-sleeves form of psychology and, through the efforts of James, Hall, Cattell, and other American pioneers, it was to have and use it most effectively, in the *ganz Amerikanisch* direct, bold, and aggressive fashion.

The exciting, vibrant, and dynamic development of American psychology is one of the most striking events in science during the period 1880–1900. In 1880 there were no laboratories; by 1895 there were 24. In 1880 there were no journals; by 1895 there were three. In 1880 Americans were still going to Germany to study psychology; by 1900 they could study it in a growing number of their own universities.

Psychology was flourishing in the universities and it made its debut before the general public at, of all places, the Chicago World's Fair in 1893. Two psychologists, Hugo Münsterberg (James's import from Germany) and Joseph Jastrow, set up exhibits of apparatus, as well as a testing laboratory in which people could learn something of their capacities.

Such popular display would not have found favor with Wundt (nor did it with James who called it "Münsterberg's Circus"). This attempt at propaganda, at securing a favorable public image for psychology, would no doubt have been characterized as *ganz Amerikanisch* by both Wundt and James. And so it was, again reflecting the unique American temperament which transformed structuralism into functionalism.

Partly as a result of this orientation, psychology's growth was much more rapid in America than in Europe. Indeed, less than 40 years after psychology began in Europe, America had assumed the lead, at least in a quantitative sense (this too is *ganz Amerikanisch*).

Joncich (1968) notes that the English publication *Who's Who in Science* showed, in 1913, "the United States already doing the heaviest volume of the world's psychological work. With eighty-four of the world's leading psychologists (more than Germany, England and France combined), among all the sciences only in psychology does this nation hold predominance [p. 444]."

Psychology became firmly established in America, not only in college catalogues, but in the lives of average citizens who were influenced and affected by its practical application to a degree not thought possible by the American pioneers of functionalism.

SUGGESTED FURTHER READINGS

Early Psychology in America
Jastrow, J. American psychology in the '80s and '90s. *Psychological Review*, 1943, **50**, 65–67.

Influence of Evolution on American Psychology
Boring, E. G. The influence of evolutionary theory upon American psychological thought. In S. Persons (Ed.), *Evolutionary thought in America*. New Haven, Connecticut: Yale Univ. Press, 1950. Pp. 267–298.

James
Allen, G. W. *William James*. New York: Viking Press, 1967.
Allport, G. W. The productive paradoxes of William James. *Psychological Review*, 1943, **50**, 95–120.
Allport, G. W. William James and the behavioral sciences. *Journal of the History of the Behavioral Sciences*, 1966, **2**, 145–147.
Harper, R. S. The first psychological laboratory. *Isis*, 1950, **41**, 158–161.
Perry, R. B. *The thought and character of William James: as revealed in unpublished correspondence and notes, together with his published writings*. Vol. 1, *Inheritance and vocation;* Vol. 2, *Philosophy and psychology*. Boston, Massachusetts: Little, Brown, 1935.

Hall
Burnham, W. H. The man, G. Stanley Hall. *Psychological Review*, 1925, **32**, 89–102.
Dennis, W., & Boring, E. G. The founding of APA. *American Psychologist*, 1952, **7**, 95–97.
Hall, G. S. *Life and confessions of a psychologist*. New York: Appleton, 1923.
Ross, D. *Granville Stanley Hall: The psychologist as prophet*. Chicago, Illinois: Univ. of Chicago Press, 1972.

Cattell
Poffenberger, A. T. (Ed.) *James McKeen Cattell—man of science*. Vol. 1, *Psychological research;* Vol. 2, *Addresses and formal papers*. Lancaster, Pennsylvania: Science Press, 1947.
Woodworth, R. S. J. McKeen Cattell, 1860–1944. *Psychological Review*, 1944, **51**, 201–209.

8

Functionalism:
Formal Development

The Founding of Functionalism

In Chapters 6 and 7 we have discussed the major themes of the functionalist movement. To briefly reiterate, we have seen that functionalism is concerned with the operation and processes of conscious phenomena, rather than with their structure. Further, its interest is with the utility or purpose of mental processes to the living organism in its continuing attempt to adapt to its environment. Mental processes are regarded as activities leading to highly practical consequences, not as elements in some kind of composition. Functionalism's practical cast inevitably led to an interest in the application of science to the affairs of the world. Thus, applied psychology, disdained by Wundt and Titchener, was well accepted and practiced by the functionalists.

These themes of functionalism were developed and practiced both in the laboratory and the real world by American psychologists such as Hall, Cattell, and James. They shaped this new movement (or approach or attitude) from the work of Darwin, Galton, and Wundt without feeling the need to formalize it; that is, to make of it a firm doctrine, characterized by the rigidity and narrowness such formalization usually entails.

There was, then, no formal school of functionalism by the end of the nineteenth century, even though the idea had rather well permeated American psychology by that time. How, then, did this general attitude, loosely structured around several universities and individuals, take on the characteristics of a formal school of thought?

As mentioned in Chapter 6, those men associated with the "founding" of functionalism were not ambitious to start a new school of psychology in the sense that Wundt had been. To be sure, they did protest against the strictures of structuralism as they saw them, but again, their intent was not to replace structuralism with an "ism" of a different name.

It seems that the formalization of their movement of protest—the "founding" of functionalism—was partly forced upon them by, of all people, E. B. Titchener.

Paradoxically, it can almost be suggested that Titchener "founded" functional psychology, for he adopted the word *structural* as opposed to *functional* in a paper published in 1898, entitled "The Postulates of a Structural Psychology."

In this paper, Titchener pointed out the differences between a structural and a functional psychology, and argued that structuralism was the only proper province of psychology. But, by setting up functionalism as an opponent, Titchener unwittingly served to bring it into a clearer focus than it had hitherto enjoyed.

"What Titchener was attacking was in fact nameless until he named it; hence he thrust the movement into high relief and did more than anyone else to get the term *functionalism* into psychological currency [Harrison, 1963, p. 395]."

Of course, all the credit for founding functionalism cannot go to Titchener, but at the very least he shares credit with those whom history has labeled the founders of the school. Those men, to whom we now turn, were reluctant founders at best.

The Chicago School

In 1894, John Dewey and James Angell came to the newly organized University of Chicago. The combined influence of the two men was largely responsible for the university's becoming a leading center of functionalism. And, as Heidbreder noted, the University itself played a role in the founding.

> It is appropriate, surely, that the first distinctively American school of psychology arose at the new university that was itself an expression

of so much that is characteristically American. The almost incredible feat of creating a great university outright—of actualizing a plan, of assembling a distinguished faculty, of bringing into being the whole complex organization, body and soul—gave the place an air of great things accomplished and about to be accomplished; and it is not surprising that a school of thought, starting in such circumstances, should thrive and grow [1933, p. 204].

John Dewey (1859–1952)

When functionalism is considered as a distinct school of psychology, rather than as an orientation or attitude, John Dewey is usually credited with sparking its development. An 1896 paper by Dewey is generally considered the most important landmark in the formal establishment of functionalism. He exerted a great influence on this school although his years of active contribution to psychology were few.

Born in Vermont, Dewey had a rather undistinguished early life and showed no great intellectual promise until his junior year at the University of Vermont. After graduation, he taught high school for a few years and studied philosophy on his own, publishing several scholarly articles. He went to graduate school at Johns Hopkins, studying under Hall, and received his doctorate in 1884, in philosophy, after which he taught at the University of Michigan and the University of Minnesota. In 1886, he published the first American textbook in psychology (called, appropriately, *Psychology*), which became very popular, though it was soon eclipsed by James's *Principles*.

In 1894, Dewey was invited to the University of Chicago, where he remained for 10 years, during which time he became a moving force in psychology. At Chicago he also began his experimental or laboratory school, which at the time was a radical innovation in education. It served as the cornerstone for the modern progressive education movement, which made him quite famous and controversial.

In 1904, he left Chicago for Columbia University, where he remained until his retirement in 1930, no longer working in psychology proper but applying psychology to the educational and philosophical problems with which he was then concerned.

Dewey's short paper, "The Reflex Arc Concept in Psychology" (1896) was the point of departure for the new movement. In this, his most important (and, unfortunately, last) contribution to psychology proper, Dewey attacked the psychological molecularism, elementism, and reductionism of the reflex arc with its distinction between stimulus and response. He argued that the behavior involved in a reflex response cannot be meaningfully reduced to its basic sensory–motor elements any more than consciousness can be meaningfully analyzed into its elementary components.

When this form of artificial analysis and reduction of behavior is undertaken, the behavior loses all meaning. All that is left are abstractions that exist in the minds of the psychologists performing the dissection. Dewey said that behavior should not be treated as an artificial scientific construct, but rather in terms of its significance to the organism in adapting to the environment. Hence, Dewey argued that the proper subject matter for psychology is the study of the total organism functioning in its environment.

Dewey was very strongly influenced by the theory of evolution and his philosophy was based on the notion of social change. He was against things remaining static, and he was in favor of progress gained through the struggle of man's intellect with reality. In this struggle for survival, both consciousness and activity function for the organism, with consciousness bringing about the appropriate activity that enables the organism to survive and progress. A function is a total coordination of an organism toward achieving an end—survival. Functional psychology is thus the study of the organism "in use."

Dewey's philosophical position brought him more fame than his psychological studies. As a social philosopher, Dewey was greatly concerned with the welfare of man and his physical, social, and moral adjustment. He considered man's psychological processes, such as thinking and learning, to be of paramount importance in his adjustment to life. Thinking, he said, was a tool used by man to meet the exigencies of life: Man thinks in order to live.

Dewey argued that the human effort to survive results in knowledge and knowledge is also a weapon in the fight for survival, a tool in the adjustment process. Since life is learning, he regarded the problem of learning as the most important issue in psychology.

Unfortunately, the time Dewey spent in psychology was all too short. In keeping with his functional orientation, he devoted most of his efforts to education. His program for the progressive education movement is spelled out in a paper, "Psychology and Social Change" given in 1900 on his retirement as president of the American Psychological Association. He remained titular head of the progressive education movement for the rest of his life. More than anyone else, Dewey is responsible for the application of a pragmatic spirit to education. He believed strongly that teaching should be oriented toward the student rather than the subject matter.

Dewey's significance for psychology lies in his stimulation of others and his development of the philosophical framework for functionalism. When he left Chicago, the leadership of functionalism went to James Rowland Angell.

James Rowland Angell (1869–1949)

Angell molded the functionalist movement into a working school and, in the process, made the psychology department at Chicago the most important and influential one of the day; it became the major training ground for functional psychologists.

Angell was born in Vermont into an academic family. His grandfather had been president of Brown University and his father president of the University of Vermont, and later of the University of Michigan. He did his undergraduate work at Michigan, where he studied under Dewey; he then worked under James for a year at Harvard, receiving his M.A. in 1892. He continued his graduate work at Halle, in Germany, but did not obtain his Ph.D. His thesis was accepted, subject to revision (rendering it into better German), but to undertake this task he would have had to remain at Halle without remuneration. He chose instead to accept an appointment at the University of Minnesota, where the salary, though small, was sufficient for him to marry. It is interesting to note that although he did not earn his Ph.D., he was instrumental in the granting of many doctorates to others and, in the course of his career, was awarded some 23 honorary doctoral degrees!

After 1 year at Minnesota, Angell went to Chicago, where he remained for 25 years. Following in the family tradition, he became president of Yale (the first non-Yale man to do so) and helped to develop the Institute of Human Relations there. In 1906, he was elected the fifteenth president of the American Psychological Association. After his retirement from academic life, he served as an officer of the National Broadcasting Company.

Angell published a text in 1904 that embodied the functionalist approach to psychology. The book was so successful that it went through four editions by 1908 which indicates something of the appeal of the functionalist position by that time. In it he maintained that the basic function of consciousness is to improve the adaptive activities of the organism, and that psychology must study how the mind aids this adjustment of the organism to its environment. A more important contribution to functional psychology was his presidential address to the American Psychological Association in 1906 (published in 1907) entitled "The Province of Functional Psychology," which clearly spelled out the functionalist position.

He began the paper by noting that

> functional psychology is at the present moment little more than a
> point of view, a program, an ambition. It gains its vitality primarily
> perhaps as a protest against the exclusive excellence of another start-
> ing point for the study of the mind, and it enjoys for the time being
> at least the peculiar vigor which commonly attaches to Protestantism
> of any sort in its early stages before it has become respectable and
> orthodox [Angell, 1907, p. 61].

As noted earlier, a new movement gains its vitality and momentum
only with reference to, or in opposition to, the established position. Angell
clearly set out the battle lines from the very beginning, but then concluded his introductory remarks with a modest proposal: "I formally
renounce any intention to strike out new plans; I am engaged in what
is meant as a dispassionate summary of actual conditions."

Functional psychology, he argued, was not at all new but had indeed
been a significant part of psychology from the earliest times. It was
structural psychology that had set itself apart from the older and more
truly pervasive functional form of psychology.

Angell then brought together the three conceptions of functionalism
that he considered the major themes of the movement.

1. Functional psychology is the psychology of mental operations in
contrast to the psychology of mental elements, as in structuralism. The
Wundtian and Titchenerian elementism was still quite strong and Angell
promoted functionalism in direct and open opposition to it. The task
of functionalism is to discover how a mental process operates, what it
accomplishes, and under what conditions it appears. Angell argued that
a mental function, unlike a given moment of consciousness studied by
the structuralists, is not a momentary perishable thing. Rather, it persists
and endures in the same manner as do biological functions. Just as a
physiological function may operate through different structures, a mental
function may operate through ideas that are markedly different in their
content.

2. Functionalism is the psychology of the fundamental utilities of consciousness. Consciousness, viewed in this utilitarian spirit, serves an end:
It mediates between the needs of the organism and the demands of its
environment. Thus, functionalism studies mental processes not as isolated
and independent events, but as an active ongoing part of the larger biological activity and, indeed, as part of the larger movement of organic
evolution. Structures and functions of the organism exist as they are
because by adapting the organism to the conditions of its environment
they have enabled it to survive. Angell believed that since consciousness

has survived, it too must perform an essential service that the organism could not otherwise accomplish. Functionalism had to discover precisely what this service is, for consciousness as well as for more specific mental processes, such as judging and willing.

3. Functional psychology is the psychology of psychophysical relations concerned with the total relationship of the organism to the environment. Thus, functionalism includes all mind–body functions. This point leaves open the study of nonconscious or habitual behavior. Functionalism assumes some sort of interrelationship between the mental and the physical, an interplay of the same sort as occurs in the relation between forces in the physical world. Functionalism finds no real palpable distinction between the mind and the body, considering them not as two different entities but as belonging to the same order, and assuming an easy transfer from one to the other.

Angell's address was given at a time when the spirit of functionalism was already an established force that had attained considerable popularity and influence. Angell shaped this force into an active, prominent enterprise with a laboratory, a body of research data, a vital and enthusiastic staff of teachers, and a core of graduate students. In guiding functionalism to the status of a formal school, he gave it the focus and formalization necessary to make it effective.

As mentioned earlier, Angell insisted that functionalism did not really constitute a school and should not be identified exclusively with the psychology taught at Chicago. He believed that the movement was much too broad in scope to be encompassed adequately within the framework of any one school. Despite Angell's protestations, the school of functionalism flourished and was definitely associated with the kind of psychology practiced at Chicago.

Harvey A. Carr (1873–1954)

The work of Carr represents functionalism when it ceased to be a crusade against structuralism, but had become a recognized system in its own right. Carr received his doctorate at Chicago in 1905 and succeeded Angell as chairman of the psychology department from 1919 to 1938, awarding some 150 doctorates during that time. Under Carr, Chicago functionalism reached its zenith as a formally defined system. He took the position that functional psychology is the American psychology. The work being done at Chicago was considered the psychology of the time, and as such had little need for a highly developed systematic formulation.

Alternative approaches to psychology, such as behaviorism, Gestalt psychology, and psychoanalysis, were regarded as needlessly exaggerated developments operating on more limited aspects of psychology. It was thought that these other schools had little to add to the all-encompassing functionalist psychology.

Because Carr's *Psychology* (1925) is an expression of the finished form of functionalism, it is instructive for us to consider two of its major points. Carr defined the subject matter of psychology as mental activity, that is, processes such as memory, perception, feeling, imagination, judgment, and will. The function of mental activity is to acquire, fixate, retain, organize, and evaluate experiences, and to use these experiences in the determination of action. Carr called the specific form of action in which mental activities appear adaptive or adjustive behavior.

Thus, we see a by now familiar emphasis, not on the elements and content of consciousness, but rather on mental processes. And we see a description of mental activity in terms of what it accomplishes in enabling the organism to adapt or adjust to its environment. It is significant that by 1925 these points were discussed dispassionately as statements of fact, not as matters for argument.

Discussing the methods of studying mental activity, Carr recognized the validity of both introspective and objective observation. He noted that the experimental method is the more highly desirable but admitted that adequate experimental investigation of the mind is extremely difficult, if not impossible. Carr also felt that the study of cultural products, such as literature, art, language, or social and political institutions, can provide information on the kind of mental activities that produced them. He also recognized the value of knowledge of the physiological processes involved in mental activity.

Obviously then, functionalism did not adhere to any one method of study, as had structuralism. In actual practice, however, there was a marked emphasis on objectivity in the functionalists' research. A great deal of the research undertaken at Chicago did not use introspection, and in those cases where it was used, it was checked as much as possible by objective controls. It is important to note that animal as well as human studies were carried out at Chicago.

The Chicago school of functionalism produced at least the beginning of a shift away from the exclusive study of the subjective (mind, consciousness) to include the study of the objective (overt behavior). In part for this reason, functionalism helped prepare the way for American psychology to go to the opposite extreme from the structuralists; that is, to focus only on the study of behavior, dropping the study of the mind altogether. The functionalists thus provided a bridge between structuralism and behaviorism.

Original Source Material on Functionalism:
From *Psychology* by H. A. Carr

The following discussion is reprinted from the first chapter of Carr's *Psychology* of 1925[1] and indicates the finished form of functionalism. The discussion covers functionalism's subject matter and methodology as well as the psychophysical nature of mental activity and the relation of psychology to other sciences, as the functionalists viewed the matter.

The Subject Matter of Psychology. Psychology is primarily concerned with the study of mental activity. This term is the generic name for such activities as perception, memory, imagination, reasoning, feeling, judgment, and will. The essential features of these various activities can hardly be characterized by a single term, for the mind does various things from time to time. Stated in comprehensive terms, we may say that mental activity is concerned with the acquisition, fixation, retention, organization, and evaluation of experiences, and their subsequent utilization in the guidance of conduct. The type of conduct that reflects mental activity may be termed adaptive or adjustive behavior. . . . An adaptive act is a response on the part of an organism in reference to its physical or social environment of such a character as to satisfy its motivating conditions. Illustrations of these mental operations may be drawn from the professional education of a physician. At times his mind is mainly engaged in the task of acquisition from lectures, books, and clinics, or from his experiences as a practitioner. At other moments his mind is primarily engaged in the attempt to memorize certain important data. Again, the reflective activities may predominate, and his mind is concerned with the task of analyzing, comparing, classifying, and relating the data in hand to other aspects of his medical knowledge. Finally comes the aspect of adaptive conduct—the use of this knowledge and skill in diagnosis, treatment, or surgical operation.

Every mental act is thus more or less directly concerned with the manipulation of experience as a means of attaining a more effective adjustment to the world. Every mental act can thus be studied from three aspects—its adaptive significance, its dependence upon previous experience, and its potential influence upon the future activity of the organism. For example, perception is a constituent part of a larger act; it is a process of cognizing objects on the basis of what we are doing, or in terms of their relation to some contemplated mode of behavior. Perception also involves the use of past experience, for the significance of any object can be appreciated only in

[1] Harvey A. Carr, *Psychology*. (New York: Longmans, Green, 1925), pp. 1–14.

terms of our previous experiences connected with that object. Likewise every experience with an object is likely to exert some effect upon the way in which that object is apprehended on subsequent occasions.

The importance of these various aspects of mental activity is apparent on a moment's reflection. Retention is essential to all learning, mental development, and social progress. The acquisition of an act of skill involves a series of successive trials or practice periods during which the act is gradually perfected and established. Each step of progress is a result of the preceding trials. The effects of each practice period are retained and it is these accumulated effects that render the succeeding attempts more facile. Without retention there could be no mind. If any individual should suddenly lose all his past experiences, he would become almost as helpless as an infant.

Our experiences must be properly organized and systematized in order to be utilized effectively. In popular speech, we often say that an insane person has lost his mind. As a matter of fact these people do have minds. They accumulate, organize, and evaluate their experiences in some sort of fashion, and they react to the world on the basis of these experiences. These people have disordered minds. Their experiences are improperly organized and evaluated. Theoretically, any group of experiences can be organized in various ways. An individual's manner of thinking and the character of his conduct are functions to a large extent of his previous organization. Certain types of organization are conducive to irrational modes of thought and to anti-social forms of behavior. Experiences must not only be organized, but they must be properly organized in order to be utilized effectively in reacting to the world in an intelligent and rational fashion.

The mind is also continuously evaluating the various aspects of experience. The mind not only labels things as good, bad, and indifferent, but it also arranges the good things of life in a crude scale of relative worth. Aesthetic appreciation in the realms of literature, music, and the graphic arts illustrates this function. Ethical values may also be cited. We label social conduct as right and wrong and develop concepts of such virtues as charity, chastity, honesty, sobriety, and punctuality. An individual's system of values constitutes perhaps the most important aspect of his personality. Some students over-emphasize the relative value of study and become bookworms and grinds. Some boys attach too great an importance to the value of financial independence, and leave school to seek a job. Some people under-estimate the importance of neatness of dress, correct habits of speech, courtesy, kindliness, and many other traits that make for an effective personality in social relations. Some individuals take their politics, their religion, or their science too seriously, and over-estimate the relative importance of those aspects of life. . . . The mind does evaluate its experiences, and . . . an individual's conduct is to a large extent a function of his ideals and system of values.

All experiences of an individual during life are thus organized into a complex but unitary system of reaction tendencies that determine to a large extent the nature of his subsequent activity. The reactive disposition of an individual, i.e., what he does and what he can and can not do, is a function of his native equipment, of the nature of his previous experiences, and of the way in which these have been organized and evaluated. The term "self" is generally employed to characterize an individual from the standpoint of his reactive disposition. We also speak of an individual's personality when we wish to refer to all those traits and characteristics of his self that make or mar his efficiency in dealing with other individuals, while the term "mind" is used when we wish to characterize an individual from the standpoint of his intellectual characteristics and potentialities. . . . Psychology is thus concerned with the study of personality, mind, and the self, but these are conceptual objects that can be studied only indirectly through their manifestations—only insofar as they express themselves in the reactions of the individual. The various concrete activities involved in an act of adjustment are the observable data and the subject matter of psychology.

The Psycho-physical Nature of Mental Activity. These various mental operations that are involved in the performance of an adjustive response are usually termed psycho-physical processes. By their psychical character, we mean that they are acts of which the individual has some knowledge. For example, an individual not only perceives and reacts to an object, but he is at least aware of the fact and he may have some knowledge of the nature and significance of those acts. Individuals are not accustomed to reason, make decisions and react on the basis of those decisions and be wholly oblivious of the fact. The performance of any mental act on the part of an individual implies some sort of experiential contact with that act. For this reason we shall refer to these mental acts from time to time as experiences or as experiential activities. These acts are not only experienced, but they are also the reactions of a physical organism. They are acts that directly involve such structures as the sense organs, muscles, and nerves. The participation of sense organs and muscles in such activities as perception and voluntary acts is obvious. The nervous system is also concerned in every mental act. While this fact is not one of the obvious sort, yet the truth of the doctrine has been thoroughly established. The integrity of these structures is essential to normal mental activity. An excision or lesion in any part of the brain is usually correlated with some sort of a mental disturbance. All conditions that affect the metabolism of these structures also influence the character of the mental operations. We shall make no attempt to explain the nature of this psycho-physical relationship. We merely note the fact that these mental acts are psycho-physical events and insist that they must be studied as such.

In contrast with our conception, mental acts are often identified with the psychical aspects of these adjustive activities. This doctrine assumes that these psycho-physical activities are composed of two parallel series of processes that belong to different orders of reality. There are the "conscious" or immaterial processes on the one hand, and the organic or material processes on the other. The conscious processes constitute the subject matter of psychology, while the latter belong to the domain of physiology. Mind is thus defined in purely psychical or immaterial terms. Mental acts are regarded as a series of immaterial or psychical events that can occur only in conjunction with a series of physiological processes.

Two objections may be urged against this doctrine. 1. When we speak of the psychical or conscious characteristic of an act, we are dealing with an abstract or conceptual object that has no independent existential reality. This doctrine thus involves the logical fallacy of assuming that these conceptual objects are independent entities. Consciousness is an abstraction that has no more independent existence than the grin of a Cheshire cat. 2. By identifying mental acts with the psychical aspects of these adaptive activities, the exponents of this doctrine are logically confronted with the problem of explaining how these mental processes can exert any effect upon conduct. In other words, this conception necessarily raises the problem of the nature of the psycho-physical relation. We do not deny the validity of this problem, but we do assert that it is a metaphysical or philosophical problem that does not belong to the domain of an empirical or natural science.

According to our conception, psychology can not be differentiated from physiology in terms of the metaphysical character of its subject matter. Both psychology and physiology are concerned with the study of the functional activities of organisms. Psychology is concerned with all those processes that are directly involved in the adjustment of the organism to its environment, while physiology is engaged in the study of the vital activities such as circulation, digestion, and metabolism that are primarily concerned with the maintenance of the structural integrity of the organism. Psychology and physiology are thus concerned with two mutually related and interactive groups of organic processes . . . .

Methods of Approach. Mental acts can be studied from several avenues of approach. Mental acts can be directly observed, they can be studied indirectly through their creations and products, and finally they can be studied in terms of their relation to the structure of the organism.

Mental acts may be subjectively or objectively observed. Objective observation refers to the apprehension of the mental operations of another individual insofar as these are reflected in his behavior. Subjective observation refers to the apprehension of one's own mental operations. Subjective observation is often termed introspection, and in times past it was regarded as an unique mode of apprehension different in kind from that involved in perceiving an external event. As a matter of fact, the two processes are essentially alike in nature and they can be differentiated only in terms of the objects cognized. Each mode of observation possesses certain advantages and limitations.

1. Introspection gives us a more intimate and comprehensive knowledge of mental events. Some mental events can not be objectively apprehended. For example, we might know from an individual's behavior that he is engaged in thought without being able to tell what he is thinking about. The individual himself not only knows that he is thinking but is keenly aware of the topic under consideration. Neither will objective observation give us any clue as to whether these thoughts are mediated in terms of words or visual imagery.

Introspection often reveals the motives and considerations derived from past experience that influence us in any particular act. It would be very difficult to obtain knowledge of this character by the exclusive use of the objective method.

2. Subjective observations are rather difficult. Many mental operations consist of a series of complex and rapidly shifting events that are difficult to analyze and apprehend in a comprehensive manner. Inasmuch as our minds are usually engaged in dealing with objective situations, many people encounter a considerable amount of difficulty in the attempt to break this habit and become introspective.

3. The validity of a subjective observation can not always be tested. Given a report by a subject that he thinks by means of visual imagery, any verification or disproof of this statement is practically impossible inasmuch as this particular mental event can be observed only by that individual. Neither can we decide that the statement is untrue because other people assert that they think in verbal terms, for it is possible that individuals may differ in their manner of thinking. On the other hand, any objective act can be observed by several people and their reports compared.

4. Naturally the use of the subjective method must be confined to subjects of training and ability. Psychology must thus rely upon the objective method in the study of animals, children, primitive peoples, and many cases of insanity.

5. Instruments may be used to record and measure any of the objective manifestations of mind. These records can then be analyzed at leisure. Acts can be detected in this manner that would otherwise escape our notice. For example, photography has been utilized as a means of studying the finer eye movements that are involved in an act of perception. This method has been extensively employed in the study of the perceptual activities involved in reading and in certain visual illusions.

Subsidiary to observation is the method of experimentation. In an experiment, the mental operations are observed under certain prescribed and defined conditions. An experiment is often called a controlled observation. An experiment may be relatively simple or quite complex according to the degree of control that is exercised. As an illustration of a simple type of experiment, we may cite the case of memorizing a list of words for the purpose of analyzing this process and discovering some of the conditions that influence our ability to recall this material on some subsequent occasion. In general, the performance of any mental act for the purpose of studying that act may be termed an experiment. A psychological experiment does not necessarily involve the employment of an elaborate technique and complicated forms of apparatus. The character of the apparatus is a function of the problem. Instruments are employed as a means of controlling the experimental conditions, or as a means of measuring and recording any feature of the experimental situation. The primary value of an experiment depends upon the fact that the observations are made under certain prescribed and specified conditions. An experiment is thus a means of discovering facts and relations that would escape detection during the ordinary course of experience. Furthermore the results of any experiment can be tested by other investigators. The experimental method has its limitations in the field of psychology. Not all aspects of the human mind are subject to control. An individual's mental reactions are to a very large extent a function of his previous experiences. A complete experimental control of a human mind implies a freedom in manipulating its development throughout life in ways that are both impossible and socially undesirable.

The nature of mind may also be studied indirectly through its creations and products—industrial inventions, literature, art, religious customs and beliefs, ethical systems, political institutions, etc. This method might well be termed the social avenue of approach. Naturally this method will not be used when the mental operations themselves can be studied. Consequently the method is mainly utilized in the study of primitive races or of past civilizations. The method in practice is essentially historical or anthropological. Obviously our knowledge of the human mind would be exceedingly limited if we were forced to rely exclusively upon such data. Facts of this character, however, are significant for an understanding of the developmental aspects of mind.

Mental acts can also be studied from the standpoint of anatomy and physiology. The structure of any organ and its functional possibilities are intimately related. The neurologist attempts to conceive of the structural arrangements of the nervous system in terms of their relation to the various activities in which they are involved. A study of the mutual relations between mental acts and the architectural features of the nervous system will obviously clarify the conceptions of both psychology and neurology. We know that the character of mental acts is influenced by the metabolic conditions of the nervous system. Neural defects are frequently correlated with disturbances of perception, memory, recall, and voluntary activity. A considerable portion of our accurate and detailed knowledge of the relation of mental operations to the nervous structures has been gained in this way. Certain parts of the nervous structures are excised in animals and the effect of this loss of nerve tissue upon the subsequent ability of the organism is noted. Many features of mind must be explained in terms of the physiological peculiarities of the nervous system. The fact of retention, certain temperamental peculiarities of mind, and some aspects of the process of forgetting must be explained in this manner.

It is thus apparent that any fact is a psychological datum whenever it can be utilized in comprehending the nature and significance of the mental operations. The same fact may be significant to several sciences such as neurology, psychology, and physiology, and such a fact will constitute a part of the data of each of these branches of knowledge. Psychology like the other sciences utilizes any fact that is significant for its purposes irrespective of how or where or by whom it was obtained. No single avenue of approach can give a complete knowledge of a mental act. The various sources of knowledge supplement each other and psychology is concerned with the task of systematizing and harmonizing the various data in order to form an adequate conception of all that is involved in the operations of mind.

Facts of common observation constitute perhaps the major portion of the factual data upon which the present conceptions of psychology are based. Psychology differs from most of the natural sciences in that it deals to a considerable extent with the obvious facts of everyday life. Mental acts are experienced events, and naturally everyone must acquire a certain amount of knowledge concerning his own mental operations during the course of life. A considerable portion of our time and energy is also devoted to the task of dealing with other minds. Everyone thus acquires a certain amount of psychological knowledge of a practical sort. Psychology as a science differs from the common sense variety in several respects. It observes and analyzes mental operations more carefully and systematically, it employs the experimental method whenever possible, it gathers its factual data from a greater variety of sources, and it attempts to construct a more adequate system of conceptions for comprehending these data. Any such system of conceptions is valuable only insofar as the student utilizes them in comprehending his own mental operations or in understanding the actions of others. To a large extent a student must regard a textbook of psychology merely as a guide to the study of his own mind. . . .

Relation to Other Sciences. So far as its systematic relations are concerned, psychology must be classed with the biological group of sciences which deal with the phenomena of living organisms. Psychology finds its closest kinship with physiology in that both are engaged in studying the reactions of animal organisms. There are no fixed lines of demarcation between the two fields. Psychology is interested in the adaptive reactions of organisms in reference to their environmental conditions insofar as those reactions are dependent upon their previous experiences. Physiologists have evinced but little systematic interest in this topic. They have been concerned for the most part with the study of the vital activities. If physiology be arbitrarily defined as the study of organic functions, psychology must naturally be regarded as a special branch of physiology. However, it is wholly immaterial whether psychology be regarded as subordinate to or coördinate with physiology. As a matter of fact, the two sciences do study different aspects of organic activity.

Psychology gathers materials from a great many fields of human endeavor. Psychology appropriates any facts that are significant for an understanding of mind. A professional psychologist naturally encounters a very limited range of mental phenomena and hence must gather his materials from a great variety of sources. Psychology takes facts from sociology, education, neurology, physiology, biology, and anthropology, and hopes in time to be able to borrow from biochemistry. Most of our factual knowledge concerning the great variety of mental disorders has been contributed by physicians and psychiatrists. Peculiar facts of mind and personality are frequently contributed by the legal profession. The various practices of business and industry contribute many suggestive data. In fact, psychological materials can be gathered from any line of human endeavor.

Psychology in turn is interested in making whatever contributions it can to all allied fields of thought and endeavor such as philosophy, sociology, education, medicine, law, business, and industry. Naturally any knowledge of human nature will be extremely serviceable to any field of endeavor that is in any way concerned with human thought and action. While psychology has exerted a considerable amount of influence upon certain of these fields, yet this practical program must be regarded as somewhat of an ideal, for psychology has not as yet attained any very adequate or complete knowledge of human nature.

Functionalism at Columbia:
Robert Sessions Woodworth (1869–1962)

We have discussed Cattell's work, with its functionalistic orientation, while he was at Columbia University. Two of Cattell's students are also of great importance because of the functionalist cast of their work. They are E. L. Thorndike (see Chapter 9) and Robert S. Woodworth.

At the outset it must be noted that Woodworth did not belong formally to the functionalist school in the tradition of Angell and Carr. Indeed, Woodworth expressed great dislike for the constraints imposed by membership in any single school of thought. As he said in 1930, the kind of psychology that he developed "does not aspire to be a school. That is the very thing it does not wish to be. Personally, I have always balked on being told, as we have been told at intervals for as long as I can remember, what our marching orders are—what as psychologists we ought to be doing, and what in the divine order of the sciences psychology must be doing [p. 327]." Thus we cannot label Woodworth as a strict functionalist. Yet his work is appropriately discussed in a chapter on American functionalism because he did express and reflect a very broad, free form of functionalism that was, and still is, characteristic of American psychology. Much of what Woodworth had to say about psychology is in the functionalist spirit of the Chicago school, but he added an important new ingredient to it.

Woodworth was active in psychology for over 70 years as a researcher, beloved teacher, writer, and editor. After receiving his B.A. from Amherst, he taught high school science for 2 years, and then mathematics in a small college for 2 more years, before beginning his graduate work. He received his M.A. from Harvard, and Ph.D. from Columbia under Cattell in 1899. He taught physiology in New York City hospitals for 3 years, and then spent a year with the famous physiologist, Sherrington in England. In 1903, he returned to Columbia, where he remained until his first retirement in 1945. In 1958, at the age of 89, he retired from Columbia a second time, having continued to lecture to large classes since his first retirement!

Woodworth's list of publications is lengthy and his work has greatly influenced several generations of students to the present day. His position is put forth in a number of journal articles and given fuller treatment in *Dynamic Psychology* (1918) and *Dynamics of Behavior* (1958). In 1911 he revised Ladd's *Physiological Psychology*, then wrote an introductory text, *Psychology*, that first appeared in 1921 and went through five editions by 1947. This book was so popular that it outsold every other psychology text for 25 years (Boring, 1950). His *Experimental Psychology*, written in 1938 and revised in 1954 with Harold Schlosberg, is a classic in that area. In 1931, he wrote *Contemporary Schools of Psychology*, revised in 1948 and again in 1964 with Mary Sheehan (appearing posthumously). The last two books are standard texts in many colleges and universities today.

In 1956, Woodworth received the first Gold Medal Award of the American Psychological Foundation and was cited as having made "unequaled contributions to shaping the destiny of scientific psychology," and as an "integrator and organizer of psychological knowledge [American Psychological Foundation, 1956, p. 58]."

Woodworth maintained that his approach was not really new, but was the one followed by "good psychologists" even in the days before psychology became a science.

Psychological knowledge must begin, he said, with an investigation of the nature of the stimulus and the response; that is, with objective external events. However, when psychology considers only the stimulus and the response in attempting to explain behavior, it is missing perhaps the most important element of all—the living organism itself. The stimulus, he said, is not the complete cause of a particular response; the organism, with its varying energy levels, its current and past experience, etc., also acts to determine the response.

> Even in a machine like a loaded gun, the action is not determined solely by the stimulus (the blow of the trigger); the structure of the gun and its stored energy (the gunpowder) must also be taken into account. In the human organism, as in the loaded gun, a stimulus, corresponding to the blow of the trigger, is necessary to start action; but the nature of the action is determined quite as much by the structure and condition of the organism itself as by the stimulus that initiates it [Heidbreder, 1933, p. 300].

Thus, according to Woodworth, psychology must consider the organism itself as interpolated between the stimulus and response. It follows that the subject matter for psychology must be both consciousness and behavior. The external stimulus as well as the overt response are both discovered by objective observation of behavior, but what happens inside the organism can be known only through introspection. Woodworth accepted introspection as a useful method for psychology, but he also made full use of observation and experimentation.

Woodworth introduced into functionalism a dynamic psychology that seemed, in a way, a continuation of the teachings of James and Dewey. The word "dynamic" had been used as early as 1884 by Dewey and 1908 by James. The concept of a dynamic psychology (a psychology concerned with change and with the interpretation of the causal factors in change) represents an interest in motivation. Woodworth had said, in 1897, that he wanted to develop a "motivology."

The first expression of Woodworth's systematic position is in his *Dynamic Psychology* of 1918, a plea for a functional kind of psychology but with the area of motivation added to it. Although there are many similarities between Woodworth's position and that of the Chicago functionalists, Woodworth more heavily stressed the physiological events underlying behavior. His dynamic psychology or motivology is concerned with cause and effect relationships though, he was quick to point out, his interest was not in ultimate causes of man's conduct, but in more immediate causes. He believed that psychology's real interest should be in determining why people behave as they do; why they feel and act in certain ways. Hence, his primary concern is with the so-called driving forces that activate the organism.

In discussing causal sequences in behavior, Woodworth distinguished two kinds of events: mechanisms and drives. A mechanism is concerned with how a task is performed, such as the mechanical aspects of a physical movement. A drive is concerned with the question of why the task was performed. Mechanisms and drives are, however, essentially alike in that they are both responses of an organism. Mechanisms may become drives and vice versa.

This brief discussion of Woodworth's position indicates his eclectic viewpoint in psychology. He did not want to adhere to any single system, nor did he want to develop a rigid system or school of his own. His position was built not on protest but rather on growth, elaboration, and synthesis. He sought out the best features of each system of thought, and found in them common interests and goals.

Criticisms of Functionalism

Critical attacks on the functionalist movement came quickly and vehemently from the structuralist camp. For the first time, at least in America, the new psychology—so recently independent of philosophy—was divided into warring factions.

Some saw this division as valuable, as an indication that the new field was resisting pressures to become solidified and narrow within the confines of a single point of view. Opposition within the field meant, to some, a vitality and flexibility—an ability to explore new concepts, goals, and approaches.

To others, of course, the division was disturbing for it indicated to them a lack of maturity relative to the natural sciences. These older sciences, they argued, did not break up into differing camps, espousing varying approaches and viewpoints.

Cornell and Chicago became, for a time, headquarters for the respective "enemy camps," and accusations, charges, and countercharges were flung back and forth with all the sincerity and righteousness characteristic of those who *know* they are right.

One point of criticism directed against functionalism was what its opponents considered the vague definition of the term *functionalism*.

In 1913, C. A. Ruckmick, a student of Titchener's, examined 15 general psychology textbooks to determine how *function* was defined by the various writers. The two most common usages were an activity or process, and a service to other processes or to the whole organism. In the first usage, function is essentially the same as activity; for instance, remembering and perceiving are functions. In the second case, function is defined in reference to the utility of some activity to the organism, such as the function of digestion or breathing. Ruckmick suggested that the functionalists sometimes used the word function to describe an activity, and at other times to refer to the utility of an activity. It followed that one could speak of the function of an activity, or the function of a function.

It was some years before this charge of inconsistent and ambiguous definition was answered. Carr (1930) argued that the two different usages were not really inconsistent and that the same two uses are found in biology. He believed that both kinds of definition really referred to the same processes. Functionalism was interested in a particular activity for its own sake (as in the first definition) as well as in the relationship of the activity to other conditions or activities (as in the second).

It is instructive to note that Carr's analysis of this problem came quite some time (17 years) after the criticism was first made. As Heidbreder (1933) noted, "Functionalism used the concept first and defined it later; and this sequence of events is characteristic of the movement. . . . functionalism has never been disposed to place definition and systematization in the foreground [p. 228]."

Another criticism, particularly from Titchener, related to the definition of psychology itself. The structuralists charged that functionalism was not really psychology at all, for it was not restricted to the subject matter and methodology of structuralism. Anything other than introspective analysis of the mind into elements simply was not psychology for those who followed Titchener. Of course, it was this very definition of psychology that the functionalists were questioning. To criticize functionalism because it did not follow the system it had purposely discarded seems to be a point not worth pursuing.

Other critics found fault with the functionalists' interest in activities of a practical or applied nature, continuing the old rivalry between pure and applied science. The structuralists, we noted, did not look favorably on the application of psychology. The functionalists, however, were never really concerned with remaining "pure" and certainly never apologized for their practical interests. Carr suggested that rigorous scientific procedures can be adhered to in both pure and applied psychology; that equally valid research can be performed in an industrial setting and in a university laboratory. In the final analysis, Carr noted, it is the method and not the subject matter that determines how "scientific" a field of inquiry is. This controversy between pure and applied science no longer exists in such an extreme form in contemporary American psychology. Indeed, this aspect of functionalism might be seen today as a positive feature of the school, and not as a point of criticism.

Functionalists were also criticized for their eclecticism. They certainly were not as dogmatic as the structuralists; rather, they consistently made use of any theoretical or methodological approach considered appropriate to the solution of the problem at hand. Many see virtue in this more flexible approach to psychology, particularly since it coexisted with tough-minded insistence on proper scientific control and methodology. It is difficult to see why their more open-minded eclecticism made them any less scientifically respectable than the more close-minded structuralists.

Contributions of Functionalism

As an attitude or general viewpoint, functionalism was so successful that it became part of the mainstream of psychology. Its early vigorous opposition to structuralism was of immense value to American psychology at a time when the new science was beginning to develop. The long-range consequences of the shift in emphasis from structure to function were also extremely important. One result was that the rapidly increasing research on animal behavior became a vitally important part of psychology. Animal research was in accord with a functional psychology, but was irrelevant to structural psychology, for which introspection was the indispensable tool. It was, after all, difficult to get animals to report on their experiences.

In addition to studies of animals, the functionalists' broadened definition of psychology was able to incorporate studies of children, the mentally retarded, and the insane. It also allowed psychologists to supplement the method of introspection with other ways of securing data, such as physiological research, mental tests, questionnaires, and objective descriptions of behavior. All of these methods, which were anathema to the structuralists, became respectable sources of information to psychology.

By the time Wundt died in 1920, his structural form of psychology had been overshadowed in the United States by the broader, more practical approach of the functional school. The functionalist victory was undeniably complete by 1930, and in the United States today, psychology remains definitely functional in orientation, even though functionalism no longer exists as a separate school of thought. Because of its very success, there was no longer any need for it to retain the characteristics of a school.

SUGGESTED FURTHER READINGS

Dewey
Boring, E. G. John Dewey: 1859–1952. *American Journal of Psychology,* 1953, **66,** 145–147.

Angell
Miles, W. James Rowland Angell, 1869–1949, psychologist–educator. *Science,* 1949, **110,** 1–4.

Woodworth
Poffenberger, A. T. Robert Sessions Woodworth: 1869–1962. *American Journal of Psychology,* 1962, **75,** 677–692.

General
Angell, J. R. *Psychology: An introductory study of the structure and function of the human consciousness.* New York: Holt, 1904.
Carr, H. A. Functionalism. In C. Murchison (Ed.), *Psychologies of 1930.* Worcester, Massachusetts: Clark Univ. Press, 1930. Pp. 59–78.
Harrison, R. Functionalism and its historical significance. *Genetic Psychology Monographs,* 1963, **68,** 387–423.
James, W. The Chicago school. *Psychological Bulletin,* 1904, **1,** 1–5.

9

Behaviorism:
Antecedent Influences

Introduction

In the second decade of this century, less than 40 years after Wundt formally launched psychology, the science had undergone drastic revisions, as we have seen. While structuralism was still a vital and strong position attracting its share of loyal adherents, the new movement of functionalism had seriously eroded the earlier school's position of primacy in the field, particularly in America.

No longer did all psychologists agree on the value of introspection, on the existence of elements of the mind, or on the necessity of psychology's remaining "pure." The functionalists were rewriting the rules of psychology, experimenting upon and applying psychology in ways that could not be admitted into Leipzig or Cornell.

The movement, this change from structuralism to functionalism, was less revolutionary than it was evolutionary. The functionalists did not set out to totally destroy the establishment of Wundt and Titchener, rather they modified it, adding a bit here, changing a bit there, so that slowly, over a number of years, a new psychology emerged. It was more a chipping away from within than a deliberate attack from without.

The leaders of the functionalist movement did not even feel the need to solidify or formalize their position into a school. It was, after all, not a complete departure from what had gone on before; not a break with the past but a building and growing upon the past.

The change from structuralism to functionalism was, therefore, not abrupt and traumatic, but gradual and not all that noticeable at the time it was taking place. There was no one particular day or year that we can point to as the start of functionalism—a time when psychology changed overnight. Indeed, it is difficult, as we have seen, to point to a particular individual as *the* founder of functionalism.

This was the situation, then, in the second decade of the twentieth century: functionalism growing to maturity and structuralism still holding a strong but no longer exclusive position.

Then, in 1913, a revolution erupted, directed against both of these positions. This was truly a revolt, an open break, a total war against the establishment, intent on shattering both points of view. There was nothing gradual or smooth about this transition. It was sudden, traumatic, dramatic—no modification of the past, but a destruction of what had gone before—no compromise, only total change.

The new movement was called *behaviorism* and its leader was the 35-year-old psychologist John Broadus Watson. Just 10 years earlier, Watson had received his Ph.D. under Angell at the University of Chicago—the center for one of the two movements he was out to smash.

Watson inaugurated his revolution with an article in the *Psychological Review*. The manifesto he wrote was a broad, slashing attack on the existing systems of psychology. The old order, he stated, was a failure and had to give way to behaviorism if psychology were to advance. In relatively little time, the older views were largely abandoned, and behaviorism became the most important and controversial American system of psychology, a position it continues to enjoy today. Moreover, it assumed a prominent role in the cultural and social life of the times.

The basic tenets of Watson's behaviorism were simple, direct, and bold. He called for a totally objective psychology—a *science of behavior*—dealing only with observable behavioral acts that could be objectively described in terms such as stimulus and response. He wanted to apply to human beings the experimental procedures and principles of animal psychology, a field in which he had been active.

Watson's positive interests shed light on what he wanted to discard. If behavioristic psychology was to be an objective science, then all mentalistic concepts and terms had to be rejected. Such words as "image," "mind," and "consciousness"—carry-overs from mental philosophy—were meaningless, and the technique of introspection, which assumed the existence of conscious processes, was irrelevant.

These were the basic points forcibly proposed and propounded by the founder of behaviorism. Of course, as discussed earlier, founding is different from originating. The tenets of the behavioristic revolution that was soon to sweep over psychology were not original with Watson. They had been developing in psychology and biology for some years prior to 1913.

It is no criticism of Watson to note that he, like Wundt (like all founders), promoted, organized, and integrated ideas and schemas already in existence. From this amalgamation he constructed his new system of psychology. The point is worth reiterating. Sarton reminded us: "Creations absolutely *de novo* are very rare, if they occur at all; most novelties are only novel combinations of old elements, and the degree of novelty is thus a matter of interpretation [1936, p. 36]."

The purpose of the present chapter is to examine behaviorism's antecedent influences, the "old" elements Watson so effectively brought together to form his new psychology. At least three major trends served to influence Watson: (1) the philosophical tradition of objectivism and mechanism, (2) animal psychology, and (3) functionalism.

Of these three influences, animal psychology and functionalism exerted the most direct and obvious impact. The philosophical traditions of objectivism and mechanism had been developing for quite some time and they favored and reinforced the growth of both functionalism and animal psychology.

Watson's insistence on the need for increased objectivity in psychology was by no means novel by 1913. The movement has a long history, beginning perhaps with Descartes, whose attempts at mechanistic explanations of the body and mind were among the first steps in the direction of greater objectivity.

More important in the history of objectivism is Auguste Comte (1798–1857), founder of the movement called *positivism*, which emphasized positive knowledge, the truth of which is not debatable (see Chapter 2). According to Comte, the only valid knowledge is that which is social in nature and objectively observable. These criteria rule out introspection, which depends on a private consciousness that cannot be objectively observed. Comte vigorously protested against mentalism and subjective methodology.

By the beginning of the twentieth century, objectivism, mechanism, and materialism had grown strong. Their influence was so pervasive that they led inexorably to a new kind of psychology; one without "consciousness" or "mind" or "soul"; one that focused on only what could be seen and heard and touched. The science of behavior—man as a machine—was the inescapable result.

We now turn to a more detailed discussion of the influence of animal psychology and functionalism on the founding of behaviorism, as both were infused and guided by the mechanistic, materialistic, and positivistic climate of the times.

Animal Psychology

Watson himself stated most succinctly the relationship between animal psychology and behaviorism when he wrote: "Behaviorism is a direct outgrowth of studies in animal behavior during the first decade of the twentieth century [1929, p. 327]."

Clearly the most important single antecedent to the development of Watson's program was animal psychology, which, as we have seen, grew out of evolutionary theory. It led to attempts to demonstrate the presence of mind in lower organisms and the continuity between the human and animal minds.

We have discussed the work of two pioneer animal psychologists, George Romanes and C. Lloyd Morgan (see Chapter 6). Another influential animal researcher who worked mainly in this country was the German zoologist and physiologist Jacques Loeb (1859–1924). Loeb developed an explanatory theory of animal behavior based on the concept of *tropism* or forced movement. According to tropistic theory, the animal's response is a direct function of the stimulus. In this sense, the behavior is forced and does not require an explanation in terms of consciousness.

More important for our purposes than the content of Loeb's work is its theoretical significance. More than any other previous individual, Loeb fashioned an absolute and total mechanistic psychology which was highly influential in the biological sciences.

Watson took several courses with Loeb at the University of Chicago and expressed the desire to do research under him, certainly indicating a sympathy with, or at least curiosity about Loeb's highly mechanistic views.[1]

By the beginning of the twentieth century, the study of animal behavior within a biological framework had become widespread. During this same time, experimental animal psychology—most notably the work of Thorndike—developed rapidly. Robert Yerkes began animal studies in 1900 and his work, using a wide range of animals, greatly strengthened the position and influence of comparative psychology. Also in 1900, the

---

[1] Angell and another faculty member, the neurologist H. H. Donaldson, talked Watson out of this desire, arguing that Loeb was "unsafe"; a word open to interpretation, but perhaps indicating objection to Loeb's uncompromising objectivism.

rat maze was introduced by W. S. Small, and the white rat and maze became a standard method of studying learning.

Laboratories of comparative psychology were established and many universities offered courses in the subject. In 1911, the *Journal of Animal Behavior* (later the *Journal of Comparative Psychology*) was begun. In 1909, Pavlov's work, which greatly supported objective psychology in general and Watson's behaviorism in particular, became known in the United States through an article written by Yerkes and a Russian student, S. Morgulis (1909).

Because their influence was so important in the development of behaviorism, we shall consider in detail the work of E. L. Thorndike and Ivan Pavlov.

Edward Lee Thorndike (1874–1949)

Thorndike is one of the most important men in the development of animal psychology. He was the first to introduce true experimental investigation of animals. His precursors, notably Romanes and Morgan, used certain aspects of experimental research but, for the most part, their observations were made under natural conditions rather than the well-controlled conditions of the psychological laboratory.

Thorndike developed an objective and mechanistic theory of learning, focusing only on overt behavior, with minimal reference to consciousness or mental processes. He strongly believed that psychology must study only behavior, not mental elements or conscious experience in any form.

Thus, he reinforced the already growing trend toward greater objectivity that the functionalists were bringing to psychology, and interpreted learning not in terms of highly subjective ideas, but rather in terms of concrete connections between stimuli and responses.

The work of Thorndike and Pavlov is another example of simultaneous independent discovery. Pavlov's *law of reinforcement* was developed in 1902 and Thorndike's similar *law of effect* in 1898, though it was many years before the great resemblance between the two was recognized.

Thorndike was one of the first American psychologists to receive all of his education in the United States. It is highly significant that this was possible just two decades after psychology had begun.

The Life of Thorndike

Thorndike's interest in psychology was awakened (as it was for many others) when he read James's *Principles* while an undergraduate at Wesleyan University. He later studied under James at Harvard where he began his investigation of animal learning. His initial research was with chicks, which he trained to run through mazes improvised by placing books on end. The story is often told of Thorndike's difficulties in finding room for his chicks. Since his landlady took a dim view of his raising them in his bedroom, he turned to James for help. James was unsuccessful in finding space in either the laboratory or the museum, so he took Thorndike and chicks into the basement of his home, apparently to the delight of the James children.

Thorndike did not complete his education at Harvard for personal reasons. Believing that a certain young lady did not return his strong feelings, he applied to Cattell at Columbia in order to get away from the Boston area. It was not what he really wanted to do; rather, it was "a move born of youthful despair and deeply felt frustration [Joncich, 1968, p. 103]." He later married the girl in question.

Offered a fellowship by Cattell at Columbia, Thorndike went to New York, taking his two best-trained chicks with him. He continued his animal research at Columbia, working with cats and dogs and using puzzle boxes of his own design. He was awarded his doctorate in 1898. His thesis, *Animal Intelligence; An experimental study of the associative processes in animals*, was subsequently published along with other research on associative learning in chicks, fish, and monkeys.

Thorndike became an Instructor in Psychology at Teachers College, Columbia, in 1899, and remained there for the rest of his career. At Cattell's suggestion, Thorndike applied his animal research techniques to children and young people; thereafter, he worked more and more with human subjects. Most of the rest of his career was spent in the areas of human learning, education, and mental testing, and he is considered a leader in the mental testing movement.

Thorndike was very prolific and his 50 years at Columbia are among the most productive ever recorded for one man. His bibliography includes 507 items, many of which are lengthy books and monographs. He "retired" in 1939, but continued working quite actively until his death 10 years later.

Thorndike's Connectionism

Thorndike created an experimental approach to associationism, which he called connectionism and which included several important departures from the more classical tradition. In 1931, he said that if he were to analyze man's entire mind he would:

> find connections of varying strength between (a) situations, elements of situations, and compounds of situations and (b) responses, readi-

nesses to respond, facilitations, inhibitions, and directions of responses. If all these could be completely inventoried, telling what the man would think and do and what would satisfy and annoy him, in every conceivable situation, it seems to me that nothing would be left out. . . . Learning is connecting. The mind is man's connection-system [Thorndike, 1931, p. 122].

This associationistic position was a direct descendant of the older philosophical associationism with one significant difference. Instead of talking about associations or connections between ideas, Thorndike talked about connections between situations and responses. Thus, he was able to incorporate a totally objective frame of reference into his psychological theory. His study of learning also differed from classical associationism in that his subjects were animals rather than humans; this method had become acceptable as an aftermath of the Darwinian notion of continuity of species.

It is important to note the mechanistic nature of Thorndike's approach. To study behavior, it must be broken down or reduced to its simplest elements: stimulus–response units. He therefore shared with the structuralists an analytic and atomistic point of view. The stimulus–response units are the elements of behavior (not of consciousness), the building blocks out of which more complex behaviors are compounded.

Thorndike's conclusions were derived through the use of new research apparatus, the "puzzle box." An animal placed in the box was required to learn to operate a latch in order to escape. Thorndike's extensive research with cats is perhaps the best known. The experiments involved placing the cat, which had been deprived of food, in the slatted puzzle box. Food was placed outside the box as a reward for escaping. The door of the box was fastened by several latches. In order for the cat to open the door it had to pull on a lever or a chain, and sometimes engage in several such acts in succession. At first, the cat displayed a general, random, rather chaotic behavior as it poked and sniffed and clawed in every direction to get to the food. Eventually the cat hit upon the correct behavior and the door opened. During the first trial, the correct behavior occurred, of course, quite by accident. On subsequent trials, the random chaotic behaviors were displayed less frequently until finally, when learning was complete, the cat would display the correct behavior as soon as it was placed in the box.

Thorndike used definite quantitative measures of learning. One technique was to record the number of "wrong" behaviors—behaviors that did not lead to escaping from the box. Over a series of trials, these diminished in number.

Another technique was to record the time elapsed from the moment the cat was placed in the box until it succeeded in getting out. As learning took place, this time period decreased.

Thorndike wrote of the "stamping in" or "stamping out" of a response tendency by its favorable or unfavorable results. He noted that all the nonsuccessful response tendencies (those that do nothing to get the cat out of the box) are stamped out over a number of trials. On the other hand, response tendencies that do lead to success are stamped in after a number of trials.

This kind of learning has been called "trial and error learning," though Thorndike preferred to call it "trial and accidental success" (Joncich, 1968, p. 266).

This stamping in or out of a response tendency was formalized in 1905 as Thorndike's famous law of effect.

> Any act which in a given situation produces satisfaction becomes associated with that situation, so that when the situation recurs the act is more likely than before to recur also. Conversely, any act which in a given situation produces discomfort becomes disassociated from that situation, so that when the situation recurs the act is less likely than before to recur [Thorndike, 1905, p. 203].

A companion law is the law of exercise or of use or disuse, which states that any response made in a particular situation becomes associated with the situation. The more the response is used in the situation, the more strongly it becomes associated with it. Conversely, prolonged disuse of the response tends to weaken the association. In other words, sheer repetition of any response in the situation tends to strengthen that response. Thorndike's later research convinced him that sheer repetition of a response is relatively ineffective compared to the reward consequences of the response.

In the early 1930s, Thorndike further examined his law of effect in an extensive program of research using human subjects. The results revealed that rewarding a response did indeed strengthen that response but punishment of a response did not produce a comparable negative effect. He revised the law of effect in the light of these results, placing a much greater emphasis on reward than on punishment.

Comment

Thorndike's pioneer investigations into the fields of human and animal learning are among the greatest in the history of psychology. His theory of association or learning served to herald the rapid rise of learning theory to its present prominent position in American psychology. Although new learning theories and models have appeared since Thorndike's work, the significance of his contributions remains secure. His influence declined with the advent of more sophisticated learning systems, but his work remains a cornerstone of associationism and the objective spirit within which he conducted his research constitutes an important antecedent to behaviorism.

Even the great Pavlov paid tribute to Thorndike's work.

> Some years after the beginning of the work with our new method I learned that somewhat similar experiments had been performed in America, and indeed not by physiologists but by psychologists. Thereupon I studied in more detail the American publications, and now I must acknowledge that the honour of having made the first steps along this path belongs to E. L. Thorndike. By two or three years his experiments preceded ours and his book [*Animal Intelligence*] must be considered a classic, both for its bold outlook on an immense task and for the accuracy of its results [Pavlov, 1928; cited by Joncich, 1968, pp. 415–416].

Ivan Petrovitch Pavlov (1849–1936)

The influence of Ivan Pavlov is felt keenly in many areas of contemporary psychology. His work in the area of association or learning helped bring about the shift of associationism from its traditional application to subjective ideas, to completely objective and quantifiable glandular secretions and muscular movements. As a result, Pavlov's work provided Watson with a new way of investigating behavior as well as a means of attempting to control and modify behavior.

The Life of Pavlov

Pavlov was born in a provincial town in central Russia, the eldest of 11 children of a village priest. His position in such a large family brought him responsibility and hard work at a very early age, characteristics he retained all his life. He was unable to attend school until the age of 11, due to an accident involving a severe blow to the head 4 years earlier.

His father tutored him at home, however, and in 1860 he entered the local theological seminary, intending to prepare for the priesthood. He changed his mind, though, and in 1870 went to the University of St. Petersburg, where he specialized in animal physiology. Miller (1962) commented that because of the university training, Pavlov joined the newly emerging third class in Russian society—the intelligentsia:

> too well-educated and too intelligent for the peasantry from which he came, but too common and too poor for the aristocracy into which he could never rise. These social conditions often produced an especially dedicated intellectual, one whose entire life was centered on the intellectual pursuits that justified his existence. And so it was with Pavlov, whose almost fanatic devotion to pure science and to experimental research was supported by the energy and simplicity of a Russian peasant [p. 177].

He obtained his degree in 1875, and then began medical training, not to practice medicine, but in the hope of furthering his aim of a career in physiological research. He then studied in Germany for 2 years, and returned to St. Petersburg for several hard years as a laboratory research assistant.

Pavlov's dedication to research was of paramount importance in his life. His single-mindedness of purpose was not distracted by practical issues such as salary, clothing, or living conditions. Luckily, his wife, whom he married in 1881, devoted her entire life to protecting him from mundane matters. (Characteristic of his indifference to practical affairs is the story that his wife often had to remind him when it was time to collect his salary.)

They lived in great poverty until 1890 when, at the age of 41, he finally obtained the post of Professor of Pharmacology at the Military Medical Academy at St. Petersburg. For a time after his marriage he slept on a cot in his laboratory while his wife lived with a relative; they could not afford an apartment. In 1883, when Pavlov was preparing his doctoral thesis, their first child was born. Frail and sickly, he would not live, the doctor said, unless mother and child could rest in the country. After a great struggle, they were able to borrow enough money for the expensive journey to a relative. But it was too late; the child died. Six years later they were still so destitute that his wife and second son had to live with relatives once again because they could no longer maintain an apartment. A group of Pavlov's students, knowing of his financial problems, gave him some money on the pretext of covering the expenses of lectures they had asked him to give. Pavlov immediately spent the money on new experimental animals and kept none for himself.

So strong was his dedication to his work, so deeply was he committed to it, that he was not particularly bothered by his hardships. He once said that it never caused him "any undue worry."

In his relations with others, he was given to explosive emotional tirades, most often directed at his research assistants. The anecdote is told that during the Russian revolution (1917) Pavlov bitterly chastised one of his assistants for being 10 minutes late for an experiment; pitched battles in the streets were not to interfere with research. Usually, however, these outbursts were quickly forgotten. His students knew exactly what was expected of them—Pavlov never hesitated to tell them. He was always completely honest and direct, if not always considerate, in his dealings with other people.

He was known as an excellent teacher with a good sense of humor, capable of enthralling an audience of students or peers. Merciless in an argument, he was nevertheless willing to admit if he had been in error (though this was a rare occurrence indeed).

His relations with the Soviet regime were complicated and difficult, since he was openly critical of the revolution and the Soviet government. He wrote dangerously strong, angry letters of protest to Stalin and even boycotted Russian scientific meetings to demonstrate his disapproval of the government. By 1933, he finally accepted the government and acknowledged that it had achieved some success in uniting the Russian people. For the last 3 years of his life he lived in peace with the government of which he had been so critical for 16 years. However, despite Pavlov's attitude, he received generous government support throughout his career for his research, and was largely free of governmental pressure.

The following passage from Pavlov's autobiography sums up his attitude toward his life.

> Looking back on my life I would describe it as being happy and successful. I have received all that can be demanded of life: the complete realization of the principles with which I began life. I dreamed of finding happiness in intellectual work, in science—and I found it. I wanted to have a kind person as a companion in life and I found this companion in my wife . . . who patiently endured all the hardships of our existence before my professorship, always encouraged my scientific aspirations and who devoted herself to our family just as I devoted myself to the laboratory. I have renounced practicality in life with its cunning and not always irreproachable ways, and I see no reason for regretting this; on the contrary, precisely in this I find now certain consolation [1955, p. 46].

Pavlov's Research

During his distinguished and productive career, Pavlov worked on three research problems. The first problem was concerned with the function of the nerves of the heart and the second with the primary digestive glands. This brilliant research on digestion won for him both world-wide recognition and, in 1904, the Nobel Prize. His third research area, the one for which he is best known, and for which he occupies such a vital role in the history of psychology, was the study of the higher nervous centers in the brain. He pursued this study with characteristic energetic determination and devotion from 1902 until his death in 1936. In his attack on this problem he made use of conditioning, which was his greatest scientific achievement. It is instructive to consider how Pavlov developed this technique, which completely changed the direction of his own career and profoundly influenced the development of psychology.

The notion of conditioned reflexes originated (as have so many scientific breakthroughs) in an accidental discovery. In his work on digestive glands, Pavlov used the method of surgical exposure of the subjects (dogs) to permit the collection and measurement of the digestive secretions outside the body where they could be observed, measured, and recorded. The surgical operations necessary to divert the secretion of a particular gland through a tube to the outside of the body without in any way damaging the nerves and the blood supply were extremely difficult. Pavlov displayed amazing ingenuity and technical skill in performing these operations.

One aspect of his work dealt with the function of saliva, which would be involuntarily secreted when food was placed in the dog's mouth. But Pavlov observed that sometimes saliva would be secreted before the food was given to the animal; there was, in other words, an anticipatory saliva flow. The dogs salivated when they saw the food or the man who regularly fed them, and even when they heard his footsteps! The reflex of secretion with its unlearned response of salivation had somehow become attached to, or conditioned to, stimuli that had previously been associated with feeding. These "psychic" reflexes (as Pavlov originally called them) were aroused in the animal by stimuli other than the original one (food), and Pavlov realized that this happened because these other stimuli (sight and sound of the attendant, etc.) had so often been associated with the ingestion of food. The associationists called this phenomenon "association by frequency of occurrence."

After a long period of doubt and indecision as to whether he should follow up this observation because of its psychical nature, Pavlov decided in 1902 to investigate these psychic reflexes, and became completely absorbed in the new research.

He wrote:

> At first in our psychical experiments with the psychical glands . . .
> we conscientiously endeavored to explain our results by imagining

the subjective state of the animal. But nothing came of this except sterile controversy and individual views that could not be reconciled. And so we could do nothing but conduct the research on a purely objective basis [Cuny, 1965, p. 65].

His research then became a model of objectivity and precision. His first experiments were quite simple. Pavlov showed a dog a piece of bread in his hand before giving it to the dog to eat. In time, salivation began as soon as the dog saw the bread. The dog's response of salivation at the placing of the bread in his mouth is a natural reflexive response of the digestive system—no learning is necessary for it to occur. Accordingly, Pavlov called this an inborn or "unconditioned reflex." Salivation at the sight of food, however, is not a reflexive response but rather one that must be learned. This response he called a "conditional reflex" (having dropped the too mentalistic term "psychic reflex") because it was conditional on the formation of an association between the sight of food and the subsequent eating of it.

Pavlov soon discovered that any stimulus could produce the conditioned salivary response so long as it was capable of attracting the animal's attention without arousing fright or anger. He variously used such stimuli as a bell, buzzer, light, and the tick of a metronome. His typical thoroughness and precision are evidenced by the elaborate and sophisticated technique he used to collect saliva. A rubber tube was connected to the fistula; saliva flowed through this tube and onto a very delicate platform resting on a sensitive spring. As each drop struck the platform, it caused a movement that was recorded by a delicate marker on a revolving drum. This arrangement, which made it possible to record the exact number of drops as well as the precise moment at which each drop fell, is but one example of Pavlov's painstaking efforts to standardize experimental conditions, use rigid controls, and eliminate sources of error.

He was so concerned about preventing intrusions from the environment that he designed special cubicles for his research. The experimental animal was placed in a harness in one cubicle while the experimenter occupied the other. In that way, the experimenter could operate the various conditioning stimuli, collect the saliva, and present the food without being seen by the animal.

Even these precautions did not satisfy Pavlov, however; extraneous stimuli were still capable of reaching the animals. Therefore, he designed a three-story research building that came to be known as the "Tower of Silence" (Cuny, 1965, p. 67). The windows were covered with extra thick sheets of glass; each room had double steel doors which sealed hermetically when closed; and the steel girders which supported the floors were embedded in sand. A deep moat filled with straw encircled the building. Thus, vibration, noise, temperature extremes, odors, even drafts were eliminated. Nothing could influence the animals except the conditioning stimuli to which they were exposed.

A typical conditioning experiment would run as follows. The conditioned stimulus (a light, let us say) is turned on. Immediately, the food (the unconditioned stimulus) is presented. After a number of pairings of the light followed by the food, the animal salivates at the sight of the light. The animal has thus become conditioned to respond to the conditioned stimulus. An association or bond has been formed between the light and the food. Learning or conditioning will not occur unless the light is followed by the food a number of times. Thus, reinforcement (being fed) is necessary in order for learning to take place.

In addition to studying the formation of conditioned responses, Pavlov and his associates investigated other phenomena: reinforcement, extinction, spontaneous recovery, generalization, discrimination, and higher-order conditioning (all household words in the language of psychology today).

Some 200 collaborators came to work with Pavlov, and the experimental program extended over a longer period of time and involved more people than any research effort since Wundt. The conditioning situation itself was quite simple, but it generated so many specific questions about its nature that answers could come only through years of patient and thorough experimentation.

Pavlov presented a preliminary report on his findings in 1923, after 20 years of research. In 1926, at the age of 77, he published a more systematic account of his work. This long interval between the beginning of his research and the two reports of his findings testifies not only to the enormous scope of the problem, but also to Pavlov's scientific integrity. He wanted to be certain of the accuracy and validity of his findings before making them generally known.

Comment

With Pavlov, more precise, objective measures and terminology were introduced into the study of association or learning. Also, Pavlov demonstrated that higher mental processes could be effectively studied in physiological terms and with the use of animal subjects. Thus, he greatly influenced psychology's shift to greater objectivity in subject matter and methodology. The effects of this shift are seen most strikingly in the development of behaviorism, in which the conditioned reflex forms a central part. This concept provided the science of psychology with a basic element or atom of behavior, a workable, concrete unit to which the highly complex behavior of man could be reduced and experimented with under laboratory conditions. As we shall see, Watson seized upon this unit of behavior and made it the central core of his program.

It seems quite ironic that Pavlov's greatest influence has been in psychology, a field toward which he was not altogether favorable. He believed that psychology would never achieve the status of an independent science and so excluded psychology completely from his own work; he even fined workers in his laboratory who used psychological rather than physiological terminology. Woodworth (1948) noted that in his lectures Pavlov frequently made such remarks as:

> In conclusion we must count it an uncontested fact that the physiology of the highest part of the nervous system of higher animals cannot be successfully studied, unless we utterly renounce the untenable pretensions of psychology [p. 60].

When he was invited to attend the International Congress of Psychology in 1929, Pavlov replied that he did not believe psychologists would really be interested in what he had to say! This attitude did not, of course, prevent psychology from making very effective use of his work. At first, psychologists used the conditioned response to measure sensory discrimination in animals (it is still used for that purpose today). During the 1920s it began to be used, primarily in America, as the foundation for learning theories. Since then, it has generated much experimentation and theory as well as controversy.

Pavlov's immense contributions to science are widely recognized and respected, but the social and philosophical implications of his research and its effects on the conception of human nature have often been sharply attacked. Many find the idea of human beings conditioned to respond to various stimuli to be highly offensive to their vision of man as a figure far removed from animals, and possessing a free will.

Vladimir M. Bekhterev (1857–1927)

Another important figure in the shift of associationism from subjective ideas toward objectively observed overt behavior is Vladimir Bekhterev. Though generally less well known than Pavlov, this Russian physiologist, neurologist, and psychiatrist pioneered a number of important research areas. He was a contemporary and rival of Pavlov in the opening years of this century, and became interested in conditioning independently of Pavlov.

Bekhterev received his degree from the Military Medical Academy in St. Petersburg in 1881. He studied abroad in Leipzig, Berlin, and Paris, and then returned to Russia to the chair of mental diseases at the University of Kazan. In 1893, he returned to the Military Medical Academy in St. Petersburg to the chair of mental and nervous diseases, and he organized a mental hospital. In 1907, he founded the Psychoneurological Institute, where he conducted a great deal of neurological research.

While Pavlov's conditioning research had been conducted almost exclusively on glandular secretions, Bekhterev was interested in the motor conditioning response, a concern that thus extended the Pavlovian conditioning principle to striped muscles. His prime concept was the "associated reflex" as revealed through the study of motor responses. He found that reflexive movements, such as withdrawing a finger from electric shock, could be elicited not only by the unconditioned stimulus (electric shock) but also by stimuli that had become associated with the original response-eliciting stimulus. For instance, the visual and auditory cues present at the time the reflex occurred soon elicited the response by themselves.

The associationists had explained such connections in terms of the operation of some sort of mental process. Bekhterev, however, considered such reactions totally reflexive in nature. He felt that higher-level behaviors of greater complexity could be explained in the same way as a compounding of the low-level motor reflexes. To Bekhterev, thought processes themselves were of the same character in that they depended on inner activities of the speech musculature. He argued for a completely objective approach to psychological phenomena and against the use of mentalistic terms and concepts. His stand was expressed in *Objective Psychology*, published in 1907 and translated into German and French in 1913. A third edition was published in English in 1932 and called *General Principles of Human Reflexology*.

Comment

From the beginnings of animal psychology in the work of Romanes and Morgan one can see a steady and rapid trend toward greater objectivity in both subject matter and methodology. The early work in the field invoked the concepts of consciousness and mental processes and used research methods that were equally subjective.

By the beginning of the twentieth century, however, animal psychology was completely objective in subject matter and methodology. Glandular secretions, conditioned reflexes, responses, acts, behavior—such terms left no doubt that animal psychology had discarded its subjective past.

Animal psychology was shortly to serve as a model for behaviorism, whose leader much preferred animal to human subjects for psychological research. Watson used the findings and methods of the animal psychologists as a foundation for the development of a science of behavior applicable to both man and animal.

Functionalism

The second direct antecedent of behaviorism is functionalism. Although functional psychology was not totally objective, in Watson's day it did represent greater objectivity than its predecessors. Cattell and other functionalists who moved in the direction of emphasizing behavior and more objective methods had expressed dissatisfaction with introspection. The various applied areas of interest to the functionalists had little use for consciousness and introspection, and essentially constituted an objective functional psychology.

Thus, the functional psychologists had moved a good bit away from the pure psychology of content of Wundt and Titchener before Watson came on the scene. In their writings and lectures, certain functional psychologists were quite specific in arguing for an objective psychology—a psychology that would focus on behavior instead of consciousness.

In one such statement, Cattell, speaking at the World's Fair in St. Louis, Missouri, in 1904, commented:

> I am not convinced that psychology should be limited to the study of consciousness as such. . . . the rather wide-spread notion that there is no psychology apart from introspection is refuted by the brute argument of accomplished fact. It seems to me that most of the research work that has been done by me or in my laboratory is nearly as independent of introspection as work in physics or in zoology. . . . I see no reason why the application of systematized knowledge to the control of human nature may not in the course of the present century accomplish results commensurate with the nineteenth century applications of physical science to the material world.

Burnham (1968) reported that Watson heard this address at the World's Fair and that the similarity between his later position and Cattell's statement was so striking that Cattell could be called "the grand-father of Watson's behaviorism [p. 149]."

James Angell, perhaps the most forward-looking functionalist, also fore-saw that American psychology, already functional, was ready to move even further in the direction of objectivity. In 1910, for example, he commented that it seemed highly possible that the term *consciousness* would disappear from psychology much as had the term *soul*. In 1913, shortly before Watson's manifesto, Angell elaborated on this point, sug-gesting that it would be profitable if the "possible existence" of conscious-ness were forgotten and that animal and human behavior be described objectively instead.

In 1911, Walter Pillsbury defined psychology in his textbook, *Essentials of Psychology*, as the "science of human behavior" and argued that it was possible to treat man as objectively as any aspect of the physical universe.

In the decade before Watson formally began behaviorism, we can see that the *Zeitgeist* was obviously favoring and reinforcing the idea of a totally objective psychology. Clearly, the overall movement of American psychology was toward a thoroughgoing behaviorism.

Watson foresaw, perhaps more clearly than anyone else, what the times were calling for, and he responded vigorously and articulately as the agent of a movement whose inevitability and success were already assured.

SUGGESTED FURTHER READINGS

Antecedents to Behaviorism
Diserens, C. M. Psychological objectivism. *Psychological Review*, 1925, **32**, 121–152.

Early Animal Psychology
Warden, C. J., & Warner, L. H. The development of animal psychology in the U.S. during the past three decades. *Psychological Review*, 1927, **34**, 196–205.

Pavlov
Babkin, B. P. *Pavlov: A biography*. Chicago, Illinois: Univ. of Chicago Press, 1949.
Cuny, H. *Ivan Pavlov: The man and his theories*. New York: Paul S. Eriksson, 1965.
Pavlov, I. P. *Selected works*. Translated by S. Belsky. Moscow: Foreign Languages Publishing House, 1955.
Pavlov, I. P. *Lectures on conditioned reflexes*. Translated by W. Gantt. New York: Liveright, 1928.
Pavlov, I. P. *Conditioned reflexes*. Translated by G. Anrep. New York: Oxford Univ. Press, 1927.

Thorndike
Joncich, G. *The sane positivist: A biography of Edward L. Thorndike.* Middletown, Connecticut: Wesleyan Univ. Press, 1968.
Postman, L. The history and present status of the Law of Effect. *Psychological Bulletin,* 1947, **44**, 489–563.

Behaviorism
Burnham, J. On the origins of behaviorism. *Journal of the History of the Behavioral Sciences,* 1968, **4**(2), 143–151.

10

Behaviorism: The Beginning

Introduction: John B. Watson (1878–1958)

As we saw in the last chapter, there were several antecedent influences that J. B. Watson used to construct his new behavioristic school of thought. Founding, as noted earlier, is not the same as originating—a point Watson recognized when he described his efforts as a "crystallization of the behavioristic trend [Burnham, 1968, p. 150]" that was already extant in psychology.

Watson, like psychology's first promoter–founder, Wundt, set out quite deliberately to found a new school of thought. This quality of intention sets him apart from others whom history now labels as precursors of behaviorism.

Watson was born on a farm outside of Greenville, South Carolina, where his early education was conducted in a one-room schoolhouse. The Watsons later moved into Greenville and 12-year-old John attended public schools. Watson described himself as being somewhat lazy and insubordinate and as never earning more than just passing grades. His teachers remember him as indolent, argumentative, and not easily controlled. He grew up in what Bakan (1966) described as a state of semi-delinquency. He fought a great deal and was twice arrested, once for shooting firearms within the city limits. It was not exactly a promising beginning! Nevertheless, he entered Furman University in Greenville at age 16 and obtained an M.A. in 5 years.

An interest in philosophy led Watson to pursue graduate study at the University of Chicago under John Dewey. He reported that he found Dewey "incomprehensible." ("I never knew what he was talking about then, and unfortunately for me, I still don't know [J. B. Watson, 1936, p. 274].") His enthusiasm for philosophy rather quickly diminished, though he did continue it as a minor. Watson became interested in psychology under the influence of Angell, and he took a second minor in neurology; in addition, he studied biology and physiology under Jacques Loeb. Beside his courses, he worked at various jobs, such as a waiter in a fraternity house, a rat caretaker, and an assistant (!) janitor. Toward the end of his graduate studies he suffered a breakdown during which he experienced acute attacks of anxiety and an inability to sleep without a light on, among other symptoms.

In 1903, he received his Ph.D., married, and remained at the University of Chicago as an instructor until 1908. In his years at Chicago as both student and instructor, Watson engaged in much research, demonstrating early his preference for animal subjects. As he stated in his autobiographical sketch:

> I never wanted to use human subjects. I hated to serve as a subject. I didn't like the stuffy, artificial instructions given to subjects. I always was uncomfortable and acted unnaturally. With animals I was at home. I felt that, in studying them, I was keeping close to biology with my feet on the ground. More and more the thought presented itself: Can't I find out by watching their behavior everything that the other students are finding out by using O's [observers] [J. B. Watson, 1936, p. 276]?

In 1908, Watson had become eligible for an assistant professorship at Chicago when he was offered a full professorship at Johns Hopkins University. He was reluctant to leave Chicago but the opportunity to direct the laboratory, the increase in rank, and the substantial increase in salary offered by Hopkins left him little choice. He remained at Hopkins until 1920 and those 12 years were to be his most productive in psychology.

Watson said that he began thinking about a more objective approach to psychology around 1903. His thoughts on the subject were expressed publicly for the first time in 1908 in a lecture at Yale University. In 1912, he again spoke on the subject in a series of lectures given at Columbia University at the invitation of Cattell. The following year saw the publication of his famous position paper, and behaviorism was officially launched.

Watson's first book, *Behavior: An Introduction to Comparative Psychology*, appeared in 1914. It argued strongly for the acceptance of animal psychology and stressed the advantages of using animals as subjects in psychological research. Watsonian behaviorism appealed to many younger psychologists who felt that Watson was cleansing the muddled atmosphere of psychology by casting off the long-standing mysteries and uncertainties carried over from philosophy. The rapid acceptance of his position was evidenced by his election to the presidency of the American Psychological Association in 1915—just 2 years after his paper appeared. He was then 37 years of age.

Watson's professional activities were interrupted by his tour in the Army Aviation Service as a major during World War I. After the war, in 1918, Watson conducted research on young children, one of the earliest attempts at experimental work on human infants. His second book, *Psychology from the Standpoint of a Behaviorist*, appeared in 1919.

This book represented a much more complete statement of his position. In it he argued that the methods and principles that he had earlier espoused for animal psychology are equally applicable and legitimate for the study of man.

Watson's highly promising academic career lasted only 17 years; it ended abruptly and tragically in 1920. The sensationalized nationwide publicity accorded divorce proceedings brought against him resulted in his forced resignation from Johns Hopkins University, and he never returned to a full-time university position. Shortly thereafter he married his former laboratory assistant, who had worked with him on studies of infant behavior (including the famous "Albert" study of conditioned fear).

Many of his academic colleagues (including his former mentor, Angell) publicly criticized Watson on personal grounds during this difficult time and, understandably, he became somewhat embittered toward them. Strangely, in view of his radically different personal temperament and theoretical position, Titchener was of great help to Watson during this crisis. "You have done more for me than all the rest of my colleagues put together," Watson wrote to Titchener in 1922 (Larson & Sullivan, 1965, p. 346).

In 1921, Watson began an entirely new professional career in the field of advertising. He joined the J. Walter Thompson agency, worked in every department, and made house-to-house surveys, sold coffee, and clerked in Macy's Department Store in order to learn about the business world. With characteristic enterprise and success, Watson was made vice-president in only 3 years time. In 1936, he joined another advertising agency where he remained as vice-president until his retirement in 1945.

After 1920, Watson's contact with psychology became less direct. Indeed, he spent a great deal of time presenting his case for behaviorism to the general public. He lectured and wrote several articles for such popular magazines as *Harper's, Cosmopolitan, McCalls, Colliers,* and *The Nation.* The fact that editors of these publications urged him to write for them attests to the great public interest in behaviorism. His new wife even wrote an article for *Parents Magazine* entitled, "I Am the Mother of a Behaviorist's Sons."

Watson lectured at the New School for Social Research in New York for awhile, and out of these lectures came his semipopular book, *Behaviorism* (1925), which contained a positive program for the improvement of society. This book attracted considerable attention, both favorable and unfavorable, from the lay public. In 1928, he published a book on child care (*Psychological Care of the Infant and Child*), in which he presented a regulatory, as opposed to a permissive, system of child-rearing in keeping with his strong environmentalistic position. This was "a book he later publicly regretted [Skinner, 1959, p. 198]." In 1930, he revised *Behaviorism*—his last professional activity in psychology.

Watson possessed a most attractive combination of personal characteristics and abilities. Certainly intelligent and articulate, his handsome appearance and legendary charm would probably have made him a charismatic leader in today's media-oriented culture.

He was a man very much in the public eye throughout most of his life; he courted and relished publicity. Larson and Sullivan (1965, p. 352), noted that "In Watson's later life he did things in great style and loved to show a display of power."

His last years were spent on a farm in Connecticut. In 1957, a year before he died, the American Psychological Association honored him with a citation lauding his work as "one of the vital determinants of the form and substance of modern psychology . . . the point of departure for continuing lines of fruitful research." Although his health was poor (he was 79 years old) and he was unable to receive the award in person, he was reported to be pleased by this official recognition.

It is tragic that Watson was forced to leave the academic world at the age of 42. From the mid-1920s on, he produced nothing new, and by 1930 had completely abandoned the science of psychology for his business career.

Original Source Material on Behaviorism:
From "Psychology as the Behaviorist Views It"
by J. B. Watson

There is probably no better starting point for a discussion of Watson's behaviorism than the article that began the movement—"Psychology as the Behaviorist Views It"[1]—from the *Psychological Review* of 1913.

Psychology as the behaviorist views it is a purely objective experimental branch of natural science. Its theoretical goal is the prediction and control of behavior. Introspection forms no essential part of its methods, nor is the scientific value of its data dependent upon the readiness with which they lend themselves to interpretation in terms of consciousness. The behaviorist, in his efforts to get a unitary scheme of animal response, recognizes no dividing line between man and brute. The behavior of man, with all of its refinement and complexity, forms only a part of the behaviorist's total scheme of investigation.

It has been maintained by its followers generally that psychology is a study of the science of the phenomena of consciousness. It has taken as its problem, on the one hand, the analysis of complex mental states (or processes) into simple elementary constituents, and on the other the construction of complex states when the elementary constituents are given. The world of the physical objects (stimuli, including here anything which may excite activity in a receptor), which forms the total phenomena of the natural scientist, is looked upon merely as means to an end. That end is the production of mental states that may be "inspected" or "observed." The psychological object of observation in the case of an emotion, for example, is the mental state itself. The problem in emotion is the determination of the number and kind of elementary constituents present, their loci, intensity, order of appearance, etc. It is agreed that introspection is the method *par excellence* by means of which mental states may be manipulated for purposes of psychology. On this assumption, behavior data (including under this term everything which goes under the name of comparative psychology) have no value *per se*. They possess significance only in so far as they may throw light upon conscious states. Such data must have at least an analogical or indirect reference to belong to the realm of psychology. . . .

I do not wish unduly to criticize psychology. It has failed signally, I believe, during the fifty-odd years of its existence as an experimental discipline to make its place in the world as an undisputed natural science. Psychology, as it is generally thought of, has something esoteric in its methods. If you fail to reproduce my findings, it is not due to some fault in your apparatus or in the control of your stimulus, but it is due to the fact that your introspection is untrained. The attack is made upon the observer and not upon the experimental setting. In physics and in chemistry the attack is made upon the experimental conditions. The apparatus was not sensitive enough, impure chemicals were used, etc. In these sciences a better technique will give reproducible results. Psychology is otherwise. If you can't observe 3–9 states of clearness in attention, your introspection is poor. If, on the other hand, a feeling seems reasonably clear to you, your introspection is again faulty. You are seeing too much. Feelings are never clear.

The time seems to have come when psychology must discard all reference to consciousness; when it need no longer delude itself into thinking that it is making mental states the object of observation. We have become so enmeshed in speculative questions concerning the elements of mind, the nature of conscious content (for example, imageless thought, attitudes, . . . etc.) that I, as an experimental student, feel that something is wrong with our premises and the types of problems which develop from them. There is no longer any guarantee that we all mean the same thing when we use the terms now current in psychology. Take the case of sensation. A sensation is defined in terms of its attributes. One psychologist will state with readiness that the attributes of a visual sensation are *quality, extension, duration,* and *intensity.* Another will add *clearness.* Still another that of *order.* I doubt if any one psychologist can draw up a set of statements describing what he means by sensation which will be agreed to by three other psychologists of different training. Turn for a moment to the question of the number of isolable sensations. Is there an extremely large number of color sensations— or only four, red, green, yellow and blue? Again, yellow, while psychologically simple, can be obtained by superimposing red and green spectral rays upon the same diffusing surface! If, on the other hand, we say that every just noticeable difference in the spectrum is a simple sensation, and that every just noticeable increase in the white value of a given color gives simple sensations, we are forced to admit that the number is so large and the conditions for obtaining them so complex that the concept of sensation is unusable, either for the purpose of analysis or that of synthesis. Titchener, who has fought the most valiant fight in this country for a psychology based upon introspection, feels that these differences of opinion as to the number of sensations and their attributes; as to whether there are relations (in the sense of elements) and on the many others which seem to be fundamental in every attempt at analysis, are perfectly natural in the present undeveloped state of psychology. While it is admitted that every growing science is full of unanswered questions, surely only those who are wedded to the system as we now have it, who have fought and suffered for it, can confidently believe that there will ever be any greater uniformity than there is now in the answers we have to such questions. I firmly believe that two hundred years from now, unless the introspective method is discarded, psychology will still be divided on the question as to whether auditory sensations have the quality of "extension," whether intensity is an attribute which can be applied to color, whether there is a difference in "texture" between image and sensation and upon many hundreds of others of like character.

The condition in regard to other mental processes is just as chaotic. Can image type be experimentally tested and verified? Are recondite thought processes dependent mechanically upon imagery at all? Are psychologists agreed upon what feeling is? One states that feelings are attitudes. Another finds them to be groups of organic sensations possessing a certain solidarity. Still another and larger group finds them to be new elements correlative with and ranking equally with sensations.

My psychological quarrel is not with the systematic and structural psychologist alone. The last fifteen years have seen the growth of what is called functional psychology. This type of psychology decries the use of elements in the static sense of the structuralists. It throws emphasis upon the biological significance of conscious processes instead of upon the analysis of conscious states into introspectively isolable elements. I have done my best to understand the difference between functional psychology and structural psychology. Instead of clarity, confusion grows upon me. The terms sensation, perception, affection, emotion, volition are used as much by the functionalist as by the structuralist. The addition of the word "process" ("mental act as a whole," and like terms are frequently met) after each serves in some way to remove the corpse of "content" and to leave "function" in its stead. Surely if these concepts are elusive when looked at from a content standpoint, they are still more deceptive when viewed from the angle of function, and especially so when function is obtained by the introspection method. It is rather interesting that no functional psychologist has carefully distinguished between "perception" (and this is true of the other psychological terms as well) as employed by the systematist, and "perceptual process" as used in functional psychology. It seems illogical and hardly fair to criticize the psychology which the systematist gives us, and then to utilize his terms without carefully showing the changes in meaning which are to be attached to them. I was greatly surprised some time ago when I opened Pillsbury's book and saw psychology defined as the "science of behavior." A still more recent text states that psychology is the "science of mental behavior." When I saw these promising statements I thought, now surely we will have texts based upon different lines. After a few pages the science of behavior is dropped and one finds the conventional treatment of sensation, perception, imagery, etc., along with certain shifts in emphasis and additional facts which serve to give the author's personal imprint.

I believe we can write a psychology, define it as Pillsbury, and never go back upon our definition: never use the terms consciousness, mental states, mind, content, introspectively verifiable, imagery, and the like. . . . It can be done in terms of stimulus and response, in terms of habit formation, habit integrations and the like. Furthermore, I believe that it is really worth while to make this attempt now.

The psychology which I should attempt to build up would take as a starting point, first, the observable fact that organisms, man and animal alike, do adjust themselves to their environment by means of hereditary and habit equipments. These adjustments may be very adequate or they may be so inadequate that the organism barely maintains its existence; secondly, that certain stimuli lead the organisms to make the responses. In a system of psychology completely worked out, given the response the stimuli can be predicted; given the stimuli the response can be predicted. Such a set of statements is crass and raw in the extreme, as all such generalizations must be. Yet they are hardly more raw and less realizable than the ones which appear in the psychology texts of the day. I possibly might illustrate my point better by choosing an everyday problem which anyone is likely to meet in the course of his work. Some time ago I was called upon to make a study of certain species of birds. Until I went to Tortugas I had never seen these birds alive. When I reached there I found the animals doing certain things: some of the acts seemed to work peculiarly well in such an environment, while others seemed to be unsuited to their type of life. I first studied the responses of the group as a whole and later those of individuals. In order to understand more thoroughly the relation between what was habit and what was hereditary in these responses, I took the young birds and reared them. In this way I was able to study the order of appearance of hereditary adjustments and their complexity, and later the beginnings of habit formation. My efforts in determining the stimuli which called forth such adjustments were crude indeed. Consequently my attempts to control behavior and to produce responses at will did not meet with much success. Their food and water, sex and other social relations, light and temperature conditions were all beyond control in a field study. I did find it possible to control their reactions in a measure by using the nest and egg (or young) as stimuli. It is not necessary in this paper to develop further how such a study should be carried out and how work of this kind must be supplemented by carefully controlled laboratory experiments. Had I been called upon to examine the natives of some of the Australian tribes, I should have gone about my task in the same way. I should have found the problem more difficult: the types of responses called forth by physical stimuli would have been more varied, and the number of effective stimuli larger. I should have had to determine the social setting of their lives in a far more careful way. These savages would be more influenced by the responses of each other than was the case with the birds. Furthermore, habits would have been more complex and the influences of past habits upon the present responses would have appeared more clearly. Finally, if I had been called upon to work out the psychology of the educated European, my problem would have required several lifetimes. But in the one I have at my disposal I should have followed the same general line of attack. In the main, my desire in all such work is to gain an accurate knowledge of adjustments and the stimuli calling them forth. My final reason for this is to learn general and particular methods by which I may control behavior. My goal is not "the description and explanation of states of consciousness as such," nor that of obtaining such proficiency in mental gymnastics that I can immediately lay hold of a state of consciousness and say, "this, as a whole, consists of gray sensation number 350, of such and such extent, occurring in conjunction with the sensation of cold of a certain intensity; one of pressure of a certain intensity and extent," and so on *ad infinitum*. If psychology would follow the plan I suggest, the educator, the physician, the jurist and the business man could utilize our data in a practical way, as soon as we are able, experimentally, to obtain them. Those who have occasion to apply psychological principles practically would find no need to complain as they do at the present time. Ask any physician or jurist today whether scientific psychology plays a practical part in his daily routine and you will hear him deny that the psychology of the laboratories finds a place in his scheme of work. I think the criticism is extremely just. One of the earliest conditions which made me dissatisfied with psychology was the feeling that there was no realm of application for the principles which were being worked out in content terms.

What gives me hope that the behaviorist's position is a defensible one is the fact that those branches of psychology which have already partially withdrawn from the parent, experimental psychology, and which are consequently less dependent upon introspection are today in a most flourishing condition. Experimental pedagogy, the psychology of drugs, the psychology of advertising, legal psychology, the psychology of tests, and psychopathology are all vigorous growths. These are sometimes wrongly called "practical" or "applied" psychology. Surely there was never a worse misnomer. In the future there may grow up vocational bureaus which really apply psychology. At present these fields are truly scientific and are in search of broad generalizations which will lead to the control of human behavior. For example, we find out by experimentation whether a series of stanzas may be acquired more readily if the whole is learned at once, or whether it is more advantageous to learn each stanza separately and then pass to the succeeding. We do not attempt to apply our findings. The application of this principle is purely voluntary on the part of the teacher. In the psychology of drugs we may show the effect upon behavior of certain doses of caffeine. We may reach the conclusion that caffeine has a good effect upon the speed and accuracy of work. But these are general principles. We leave it to the individual as to whether the results of our tests shall be applied or not. Again, in legal testimony, we test the effects of recency upon the reliability of a witness's report. We test the accuracy of the report with respect to moving objects, stationary objects, color, etc. It depends upon the judicial machinery of the country to decide whether these facts are ever to be applied. For a "pure" psychologist to say that he is not interested in the questions raised in these divisions of the science because they relate indirectly to the application of psychology shows, in the first place, that he fails to understand the scientific aim in such problems, and secondly, that he is not interested in a psychology which concerns itself with human life. The only fault I have to find with these disciplines is that much of their material is stated in terms of introspection, whereas a statement in terms of objective results would be far more valuable. There is no reason why appeal should ever be made to consciousness in any of them. Or why introspective data should ever be sought during the experimentation, or published in the results. In experimental pedagogy especially one can see the desirability of keeping all of the results on a purely objective plane. If this is done, work there on the human being will be comparable directly with the work upon animals. For example, at Hopkins, Mr. Ulrich has obtained certain results upon the distribution of effort in learning—using rats as subjects. He is prepared to give comparative results upon the effect of having an animal work at the problem once per day, three times per day, and five times per day. Whether it is advisable to have the animal learn only one problem at a time or to learn three abreast. We need to have similar experiments made upon man, but we care as little about his "conscious processes" during the conduct of the experiment as we care about such processes in the rats.

I am more interested at the present moment in trying to show the necessity for maintaining uniformity in experimental procedure and in the method of stating results in both human and animal work, than in developing any ideas I may have upon the changes which are certain to come in the scope of human psychology. Let us consider for a moment the subject of the range of stimuli to which animals respond. I shall speak first of the work upon vision in animals. We put our animal in a situation where he will respond (or learn to respond) to one of two monochromatic lights. We feed him at the one (positive) and punish him at the other (negative). In a short time the animal learns to go to the light at which he is fed. At this point questions arise which I may phrase in two ways: I may choose the psychological way and say "does the animal see these two lights as I do, i.e., as two distinct colors, or does he see them as two grays differing in brightness, as does the totally color blind?" Phrased by the behaviorist, it would read as follows: "Is my animal responding upon the basis of the difference in intensity between the two stimuli, or upon the difference in wave-lengths?" He nowhere thinks of the animal's response in terms of his own experiences of colors and grays. He wishes to establish the fact whether wave-length is a factor in that animal's adjustment. If so, what wave-lengths are effective and what differences in wave-length must be maintained in the different regions to afford bases for differential responses? If wave-length is not a factor in adjustment he wishes to know what difference in intensity will serve as a basis for response, and whether that same difference will suffice throughout the spectrum. Furthermore, he wishes to test whether the animal can respond to wave-lengths which do not affect the human eye. He is as much interested in comparing the rat's spectrum with that of the chick as in comparing it with man's. The point of view when the various sets of comparisons are made does not change in the slightest.

However we phrase the question to ourselves, we take our animal after the association has been formed and then introduce certain control experiments which enable us to return answers to the questions just raised. But there is just as keen a desire on our part to test man under the same conditions, and to state the results in both cases in common terms.

The man and the animal should be placed as nearly as possible under the same experimental conditions. Instead of feeding or punishing the human subject, we should ask him to respond by setting a second apparatus until standard and control offered no basis for a differential response. Do I lay myself open to the charge here that I am using introspection? My reply is not at all; that while I might very well feed my human subject for a right choice and punish him for a wrong one and thus produce the response if the subject could give it, there is no need of going to extremes even on the platform I suggest. But be it understood that I am merely using this second method as an abridged behavior method. We can go just as far and reach just as dependable results by the longer method as by the abridged. In many cases the direct and typically human method cannot be safely used. Suppose, for example, that I doubt the accuracy of the setting of the control instrument, in the above experiment, as I am very likely to do if I suspect a defect in vision? It is hopeless for me to get his introspective report. He will say: "There is no difference in sensation, both are reds, identical in quality." But suppose I confront him with the standard and the control and so arrange conditions that he is punished if he responds to the "control" but not with the standard. I interchange the positions of the standard and the control at will and force him to attempt to differentiate the one from the other. If he can learn to make the adjustment even after a large number of trials it is evident that the two stimuli do afford the basis for a differential response. Such a method may sound nonsensical, but I firmly believe we will have to resort increasingly to just such a method where we have reason to distrust the language method.

There is hardly a problem in human vision which is not also a problem in animal vision: I mention the limits of the spectrum, threshold values, absolute and relative, flicker, Talbot's law, Weber's law, field of vision, the Purkinje phenomenon, etc. Every one is capable of being worked out by behavior methods. Many of them are being worked out at the present time.

I feel that all the work upon the senses can be consistently carried forward along the lines I have suggested here for vision. Our results will, in the end, give an excellent picture of what each organ stands for in the way of function. The anatomist and the physiologist may take our data and show, on the one hand, the structures which are responsible for these responses, and, on the other, the physico–chemical relations which are necessarily involved (physiological chemistry of nerve and muscle) in these and other reactions.

The situation in regard to the study of memory is hardly different. Nearly all of the memory methods in actual use in the laboratory today yield the type of results I am arguing for. A certain series of nonsense syllables or other material is presented to the human subject. What should receive the emphasis are the rapidity of the habit formation, the errors, peculiarities in the form of the curve, the persistence of the habit so formed, the relation of such habits to those formed when more complex material is used, etc. Now such results are taken down with the subject's introspection. The experiments are made for the purpose of discussing the mental machinery involved in learning, in recall, recollection and forgetting, and not for the purpose of seeking the human being's way of shaping his responses to meet the problems in the terribly complex environment into which he is thrown, nor for that of showing the similarities and differences between man's methods and those of other animals.

The situation is somewhat different when we come to a study of the more complex forms of behavior, such as imagination, judgment, reasoning, and conception. At present the only statements we have of them are in content terms. Our minds have been so warped by the fifty-odd years which have been devoted to the study of states of consciousness that we can envisage these problems only in one way. We should meet the situation squarely and say that we are not able to carry forward investigations along all of these lines by the behavior methods which are in use at the present time. In extenuation I should like to call attention to the paragraph above where I made the point that the introspective method itself has reached a *cul-de-sac* with respect to them. The topics have become so threadbare from much handling that they may well be put away for a time. As our methods become better developed it will be possible to undertake investigations of more and more complex forms of behavior. Problems which are now laid aside will again become imperative, but they can be viewed as they arise from a new angle and in more concrete settings.

Will there be left over in psychology a world of pure psychics, to use Yerkes' term? I confess I do not know. The plans which I most favor for psychology lead practically to the ignoring of consciousness in the sense that that term is used by psychologists today. I have virtually denied that this realm of psychics is open to experimental investigation. I don't wish to go further into the problem at present because it leads inevitably over into metaphysics. If you will grant the behaviorist the right to use consciousness in the same way that other natural scientists employ it—that is, without making consciousness a special object of observation—you have granted all that my thesis requires.

In concluding, I suppose I must confess to a deep bias on these questions. I have devoted nearly twelve years to experimentation on animals. It is natural that such a one should drift into a theoretical position which is in harmony with his experimental work. Possibly I have put up a straw man and have been fighting that. There may be no absolute lack of harmony between the position outlined here and that of functional psychology. I am inclined to think, however, that the two positions cannot be easily harmonized. Certainly the position I advocate is weak enough at present and can be attacked from many standpoints. Yet when all this is admitted I still feel that the considerations which I have urged should have a wide influence upon the type of psychology which is to be developed in the future. What we need to do is to start work upon psychology, making *behavior*, not *consciousness*, the objective point of our attack. Certainly there are enough problems in the control of behavior to keep us all working many lifetimes without ever allowing us time to think of consciousness *an sich*. Once launched in the undertaking, we will find ourselves in a short time as far divorced from an introspective psychology as the psychology of the present time is divorced from faculty psychology.

Comment

This vigorous attack on the old psychology and the call for a dramatic "new" approach was a stirring appeal to many psychologists. Consider the major points. Psychology is to be the science of behavior (and not the introspective study of consciousness)—a purely objective experimental branch of natural science. Both human and animal behavior will be investigated. The new psychology will discard all mentalistic concepts, and use only behavior concepts such as stimulus and response. The goal of psychology is the prediction and control of behavior.

As we have seen, these points were not new with Watson. Objective experimental methods had been employed for some time, and functional concepts had certainly been highly influential, indeed, dominant, in America. Research on animal learning had begun to yield data applicable to human learning, and objective tests had been developed and used with some success to predict and control behavior. Even Watson's definition of psychology as the science of behavior had been anticipated.

Thus, Watson's positive points were not new. What was unique and provocative about his program was his pronounced negative emphasis— drop the mind and consciousness, do away with mentalistic concepts, stop speculating about what might be occurring in the brain, and stop using introspection. He was "a breath of fresh air, clearing away the musty accumulation of 'the centuries [R. I. Watson, 1971, p. 442]."

The Methods of Behaviorism

As Watson stated, only objective methods of investigation are admissible in the behavioristic laboratory. Watson stated quite explicitly the methods to be used in research: (*a*) observation, with and without the use of instruments, (*b*) the conditioned reflex method, (*c*) the verbal report method, and (*d*) testing methods.

The method of observation, self-explanatory and fundamental, is a necessary basis for the other methods. Objective tests were already in use but Watson proposed that test results be treated as samples of behavior, and not as measures of mental qualities. To Watson, a test did not measure intelligence or personality, rather it measured the responses the subject made to the stimulus situation of the test, and nothing more. Also, as we have seen, conditioning methods were in use before the advent of behaviorism, although their use in America had been limited and Watson was largely responsible for their subsequent widespread application in American psychological research.

The verbal report method is unique in Watson's system and deserves extra comment, indeed perhaps even justification. Watson was, as noted, violently opposed to introspection. In view of this opposition, his admission of verbal reporting into the laboratory was regarded by some as a questionable compromise whereby he admitted introspection at the back door after having vigorously thrown it out the front. His system was particularly sensitive to this criticism.

Let us first consider why Watson was so opposed to introspection. That introspection could not be used by those who performed research on animals (as Watson did) obviously caused him to look upon it with disfavor. He also distrusted the accuracy of introspection. If even the most highly trained introspectionists could not agree on what they observed, Watson asked, how was psychology to progress? More fundamental was the objection that a behaviorist could not tolerate anything in his laboratory that could not be objectively observed. Watson wanted to deal only with tangibles and he objected strongly to the introspectionists' pretensions of reporting on occurrences within an organism which could not be verified through objective observation.

In spite of his opposition to introspection, Watson felt he could not rule out all the work in psychophysics, which made use of introspection. He therefore suggested that speech reactions are, after all, objectively observable, and hence are as meaningful to the behaviorist as any other type of motor reaction:

> Now what can we observe? We can observe *behavior—what the organism does or says*. And let us point out at once: that *saying* is doing—that is, *behaving*. Speaking overtly or to ourselves (thinking) is just as objective a type of behavior as baseball [J. B. Watson, 1930, p. 6].[2]

The use of verbal report in the methodology of behaviorism was a concession that was much debated by Watson's critics, who contended that, in this respect, Watson was asking for mere semantic changes, not a genuine alteration of research procedures. It is noted that Watson

[2] This quote and the quotes on pp. 212–215, 217, and 218 are reprinted from *Behaviorism* by John B. Watson, by permission of W. W. Norton & Company, Inc. Copyright 1924, 1925, 1930 by W. W. Norton & Company, Inc. Copyright renewed 1952, 1953, 1958, by John B. Watson.

(1914) considered verbal report to be an "inexact" method and not a satisfactory substitute for more objective methods of observation. He wanted to limit the use of verbal report to those situations in which it was totally accurate and capable of verification, as for example in observing differences in tones. Unverifiable verbal reports, such as imageless thoughts or comments about feeling states, were ruled out. While indicating that he would severely restrict the use of verbal report, he never said exactly how he would do so.

The most important research method of the behaviorists—the conditioned reflex method—was not adopted until 1915, 2 years after behaviorism's formal beginning. In his later writings, Watson acknowledged his debt to both Pavlov and Bekhterev for the conditioning method. Watson wrote of conditioning in terms of "stimulus substitution." A response, he said, is conditioned when it becomes attached or connected to a stimulus other than the one which originally aroused it. (Pavlov's dogs salivating to the sound of a bell instead of the sight of food is a conditioned response.)

Watson seized upon this approach because it provided him with a totally objective method of analyzing behavior, that is, reducing behavior to its most elementary units, the stimulus–response (S–R) bonds. All behavior, he argued, could be reduced to these elements, providing a method for laboratory investigation of man's complex behavior.

Thus, Watson continues in the atomistic and mechanistic tradition established by the British empiricists and used by Wundt. Psychologists must study man in the same way physical scientists study the universe, by breaking it down into the component elements or atoms.

This exclusive focus on the use of objective methods and the elimination of introspection meant a change in the nature and role of the human subject in the psychological laboratory. In Wundt's and Titchener's structuralist system, the subject (the reagent) was both the observer and the observed; he observed his own conscious experience.

In behaviorism, the subject assumes a different and less important role; the subject no longer observes, rather he is the one being observed by the experimenter. The true observer (the experimenter) sets up the conditions of the experiment and observes how the subject responds to these conditions.

Therefore the human subject is demoted in status—he no longer observes, he merely behaves, and thus becomes the object of observation. And almost anyone can behave: children, the mentally ill, animals.

This changed viewpoint reinforced psychology's image or model of man as "a stimulus–response machine: you put a stimulus in one of the slots, and out comes a packet of reactions [Burt, 1962, p. 232]."

Initially, Watson's arguments for the use of only objective methods (the so-called "methodological behaviorism") seemed to many to be a major advance. Retrospective analysis, however, suggests that the behaviorists actually contributed little that was positive in this regard because objective methodology had characterized psychology since its beginnings as a science. For example, studies in psychophysics, memory, and conditioning were already using objective methods. Therefore, the contributions of the behaviorists were more in terms of extending and refining existing methods than developing new ones.

The Subject Matter of Behaviorism

In the long run, Watson's "conceptual behaviorism" (the spirit or basic notion of behaviorism) has proved to be of greater importance for psychology than his methodological behaviorism. The primary subject matter or data must always be items of behavior—muscular movements or glandular secretions. Watson said that these responses constitute evidence of the organism's ability to react in discriminate fashion to its environment. Psychology, as the science of behavior, must deal only with acts that can be described objectively in terms of stimulus and response, habit formation, habit integration, etc. All human and animal behavior can be described in these terms without resorting to mentalistic concepts and terminology. Through the objective study of behavior, behavioristic psychology can fulfill its aim of predicting the response given the stimulus, and predicting the antecedent stimulus given the response. Human and animal behavior can therefore be effectively understood, predicted, and controlled by reducing the behavior to the stimulus–response level.

Despite this reduction of behavior to stimulus–response units, Watson argued that behaviorism deals with the overall behavior of the whole organism. While a response can be something as simple and low-level as a knee jerk or other reflex, it can also be much more complex, in which case the term "act" is applied. For example, Watson considered response acts to include such things as the taking of food, writing a book, playing baseball, or building a house. Thus, an act involves the organism's response through movement in space such as talking, reaching, walking, etc. Watson seemed to have thought of a response in terms of accomplishing some result in the environment, rather than as an assemblage of muscular elements, that is, in more molar than molecular terms.

Nevertheless, these behavioral acts, no matter how complex, can be reduced to lower-level motor or glandular responses. Responses are classified in two ways: learned or unlearned, and explicit or implicit. Watson considered it important for behaviorism to distinguish between innate responses and those that are learned, and to discover for the latter the laws of learning.

Explicit responses are overt and therefore directly observable. Implicit responses, such as visceral movements, glandular secretions, and nerve impulses, take place inside the organism. Though such movements are not overt, they are nonetheless items of behavior. In introducing this notion of implicit behavior, Watson modified somewhat his initial requirement that all the subject matter of psychology be *actually* observable and said instead that everything must be *potentially* observable (Woodworth, 1948, p. 75). The movements or responses occurring within the organism are theoretically observable through the use of instrumentation.

The exciting stimuli, like the responses with which the behaviorist deals, may be complex. A stimulus may, of course, be something relatively simple, such as light waves striking the retina, but it can also be a physical object in the environment, or total situations (or constellations of specific stimuli). Just as the constellation of responses involved in an act can be reduced to particular responses, so the "stimulus situation" can be resolved into its component specific stimuli.

Thus, behaviorism deals with the behavior of the whole organism in relation to its environment. Specific laws of behavior can be worked out through the analysis of the total stimulus and response complexes into their more elemental stimulus and response segments. This analysis was not to be as minute and detailed as that performed by the physiologist in determining the structure and organization of the central nervous system. Because of the inaccessibility of the "mystery box" (Watson's term for the brain), he had little interest in cortical functioning. Behavior, to Watson, was concerned with the total organism and could not be restricted to the nervous system alone. Watson focused on larger units of behavior—the whole response of the organism to a given situation.

In both subject matter and methodology, the new psychology of John B. Watson was an attempt to construct a science that was completely free of mentalistic notions and subjective methods, a science as objective as physics.

We now consider Watson's treatment of some of the traditional topics in psychology: instinct, learning, emotion, and thinking.

Specific Views and Concepts

Like all systematic theorists, Watson developed his psychology in accordance with his fundamental theses. All areas of behavior, emotions, feelings, thought, etc., were to be treated in objective stimulus–response terms.

Instinct

Watson's position on the role of instinct in behavior changed from an initial acceptance of instincts to a categorical denial of their existence in humans—the latter position announced in 1925. All those aspects of human behavior that seem instinctive, Watson argued, are in reality socially conditioned responses. With his position that learning is the key to understanding the development of human behavior, Watson became an extreme environmentalist. He went beyond just denying instincts and refused to admit that there were inherited capacities, temperaments, or talents of any kind.

Those things that seem inherited

> depend on training that goes on mainly in the cradle. The behaviorist would *not* say: "He inherits his father's capacity or talent for being a fine swordsman." He would say: "This child certainly has his father's slender build of body, the same type of eyes . . . ." And he would go on to say: "—and his father is very fond of him. He put a tiny sword into his hand when he was a year of age, and in all their walks he talks sword play, attack and defense, the code of duelling and the like." A certain type of structure, plus early training—*slanting*—accounts for adult performance [J. B. Watson, 1930, p. 94].

This emphasis on the overwhelming influence of the environment, and its corollary that one can train a child to be whatever one wants him to be, was at least part of the reason for Watson's large public following.

Learning

Since, according to Watson, there are no instincts or inherited capacities or talents of any kind—the adult is strictly a product of childhood conditioning—learning plays a major role in behaviorism.

Watson's views on learning showed a progressive change in the direction of the incorporation of conditioning as a basic part of his system. In his 1913 article there is no mention of conditioning, and his first book, *Behavior: An Introduction to Comparative Psychology* (1914), gives but slight emphasis to Pavlov's conditioning experiments, even expressing doubt that the method can be used with primates.

In his 1915 presidential address to the American Psychological Association, however, he suggested that the conditioned reflex method should displace introspection. From then on it was one of the chief methods of the behaviorists. Surprisingly, however, Watson never completely developed a satisfactory theory of learning, and conceptually seemed to belong with the rather antiquated pre-Thorndikian associationists. He rejected Thorndike's law of effect and relied primarily on the older laws of contiguity, frequency, and recency. He maintained that the correct response was the most recent one and that it occurred more and more frequently during the process of learning.

In spite of his enthusiasm for classical conditioning, Watson failed to recognize the importance of Pavlov's law of reinforcement and its similarity to Thorndike's law of effect. Thus, while accepting conditioning principles and using them in his research, he continued to cling to a law of exercise and to emphasize frequency and recency as primary factors of learning.

Emotion

Emotions, to Watson, are nothing more than bodily responses to specific stimuli. The stimulus (the presence of danger, for instance) produces internal body changes and the appropriate learned overt responses. This notion, of course, implies no conscious perception of the emotion nor any mass of sensations from the internal organs. Each separate emotion involves its particular pattern of changes in the general body mechanism, particularly in the visceral and glandular systems. Although Watson recognized that all emotional responses involve overt movements, for example, of the arms and legs, the internal responses predominate in his concept. Emotion, then, is a form of implicit behavior in which the hidden visceral responses are evident, at least to some extent, as changes in pulse and breathing, blushing, etc.

Watson's theory of emotion is much simpler than that of James, discussed earlier. In James's theory, the bodily changes follow immediately upon the perception of the exciting stimulus, and the feeling of these bodily changes is the emotion. Watson was highly critical of this position, saying that "James gave to the psychology of the emotions a setback from which it has only recently begun to recover [1930, p. 140]."

Watson discarded the conscious processes of perception of the situation and the feeling state and said simply that emotions can be understood in terms of the objective stimulus situation, the overt bodily response, and the internal visceral changes.

A famous study of Watson's was his investigation of the stimuli that produce emotional responses in infants. He found what he believed to be the three fundamental emotions: fear, rage, and love. Fear is produced by loud sounds and sudden loss of support, rage by hampering of body movement, and love by stroking the skin, rocking, and patting. He also found characteristic reaction patterns to these stimuli.

Watson believed that fear, rage, and love are the only unlearned emotional responses. All the remaining human emotional responses are built up from these basic three through the process of conditioning. He felt that the basic emotional responses may become attached, through conditioning, to a variety of environmental stimuli that were not originally capable of eliciting them.

Watson experimentally demonstrated this in his study, mentioned earlier, of Albert, who at 11 months of age was conditioned to fear a white rat that he had not feared prior to the conditioning trials. The fear was established quite easily by presenting a very loud noise (striking a steel bar with a hammer) behind Albert's head whenever the rat was presented. In a short time, just the sight of the rat produced signs of fear and discomfort in the child. Watson went on to demonstrate that this conditioned fear could be generalized to other somewhat similar stimuli, such as a rabbit, a white fur coat, and Santa Claus whiskers. Watson believed that adult fears, aversions, and anxieties are conditioned in like manner in early childhood.

Having demonstrated that fears could be conditioned, Watson then turned to the problem of eliminating them. Several rather common techniques, such as disuse and verbal appeal, and frequent application of the fear stimulus, were tried but proved unsuccessful. Success was reached through the use of the unconditioning or reconditioning technique. The subject was a child (not Albert) who showed a fear of rabbits that had not been conditioned in the laboratory. While the child was eating, the rabbit was brought into the room, but kept at a distance great enough so as to not elicit the fear response. Thereafter, the rabbit was brought progressively closer to the child, always while the latter was eating. The point was finally reached at which the child could handle the rabbit without fear. Watson also found that generalized fear responses to other similar objects could be eliminated by this procedure.

Watson's behavioristic approach to the emotions and his interest in the physiological changes that accompany emotional behavior stimulated a great deal of research on emotional development in children and on the specific reaction patterns for the specific emotions.

Thought

Prior to the advent of behaviorism, the traditional point of view with regard to thought processes was the so-called "centralist" theory of thinking, which held that thought processes occurred in the brain "so faintly that no neural impulse passes out over the motor nerve to the muscle, hence no response takes place in the muscles and glands [J. B. Watson, 1930, p. 239]." According to this view, thought processes, because they occur in the absence of muscular movements, are not considered accessible to observation and experimentation. Hence, thought is regarded as intangible; something exclusively mental in nature with no physical referents. The concept of image, as used by the structuralists, is an example of this conception of thought.

Watson's "peripheral theory of thinking," perhaps his most famous theory, takes issue with this older notion and attempts to reduce thinking to nothing more than implicit motor behavior. Thinking, he argued, must be, like all other aspects of human functioning, sensorimotor behavior of some sort. He reasoned that the behavior of thinking must be implicit speech movements. Verbal thinking, then, is reduced to subvocal talking involving muscular habits learned in overt speech. These muscular habits become inaudible as the child grows up, as described by Watson (1930):

> The child talks incessantly when alone. At three he even plans the day *aloud*, as my own ear placed outside the key hole of the nursery door has very often confirmed. Soon society in the form of nurse and parents steps in. "Don't talk aloud—daddy and mother are not always talking to themselves." Soon the overt speech dies down to whispered speech and a good lip reader can still read what the child thinks of the world and of himself. Some individuals never even make this concession to society. When alone they talk aloud to themselves. A still larger number never go beyond even the whispering stage when alone. Watch people reading on the street car; peep through the key hole sometime when individuals not too highly socialized are just sitting and thinking. But the great majority of people pass on to the third stage under the influence of social pressure constantly exerted. "Quit whispering to yourself," and "Can't you even read without moving your lips?" and the like are constant mandates. Soon the process is forced to take place behind the lips. Behind these walls you can call the biggest bully the worst name you can think of without even smiling. You can tell the female bore how terrible she really is and the next moment smile and overtly pay her a verbal compliment [pp. 240–241].

After we learn to talk (by conditioning), thought becomes nothing more than talking silently to ourselves. Watson suggested that the focal points for much of this implicit behavior are the muscles of the larynx and the tongue. In fact, Watson's equivalent term for thinking was "laryngeal habits," and, initially, the larynx was considered to be the "organ of thought." In addition to these laryngeal habits, language or thought is also mediated by gestures, frowns, shrugs, etc., which symbolize more overt reactions to situations.

One obvious source of corroboration for Watson's hypothesis is that most of us are aware that we often talk to ourselves while thinking. This is inadmissible evidence, however, since it is purely introspective, and Watson could hardly use introspection to support a tenet of behaviorism. Behaviorism required objective evidence of these implicit speech movements, and attempts were made to record movement in the tongue and larynx during thought. Such measurements revealed slight movements part but not all of the time that the subjects were thinking. Similarly, measurements taken from the hands and fingers of deaf mutes revealed movement some of the time during thought. In spite of the inability to always secure positive results in these studies, Watson was convinced that implicit speech movements existed and that their clear demonstration awaited only the development of more sophisticated instrumentation.

Watson's Popular Appeal

Watson's bold pronouncements won him a large following not only among psychologists, but among the lay public as well. Why this public acclaim? Surely people were not distressed because some psychologists practiced introspection, whereas others refuted its use; or because some psychologists pretended to be conscious while others joyously proclaimed that psychology had finally lost its mind; or whether thinking took place in the head or in the neck. While these issues aroused comment and controversy among psychologists, they would hardly concern the general public.

What did stir the public was Watson's call for a world based on scientifically shaped and controlled behavior, free from myths, customs, and conventions. This appeal offered hope to many people who had become disenchanted with the older guiding creeds. In fervor and faith it had many of the aspects of a religion.

Some of the excitement generated by Watson's ideas can be appreciated from the newspaper reviews of *Behaviorism*. The *New York Times* said dramatically, "It marks an epoch in the intellectual history of man [August 2, 1925]"; the *New York Herald Tribune* commented, "Perhaps this is the most important book ever written. One stands for an instant blinded with a great hope [Woodworth, 1948, p. 93]."

The "great hope" stemmed in part from Watson's extreme environmentalistic position, as reflected in what is probably his most famous passage:

> Give me a dozen healthy infants, well-formed, and my own specified world to bring them up in and I'll guarantee to take any one at random and train him to become any type of specialist I might select—doctor, lawyer, artist, merchant-chief and, yes, even beggar-man and thief, regardless of his talents, penchants, tendencies, abilities, vocations, and race of his ancestors [1930, p. 104].

Watson's conditioning experiments, such as the study of Albert, convinced him that emotional disturbances in adults cannot be traced back to sex alone, as Freud held. Instead, Watson argued, these adult disturbances can be traced to conditioned and transferred responses established in infancy and youth. If such disturbances are a function of faulty conditioning in childhood, then a proper program of childhood conditioning should prevent their emergence. Watson believed that such practical control of infant behavior (and hence of the adult) is not only possible, but absolutely necessary. Toward this end, he developed a plan for social improvement—a program of "experimental ethics" based on the principles of behaviorism.

No one gave him "a dozen healthy infants" so that he might test his claim, and he admitted that in making it he was going beyond the known facts. He noted, however, that those who believed in the predominance of heredity had been arguing their case for thousands of years and still had no real supporting evidence.

The following passage from the end of *Behaviorism* (1930) reveals some of the fervor with which Watson described his program for living under the banner of behaviorism, and perhaps explains why it became a new "religion" to so many people.

> Behaviorism ought to be a science that prepares men and women for understanding the principles of their own behavior. It ought to make men and women eager to rearrange their own lives, and especially eager to prepare themselves to bring up their own children in a healthy way. I wish I could picture for you what a rich and wonderful individual we should make of every healthy child if only we could let it shape itself properly and then provide for it a universe in which it could exercise that organization—a universe unshackled by legendary folk-lore of happenings thousands of years ago; unhampered by disgraceful political history; free of foolish customs and conventions which have no significance in themselves, yet which hem the individual in like taut steel bands. I am not asking here for revolution; I am not asking people to go out to some God-for-saken place, form a colony, go naked and live a communal life, nor am I asking for a change to a diet of roots and herbs. I am not asking for "free love." I am trying to dangle a stimulus in front

of you, a verbal stimulus which, if acted upon, will gradually change this universe. For the universe will change if you bring up your children, not in the freedom of the libertine, but in behavioristic freedom—a freedom which we cannot even picture in words, so little do we know of it. Will not these children in turn, with their better ways of living and thinking, replace us as society and in turn bring up their children in a still more scientific way, until the world finally becomes a place fit for human habitation [pp. 303–304]?

This "great hope" remained only a hope on Watson's part, for his program of experimental ethics to replace the older speculative ethics based on religion was never carried out. He outlined his plan in rather brief terms and left it as a framework for future research.

As we shall see in Chapter 11, a contemporary behaviorist, B. F. Skinner, has formulated a detailed program for a scientifically shaped utopia that certainly seems in the spirit of the one which Watson espoused.

A Final Note

Although Watson's productive career in psychology lasted less than 20 years, he profoundly influenced the course of psychology. Indeed, his impact compels us to count him among psychology's great men. As noted earlier, Watson was an effective agent of the *Zeitgeist*, and the times were changing not only in psychology but in general scientific attitudes as well. The nineteenth century had produced magnificent advances in every branch of science. The twentieth century promised even more marvels. It was thought that science was capable of finding an answer to everything, if given enough time. It was an era in which idealism was rapidly yielding to a spirit of tough-minded realism. Watson's behavioristic crusade helped American psychology in its ongoing transition from concentration on consciousness and subjectivism to materialism and objectivism in the study of behavior.

While Watson's program did not realize his ambitious goals, the behavioristic orientation in general remains a strong and active force in modern psychology.

Criticisms of Watsonian Behaviorism

Any systematic program that so blatantly attacks the existing order of things (indeed, suggests the complete discarding of the earlier version of the truth) and proposes such radical and sweeping revisions is bound to come under criticism. As we have seen, American psychology was already moving in the general direction of increased objectivity when Watsonian behaviorism formally began, but not all psychologists were pleased at the extreme form of objectivity that Watson proposed. Many, including some who generally supported the objective movement, felt that important components of psychology, such as sensory and perceptual processes, were being left out.

One of Watson's outstanding opponents was William McDougall (1871–1938), an English psychologist who came to this country in 1920. McDougall is probably most important for his espousal of an instinct theory of behavior, a theory that states that all human action results from innate tendencies to thought and action. He is also well known for the impetus his most influential book, *Introduction to Social Psychology*, gave to that area. This book, published in 1908, went through 14 editions by 1921.

McDougall's instinct theory enjoyed considerable initial success among social scientists, but rapidly lost ground when behaviorism came to the fore. In addition to his instinct theory, McDougall was an ardent supporter of a number of unpopular causes, such as freedom of the will, Nordic superiority, and psychic research.

By 1925 Watson had rejected the notion of instincts, and on this issue a pitched battle was joined between Watson and McDougall. The debate reached such proportions that much of it was published in 1929 in *The Battle of Behaviorism*, by Watson and McDougall.

McDougall began the debate on a falsely optimistic (yet amusing) note: "I have an initial advantage over Dr. Watson, an advantage which I feel to be so great as to be unfair; namely, all persons of common-sense will of necessity be on my side from the outset [Watson & McDougall, 1929, p. 40]."

McDougall agreed with Watson that the data of behavior are necessary in the science of psychology, but he argued forcefully that the data of consciousness are equally indispensable. He (and other critics as well) emphasized that psychology must use both kinds of data.

Without the use of introspection, McDougall asked, how can psychology determine the meaning of a subject's response, or the accuracy of speech behavior (verbal report), or know anything of the world of daydreams and fantasies, or understand (or even appreciate) aesthetic experiences?

In one of his most eloquent challenges to Watson, McDougall asked how a strict behaviorist would account for the experience of musical enjoyment:

I come into this hall and see a man on this platform scraping the guts of a cat with hairs from the tail of a horse; and, sitting silently in attitudes of rapt attention, are a thousand persons, who presently break into wild applause. How will the Behaviorist explain these strange incidents? How explain the fact that the vibrations emitted by the cat-gut stimulate all the thousands into absolute silence and quiescence; and the further fact that the cessation of the stimulus seems to be a stimulus to the most frantic activity? Common sense and psychology agree in accepting the explanation that the audience heard the music with keen pleasure, and vented their gratitude and admiration for the artist in shouts and handclappings. But the Behaviorist knows nothing of pleasure and pain, of admiration and gratitude. He has relegated all such "metaphysical entities" to the dust heap, and must seek some other explanation. Let us leave him seeking it. The search will keep him harmlessly occupied for some centuries to come [Watson & McDougall, 1929, pp. 62–63].[3]

Another point of criticism from McDougall was in regard to Watson's assumption that man's behavior is fully determined; that everything he does is the direct result of past experience and hence can be predicted when the past events are known. Such a psychology leaves no room for what has been called "free will" or freedom of choice, for all our behavior is predetermined. This important issue did not begin with Watson and McDougall. There is long-standing opposition between advocates of determinism and those of free will. Science accepts a strictly determined natural world, while theology and some philosophies accept freedom of the will. Watson, of course, belongs in the determinist camp. Since all behavior is interpretable in physical terms, all acts of behavior must be physically predetermined. Watson believed that people are not personally responsible for their actions, in terms of having a free will. This belief has important social implications, particularly for the treatment of criminals, who, according to Watson, should not be punished for their actions but rather should be reconditioned.

McDougall (and many others) argued that if the deterministic position were true—that people have no free will and cannot be held responsible for their actions—then there is no such thing as human striving, effort, or desire to improve oneself and society. No one, he argued, would make any effort to prevent war, alleviate injustice, or achieve other personal or social ideals.

The free will–determinist controversy cannot be resolved at this time and may never be. A point worth noting is that many determinists,

---

[3] From J. B. Watson and W. McDougall, *The Battle of Behaviorism* (New York: Norton, 1929). Reprinted by permission.

notably Watson and B. F. Skinner, have made "determined" efforts (no pun intended—I think) to bring about improvements in the individual and society.

Mention has already been made of the criticism directed at Watson's admission of verbal report as a method of research. Critics argued that its use was discriminatory; that he used it only when it could be verified and rejected it when it could not. Of course, that was Watson's point— the point of the entire behavioristic movement—to use only verifiable data.

The criticisms of Watsonian behaviorism were many and varied and are still voiced today, in modified form, against the newer varieties of behaviorism that derived from Watson's work.

The Watson–McDougall debates were held in 1924, 11 years after behaviorism formally began. McDougall ended his criticisms on a very optimistic note, predicting that in a few years Watson's position would disappear without a trace.

A few years later, in a postscript to the published version of the debate, McDougall wrote that his forecast had been "too optimistic; it was founded upon a too generous estimate of the intelligence of the American public. . . . Dr. Watson continues, as a prophet of much honor in his own country, to issue his pronouncements [Watson & McDougall, 1929, pp. 86, 87]."

Contributions of Watsonian Behaviorism

Watson's primary lasting contribution was his advocacy of a completely objective science of behavior. He exerted an enormous influence in rendering psychology more objective, in both methods and terminology. Methodological behaviorism is so much a part of American psychology today that it "has conquered itself to death. It . . . has become a truism. Virtually every American psychologist, whether he knows it or not, is nowadays a methodological behaviorist [Bergmann, 1956, p. 270]."

Although his positions on specific topics have stimulated a great deal of research, Watson's original formulations on these topics are no longer of use. Behaviorism as a separate school has been replaced by newer forms of psychological objectivism that built upon it. Boring said in 1929 that behaviorism was already past its prime as a movement. Since movements depend on protest for their strength and very existence, it is a most effective tribute to Watsonian behaviorism that only 16 years after its inception, it no longer needed to protest. Objective methodology and terminology have largely become the American psychology, and behaviorism died, as have other successful movements, by being incorporated into the main body of thought, where it continues to reside today.

To some degree, the acceptance of Watsonian behaviorism was a function of the clarity and force of the man himself. As noted earlier, he was a charming, charismatic figure who wrote with great enthusiasm, optimism, self-confidence, and clarity. He was a bold and appealing revolutionary who scorned tradition and rejected the older version of psychology. These personal characteristics, interacting with the spirit of the times which he reflected so well, define J. B. Watson as one of psychology's great figures.

SUGGESTED FURTHER READINGS

Watson

Bergmann, G. The contributions of John B. Watson. *Psychological Review,* 1956, 63, 265–276.

Skinner, B. F. John Broadus Watson, behaviorist. *Science,* 1959, 129, 197–198.

Woodworth, R. S. John Broadus Watson: 1878–1958. *American Journal of Psychology,* 1959, 72, 301–310.

General

Bakan, D. Behaviorism and American urbanization. *Journal of the History of the Behavioral Sciences,* 1966, 2, 5–28.

Schultz, D. The human subject in psychological research. *Psychological Bulletin,* 1969, 72, 214–228.

Watson, J. B., & McDougall, W. *The battle of behaviorism.* New York: Norton, 1929.

11

Behaviorism:
After the Founding

Early Behaviorists

In the early 1920s behaviorism seemed to capture the attention and imagination of nearly all American psychologists except those few who remained loyal to Titchener. However, not everyone in this new generation of behaviorists adopted the strict Watsonian viewpoint. Some developed their own approaches and were more receptive to divergent views than Watson had been. Although Watson was both the founder of behaviorism and its most effective leader for a time, other psychologists had reached the same general point of view at the same time, but had attempted to move in somewhat different directions. We will discuss several of these men, and then consider the work of more contemporary psychologists who might appropriately be called neobehaviorists.

Edwin B. Holt (1873–1946)

Holt received his Ph.D. at Harvard in 1901 and spent his academic career there and at Princeton. His main line of influence was in terms of the philosophical framework that he provided for behaviorism. His was a rather unorthodox view of behaviorism, probably because he was, as Boring (1950) noted, half an experimentalist and half a philosopher. Holt did not agree with Watson's complete rejection of consciousness and mental phenomena. Rather, he suggested that consciousness should be related to epistemological realism, according to which objects exist as perceived even when we are not perceiving them.

Holt believed that consciousness was simply a label given to the process of sensorimotor adjustment to a physical object. Thus, to be conscious of an object involves the relation of the sensorimotor aspects of the organism to that object, such as the oculomotor movements necessary to focus clearly on an object. Physical objects in the environment, then, have essentially similar qualities to those within consciousness, according to Holt. There were, therefore, physical referents for what was called conscious experiencing.

Holt agreed with Watson on the relative unimportance of heredity in shaping human behavior. He believed that an individual's behavior patterns are developed in two ways. The primary way is through learning, which occurs in response to what Holt called inner or outer motivation. Outer motivation refers to external forms of stimulation, whereas inner motivation refers to inner needs or drives, such as hunger, thirst, and so on. The latter point anticipated the development of Hull's learning theory with its emphasis on internal drive reduction as a necessary condition for learning. The second way in which behavior patterns are acquired is through the preservation in adulthood of childhood patterns of behavior.

Holt did not believe that psychology should attempt to reduce behavior to elemental units, whether stimulus–response connections or anything else. He wanted to deal with responses on a more molar level, as wholes accomplishing some end. He was concerned with behavior on a larger scale, behavior that had both a unity and a purpose, concepts that Watson could not allow in his system.

Holt's unorthodox form of behaviorism enabled him to use a great variety of sources and to take an interest in problems outside the mainstream of American behaviorism. For instance, in one of his books, *The Freudian Wish and Its Place in Ethics* (1915), he attempted to synthesize the major features of behaviorism and psychoanalysis. Probably his greatest single influence is, as we shall see, his role as a stimulus for a later behaviorist, E. C. Tolman.

Albert P. Weiss (1879–1931)

Born in Germany, Weiss came to the United States when he was very young, received his Ph.D. in 1916 at the University of Missouri, and pursued his career as a behaviorist, primarily studying child development at Ohio State University. His book, *A Theoretical Basis of Human Behavior* (1925), outlines his program of unabashed behaviorism. He strongly believed that psychology must operate as a natural science. All reference to conscious and mental phenomena had to be eliminated along with the subjective method of introspection; anything not accessible to a natural science approach had no place in psychology.

Weiss's behaviorism stressed an extreme form of reductionism that urged psychology to deal only with those elements of matter dealt with in physics. Thus, all behavior was seen as capable of analysis and reduction to physical–chemical entities. Weiss believed that psychology was actually a branch of physics and, as such, should not claim a nonphysical entity (consciousness) as its subject matter. Thus, we see in Weiss's system a strong emphasis on biological components of behavior, which in turn are reducible to physical elements. If this were his complete system, we might reasonably label him a physiologist, not a psychologist. But there was more: Man is not only biological, but social as well. Weiss argued that man is a product of both forces and he coined the term "biosocial" to denote this.

The organism is a solely biological entity only during early infancy, according to Weiss. As it matures and develops, its behavior is shaped and modified by social forces encountered in its interaction with other people. The importance of biological forces does not diminish, however; behavior is just as capable of reduction to physical–chemical units whether the individual is alone or influenced by other people. Weiss believed that psychology must study both physiological and social processes and that its primary task is to understand how the infant develops into a social adult. He outlined a program of research on child development and learning that, because of his early death, was never implemented.

Karl Lashley (1890–1958)

A prominent physiological psychologist, Lashley was a student of Watson's at Johns Hopkins University, where he received his Ph.D. in 1915. His productive career took him to the Universities of Minnesota and Chicago, then to Harvard, and finally to the Yerkes Laboratory of Primate Biology. An ardent supporter of behaviorism, Lashley vigorously championed increased objectivism in psychology and opposed the study of consciousness through introspection.

His own thorough research produced some results that differed from Watson's position on certain points. Specifically, he believed that S–R connections developed through conditioning were not the most effective approach to the analysis of behavior. However, Lashley's adherence to the basic tenets of behavioristic psychology never wavered; only his attitude toward some of Watson's secondary points changed.

Lashley is perhaps best known for his work involving brain extirpation of rats and other animals. He devoted many years to patient research on the role of the brain in the learning process. His initial studies were conducted with his former teacher, S. I. Franz, who, with Thorndike, had studied under Cattell.

Conceptually, the basic research procedure followed by Lashley and Franz was a simple one. After an animal had successfully learned a certain behavior, such as escaping from puzzle boxes of the type used by Thorndike, different parts of the brain were extirpated to determine the effect on the learned behavior. Would the animal be able to retain and perform the behavior with portions of the cortex no longer operative?

The results of this program were surprising and somewhat disturbing because they were at variance with the then accepted views on localization of function within the cortex. Earlier investigators had demonstrated specific sensory and motor areas in the cortex. Lashley's research showed that, even though destruction of large cortical areas resulted in slower learning, it seemed not to matter which specific cortical area was destroyed. That is, animals were able to learn just as well with one part of the cortex as with another. This perplexing finding seemed to indicate that other cortical centers were capable of taking over the functions performed by destroyed centers. Lashley thus concluded that the brain must function as a whole.

Lashley summarized his research findings in *Brain Mechanisms and Intelligence* (1929), in which he plotted errors in learning against (*a*) amount of cortical tissue destroyed, and (*b*) the difficulty of the learning task. His results led him to postulate two famous principles: mass action and equipotentiality. The law of mass action states that the efficiency of learning is a function of the total mass of the cortex left intact. In other words, the more cortical tissue available, the better the learning.

Thus, learning depends on the amount of cortex left functioning rather than on the integrity of a particular part; or, expressed as Lashley's principle of equipotentiality, one part of the cortex is essentially equal to another in terms of its contribution to tasks such as maze learning. There are, however, some exceptions to this principle: Visual perception of a shape or pattern, for instance, requires that a certain part of the cortex be intact, though within that specific cortical area, the subparts are to a large degree equal in potential.

Lashley had expected to find in his research specific pathways and connections between sensory and motor apparatus with definite points of localization in the cortex. Such findings would have supported the primacy of the reflex arc as an elemental unit of behavior. His results, however, challenged the Watsonian notion of a simple point-to-point connection in reflexes, according to which the brain merely serves to switch incoming sensory nerve impulses into outgoing motor impulses. Lashley's results suggested that the brain has a more active role in learning and challenged Watson's assumption that behavior is compounded bit by bit through conditioned reflexes.

Thus, while discrediting a basic point of Watson's system, Lashley's work did not weaken the behaviorists' fundamental contention that only completely objective methods should be used. Quite the contrary, his work was an excellent demonstration of the great value of objective methods in psychological research.

The Influence of Operationism

Beginning in the mid-1920s, new behavioristic systems appeared on the scene. The movement began to branch out into distinct subsystems, generating much controversy that has continued up to the present day, particularly with regard to theories of learning.

The increasingly dominant behavioristic movement in American psychology was further strengthened by the development of the principle known as operationism. Actually, the relationship between this principle and behaviorism was somewhat circular: On the one hand, as just noted, behaviorism was fortified by operationism, while on the other, the increasingly objective framework of behavioristic psychology prepared the way for the acceptance of operationism.

Operationism is more an attitude or general principle than a formal school in the sense in which we have been using the term. Its purpose is to render the language and terminology of science more objective and precise and to rid science of those problems that are not actually observable or physically demonstrable (the so-called pseudo-problems). Briefly, operationism holds that the validity of a given scientific finding or theoretical construct is dependent on the validity of the operations used in arriving at that finding or construct.

The operationist viewpoint was championed by the well-known Harvard physicist Percy W. Bridgman, who wrote *The Logic of Modern Physics* (1927). In this book, which quickly captured the attention of many psychologists, Bridgman proposed that physical concepts must be defined in more precise and rigid terms and that all concepts lacking physical referents must be promptly discarded. Bridgman's own terms are perhaps more precise:

> The new attitude toward a concept is entirely different. We may illustrate by considering the concept of length: what do we mean by the length of an object? We evidently know what we mean by length if we can tell what the length of any and every object is, and for the physicist nothing more is required. To find the length of an object, we have to perform certain physical operations. The concept of length is therefore fixed when the operations by which length is measured are fixed: that is, the concept of length involves as much as and nothing more than a set of operations; *the concept is synonymous with the corresponding set of operations* [1927, p. 5].

Thus, a physical concept is the same as the set of operations or procedures by which it is determined. Many psychologists quickly found this principle to be of great use in the science of psychology, and some applied it with great eagerness. But as promptly as it was accepted by some psychologists, it provoked opposition from others.

Bridgman's concern with pseudo-problems, or questions that defy answer by any known objective test, is especially noteworthy. Notions or propositions that cannot be put to experimental test are meaningless for science (hence the label *pseudo*-problem). An example of a pseudo-problem is the problem of the existence and nature of the soul. What is this thing "soul?" Can it be observed in the laboratory? Can it be measured and manipulated under controlled conditions to determine its effects on behavior? If something cannot be so observed, measured, manipulated, etc., it has absolutely no use, no meaning, and no relevance for science. It follows that the concept of an individual and private consciousness is a pseudo-problem in psychology, for neither its existence nor its characteristics can be determined or investigated through objective methods. Consciousness, therefore, has no place in a scientific psychology.

It can be argued that operationism is not really new; that it is little more than a formal statement of methods that had already been used in psychology when the meanings of words or concepts were defined in terms of their physical referents. Indeed, as Turner (1967) points out, there is very little in operationism that cannot be found in the works of the British empiricists. We have already noted the long-term trend in American psychology toward an increasing objectification of methods and subject matter. Thus, it can be said that the spirit of operationism—as a basic attitude and as the framework within which to conduct research and formulate theories—had already been in use by a number of American psychologists for some years before the publication of Bridgman's book in 1927. Since the time of Wundt, however, physics had been the paragon of scientific respectability for the newer psychology and when physics favored operationism as a formal doctrine, psychology quickly followed suit.

As we mentioned earlier, operationism did not win universal recognition in psychology, nor is it universally accepted even today. Controversy continues about the relative utility or futility of limiting psychology's subject matter to only that which has empirical reference.

Also, as Boring (1950) pointed out, "The reduction of concepts to their operations turned out to be dull business. No one wants to trouble with it when there is no special need [p. 658]."

Turner (1967), among others, takes the position that operationism is no longer the orthodoxy it was in the 1920s and 1930s, and even Bridgman seems to have second thoughts about the concept, or at least the use made of it. Writing 27 years after proposing the operationist viewpoint, he said, "I feel that I have created a Frankenstein which has certainly gotten away from me. I abhor the word *operationalism* or *operationism*. . . . The thing I have envisaged is too simple to be so dignified by so pretentious a name . . . [Bridgman, 1954, p. 224]."

This appears to be another case of disciples becoming more fanatical in their zeal than their leader. At any rate, the important point about operationism for our purpose is that the generation of behaviorists that came of age in the late 1920s and 1930s characteristically included operationism in their approach to psychology.

More Recent Behaviorists

Edward Chace Tolman (1886–1959)

One of the very early adherents to behaviorism, Tolman originally studied engineering at the Massachusetts Institute of Technology. He then changed to psychology and studied under Holt at Harvard, where he received his Ph.D. in 1915. Also, in the summer of 1912, he studied under one of the Gestalt psychologists, Kurt Koffka, in Germany. In his last year of graduate work, while being trained in the Wundt–Titchener tradition, Tolman became acquainted with Watsonian behaviorism. Already questioning the scientific usefulness of introspection while still a graduate student, Tolman said in his *Autobiography* (1952) that Watson's behaviorism came as a "tremendous stimulus and relief."

After receiving his degree, Tolman became an instructor at North-western University until 1918, when he went to the University of California at Berkeley. It was at Berkeley, where he taught comparative psychology and conducted research on learning with rats, that he definitely became a behaviorist, though of a different sort than Watson.

There were two interruptions to his career at Berkeley. During World War II, he served in the Office of Strategic Services (1944–1945), and from 1950 to 1953, he was a leader in the spirited and commendable faculty opposition to the California state loyalty oath. During this time he taught at Harvard and the University of Chicago.

Tolman's Purposive Behaviorism

The most definite statement of Tolman's position is presented in his first and most important book, *Purposive Behavior in Animals and Men*, published in 1932. His system of purposive behaviorism might appear, at first glance, to be a curious blending of two contradictory terms: purpose and behavior. Attributing purpose to an organism seems to imply consciousness. Surely such a mentalistic concept can have no place in a behavioristic system.

Tolman made it clear, however, both in this book and in his careful research, that he was very much the behaviorist in both subject matter and methodology, and that he was not urging a return to consciousness for psychology. He vigorously rejected introspection of the structuralist sort. Like Watson, Tolman had no interest in assumed internal experiences that were not accessible to objective observation. Any reference to conscious processes in Tolman's system was phrased in terms of cautious inferences from observed behavior.

It is equally clear, however, that Tolman was not a Watsonian behaviorist, for the two differed in at least two important respects. First, Tolman was not interested in studying behavior at the molecular level, that is, in terms of stimulus–response connections. Thus, unlike Watson, he was not concerned with elemental units of behavior—activities of the nerves, muscles, and glands. His focus was molar behavior—the total response actions of the whole organism. In this respect, his system combines both behavioristic and Gestalt concepts (see Chapter 12).

The major point of difference between Watson and Tolman, however, and the major tenet of Tolman's system, is the introduction of the notion of purposive behavior. Purposiveness in behavior, Tolman said, can be defined in very objective behavioral terms without appeal to introspection or to how the organism might "feel" about the experience. It seemed obvious to Tolman that all behavior is goal directed; the cat tries to get out of the puzzle box, the rat learns a difficult maze, the human studies music. Behavior, he said, "reeks of purpose." All behavior is oriented toward achieving some goal object, learning the means to an end. The rat persistently goes through a maze, making fewer errors, getting to the goal faster and faster each time. In other words, the rat is learning, and the very fact of learning, in a rat or a man, is highly objective behavioral evidence of purpose. Note that Tolman is dealing with the response of the organism, and that his measures are in terms of the response behavior changing as a function of learning; these are highly objective data.

Watsonian behaviorists were quick to criticize this attribution of purpose to behavior for, they argued, did this not rest on the assumption of consciousness in the organism? Tolman's answer was that it made no difference to him whether the animal was conscious or not. The conscious experience (if any) associated with purposing did not in any way influence the behavioral responses of the organism; it was only the overt response behavior that concerned Tolman.

If there is a conscious awareness of the goal, Tolman said, this is a private matter within each individual organism and not available to the objective tools of science. Anything that is internal and cannot be observed from outside the organism is not within the realm of science. Woodworth (1948) described Tolman's argument in the following fashion.

> If I try to describe to you my sensation of the color red, I find it cannot be done. I can point to a red object, I can say that red is somewhat like orange or purple, and very different from green and blue, quite a gay, stimulating color, very nice for a tie but a little too gay for a professor's overcoat—I can put red in many such relations but I cannot describe the sensation itself. I should have the same difficulty in trying to describe my feelings of pleasantness. Now what is essentially private cannot be made the subject matter of science . . . . Only to the extent that private experience can be *reported*, made public, can it have any place in science [p. 106].

INTERVENING VARIABLES. Perhaps Tolman's most unique and, in the long run, most useful contribution to psychology is his concept of the intervening variable. As a behaviorist, Tolman believed that the initiating causes of behavior, and the final resulting behavior itself, must be capable of being objectively observed and operationally defined. He felt that the initiating causes of behavior consist of five independent variables: the environmental stimuli (S), physiological drive (P), heredity (H), previous training (T), and age (A). In the case of animal subjects, the experimenter can control these variables. He would obviously have less control with human subjects. Behavior, then, is a function of these independent variables:

$$B = f_x \ (S, \ P, \ H, \ T, \ A)$$

Between these observable independent variables and the final response measure (the observable dependent or behavior variable), Tolman postulated a set of inferred and nonobserved factors, the intervening variables, which are the actual determinants of behavior. They are the internal processes that connect the antecedent stimulus situation with the observed response. The statement S–R must now read S–O–R. The intervening variable, then, is what is going on within O (the organism) that brings about a given response in reaction to a given stimulus.

This intervening variable cannot. itself be objectively observed and therefore can be of no use to science unless it can be clearly related to both the experimental (independent) variable and the behavior (dependent) variable. The classic example is the intervening variable of hunger, which cannot be seen, as such, in another person or in a rat. Hunger can, however, be precisely and objectively related to an objective experimental variable—the length of time since the organism last had food. It can also be objectively and precisely related to an objective response variable such as the amount of food eaten or how rapidly it is consumed. Thus, this unobservable inferred variable can be given precise empirical referents and is therefore amenable to quantification and experimental manipulation.

Tolman originally proposed two kinds of intervening variables: demand variables and cognitive variables. The demand variables are essentially motives, and include sex, hunger, and demand for safety in the face of danger, for example. The cognitive (or "know-how") variables are abilities, and include perception of objects, motor skills, and the like. In 1951, Tolman revised his intervening variables and proposed three main categories: (1) *need systems*—the physiological deprivation or drive situation at a given moment in time; (2) *belief–value motives*—these represent the intensity of preference for certain goal objects and the relative strengths of these goal objects in satisfying needs; and (3) *behavior-spaces*—behavior takes place in the behavior-space of the individual. In this behavior-space, some objects attract (have a positive valence), whereas others repel (have a negative valence).

Tolman's concept of the intervening variable has been useful to many psychologists, though it has certainly not gone uncriticized. Intervening variables appear to be of value in developing an acceptable theory of behavior so long as they are empirically related to both experimental and behavior variables. Doing this comprehensively and completely, however, is a monumental task.

THEORY OF LEARNING. Tolman felt that all animal and human behavior (with the exception of tropisms and simple reflexes) is capable of modification through experience. Hence, learning plays a major role in his system. He rejected Thorndike's law of effect, saying that reward or reinforcement has little, if any, role in learning. In its place, he proposed a cognitive theory of learning in which the continued performance of a task builds up *sign Gestalts,* which are learned relationships between cues in the environment and the organism's expectations. The animal, he said, gets to know some of his environment.

Let us follow Tolman's system as we watch a hungry rat placed in a maze. The animal moves about in the maze, sometimes in correct alleys and sometimes in blind alleys. Eventually, he discovers the food. In subsequent trials in the maze, Tolman argued, purpose and direction are given to the rat's behavior by the goal. At each choice point, expectations are established. The rat comes to expect that certain cues associated with the choice point will lead on to food. If the rat's expectancy is confirmed (if he gets food), the sign Gestalt of cue expectancy associated with that choice point is strengthened. Over all the choice points in the maze, there is established an entire pattern of sign Gestalts, which Tolman called a "cognitive map." This pattern, according to Tolman, is what the animal learns—a cognitive map of the maze, not a set of motor habits. In a sense, then, the rat establishes a comprehensive "knowledge" of the maze or of any familiar environment. Something like a field map is developed in its brain, enabling it to go from one spot in the environment to another without being restricted to a fixed series of bodily movements.

More than 30 years of research was conducted in Tolman's laboratory, and it is important to consider the nature of some of the research that supports his unique theory of learning.

One of the classic experiments was to investigate the basic question of whether the rat in the maze learns a set of motor responses or a cognitive map of the maze. A cross-shaped maze was used. One set of rats always found food at the same place, even though (using different starting points) the rats had sometimes to turn to the right and other times to the left in order to get to the food. Thus, the motor responses differed, but the place or location of food remained the same.

The second group of rats always made the same response regardless of the starting point, but the food was found in different places. For example, starting from one end of the cross, the rats would find food only by turning to the right at the choice point; when started from the other end of the cross, they also found food only by turning to the right.

The results showed that the "place learners" (the first group) performed significantly better than the "response learners." Tolman said that the same thing occurred with a person who is very familiar with his town or neighborhood. He can go from one point to another by a number of different routes because of the cognitive map that he has developed of the area.

Another type of experiment involved latent learning; that is, learning that is "hidden" and cannot be observed at the time, but occurs nonetheless. A hungry rat was placed in a maze and allowed to wander about freely. There was, however, no food to be found anywhere. Was the rat learning anything in the absence of reinforcement?

After a number of no-reinforcement trials, the rat found food. His improvement thereafter in "running the maze" was extremely rapid, indicating that some learning had taken place. Indeed, his performance very quickly equalled that of a control group which had been reinforced with food on every trial.

Tolman's research on learning has proven highly stimulating to subsequent researchers and has provided considerable support for his position.

Comment

Tolman exercised great influence on psychology, particularly in the area of learning, for a period of more than 40 years; moreover, his influence is still felt in psychology today. He has been criticized for his failure to develop a fully integrated theoretical system, and many feel that he failed to adequately relate behavior to the more covert functioning, such as cognitive states. A further and more obvious point of attack relates to his language, which many feel is too subjective and mentalistic.

On the positive side, Tolman initiated many important research topics in learning and introduced the concept of the intervening variable to psychology. One point of general significance is Tolman's strong support of the use of the rat as an appropriate subject for psychological study. An essay written in 1945 clearly and delightfully states his position on this issue:

> What . . . can we now say as to the contributions of us rodent psychologists to human behavior? What is it that we rat runners

still have to contribute to the understanding of the deeds and the misdeeds, the absurdities and the tragedies of our friend, and our enemy—*homo sapiens?* The answer is that, whereas man's successes, persistences, and socially unacceptable divagations . . . are all ultimately shaped and materialized by specific cultures, it is still true that most of the formal underlying laws of intelligence, motivation, and instability can still be studied in rats as well as, and more easily than, in men.

And, as a final peroration, let it be noted that rats live in cages; they do not go on binges the night before one has planned an experiment; they do not kill each other off in wars; they do not invent engines of destruction, and, if they did, they would not be so inept about controlling such engines; they do not go in for either class conflicts or race conflicts; they avoid politics, economics, and papers on psychology. They are marvelous, pure, and delightful. And, as soon as I possibly can, I am going to climb back again out on that good old phylogenetic limb and sit there, this time right side up and unashamed, wiggling my whiskers at all the silly, yet at the same time far too complicated, specimens of *homo sapiens*, whom I shall see strutting and fighting and messing things up, down there on the ground below me [p. 166].[1]

Edwin Ray Guthrie (1886–1959)

After receiving his Ph.D. in 1912 from the University of Pennsylvania, Guthrie began his academic career in 1914 at the University of Washington, where he remained until his retirement in 1956. While in graduate school, he became an ardent convert to a behavioristic approach to psychology, an approach from which he never wavered. He strongly believed that science must deal only with objectively observable conditions and events. So extreme an empiricist was Guthrie that he opposed the practice of attempting to relate behavioral events to what he considered the invisible brain and nervous system. Although his basic orientation is definitely that of behaviorism, he cannot be described as a Watsonian behaviorist.

His most important influence on psychology is his formulation of an extremely simple learning theory. Variously described as the most persistent advocate of conditioning and the most radical of all those who dealt with association, Guthrie remained for several decades a forceful proponent of a theory of learning based on only one principle—contiguity.

---

[1] From E. C. Tolman, A stimulus-expectancy need-cathexis psychology. *Science,* 1945, **101**, 160–166. Reprinted by permission of the American Association for the Advancement of Science.

In accounting for the strengthening of learned responses, he rejected Thorndike's laws of effect and frequency as well as Pavlovian reinforcement. He relied, instead, on what he called "simultaneous conditioning," which he considered the most general law in psychology.

To Guthrie, all learning or behavior modification depends solely on the contiguity of stimulus and response. Thus, if a stimulus just once elicits a response, then the S–R association is established. It is, in essence, a *one-trial learning* situation, which is his most famous principle. Repetition and reinforcement form no essential part of his system. His primary, and actually his only, formal law of learning states that: "A combination of stimuli which has accompanied a movement will on its recurrence tend to be followed by that movement [1935, p. 26]." Note that there is no mention of internal drive states, of repetitions of the stimulus–response pairings, or of any form of reinforcement. One pairing of the stimulus and the resulting movement serves to establish the association: The behavior is learned.

Note also that the law refers to movements, which Guthrie carefully distinguished from acts. He defined a movement as a pattern of motor and glandular responses or actions. An act, on the other hand, is a movement or series of movements that brings about end results. Although an act is a movement, a movement is not an act. The latter is on a larger scale: Hitting a basket with a ball is an act composed of a number of separate movements. Guthrie believed that in measuring earning, the performance of the complete act is usually taken as the criterion of learning, whereas it is the movements that are actually conditioned as responses.

He considered this focus on the movements as a major distinguishing feature of his theory. He argued that Thorndike, for instance, was concerned with the total act, with the acquisition of a skill (such as a cat escaping from a puzzle box) that is a function of a number of individual muscular movements. These individual movements are developed or acquired in single trials, but learning of the total act calls for repeated practice. The movements, or individual parts of the learned act, are the basic raw data in Guthrie's system. Because they are smaller, these movements are more difficult to observe in a learning situation, which (he explained) is why they are often overlooked.

Just as the response of the organism is composed of a number of separate components, so too is the stimulation to which the organism is exposed. Since the stimulus and response comprise so many components it is necessary to have a large number of pairings of the total stimulus and response situations in order to achieve any degree of consistency in the behavior under question. So, practice is necessary to bring about improvement of the total constellation of movements (the act), but each component movement is learned after just one pairing with the stimulus.

Comment

During his active career, Guthrie seemed to prefer writing and argumentation to experimentation. He believed strongly in the importance of theory for the development of psychology, commenting that theories, not facts, endure. His several books contain evidence of an anecdotal nature, and comparatively little in the way of experimental evidence. There is, however, empirical support for his theory, mainly his own research involving stereotypy in the behavior of the cat in a puzzle box, and the research of a number of others. Compared to some other theoretical positions in neo-behavioristic psychology, however, there is relatively little empirical support. Much of the appeal of Guthrie's system probably rests upon its consistency over the years and its great simplicity. It is indeed a system that is quite easy to understand when compared to other more complex learning theories, particularly that of Hull.

Thus, the inherent simplicity of the system elicits praise from some, but it also provides a point of criticism for others. For instance, it has been suggested that the simplicity has been maintained as a result of Guthrie's failure to deal explicitly with certain major problems in learning that might defy explanation within his framework. Mueller and Schoenfeld (1954) noted, for example, that "It is undoubtedly true that many reviews of Guthrie in the literature have mistaken incompleteness for simplicity [p. 368]." Such critics suggest that a number of additional constructs and assumptions are necessary to encompass the major problem areas of learning.

Nevertheless, Guthrie was able to successfully maintain his theoretical position and stature as a leading learning theorist and his system is still a subject for serious consideration in contemporary psychology. The value of his contributions received formal recognition in 1958 when the American Psychological Foundation presented him with their Gold Medal Award. Finally, it is noted that the recent appearance of statistical models of learning are based largely on the Guthrian scheme.

Clark Leonard Hull (1884–1952)

First and foremost a behaviorist, Hull has achieved a highly respected position in contemporary psychology. Perhaps no previous psychologist had been so consistently and keenly devoted to the problems inherent in scientific method. "Few psychologists have had such a mastery of mathematics and formal logic as Hull had. Hull applied the language of mathematics to psychological theory in a manner used by no other psychologist [Wolman, 1960, p. 105]."

The Life of Hull

For most of his childhood and young adult life, Hull was plagued by poor health. Illnesses of one form or another struck him frequently, and poor eyesight affected him all of his life. At age 24 he contracted polio which left him crippled in one leg.

To add to these difficulties, his family had very little money and his education was interrupted by periods of forced teaching in order to earn money. He did have one asset, however: a driving motivation and aspiration for greatness, and he persevered in the face of many obstacles.

In 1918, at the age of 34, he received his Ph.D. from the University of Wisconsin where he had studied mining engineering before switching to psychology. He remained a member of the faculty at Wisconsin for 10 years.

His early research presaged his lifelong emphasis on objective methods and functional laws. He investigated concept formation and the effects of tobacco on behavioral efficiency, and surveyed the literature on tests and measurements, publishing an important early text in that area in 1928. He also worked on the development of practical methods of statistical analysis, and even invented a machine for calculating correlations.

Hull devoted 10 years to the study of hypnosis and suggestibility, publishing 32 papers and a book, *Hypnosis and Suggestibility* (1933), that summarized the research. In 1929, he became a research professor at Yale, where he developed his final major research interest: a theory of behavior based on Pavlov's laws of conditioning. He had first read Pavlov in 1927 and became greatly interested in the problem of conditioned reflexes and learning.

In the 1930s he wrote a number of articles on conditioning that argued that complex higher–order behaviors could be explained in terms of the basic principles of conditioning. In 1940 he published, with five colleagues, a difficult book, *Mathematico-Deductive Theory of Rote Learning: A Study in Scientific Methodology*. Though it was considered a notable achievement in the development of scientific psychology, it was extremely difficult to understand and so was read by very few.

Hull's next major publication, *Principles of Behavior* (1943), was considerably less difficult to read. In it, he outlined, in great detail and with characteristic precision, a theoretical framework so comprehensive as to include all behavior. With the publication of this book, Hull's system assumed a position of paramount importance and influence in the area of learning in this country, a position it still commands today. A great deal of research was generated by the book, and Hull soon became the most frequently cited psychologist in the field. His system underwent revision in a number of journal articles, and the final revision appeared in *A Behavior System* (1952). Hull had been ill for a number of years, and he died before reading the galley proofs of this book.

Hull's System: The Frame of Reference

Hull believed that human behavior involves a continuing interaction between the organism and the environment. The objective stimuli provided by the environment and the objective behavioral responses provided by the organism are, of course, observable facts. This interaction takes place, however, within a much larger context that cannot be totally defined in observable stimulus–response terms.

This broader context or frame of reference is the biological adaptation of the organism to its unique environment. The survival of the organism is aided by this biological adaptation. Whenever survival is in jeopardy, Hull would consider the organism to be in a state of need. Thus, need involves a situation in which the biological requirements for survival are not being met. When in a state of need, the organism behaves in a manner designed to reduce that need. The behavior, therefore, serves to reinstate the optimal biological conditions necessary for survival.

Hull's concern with biological survival grew out of his interest in certain aspects of evolutionary theory. It is also quite consistent with the functionalists' emphasis on adaptation to the environment.

Hull was, however, totally committed to a behavioristic or objective psychology, allowing no place in his system for consciousness, purpose, or any other mentalistic notion.

Hull's system was an uncompromising radical behaviorism in which he attempted to reduce every concept he used to physicalistic terms. Even though his methodological behaviorism was perhaps even more rigid than Watson's, he did allow for the notion of intervening variables. These variables, however, were closely and concretely tied to highly objective stimulus and response conditions that could be quantified and measured with precision.

His system, as his image of man, was very definitely couched in mechanistic terms. He regarded human behavior as automatic and cyclical, capable of reduction to the terminology of physics.

Overall, he persistently warned against the intrusion of "anthropomorphic subjectivism"—giving subjective interpretation of the behavior being observed. The observation and interpretation of behavior must be uncompromisingly objective, and one way of attaining this, Hull suggested, is to think in terms of the behavior of animals. However, even this has its dangers.

> [It] all too often breaks down when the theorist begins thinking what he would do if he were a rat, a cat, or a chimpanzee; when that happens, all his knowledge of his own behavior, born of years of self-observation, at once begins to function in place of the objectively stated general rules or principles which are the proper substance of science [Hull, 1943, p. 27].

There must be, then, an even more rigid safeguard against subjectivism, and Hull found it in an attitude which considers "the behaving organism as a completely self-maintaining robot, constructed of materials as unlike ourselves as may be [Hull, 1943, p. 27]."

Thus, the behaviorist should take a "robot" view of his subject matter. The spirit of mechanism from the mechanical figures of European seventeenth century gardens was faithfully followed and strengthened in Hull's work.

One advantage of this robot approach, according to Hull, is that it prevents the reifying of behavior, that is, explaining behavior by attributing it to causes other than strictly mechanical ones.

Clearly, there is little, if any, difference between psychology and physics, as far as Hull is concerned. Indeed, any such difference is, as he states, only in degree, not in kind.

METHODOLOGY. Our discussion of Hull's mechanistic, reductionistic, and totally objective behaviorism provides a clear view of what his methods of study must be. Obviously, they are characterized by as much objectivity as possible.

In addition, Hull's approach to psychology is characterized by quantification. The laws of behavior, he argued, must be stated or expressed in the precise language of mathematics. Quantification therefore became a second cornerstone on which he erected his behaviorism.

Psychologists, he said, must not only develop a thorough understanding of mathematics, they must *think* mathematics. At the end of *Principles of Behavior* (1943) Hull wrote how such a mathematically defined psychology would proceed.

> Progress . . . will consist in the laborious writing, one by one, of hundreds of equations; in the experimental determination, one by one, of hundreds of the empirical constants contained in the equa-

tions; in the devising of practically usable units in which to measure the quantities expressed by the equations; in the objective definition of hundreds of symbols appearing in the equations; in the rigorous deduction, one by one, of thousands of theorems and corollaries from the primary definitions and equations; in the meticulous performance of thousands of critical quantitative experiments . . . [pp. 400–401].

This statement provides a good indication of the high degree of rigor (and patience) needed by a follower of the Hullian system.

In terms of specific research methodology, Hull believed there were four methods that could be useful to science. Three methods then in current use included (*1*) simple observation, (*2*) systematic controlled observation, and (*3*) experimental testing of hypotheses. In addition, Hull argued for strict adherence to the *hypothetico–deductive method*, which utilizes rigorous deduction from a set of formulations that are determined in *a priori* fashion. The method involves establishing postulates from which experimentally testable conclusions can be deduced. These conclusions are then submitted to experimental test: Failure results in revision; verification allows for their incorporation into the body of science. Hull believed that if psychology was to be an objective science on the order of other natural sciences (in accord with the behavioristic program), then the only appropriate method was the hypothetico–deductive one.

DRIVES. As mentioned earlier, Hull considered bodily need arising from a deviation from optimal biological conditions as the basis of motivation. However, rather than introduce the concept of biological need as such directly into his system, he postulated the intervening variable of drive, a term that had already come into use in psychology. Drive was posited as a stimulus (S_D) that arises from a state of tissue need and that functions to arouse or activate behavior. The strength of the drive, Hull noted, can be empirically determined in terms of either the length of deprivation, or the intensity, strength, or energy expenditure of the resulting behavior. He considered the duration of deprivation a rather imperfect index, and he placed greater emphasis on behavior strength.

It is important to note that Hull considered drive as nonspecific. In other words, any kind of deprivation—food, water, sex—contributed in the same way (though perhaps in differing degrees) to the drive. This nonspecificity means that drive does not direct or guide behavior, rather it functions solely to energize behavior. All the steering or guiding of behavior is accomplished by environmental stimuli. Also, according to Hull, drive reduction is the sole basis for reinforcement.

There are two major kinds of drives in Hull's system: primary and secondary. The primary drives are associated with the biological need states and are directly and intimately involved with the organism's survival. These drives arise from a state of tissue need, and include hunger, thirst, air, temperature regulation, defecation, urination, sleep, activity, sexual intercourse, relief from pain, etc. These are basic innate processes of the organism and vitally necessary for survival.

In addition, Hull recognized that both humans and animals are also motivated by forces other than the basic primary drives. Accordingly, he postulated the secondary or learned drives. The secondary drive concept refers to situations (or other stimuli in the environment) that are associated with the reduction of primary drives and that may, as a result, become drives themselves. This means that previously neutral stimuli assume drive characteristics because they are capable of eliciting responses that are similar to those aroused by the original need state or primary drive. A simple example involves being burned by a stove. The painful burn (tissue damage) produces a primary drive (relief from pain). Other stimuli associated with this primary drive, such as the sight of the stove, may lead to the withdrawing of the hand when the visual stimulus is perceived. Thus, the sight of the stove may become the stimulus for the learned drive of fear. These secondary drives or motivating forces develop on the basis of the primary drives.

Since Hull postulated learned drives, learning obviously plays a key part in his system.

LEARNING. Hull's system is basically and primarily concerned with motivation. This may surprise those who first heard of Hull in discussions of learning. Certainly he focused great attention on problems of learning but, as Cofer and Appley (1964) noted, "learning was, in the last analysis, only an instrumentality that permitted an organism to extend the range and variety of its efforts to satisfy its needs . . . [p. 469]." In the course of developing his system, Hull became less concerned with learning and more concerned with other factors capable of influencing behavior, although he is best known and most frequently studied in terms of his theory of learning.

Probably the most important part of Hull's theory is his attempt to integrate, or at least reconcile, Thorndike's law of effect with Pavlovian conditioning. He believed that learning could not be adequately explained by the principles of recency and frequency. Instead, the major focus of his learning theory is on the principle of reinforcement, which is essentially Thorndike's effect principle.

Hull's famous law of primary reinforcement states that if a stimulus–response relationship is followed by a reduction in need, then on subsequent occasions, the probability is high that the same stimulus will evoke the same response. Note that reward or reinforcement is defined not in terms of Thorndike's notion of satisfaction, but rather in terms of reduction of a primary need. Thus, primary reinforcement, referring to the reduction of a primary drive, is the cornerstone of Hull's system of learning. Just as his system contains secondary drives, it also deals with secondary reinforcement. If a secondary or learned drive brings about a reduction in the intensity of the stimulus, it will act as a secondary reinforcement. As Hull stated it:

> It follows that any stimulus consistently associated with a reinforcement situation will through that association acquire the power of evoking the conditioned inhibition, i.e., reduction in stimulus intensity, and so of itself producing the resulting reinforcement. Since this indirect power of reinforcement is acquired through learning, it is called *secondary reinforcement* [1951, pp. 27–28].

Hull believed that the stimulus–response connection is strengthened by the number of reinforcements that have taken place. He called the strength of the S–R connection habit strength, which refers to the persistence of the conditioning and is a function of reinforcement.

Learning cannot take place in the absence of reinforcement that is necessary to bring about a reduction of the drive. Because of this emphasis on reinforcement, Hull's system is called a need-reduction theory, as opposed to Guthrie's contiguity theory and Tolman's cognitive theory.

Hull's system is presented in terms of highly specific and detailed postulates and corollaries, all of which are phrased in difficult verbal and mathematical form. In his last presentation (*A Behavior System*, 1952) there are 18 postulates and 12 corollaries. Though the system was based originally upon conditioning principles, Hull believed that his fundamental position could be elaborated upon to include complex processes such as problem solving, social behavior, and forms of learning other than conditioning. He lived to see only a portion of this ambition realized.

Comment

This overview of Hull's system is, of course, far too brief to encompass the enormous scope of his work. Our purpose, when dealing with these contemporary systems, is to point out how such newer developments derive from or grow out of older ways of thinking. There is a continuity of development in psychology, and our brief discussions of contemporary derivatives of past systems are intended to provide an appreciation of the relevance of the past for the present.

Hull's system has remained in a continuous state of development, and even after his death cannot be considered "finished." His students and his students' students are still actively engaged in research. The older systems we have discussed are finished in the sense that proponents of them are no longer conducting research. Such systems *qua* systems are extinct (though, in some cases, their spirit lingers on). It remains for future books on the history of psychology to attempt to evaluate whether Hull's program will have made lasting contributions to psychological theory. It is not yet history.

The system has, however, achieved a position of such prominence that it has generated a great deal of criticism since its inception. This, in itself, constitutes evidence of its wide influence in psychology. A few of the more general points of criticism are noted.

As a leading exponent of neo-behaviorism, Hull is subject to the same general kinds of criticism aimed at Watson and others who followed the behavioristic tradition. Thus, those who oppose a behavioristic approach to psychology on methodological and theoretical grounds include Hull among those in the "enemy camp."

A specific criticism of Hull's system is its lack of generalizability. It has been asserted that, in his attempt to define his variables with such total precision in quantitative terms, he operated too specifically, functioning at times on a narrow miniature system basis. His approach was, in other words, extremely particularistic, in that he often formulated his postulates from results of single experimental situations. Many opponents argue that generalization to all behavior on the basis of such extremely specific experimental demonstrations is questionable.

As Hilgard (1956) stated the problem:

> Surely a set of laws of mammalian behavior ought not reflect in the constants of its basic postulates such specialized information as the most favorable interval for human eyelid conditioning (Postulate 2), . . . the weight in grams of food needed to condition a rat (Postulate 7), . . . or the amplitude in millimeters of galvanometer deflection in human conditioning (Postulate 15) [p. 181].

While precise quantification is certainly necessary and commendable in a natural science approach to psychology, Hull's extreme approach does tend to reduce the range of applicability of the findings.

Thus, we see that Hull's adherence to a mathematical and formal system of theory building is open to both praise and criticism at the same time. Wolman (1960) suggested that "Hull became, to a certain extent, a victim of his zest for mathematics. . . . Whenever the opportunity came, he quantified his statements, sometimes pursuing the issue *ad absurdum* . . . [p. 124]." His system is so thoroughly and minutely developed in quantitative terms that incomplete or inaccurate formulations are relatively easy to spot. Gaps and inconsistencies in a theory expressed in ordinary verbal terms can be easily filled in with appropriate illustrative examples. Some critics have found such gaps in Hull's system and argue that at least some parts of Hull's formulations are not as tightly constructed as was originally thought.

Damaging though the criticisms are, Hull's enormous influence on contemporary psychology cannot be minimized. We have already mentioned the great amount of research occasioned by Hull's work, perhaps more than by any other theory; this alone constitutes a major contribution to psychology. He provided an objective terminology that was not only well accepted but that represented a new approach to psychological data rather than a simple relabeling of older concepts.

Marx and Hillix (1973) suggest that no other psychologist has had such a pronounced and extensive effect on the professional motivation of so many other psychologists. He defended, extended, and expounded the strictly objective behavioristic approach as had never been done before.

Perhaps it is true that Hull's contribution to systematic psychological theory building in general is greater than his own theory, but as noted earlier, it is still too close in time to fully determine this. While many psychologists question parts or all of Hull's theory, there is general respect and admiration for the rigorous methods used to develop it. Lowry (1971) noted that "It is not often in any field that a true theoretical genius comes along; of the very few to whom psychology can lay claim, Hull must surely rank among the foremost [p. 183]." It is also a tribute to the greatness of the man to note a few of the more contemporary leading psychologists who are his disciples and followers: Dollard, Hovland, Kimble, Miller, Mowrer, and Spence.

Burrhus Frederick Skinner (1904–   )

B. F. Skinner has become the most important and influential individual in psychology today. His areas of interest over his long career, and their implications for modern man, are diverse.

The magazine *Psychology Today* called him "very much the man of today," and added that, "when history makes its judgment, he may well be known as the major contributor to psychology in this century [Hall, 1967, p. 21]."

For many years Skinner has been America's leading behaviorist with a large, loyal, and enthusiastic band of followers. He has developed a program for behavioral control of societies, invented an automatic crib for the care of infants, and is, more than anyone else, responsible for the large-scale use of teaching machines. In addition, he wrote a novel (*Walden Two*) which continues to be popular 25 years after publication, and, in 1971, his book, *Beyond Freedom and Dignity*, became a nationwide best seller. He has published many professional articles and books and has been compared to Sir Francis Galton in terms of the diversity and scope of his interests.

The Life of Skinner

Skinner was born and raised in a small town in northeastern Pennsylvania where he lived until he went away to college. By his own report, his childhood environment was "warm and stable." He attended the same high school from which his parents had graduated; there were only seven others in his graduating class.

He liked school and was always the first to arrive every morning. As a child and adolescent, he was interested in building things: sleds, wagons, rafts, merry-go-rounds, slingshots, model airplanes, and even a steam cannon with which he shot potato and carrot plugs over the roofs of his neighbors' houses. He spent years trying to develop a perpetual motion machine, but did not succeed.

On the advice of a family friend, Skinner enrolled in Hamilton College where, as he wrote:

> I never fitted into student life . . . I joined a fraternity without knowing what it was all about. I was not good at sports and suffered acutely as my shins were cracked in ice hockey or better players bounced basketballs off my cranium. . . . In a paper I wrote at the end of my freshman year, I complained that the college was pushing me around with unnecessary requirements (one of them daily chapel) and that almost no intellectual interest was shown by most of the students. By my senior year I was in open revolt [1967, p. 392].

As part of his "open revolt," Skinner participated in a series of hoaxes that greatly disrupted the college community, and indulged in verbal attacks on the faculty and administration. His revolt continued right up to graduation day when, at commencement ceremonies, the college president warned Skinner and his friends that if they did not settle down they would not graduate.

Skinner did graduate with a degree in English, a Phi Beta Kappa key, and a strong desire to become a writer. Even as a child, he had written poems and stories, and in 1925, at a summer writing school, Robert Frost commented favorably on his work.

For 2 years after his graduation, Skinner worked at writing, but then, deciding that he had "nothing important to say," he enrolled as a graduate student at Harvard where he developed the rigorous program of self-discipline that continues to characterize his career.

> I would rise at six, study until breakfast, go to classes, laboratories, and libraries with no more than fifteen minutes unscheduled during the day, study until exactly nine o'clock at night and go to bed. I saw no movies or plays, seldom went to concerts, had scarcely any dates and read nothing but psychology and physiology [Skinner, 1967, p. 398].

He maintained this schedule for 2 years and in 1931 received his Ph.D. His dissertation topic provides an early glimpse of the position to which he has consistently adhered throughout his career. His major proposition was that a reflex is the correlation between a stimulus and a response, and nothing more.

Following several years of postdoctoral fellowships, Skinner taught at the University of Minnesota (1936–1945) and Indiana University (1945–1947). In 1947 he returned to Harvard, where he has remained. In 1938 *The Behavior of Organisms* was published. It details the basic points of his system. *Science and Human Behavior* (1953) was written as a textbook for his behavioristic psychology.

Skinner's System: General Approach

In a number of important respects, Skinner's position represents a renewal of the older Watsonian behaviorism. As MacLeod stated, "Watson's spirit is indestructible. Cleaned and purified, it breathes through the writings of B. F. Skinner [1959, p. 34]."

Hull, as we have seen, was also a behaviorist, but there are marked differences between Hull's and Skinner's approaches to psychology. Whereas Hull stressed the importance of theory, Skinner advocates a strictly empirical system with no theoretical framework within which to conduct research. Where Hull's work consisted of postulating theory on an *a priori* basis and then checking the deduced conclusions against experimental evidence, Skinner avoids theory completely and practices instead a strict brand of positivism. Skinner begins with empirical data and then proceeds very carefully and slowly (if at all) toward tentative generalizations. Hull represents the deductive method; Skinner represents the inductive method.

His point of view is summarized in this way:

> I never attacked a problem by constructing a Hypothesis. I never deduced Theorems or submitted them to Experimental check. So far as I can see I had no preconceived Model of Behavior—certainly not a physiological or mentalistic one, and I believe not a conceptual one . . . [Skinner, 1956, p. 227].

Skinner's position is an exclusively descriptive kind of strict behaviorism devoted to the study of responses; it is atheoretical in nature. Thus, his concern is with describing behavior rather than explaining it. He deals only with observable behavior and believes that the task of scientific inquiry is to establish functional relations between the antecedent experimenter-controlled stimulus conditions and the organism's subsequent response.

Skinner is not at all concerned with theorizing or speculating about what might be going on inside the organism. His program includes no reference to presumed internal entities, whether described as intervening variables or as physiological processes. Whatever might occur between the stimulus and the response does not represent objective data for a Skinnerian behaviorist. This purely descriptive behaviorism has been called, with good reason, the "empty-organism approach."

It is important to note that while Skinner's system is atheoretical, he is not totally against theorizing. Rather, he has opposed premature theorizing—theorizing in the absence of adequate supporting data.

In an interview in 1968, he said that he looks forward "to an overall theory of human behavior which will bring together a lot of facts and express them in a general way. That kind of theory I would be very much interested in prompting . . . [Evans, 1968, p. 88]."

In contrast to much of contemporary psychology, Skinner does not believe in the use of large numbers of subjects and statistical comparisons between mean responses of groups. Instead, he has focused on the intense and thorough investigation of a single subject:

> A prediction of what the *average* individual will do is often of little or no value in dealing with a particular individual. . . . a science is helpful in dealing with the individual only insofar as its laws refer to individuals. A science of behavior which concerns only the behavior of groups is not likely to be of help in our understanding of the particular case [Skinner, 1953, p. 19].

Skinner believes that truly valid replicable results can be obtained without the use of statistical analysis if a large body of data is collected from a single subject under very well-controlled experimental conditions. He argues that the use of a large group of subjects rather much forces the experimenter to attend to the average behavior of the group. As a result, individual response behavior and individual differences in behavior will not appear as a part of the data of the experiment. In 1958, the Skinnerians established their *Journal for the Experimental Analysis of Behavior,* because of the unwritten requirements of the existing journals concerning subject sample size and statistical analysis.

OPERANT CONDITIONING. All psychology students are aware of the Skinner box and of Skinner's emphasis on operant as opposed to respondent behavior. In the Pavlovian conditioning situation, a known stimulus is paired with a response under conditions of reinforcement. The behavioral response is elicited by a specific observable stimulus situation and is called, by Skinner, a respondent behavior.

Operant behavior, on the other hand, occurs without any observable external stimuli. The organism's response is seemingly spontaneous in that it is not related to any known observable stimulus. This is not to say that there is definitely no stimulus eliciting the response, but rather that no stimulus is detected when the response occurs. Thus, as far as the experimenter is concerned, there is no stimulus because he has not applied any and cannot see any.

Another difference between the two kinds of response behavior is that operant behavior operates on the organism's environment while respondent behavior does not. The harnessed dog in Pavlov's laboratory can do nothing but respond when the experimenter presents the stimulus. The dog cannot act "on his own" to secure the stimulus. The operant behavior of the rat in the Skinner box, however, is instrumental in securing the stimulus (food): When the rat presses the bar, it secures food, and it does not get any food until it does press the bar. Skinner feels that operant behavior is much more representative of the real-life human learning situation. Hence, since behavior is mostly of the operant variety, the most effective approach to a science of behavior, according to Skinner, is the study of the conditioning and extinction of operant behaviors.

Skinner's classic experimental demonstration involved bar pressing in the Skinner box that was especially constructed to eliminate all extraneous stimuli. In this experiment, a rat that had been deprived of food was placed in the box and allowed to explore. In the course of this general exploratory behavior the rat sooner or later, and by accident, depressed a lever activating a food magazine that released a food pellet into a tray. After a few reinforcements, conditioning was usually very rapid. Note that the rat's behavior operated on the environment (pressed the lever) and was instrumental in securing food. The dependent variable in this kind of experiment is a simple and direct one; the rate of the response. A cumulative recorder attached to the Skinner box keeps a moment-by-moment record of the rate of bar pressing.

From this basic experiment, Skinner derived his law of acquisition, which states that the strength of an operant is increased when that operant is followed by presentation of a reinforcing stimulus. Although practice is important in the establishment of high rates of bar pressing, the key variable is reinforcement. Practice by itself will not increase the rate; all it does is provide the opportunity for additional reinforcement to occur.

Skinner's law of acquisition differs from the positions of Thorndike and Hull on learning. First, Skinner does not speak in terms of any pleasure–pain consequences of reinforcement, as did Thorndike. In opposition to Hull, Skinner makes no attempt to interpret reinforcement in terms of drive reduction. Whereas the systems of Thorndike and Hull are explanatory, Skinner's is descriptive. Skinner does not view drive as a stimulus or a physiological state. Rather, he considers drive as simply a set of operations that influence response behavior in a certain way. He defines drive quite objectively in terms of number of hours of deprivation.

Skinner and his followers have conducted a great deal of research on numerous problems in learning. Their studies included the role of punishment in the acquisition of responses, the effect of different schedules of reinforcement, extinction of operant response, secondary reinforcement, and generalization, among other things.

In recent years, Skinner has worked with animals other than rats, as well as with human subjects, using the same basic approach as the Skinner box. With pigeons, the operant behavior involves pecking at a spot with food as a reinforcement. The operant behavior for human subjects involves problem solving reinforced by verbal approval or by knowledge of having given the correct answer.

SCHEDULES OF REINFORCEMENT. To many psychologists, Skinner's most notable research is that devoted to the determination of schedules of reinforcement. The initial research on bar pressing in the Skinner box demonstrated the necessary role of reinforcement in operant behavior. In that situation, the rat's behavior was reinforced for every bar press; that is, it received food every time it made the correct response.

However, as Skinner points out, in the real world reinforcement is not always so consistent or continuous, and yet learning occurs and behaviors continue even when reinforced only intermittently. There are many examples.

> We do not always find good ice or snow when we go skating or skiing. . . . We do not always get a good meal in a particular restaurant because cooks are not always predictable. We do not always get an answer when we telephone a friend because the friend is not always at home. . . . The reinforcements characteristic of industry and education are almost always intermittent because it is not feasible to control behavior by reinforcing every response [Skinner, 1953, p. 99].

Think of your own lives. Even though you may study consistently well, you may not get an "A" on every examination or term paper. If you have a job, you do not receive praise or a pay increase every day. In a football pool or at a slot machine you do not win every time.

How is behavior affected by such intermittent reinforcement? Are there different schedules of reinforcement that are optimum in terms of influencing behavior? Skinner and his colleagues devoted years of research to these questions.

One set of experiments compared the response rate of animals reinforced for every response versus those reinforced only after a certain time interval. This is known as *fixed-interval reinforcement*. A reinforcement could be given, for instance, every 1 minute or every 4 minutes. The point is that the reinforcement does not in any way depend on the animal's making a certain number of responses. It depends solely on the passage of a fixed interval of time.

The research has shown that the shorter the interval between reinforcements, the more rapidly the animal will respond. Conversely, as the interval between reinforcements gets longer, the rate of responding falls off.

The frequency of reinforcement also affects the extinguishing of a response. Behaviors are extinguished more quickly when they have been reinforced continuously (and the reinforcement then stopped) as compared to a schedule of intermittent reinforcement. Some pigeons have responded as many as 10,000 times in the absence of reinforcement when they had been conditioned intermittently.

In addition to the fixed-interval schedule of reinforcement, there is the *fixed-ratio reinforcement*. In this case, reinforcement is presented not after a certain time interval, but after a predetermined number of responses. The animal thus determines how often he will be reinforced;

he must respond, for example, 20 times after the last reinforcement in order to get another.

Not surprisingly, animals on a fixed-ratio schedule respond much faster than those on a fixed-interval schedule. Responding faster on fixed-interval reinforcement will not make any difference; whether the animal presses the bar 5 times or 50 times, he will still be reinforced only when the predetermined time interval has passed.

The higher rate of responding on the fixed-ratio schedule has been found to hold true for rats and pigeons as well as man. A fixed-ratio schedule of payment is used in industry and business where a worker's pay depends on how many units he produces, or a salesman's commission is determined by how much he sells.

The fixed-ratio schedule is very effective, providing the ratio is not set at too high a level (that is, an impossible amount of work required for each unit of pay or reinforcement), and providing the reinforcement is worth the effort.

Other reinforcement schedules include variable ratios, variable intervals, and other forms of mixed schedules. The research is discussed in *Schedules of Reinforcement* (1957) by C. B. Ferster and Skinner, and *Contingencies of Reinforcement* (Skinner, 1969).

VERBAL BEHAVIOR.   Skinner has long had an interest in verbal behavior, the only area in which he sees any difference between rat and man. The sounds the human organism makes in speech, he argues, are responses that can be reinforced (by other speech sounds or gestures) in the same way a rat's bar-pressing behavior can be reinforced by food.

For the infant, the sounds that will be reinforced obviously depend on the culture in which he is being raised, but the "mechanics" of verbal behavior apply independently of the culture.

Verbal behavior, Skinner said, requires two people in interaction—one speaking and one listening. The speaker makes a response; that is, utters a sound. The listener, by his behavior in reinforcing, not reinforcing, or punishing the speaker for what he has said, can control the speaker's subsequent behavior.

For example, if every time the speaker uses a certain word or a certain category of words, the listener smiles or says, "That's nice," he increases the probability of the speaker's using that category of words again.

By the same token, if the listener responds by frowning, making angry gestures, or commenting unfavorably at certain words, he increases the probability that the speaker will avoid those words.

One can see this in the behavior of parents when their children are learning to speak. "Naughty" words or incorrect usage or poor pronunciation bring forth different reactions from correct usage and pronunciation. In this way the child is taught the proper use of speech (at least as his parents understand it).

These simple examples do not, of course, reflect the great complexity of Skinner's work in this field. The point to be established is that, to Skinner, speech is behavior and is therefore subject to contingencies of reinforcement and prediction and control. His work in this area is summarized in *Verbal Behavior* (1957).

The Machines of Skinner's Behaviorism

We have already discussed the famous Skinner box and its use in operant conditioning, but that was not the only machine Skinner developed.[2]

The Skinner box brought him prominence in psychology, but it was another invention that first gained him prominence (or at least notoriety) among the general public. In 1945, in an article in the *Ladies Home Journal*, he first described his "aircrib"—a device to mechanize the care of an infant.

It seems that when Skinner and his wife decided they wanted another child, she protested that caring for them through their first 2 years required too much attention and menial labor. And so Skinner invented a way of relieving mothers of that task. The aircribs were made available commercially but never became a big success. The aircrib

> is a large, air-conditioned, temperature controlled, germ free, sound-proof compartment in which a baby can sleep and play without blankets or clothing other than a diaper. It allows complete freedom of movement, and relative safety from the usual colds and heat rashes [Rice, 1968, p. 98].

Skinner raised his second child in an aircrib. Except for a broken leg in a skiing accident—while out of the box—she apparently suffered no ill effects, even growing to beat Skinner at chess.

Skinner's best known apparatus is the teaching machine. This too grew out of his own experience. After visiting his daughter's fourth grade class, he commented, "It's absolutely horrible. They're ruining minds over there. I can do something much better [Rice, 1968, p. 98]."

Whether he did or not is a subject of much controversy, but there is no denying that teaching machines (or "programmed learning") have been put to use in a great many areas, from elementary mathematics

[2] Skinner is reported to deplore the term "Skinner box" as a label for his "operant conditioning apparatus" (Hall, 1967, p. 22).

to music. In 1968 Skinner published the aptly titled *The Technology of Teaching*!

Walden Two—A Behavioristic Society

B. F. Skinner, more than any other behaviorist, has mapped out a program of behavioral control in which he attempts to transpose the findings from his laboratory to society at large. What he has tried to develop is a "technology of behavior." Whereas Watson talked in general terms about a "foundation for saner living" through the principles of conditioning, Skinner has outlined in detail the mechanics of such a society.

In 1948 he published a novel, *Walden Two*, which describes a 1000-member rural community in which every aspect of life, from birth on, is "controlled" by positive reinforcement. The book was both hailed and reviled in reviews, and never sold more than a few thousand copies a year until the early 1960s when, for some reason, sales increased sharply. The book continues to be popular today; it is required reading in many college courses and is voluntarily read by thousands.

A national Walden Two conference was held in 1966 and small Walden Two communities have been reported in several parts of the United States. One such community, Twin Oaks (Louisa, Virginia 23093), publishes a newsletter for those interested in how their experiment is working.[3]

The long line of thought from Galileo and Newton through the British empiricists, to Wundt and Watson, reaches its culmination in Skinner's designed society and his basic assumption about the nature of man-the-machine.

> If we are to use the methods of science in the field of human affairs, we must assume that behavior is lawful and determined. . . . that what a man does is the result of specifiable conditions and that once these conditions have been discovered, we can anticipate and to some extent determine his actions [Skinner, 1953, p. 6].

The mechanistic, analytic, and deterministic approach of natural science, reinforced by Skinner's conditioning experiments, convinces the behaviorists that human behavior can be controlled, guided, modified, and shaped by the proper use of positive reinforcement.

In the free will–determinism controversy, it is easy to see on which

---

[3] See also K. Kinkade, *A Walden Two Experiment: The First Five Years of Twin Oaks Community* (New York: Morrow, 1973). Foreword by B. F. Skinner.

side of the fence the Skinnerians sit. Skinner makes the point over and over again that

> the issue of personal freedom must not be allowed to interfere with a scientific analysis of human behavior. . . . We cannot expect to profit from applying the methods of science to human behavior if for some extraneous reason we refuse to admit that our subject matter can be controlled [1953, p. 322].

This position is discussed in *Beyond Freedom and Dignity* (1971). The book has generated a great deal of publicity, brought about Skinner's appearance on several television talk shows, and become a best seller. As with *Walden Two*, this book was praised by some and derided by others. But the fact that it was bought (and presumably read) by many thousands of laymen demonstrates a great deal of public curiosity—if not acceptance—of the Skinnerian position.

Comment

However one might view Skinner's work—as a savior or enslaver of man (and it is difficult to take a neutral position)—there is no denying the extent of his influence on contemporary psychology. As with Hull's system, Skinner's system is not yet history and so the judgment that the perspective of time allows cannot be made.

Skinner certainly has received much criticism, both from inside and outside the psychological "establishment." His attitude toward his critics is simply to ignore them. As he said when discussing a particularly scathing review of one of his books, "I read a bit of it and saw that he missed the point, so I never read the rest. I never answer any of my critics. I generally don't even read them. There are better things to do with my time than clear up their misunderstanding [Rice, 1968, p. 90]."

Perhaps the most frequent criticism is directed at Skinner's extreme brand of positivism and its accompanying opposition to theory. Opponents argue that it is impossible to eliminate all theorizing, as Skinner would have it. Since the details of an experiment are planned in advance of the actual situation, this in itself, critics claim, is evidence of theorizing, however simple. It has been noted that Skinner's acceptance of the basic principles of conditioning as the framework for his research constitutes some degree of theorizing. Further, Skinner has made very confident assertions about economic, social, political, and religious affairs of human conduct that apparently are derived from his system. This willingness to extrapolate beyond his basic data, particularly in regard to proposals about complex human problems, is also inconsistent with his antitheory stand. Certainly, critics argue, he has gone beyond the observable data when he presents large-scale blueprints for the redesign of society; this seems contrary to the principles of his system.

The narrow range of behavior actually studied in Skinnerian laboratories has also been attacked—such items as bar pressing and key pecking (with pigeons). Critics argue that numerous aspects or examples of behavior have been largely ignored.

As to which will assume precedence in the long run—the criticism or the praise (both of which are substantial)—no one can say at the present time. It can and must be said, however, that Skinner is the incontestable leader and champion of a behavioristic psychology, and that contemporary American psychology is molded more by his work than by the work of any other psychologist in history. Even most of his critics would be forced to agree with that.

Contemporary psychology has noted the magnitude of Skinner's contribution and, in 1958, the American Psychological Association granted him their Distinguished Scientific Contribution Award, with the following citation.

> An imaginative and creative scientist, characterized by great objectivity in scientific matters and by warmth and enthusiasm in personal contacts. Choosing simple operant behavior as subject matter, he has challenged alternative analyses of behavior, insisting that description take precedence over hypotheses. By careful control of experimental conditions, he has produced data which are relatively free from fortuitous variation. Despite his antitheoretical position, he is considered an important systematist and has developed a self-consistent description of behavior which has greatly increased our ability to predict and control the behavior of organisms from rat to man. Few American psychologists have had so profound an impact on the development of psychology and on promising younger psychologists [APA, Committee on Distinguished Scientific Contribution Awards, 1958b, p. 735].

In 1968 he was awarded the National Medal of Science, the highest accolade given by the United States government for distinguished contribution to science. In 1971 the American Psychological Foundation presented him its gold medal.

Concluding Commentary on Behaviorism

Behaviorism, like all the other systematic positions, has a very long past, as we have seen in these three chapters. Watson gave voice to the changing climate of the times in American psychology, revolted against its mentalistic background, and formally established a completely objective science of behavior. This vigorous Watsonian revolt marked the beginning of the strong positivistic era in American psychology, which seems to have grown even stronger with each passing year. There have followed, immediately and up to the present day, highly enthusiastic formulations of many different forms of behaviorism, and the general American acceptance of the spirit of operationism.

Although behaviorism as a formal school is dead, the neo-behavioristic spirit still flourishes, albeit as a general point of view or attitude rather than as a formal school, for behaviorism has evolved into the American tradition in experimental psychology. No psychologist today calls himself a behaviorist—it is no longer necessary to do so. To the extent that American experimental psychology is today objective, mechanistic, empirical, reductionistic, and (to some degree) environmentalistic, the spirit, if not the letter, of Watsonian behaviorism lives on. Fifty years after the publication of Watson's article, which formally began behaviorism, Skinner celebrated the anniversary with his article, *Behaviorism at Fifty* (1963), in which he noted that the tremendous progress in experimental psychology in America has been due primarily to the influence of behaviorism.

In recent years, however, a small but vocal group of psychologists has begun to question the behavioristic point of view. Their numbers appear to be growing, and they may represent the beginning of a disinclination to view psychology wholly as a science of behavior. It is still too early to assess this so-called humanistic movement (indeed, perhaps too early to call it a movement), but it does exist, and is discussed in Chapter 15.

SUGGESTED FURTHER READINGS

Lashley

Beach, F. A., Hebb, D. O., Morgan, C. T., & Nissen, H. W. (Eds.) *The neuropsychology of Lashley.* New York: McGraw-Hill, 1960.

Carmichael, L. Karl Spencer Lashley, experimental psychologist. *Science,* 1959, **129**, 1409–1412.

Operationism

Bergmann, G. Sense and nonsense in operationism. *Scientific Monthly,* 1954, **79**, 210–214.

Bridgman, P. W. Remarks on the present state of operationism. *Scientific Monthly,* 1954, **79**, 224–226.

Margenau, H. On interpretations and misinterpretations of operationalism. *Scientific Monthly,* 1954, **79**, 209–210.

Stevens, S. S. The operational basis of psychology. *American Journal of Psychology,* 1935, **47**, 323–330.

Tolman

MacCorquodale, K., & Meehl, P. E. Edward C. Tolman. In W. Estes, S. Koch, K. MacCorquodale, P. E. Meehl, C. G. Mueller, Jr., W. N. Schoenfeld, & W. Verplanck (Eds.), *Modern learning theory*. New York: Appleton, 1954. Pp. 177–266.

Tolman, E. C. Principles of purposive behavior. In S. Koch (Ed.), *Psychology: A study of a science*. Vol. 2. New York: McGraw-Hill, 1959. Pp. 92–157.

Guthrie

Guthrie, E. R. *The psychology of learning*. New York: Harper, 1935. (Rev. ed., 1952.)

Mueller, C. G., Jr., & Schoenfeld, W. N. Edwin R. Guthrie. In W. Estes, S. Koch, K. MacCorquodale, P. E. Meehl, C. G. Mueller, Jr., W. N. Schoenfeld, & W. Verplanck (Eds.), *Modern learning theory*. New York: Appleton, 1954. Pp. 345–379.

Hull

Hull, C. L. Mind, mechanism and adaptive behavior. *Psychological Review*, 1937, **44**, 1–32.

Koch, S. Clark L. Hull. In W. Estes, S. Koch, K. MacCorquodale, P. E. Meehl, C. G. Mueller, Jr., W. N. Schoenfeld, & W. Verplanck (Eds.), *Modern learning theory*. New York: Appleton, 1954. Pp. 1–176.

Skinner

Bixenstine, V. E. Empiricism in latter-day behavioral science. *Science*, 1964, **145**, 464–467.

Evans, R. *B. F. Skinner: The man and his ideas*. New York: Dutton, 1968.

Skinner, B. F. A case history in scientific method. In S. Koch (Ed.), *Psychology: A study of a science*. Vol. 2. New York: McGraw-Hill, 1959. Pp. 359–379.

Skinner, B. F. *Cumulative record*. (3rd ed.) New York: Appleton, 1972.

Skinner, B. F. *Beyond freedom and dignity*. New York: Knopf, 1971.

Contemporary Learning Theory

Deese, J., & Hulse, S. *The psychology of learning*. (2nd ed.) New York: McGraw-Hill, 1967.

Hilgard, E. R., & Bower, G. *Theories of learning*. (4th ed.) Englewood Cliffs, New Jersey: Prentice-Hall, 1974.

General

Blanshard, B. Critical reflections on behaviorism. *Proceedings of the American Philosophical Society*, 1965, **109**, 22–28.

Boring, E. G. The trend toward mechanism. *Proceedings of the American Philosophical Society*, 1964, **108**, 451–454.

Hebb, D. O. The American revolution. *American Psychologist*, 1960, **15**, 735–745.

Matson, F. (Ed.) *Without/within: Behaviorism and humanism*. Monterey, California: Brooks/Cole, 1973.

Rachlin, H. *Introduction to modern behaviorism*. San Francisco, California: Freeman, 1970.

Skinner, B. F. Behaviorism at fifty. *Science*, 1963, **140**, 951–958.

Wann, T. W. (Ed.) *Behaviorism and phenomenology: Contrasting bases for modern psychology*. Chicago, Illinois: Univ. of Chicago Press, 1964.

12

Gestalt Psychology

Introduction

We have now seen the line of development of the history of psychology stretch from the 1870s psychology of Wilhelm Wundt to the 1970s psychology of B. F. Skinner. We have seen how functionalism followed structuralism, and how behaviorism developed in opposition to both of these schools.

While these major movements were forming and growing in the United States, another movement—a revolution—was beginning in Germany. It was yet an additional protest against structuralism, further testimony to the importance of that initial school of thought as an inspiration and impetus for opposing points of view, and as an effective base from which to launch new systems of psychology.

To understand this revolution—Gestalt psychology—we must go back to around 1912—the year described by Woodworth and Sheehan (1964) as a "time of troubles" for the old theory of psychology—when behaviorism was beginning its violent attack against the Wundtian order of things, as well as against the newer functionalism. The new animal research of Thorndike and Pavlov had been on the rise for a decade. Thorndike's first full statement of his position was made in 1911–1913, and the significance for psychology of the Pavlovian conditioned reflex was soon to be acknowledged. Another fresh approach, psychoanalysis, was already over a decade old.

The Gestalt psychologists' attack on structuralism in Europe was simultaneous with, although independent of, the American movement. At the outset, both movements opposed Wundtian structuralism, but later they came to oppose each other. There were sharp differences between the Gestaltists and the behaviorists: The former accepted the value of consciousness but disallowed the attempt to analyze consciousness into elements, whereas behaviorism refused to do anything at all with consciousness, even acknowledge it.

Gestalt psychologists referred to the Wundtian approach (with a sneer) as the "brick-and-mortar psychology," with the elements (the bricks) held together by the mortar of the process of association. They argued that a person on looking out a window sees immediately the trees and the sky, not the various alleged sensory elements (brightnesses, hues, etc.) that constitute the perception of the sky and trees according to the Wundtians.

Wundtians claimed that perception of objects consists in the accumulation of elements into groups or collections (Gestaltists called this the "bundle hypothesis"). The Gestalt psychologists maintained that when sensory elements are brought together, something new is formed. Put together a number of individual musical notes and something new (a melody) emerges from their combination, something that did not exist in any of the individual notes. Put simply and succinctly, "the whole is more than the sum of its parts." This was the keynote of the Gestalt opposition to Wundtian structuralism.

Miller[1] described an imaginary visit to a psychological laboratory in Germany around this time, which points out the basic difference between the Gestalt and structural approaches to perception. As you walk into the laboratory, a psychologist asks you what you see on the table:

> "A book."
>
> "Yes, of course, it is a book," he agrees, "but what do you *really* see?"
>
> "What do you mean, 'What do I *really* see'?" you ask, puzzled. "I told you that I see a book. It is a small book with a red cover."
>
> The psychologist is persistent. "What is your perception *really*?" he insists. "Describe it to me as precisely as you can."
>
> "You mean it isn't a book? What is this, some kind of trick?"

---

[1] From pp. 103–105 in *Psychology* by George A. Miller. Copyright 1962 by George A. Miller. Reprinted by permission of Harper & Row, Publishers, Inc.

There is a hint of impatience. "Yes, it is a book. There is no trickery involved. I just want you to describe to me *exactly* what you can see, no more and no less."

You are growing very suspicious now. "Well," you say, "from this angle the cover of the book looks like a dark red parallelogram."

"Yes," he says, pleased. "Yes, you see a patch of dark red in the shape of a parallelogram. What else?"

"There is a grayish white edge below it and another thin line of the same dark red below that. Under it I see the table—" He winces. "Around it I see a somewhat mottled brown with wavering streaks of lighter brown running roughly parallel to one another."

"Fine, fine." He thanks you for your cooperation.

As you stand there looking at the book on the table you are a little embarrassed that this persistent fellow was able to drive you to such an analysis. He made you so cautious that you were not sure any longer what you really saw and what you only thought you saw. You were, in fact, as suspicious as the New England farmer who would admit only that, "It looks like a cow on this side." In your caution you began talking about what you saw in terms of sensations, where just a moment earlier you were quite certain that you perceived a book on a table.

Your reverie is interrupted suddenly by the appearance of a psychologist who looks vaguely like Wilhelm Wundt. "Thank you, for helping to confirm once more my theory of perception. You have proved," he says, "that the book you see is nothing but a compound of elementary sensations. When you were trying to be precise and say accurately what it was you really saw, you had to speak in terms of color patches, not objects. It is the color sensations that are primary, and every visual object is reducible to them. Your perception of the book is constructed from sensations just as a molecule is constructed from atoms."

This little speech is apparently a signal for battle to begin. "Nonsense!" shouts a voice from the opposite end of the hall. "Nonsense! Any fool knows that the *book* is the primary, immediate, direct, compelling, perceptual fact!" The psychologist who charges down upon you now bears a faint resemblance to William James, but he seems to have a German accent, and his face is so flushed with anger that you cannot be sure. "This reduction of a perception into sensations that you keep talking about is nothing but an intellectual game. An object is not just a bundle of sensations. Any man who goes about seeing patches of dark redness where he ought to see books is sick!"

As the fight begins to gather momentum you close the door softly and slip away. You have what you came for, an illustration that there are two different attitudes, two different ways to talk about the information that our senses provide.

Thus, the Gestalt psychologists feel there is more to perception than meets the eye (so to speak); that our perception somehow goes beyond the basic physical data provided to the sense organs. As with other movements, the basic notion of the Gestaltist protest has its historical antecedents. After examining these antecedent influences, we shall discuss the formal founding of the Gestalt movement.

Antecedent Influences

The basis of the Gestalt position—the focus on the unity of perception—can be found in the work of the German philosopher Immanuel Kant (1724–1804). This eminent man, who never ventured more than 60 miles from his place of birth, dominated philosophical thinking for more than a generation. Although less extensive than his contribution to philosophy, his contribution to psychology is important.

Kant influenced psychology through his stress on the unity of a perceptual act. He argued that when we perceive objects (or what we call objects), we encounter mental states that might seem to be composed of bits and pieces (the sensory elements of which the empiricists and associationists spoke). However, these elements are meaningfully organized in *a priori* fashion and not through the mechanical process of association. The mind, in the process of perception, forms or creates a unitary experience. According to Kant, perception is not a passive impression and combination of sensory elements, but an active organization of these elements into a unitary and coherent experience. The raw material of perception is thus given form and organization by the mind. This position obviously was contrary to the very heart of associationism.

To Kant, some of the forms imposed on experience by the mind are innate, such as space, time, and causality. That is, time and space are not derived from experience, but exist innately in the mind as *a priori* forms of perception; they are intuitively knowable.

As was the case with functionalism and behaviorism, Wundt, in his role as a target for criticism, was a precursor of Gestalt psychology. He was also a more direct influence, however, in that his principle of creative synthesis recognized that new characteristics might emerge when elements are combined into wholes. Wundt made little of this notion, however, as noted in Chapter 4.

Franz Brentano also anticipated the formal Gestalt movement through his insistence that psychology study the process or act of experiencing rather than the content of experience (elementary sensations). He considered the Wundtian method of introspection to be highly artificial and favored a less rigid and more direct observation of experience as it occurs, like the later Gestalt method.

A physicist, Ernst Mach (1838–1916), provided a more direct influence on the Gestalt revolution. In his book, *The Analysis of Sensations* (1885), Mach spoke of sensations of space–form and time–form, considering spatial patterns (such as geometrical figures) and temporal patterns (such as melodies) as sensations. These space–form and time–form sensations he considered independent of their elements. For example, a circle might be white or black, or large or small, and lose absolutely nothing of its quality of circularity.

Mach argued that one's visual or aural perception of an object does not change, even though the perceiver may change his spatial orientation with regard to the object. For example, a table remains a table in our perception whether looked at from the side or the top or from an angle. Similarly, a series of sounds, as in a melody, remains the same in our perception even though the tempo might be altered.

Mach's work was expanded by Christian von Ehrenfels (1859–1932), who is often considered the most important antecedent of the Gestalt movement (although Gestalt psychologists denied this). Von Ehrenfels suggested that there are qualities of experience that cannot be explained in terms of combinations of the traditional kinds of sensations. He called these qualities *Gestalt qualitäten*, or form qualities: perceptions based on something beyond the individual sensations. A melody, for example, is a form quality because it sounds the same even when transposed to different keys. Thus, a melody is independent of the particular sensations of which it is composed.

To von Ehrenfels, and the Austrian school of *Gestalt qualität* founded at Graz, form itself was an element (not a sensation)—a new element created by the action of the mind operating on the sensory elements. Thus, the mind creates form out of elementary sensations.

While Mach and von Ehrenfels certainly thought along the lines that came to be known as Gestalt psychology, they deviated little from the older elementistic position of the structuralists. Rather than opposing the very notion of elementism, as the Gestalt psychologists later did, they simply added a new element (form). Thus, while they attacked the same position as the Gestalt psychologists, they offered quite a different solution. We can see why Gestalt psychology denies any relationship with the two.

In America, an antecedent of Gestalt psychology is found in William

James's opposition to psychological elementism. James regarded elements of consciousness as purely artificial abstractions and noted that we see objects, not bundles of sensations.

One very important early influence is the phenomenological movement in German philosophy and psychology. As a methodological tool, phenomenology refers to a free and unbiased description of immediate experience exactly as it occurs. It is an "uncorrected" kind of observation in which an experience is accepted as it is (not analyzed into elements or otherwise artificially abstracted). It involves the almost naïve experience of common sense rather than experience as reported by a trained introspector with a special systematic orientation.

The phenomenological tradition in psychology is generally assumed to have begun with Goethe, and its active use can be traced to a number of scholars in psychology as well as other disciplines. A particularly active group of phenomenological psychologists was at G. E. Müller's laboratory at Göttingen in the years 1909–1915. Three men, Erich R. Jaensch, David Katz, and Edgar Rubin, conducted extensive phenomenological research that was supportive of, indeed anticipated, the formal Gestalt school.

Not to be neglected among antecedent influences of Gestalt psychology is the *Zeitgeist*, particularly as it operated in physics. In the closing decades of the nineteenth century, physics was becoming a good bit less atomistic, as it came to recognize and accept the notion of fields of force.

The classic example of this new "force" in physics is magnetism, a property or quality that seemed difficult to define or understand in traditional Galilean–Newtonian terms. When, for instance, iron filings are shaken onto a sheet of paper which is resting on top of a magnet, the filings become arranged in a characteristic pattern. The filings do not touch the magnet, yet they are obviously affected by the force—the field of force—around the magnet. Light and electricity were considered at the time to operate in the same way.

These fields of force were thought to possess both spatial extension and configuration or pattern. They were, in other words, seen as new structural entities, not as summations of effects of individual elements or particles.

Thus, the notion of atomism, which had been so influential for Wundt, was under serious attack in physics, which was beginning to think in terms of organic wholes—a concept congruent with the new Gestalt psychology. Therefore, the changes offered by Gestalt psychology paralleled the changes in the physics of the time. Psychology was still desirous of emulating the natural sciences.

The Founding of Gestalt Psychology

The formal movement known as Gestalt psychology grew out of a research study conducted by the German psychologist Max Wertheimer, the primary founder of the new school. While on a train on his vacation, Wertheimer had an idea for an experiment on the seeing of motion. Promptly forgetting his vacation, he left the train at Frankfurt am Main, bought a toy stroboscope,[2] and verified his insight in a preliminary way in his hotel room. He later carried out more formal research at the University of Frankfurt, which provided a tachistoscope for his use. In Frankfurt at that time were two other young German psychologists who, some years earlier, had been students with Wertheimer at the University of Berlin: Kurt Koffka and Wolfgang Köhler. Each had been working productively in psychology and they shortly embarked on a joint crusade against Wundtian elementism.

Wertheimer's research problem, on which Koffka and Köhler served as subjects, involved the perception of apparent movement: the perception of motion or movement when no actual physical movement has taken place. Using the tachistoscope, Wertheimer projected light through two slits, one vertical and the other 20 or 30 degrees from the vertical. If light was shown through one slit and then the other, with a long interval in between (over 200 milliseconds), the subjects saw two successive lights, first at one slit and then at the other. If the interval between the lights was very short, the subjects saw both lights on continuously. With an optimal interval (about 60 milliseconds) between the lights, however, the subjects saw the line of light actually move from one place to the other and back again. These findings might seem trivial and straightforward since this phenomenon, after all, had been known for many years. It might even be considered a matter of common sense.

But according to the prevailing psychological (structuralist) viewpoint, all conscious experience could be analyzed into its sensory elements. Yet how could this perception of apparent movement be explained in terms of a summation of individual sensory elements? Can one stationary stimulus be added to another to produce a sensation of movement? It could not, and this was precisely the point of Wertheimer's brilliantly simple demonstration: It defied explanation by the prevailing Wundtian system!

Wertheimer believed that the phenomenon verified in his laboratory was, in its own way, as elementary as a sensation, yet it obviously differed

[2] The stroboscope, invented about 80 years earlier by J. Plateau, was a forerunner of the motion picture camera; it is an instrument that rapidly projects a series of different pictures on the eye, producing apparent motion.

from a sensation or even a succession of sensations. Wertheimer gave the phenomenon a name befitting its unique status: the phi phenomenon.

We may reasonably ask how Wertheimer explained this phi phenomenon if the traditional introspective structuralism could not. His answer was as simple and ingenious as the verifying experiment itself: *Apparent movement did not need explaining;* it simply existed as perceived and could not be reduced to anything simpler.

According to Wundt, introspection of the stimulus would produce two successive lines and nothing else. But, no matter how rigorously one might try to introspect the two exposures, the experience of a single line in motion persisted. Any attempt at analysis was a failure. The whole (the movement) was indeed greater than the sum of its parts (the two stationary lines)! The traditional associationist–structuralist psychology, dominant for so many years, had been challenged—and it was a challenge it could not meet.

Wertheimer's results were published in 1912 in an article, *Experimental Studies of the Perception of Movement,* that is often considered to mark the beginning of the new school.

After considering the lives of the three key figures in this movement, we shall examine the basic principles of the Gestalt school.

Max Wertheimer (1880–1943)

Wertheimer was the oldest of the three original Gestalt psychologists, and the intellectual leader of the movement. Koffka and Köhler served to promote Wertheimer's more prominent position, though each was highly influential in his own right. Born in Prague, Wertheimer attended the local gymnasium until the age of 18 and then studied law for $2\frac{1}{2}$ years at the university there. He later shifted to philosophy and attended the lectures of von Ehrenfels, among others. He then studied philosophy and psychology at Berlin and finally took his degree in 1904 at Würzburg under Külpe at the height of the imageless thought controversy.

Very little is known about the years between 1904 and his arrival at Frankfurt, though it has been established that he spent his time variously at Prague, Vienna, and Berlin. He lectured at Frankfurt from 1912 until 1916, when he returned to Berlin. In 1929 he received a professorship at Frankfurt. During World War I, he participated in research of military value dealing with listening devices for submarines and harbor fortifications. Wertheimer did not write a great deal, at least not as much as Koffka and Köhler, but a paper on creative thinking was published in 1920, and in 1923 he wrote an influential article on perceptual grouping.

In 1921 the three primary Gestaltists, together with K. Goldstein and H. Gruhle, founded the journal *Psychologische Forschung*, which became the official organ of the Gestalt school. It published 22 volumes before its suspension in 1938 under the Hitler regime.

Wertheimer was among the first group of refugee scholars from Germany to arrive in New York in 1933. In 1934 he became associated with the New School for Social Research in New York City, where he remained until his death in 1943. Though his years in the United States were busy, he published little, due to increasing exhaustion and the burden of adapting to a new language and culture. His research was conducted rather informally and was communicated to his friends and to meetings.

Kurt Koffka (1886–1941)

Koffka was considered the most productive of the triumvirate.[3] He received his education at Berlin, his place of birth. During his early years he developed a strong interest in science and philosophy that was strengthened during a year at Edinburgh (1903–1904). After returning to Berlin, he studied psychology and received his degree in 1909 under Stumpf. A number of research positions followed until 1910 when he began his long and productive association with Wertheimer and Köhler in Frankfurt. In 1911, he went to the University of Giessen, some 40 miles from Frankfurt, and remained there until 1924. At Giessen he conducted a good deal of research, and during World War I he worked with brain-damaged and aphasic patients at the psychiatric clinic.

After the war, American psychology was becoming vaguely aware of the school developing in Germany and Koffka was persuaded to write an article on the new movement for the *Psychological Bulletin*. This article, *Perception: An Introduction to Gestalt-Theorie*, appeared in 1922 and presented the basic concepts along with the results and implications of much research.

In 1921, Koffka published *The Growth of the Mind*, a book in developmental child psychology that became a great success in Germany and America. He was a visiting professor first at Cornell and later at Wisconsin in 1924, and in 1927 was appointed a professor at Smith College, where he remained until his death in 1941.

In 1932, Koffka accompanied an expedition to study the people of Central Asia. While recovering from recurrent fever contracted on this

[3] Boring (1950) suggested that "the originality of these three men varied inversely with their productivity [p. 594]."

expedition, he began work on his *Principles of Gestalt Psychology*, published in 1935. It was an extremely difficult book and did not become the definitive treatment of Gestalt psychology it was intended to be.

Wolfgang Köhler (1887–1967)

The youngest of the three, Köhler was the spokesman for the Gestalt movement and became the best known (Boring, 1950). His books, written with great care and precision, became the definitive works on certain aspects of Gestalt psychology. Born in the Baltic provinces, Köhler was 5 years old when his family moved to northern Germany. His university education was at Tübingen, Bonn, and Berlin, where he received his degree in 1909 under Stumpf. He then went to Frankfurt, arriving just before Wertheimer and his stroboscope.

Köhler received considerable training in physics, some of it under the eminent Max Planck. Probably as a result, he argued strongly that psychology must ally itself with physics.

In 1913 Köhler, at the invitation of the Prussian Academy of Science, went to the Spanish island of Tenerife in the Canary Islands to study chimpanzees. Six months after his arrival, World War I began and he was unable to leave. For the next 7 years he studied learning in chimpanzees and produced the classic volume *Mentality of Apes* (1917). The book appeared in a second edition in 1924, and was then translated into English (1925) and French (1928). This work is discussed later.

In 1920 Köhler returned to Germany, and in 1922 succeeded Stumpf at Berlin, where he remained until 1935. The apparent reason for his appointment to this coveted position was the publication in 1920 of *Static and Stationary Physical Gestalts*, a difficult book that won critical acclaim for its high level of scholarship.

Köhler lectured at Clark and Harvard Universities in 1925–1926, and in 1929 published, in English, *Gestalt Psychology*, the most definitive and thorough argument for the Gestalt movement. In 1934–1935, Köhler gave the William James lectures at Harvard, and in 1935 he left Germany for good since he was in continual conflict with the Nazi regime over a courageous anti-Nazi letter he wrote to a Berlin newspaper. He went to Swarthmore College, where he remained until his retirement. His later books include *The Place of Value in a World of Facts* (1938), *Dynamics in Psychology* (1940), and *Figural After-Effects* (1944), the latter with Hans Wallach. In 1956, he received the Distinguished Contribution Award from the American Psychological Association, and in 1959 was elected president of that organization.

The Nature of the Gestalt Revolt

The Gestalt principles were in full and direct opposition to most of the academic tradition of psychology in Germany. Behaviorism was less of an immediate revolution (relative to structuralism) because functionalism had already brought about some change in American psychology. No such tempering effect paved the way for the Gestalt revolt in Germany; the pronouncements of the Gestaltists were nothing short of heresy to the German structuralist tradition. Consider the basic points of Gestalt psychology in the light of Wundt's brand of psychology: (*a*) complex mental experience can have an existence of its own, (*b*) the primary data of perception are not elements but significantly structured forms, (*c*) it is acceptable when introspecting to use simple descriptive words, that is, it is acceptable to say, "I see a book"!

The initiators of the Gestalt movement realized, as they began their revolt, that they were taking on a powerful and rigid tradition; that they were striking at the very foundation of psychology as it was then defined. Like most revolutionary movements, the Gestalt school demanded a complete revision of the old order. After the study of apparent movement, they were quick to seize upon other perceptual phenomena to support their position. The experience of perceptual constancies afforded ample corroboration. For example, if we stand directly in front of a window, it projects a rectangular image on the retina. But if we stand off to one side and look at the window, the retinal image becomes a trapezoid, yet we still perceive the window as rectangular. Thus, our perception of the window remains unchanged even though the sensory datum (the image projected on the retina) has changed.

The same thing occurs with brightness and size constancy: The actual sensory elements can change radically, yet our perception does not. There are many similar examples in everyday experience. In these cases, as with apparent movement, the perceptual experience has a quality of wholeness that is not found in any of the parts. There can exist, then, a difference between the character of the actual perception and the character of the sensory stimulation. Thus, the perception cannot be explained as a collection of sensory elements or as the mere sum of the parts.

> The perception itself shows a character of totality, a form, a *Gestalt*, which in the very attempt at analysis is destroyed; and this experience, as directly given, sets the problem for psychology. It is this experience that presents the raw data which psychology must explain, and which it must never be content to explain away. To begin with elements

is to begin at the wrong end; for elements are products of reflection and abstraction, remotely derived from the immediate experience they are invoked to explain. *Gestalt* psychology attempts to get back to naïve perception, to immediate experience "undebauched by learning"; and it insists that it finds there not assemblages of elements, but unified wholes; not masses of sensations, but trees, clouds, and sky. And this assertion it invites any one to verify simply by opening his eyes and looking at the world about him in his ordinary everyday way [Heidbreder, 1933, p. 331].

Boring (1950) commented that the word "Gestalt" has caused some difficulty because it does not clearly indicate what the movement stands for (like functionalism or behaviorism), and it has no exact English counterpart. Several "equivalents" are in common use (form, shape, configuration, for example), and in modern usage Gestalt has become part of the English language.

In Köhler's *Gestalt Psychology* of 1929, it is noted that the word "Gestalt" was used in two ways in German. One usage involved the denoting of shape or form as a property of objects. In this sense the word refers to general properties that would be expressed in such terms as "angular" or "symmetrical." It describes characteristics such as triangularity (in geometrical figures) or temporal sequences (in a melody).

The second usage denoted an entity that is concrete and has as one of its attributes a specific shape or form. In this sense, the word refers to triangles, rather than, as in the first usage, the notion of triangularity. Thus, the word is used in reference to objects rather than to the characteristic forms of these objects. In this sense, Gestalt refers to any segregated whole.

Finally, the use of the term is not restricted to the visual field or even to the total sensory field.

In fact, the concept "Gestalt" may be applied far beyond the limits of sensory experience. According to the most general functional definition of the term, the processes of learning, of recall, of striving, of emotional attitude, of thinking, acting, and so forth, may have to be included. . . . "Gestalt" in the meaning of shape is no longer the center of the Gestalt Psychologist's attention [Köhler, 1947, pp. 178–179].

And it is in this larger sense of the term that the Gestalt psychologists wanted to deal with the whole province of psychology—in terms of *Gestalten.*

Original Source Material on Gestalt Psychology:
From "Gestalt Theory" by Max Wertheimer

The following article is a lecture presented by Max Wertheimer to the Kant Society in Berlin on December 17, 1924.[4] Ranging from psychology to mathematics to philosophy and the social sciences, Wertheimer points out the differences between a Gestalt (whole) approach and that involving the reduction of the subject matter to elements. The lecture demonstrates the basic conflict between these two divergent views of the world, as represented in psychology at that time by Wertheimer and by Wundt.

What is Gestalt theory and what does it intend? . . .

The fundamental "formula" of Gestalt theory might be expressed in this way: There are wholes, the behaviour of which is not determined by that of their individual elements, but where the part-processes are themselves determined by the intrinsic nature of the whole. It is the hope of Gestalt theory to determine the nature of such wholes.

With a formula such as this, one might close, for Gestalt theory is neither more nor less than this. It is not interested in puzzling out philosophic questions which such a formula might suggest. Gestalt theory has to do with concrete research; it is not only an *outcome* but a *device*: not only a theory *about* results but a means toward further discoveries. This is not merely the proposal of one or more problems but an attempt to *see* what is really taking place in science. This problem cannot be solved by listing possibilities for systematization, classification, and arrangement. If it is to be attacked at all, we must be guided by the spirit of the new method and by the concrete nature of the things themselves which we are studying, and set ourselves to penetrate to that which is really given by nature.

There is another difficulty that may be illustrated by the following example. Suppose a mathematician shows you a proposition and you begin to "classify" it. This proposition, you say, is of such and such type, belongs in this or that historical category, and so on. Is that how the mathematician works?

"Why, you haven't grasped the thing at all," the mathematician will exclaim. "See here, this formula is not an independent, closed fact that can be dealt with for itself alone. You must see its dynamic *functional* relationship to the whole from which it was lifted or you will never understand it."

What holds for the mathematical formula applies also to the "formula" of Gestalt theory. The attempt of Gestalt theory to disclose the functional meaning of its own formula is no less strict than is the mathematician's. The attempt to explain Gestalt theory in a short essay is the more difficult

[4] From M. Wertheimer, "Gestalt Theory." In W. D. Ellis (Ed.), *A Source Book of Gestalt Psychology.* (London: Routledge & Kegan Paul, 1938; New York: Humanities Press, Inc., 1967), pp. 1–11. (Footnotes omitted.)

because of the terms which are used: part, whole, intrinsic determination. All of them have in the past been the topic of endless discussions where each disputant has understood them differently. And even worse has been the cataloguing attitude adopted toward them. What they *lacked* has been actual research. Like many another "philosophic" problem they have been withheld from contact with reality and scientific work.

About all I can hope for in so short a discussion is to suggest a few of the problems which at present occupy the attention of Gestalt theory and something of the way they are being attacked.

To repeat: the *problem* has not merely to do with scientific work—it is a fundamental problem of our times. Gestalt theory is not something suddenly and unexpectedly dropped upon us from above; it is, rather, a palpable convergence of problems ranging throughout the sciences and the various philosophic standpoints of modern times.

Let us take, for example, an event in the history of psychology. One turned from a living experience to science and asked what it had to say about this experience, and one found an assortment of elements, sensations, images, feelings, acts of will and laws governing these elements—and was told, "Take your choice, reconstruct from them the experience you had." Such procedure led to difficulties in concrete psychological research and to the emergence of problems which defied solution by the traditional analytic methods. Historically the most important impulse came from v. Ehrenfels who raised the following problem. Psychology had said that experience is a compound of elements: we hear a melody and then, upon hearing it again, memory enables us to recognize it. But what is it that enables us to recognize the melody when it is played in a new key? The sum of the elements is different, yet the melody is the same; indeed, one is often not even aware that a transposition has been made.

When in retrospect we consider the prevailing situation we are struck by two aspects of v. Ehrenfels's thesis; on the one hand one is surprised at the essentially summative character of his theory, on the other one admires his courage in propounding and defending his proposition. Strictly interpreted, v. Ehrenfels's position was this: I play a familiar melody of six tones and employ six *new* tones, yet you recognize the melody despite the change. There must be a something *more* than the sum of six tones, viz. a seventh something, which is the form-quality, the *Gestaltqualität*, of the original six. It is this *seventh* factor or element which enabled you to recognize the melody despite its transposition.

However strange this view may seem, it shares with many another subsequently abandoned hypothesis the honour of having clearly seen and emphasized a fundamental problem.

But other explanations were also proposed. One maintained that in addition to the six tones there were intervals—relations—and that *these* were what remained constant. In other words we are asked to assume not only elements but "relations-between-elements" as additional components of the total complex. But this view failed to account for the phenomenon because in some cases the relations *too* may be altered without destroying the original melody.

Another type of explanation, also designed to bolster the elementaristic hypothesis, was that *to* this total of six or more tones there come certain "higher processes" which operate upon the given material to "*produce*" unity.

This was the situation until Gestalt theory raised the radical question: Is it really true that when I hear a melody I have a *sum* of individual tones (pieces) which constitute the primary foundation of my experience? Is not perhaps the reverse of this true? What I really have, what I hear of each individual note, what I experience at each place in the melody is a *part* which is itself determined by the character of the whole. What is given me by the melody does not arise (through the agency of any auxiliary factor) as a *secondary* process from the sum of the pieces as such. Instead, what takes place in each single part already depends upon what the whole is. The flesh and blood of a tone depends from the start upon its role in the melody. . . . It belongs to the flesh and blood of the things given in experience [*Gegebenheiten*], how, in what role, in what function they are in their whole.

Let us leave the melody example and turn to another field. Take the case of threshold phenomena. It has long been held that a certain stimulus necessarily produces a certain sensation. Thus, when two stimuli are sufficiently different, the sensations also will be different. Psychology is filled with careful inquiries regarding threshold phenomena. To account for the difficulties constantly being encountered it was assumed that these phenomena must be influenced by higher mental functions, judgments, illusions, attention, etc. And this continued until the radical question was raised: Is it really true that a specific stimulus *always* gives rise to the same sensation? Perhaps the prevailing whole-conditions will themselves determine the effect of stimulation? This kind of formulation leads to experimentation, and experiments show, for example, that when I see two colours the sensations I have are determined by the whole-conditions of the entire stimulus situation. Thus, also, the same local *physical* stimulus pattern can give rise to either a unitary and homogeneous figure, or to an articulated figure with different parts, all depending upon the whole-conditions which may favour either unity or articulation. Obviously the task, then, is to investigate these "whole-conditions" and discover what influences they exert upon experience. . . .

Our next point is that my field comprises also my Ego. There is not from the beginning an Ego over-against others, but the genesis of an Ego offers one of the most fascinating problems, the solution of which seems to lie in Gestalt principles. However, once constituted, the Ego is a functional part of the total field. Proceeding as before we may therefore ask: What happens to the Ego as a part of the field? Is the resulting behaviour the piecewise sort of thing associationism, experience theory, and the like, would have us believe? Experimental results contradict this interpretation and again we often find that the laws of whole-processes operative in such a field tend toward a meaningful behaviour of its parts.

This field is not a summation of sense data and no description of it which considers such separate pieces to be *primary* will be correct. If it were, then for children, primitive peoples and animals experience would be nothing but piece-sensations. The next most developed creatures would have, in addition to independent sensations, something higher, and so on. But this whole picture is the opposite of what actual inquiry has disclosed. We have learned to recognize the "sensations" of our textbooks as products of a late culture utterly different from the experiences of more primitive stages. Who experiences the sensation of a specific red in that sense? What the man of the streets, children, or primitive men normally react to is something coloured but at the same time exciting, gay, strong, or affecting—*not* "sensations."

The programme to treat the organism as a part in a larger field necessitates the reformulation of the problem as to the relation between organism and environment. The stimulus-sensation connection must be replaced by a connection between alteration in the field conditions, the vital situation, and the total reaction of the organism by a change in its attitude, striving, and feeling.

There is, however, another step to be considered. A man is not only a part of his field, he is also one among other men. When a group of people work together it rarely occurs, and then only under very special conditions, that they constitute a mere sum of independent Egos. Instead the common enterprise often becomes their mutual concern and each works *as* a meaningfully functioning part of the whole. Consider a group of South Sea Islanders engaged in some community occupation, or a group of children playing together. Only under very special circumstances does an "I" stand out alone. Then the balance which obtained during harmonious and systematic occupation may be upset and give way to a surrogate (under certain conditions, pathological) *new* balance. . . .

The fundamental question can be very simply stated: Are the parts of a given whole determined by the inner structure of that whole, or are the events such that, as independent, piecemeal, fortuitous and blind the total activity is a sum of the part-activities? Human beings can, of course, *devise* a kind of physics of their own—e.g., a sequence of machines—exemplifying the latter half of our question, but this does not signify that *all natural* phenomena are of this type. Here is a place where Gestalt theory is least easily understood and this because of the great number of prejudices about nature which have accumulated during the centuries. Nature is thought of as something essentially blind in its laws, where whatever takes place in the whole is purely a sum of individual occurrences. This view was the natural result of the struggle which physics has always had to purge itself of teleology. Today it can be seen that we are obliged to traverse other routes than those suggested by this kind of purposivism.

Let us proceed another step and ask: How does all this stand with regard to the problem of body and mind? What does my knowledge of another's mental experiences amount to and how do I obtain it? There are, of course, old and established dogmas on these points: The mental and physical are wholly heterogeneous: there obtains between them an absolute dichotomy. (From this point of departure philosophers have drawn an array of metaphysical deductions so as to attribute all the good qualities to mind while reserving for nature the odious.) As regards the second question, my discerning mental phenomena in others is traditionally explained as inference by analogy. Strictly interpreted the principle here is that something mental is meaninglessly coupled with something physical. I observe the physical and infer the mental from it more or less according to the following scheme: I see someone press a button on the wall and infer that he wants the light to go on. There *may be* couplings of this sort. However, many scientists have been disturbed by this dualism and have tried to save themselves by recourse to very curious hypotheses. Indeed, the ordinary person would violently refuse to believe that when he sees his companion startled, frightened, or angry he is seeing only certain physical occurrences which themselves have nothing to do (in their inner nature) with the mental, being only superficially coupled with it: you have frequently seen this and this combined . . . etc. There have been many attempts to surmount this problem. One speaks, for example, of *intuition* and says there can be no other possibility, for I *see* my companion's fear. It is not true, argue the intuitionists, that I see only the bare bodily activities meaninglessly coupled with other and invisible activities. However inadmissible it may otherwise be, an intuition theory does have at least this in its favour, it shows a suspicion that the traditional procedure might be successfully reversed. But the word intuition is at best only a *naming* of that which we must strive to lay hold of.

This and other hypotheses, apprehended as they now are, will not advance scientific pursuit, for science demands fruitful penetration, not mere cataloguing and systematization. But the question is, How does the matter really stand? Looking more closely we find a third assumption, namely that a process such as fear is a matter of consciousness. Is this true? Suppose you see a person who is kindly or benevolent. Does anyone suppose that this person is feeling mawkish? No one could possibly believe that. The characteristic feature of such behaviour has very little to do with consciousness. It has been one of the easiest contrivances of philosophy to identify a man's real behaviour and the direction of his mind with his consciousness. Parenthetically, in the opinion of many people the distinction between idealism and materialism implies that between the noble and the ignoble. Yet does one really mean by this to contrast consciousness with the blithesome budding of trees? Indeed, what is there so repugnant about the materialistic and mechanical? What is so attractive about the idealistic? Does it come from the *material* qualities of the connected pieces? Broadly speaking most psychological theories and textbooks, despite their continued emphasis upon consciousness, are far more "materialistic," arid, and spiritless than a living tree—which probably has no consciousness at all. The point is not what the material pieces are, but what *kind* of whole it is. Proceeding in terms of specific problems one soon realizes how many bodily activities there are which give no hint of a separation between body and mind. Imagine a dance, a dance full of grace and joy. What is the situation in such a dance? Do we have a summation of *physical* limb movements and a *psychical* consciousness? No. Obviously this answer does not solve the problem; we have to start anew—and it seems to me that a proper and fruitful point of attack has been discovered. One finds many processes which, in their dynamical form, are identical regardless of variations in the material character of their elements. When a man is timid, afraid or energetic, happy or sad, it can often be shown that the course of his physical processes is Gestalt-identical with the course pursued by the mental processes.

Again I can only indicate the direction of thought. I have touched on the question of body and mind merely to show that the problem we are discussing also has its philosophic aspects. . . .

This brings us to the close of an attempt to present a view of the problem as illustrated by its specific appearances in various fields. In concluding I may suggest a certain unification of these illustrations somewhat as follows. I consider the situation from the point of view of a theory of aggregates and say: How should a world be where science, concepts, inquiry, investigation, and comprehension of inner unities were impossible? The answer is obvious. This world would be a manifold of disparate pieces. Secondly, what kind of world would there have to be in which a piecewise science would apply? The answer is again quite simple, for here one needs only a system of recurrent couplings that are blind and piecewise in character, whereupon everything is available for a pursuit of the traditional piecewise methods of logic, mathematics, and science generally in so far as these presuppose this kind of world. But there is a third kind of aggregate which has been but cursorily investigated. These are the aggregates in which a manifold is not compounded from adjacently situated pieces but rather such that a term at its place in that aggregate is determined by the whole-laws of the aggregate itself.

Pictorially: suppose the world were a vast plateau upon which were many musicians. I walk about listening and watching the players. First suppose that the world is a meaningless plurality. Everyone does as he will, each for himself. What happens together when I hear ten players might be the basis for my guessing as to what they all are doing, but this is merely a matter of chance and probability much as in the kinetics of gas molecules.— A second possibility would be that each time one musician played *c*, another played *f* so and so many seconds later. I work out a theory of blind couplings but the playing as a whole remains meaningless. This is what many people think physics does, but the real work of physics belies this.—The third possibility is, say, a Beethoven symphony where it would be possible for one to select one part of the whole and work from that towards an idea of the structural principle motivating and determining the whole. Here the fundamental laws are not those of fortuitous pieces, but concern the very character of the event.

Wertheimer's Principles of Organization

Perhaps the best known of all the propositions put forward by the Gestaltists are Wertheimer's principles of perceptual organization, presented in a paper in 1923. Wertheimer took the position that a person perceives objects in the same immediate and unified manner in which he perceives apparent motion—as unified wholes, not as clusters of individual sensations. These principles, which may be found in most general psychology texts today, are essentially rules or laws by which a person organizes his perceptual world.

A basic premise of Wertheimer's principles is that in perception, organization occurs instantly whenever we see (or hear) different shapes or patterns. Parts of the perceptual field become connected and these groups or collections of parts unite to form structures that are distinct from the background. This basic perceptual organization is spontaneous and inevitable whenever an organism looks about its environment. We do not have to learn to so organize, as the structuralists and associationists claimed. Higher-level perception, such as labeling an object by name, is, of course, more dependent on learning.

According to Gestalt theory, the primary brain process in visual perception is not a collection of small separate activities, but is, instead, a dynamic system. The visual area of the brain does not respond in terms of separate elements of visual input, with these elements being connected by a principle of association. Rather, the brain is a dynamic system in which all those elements active at a given time interact. Elements that are similar or close together tend to combine; elements that are dissimilar or far apart do not tend to combine.

Several of the principles of organization are listed here, and examples are given in Figure 12.1.

1. Proximity: Parts that are close together in time or space tend to be perceived together. For example, in Figure 12.1a the circles are seen in three columns rather than as one large collection.
2. Similarity: Similar parts tend to be seen together as forming a group (Figure 12.1b). Since the circles and the dots appear to "belong" together, we tend to perceive rows instead of columns.
3. Closure: There is a tendency in our perception to complete incomplete figures—to fill in gaps. In Figure 12.1c we perceive three squares even though the figures are incomplete.
4. *Prägnanz*: There is a tendency to see a figure as being as "good" as possible under the stimulus conditions. A "good" figure is one

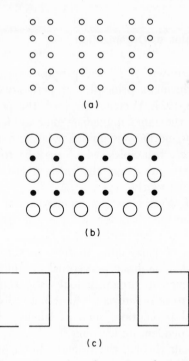

Figure 12.1. Examples of perceptual organization.

that is symmetrical, simple, and stable, and that cannot be made simpler or more orderly.

These organizing factors do not depend on the higher mental processes of the individual nor on his past experience, but are present in the stimuli themselves. While stressing these "peripheral" factors, Wertheimer did recognize that "central" factors (factors within the organism) can also influence perception. For example, the factors of familiarity and set or attitude (higher mental processes) can influence perception. In general, however, the Gestaltists tended to concentrate on the more direct and primitive peripheral factors of perceptual organization, rather than on the role of learning or experience.

Gestalt Principles of Learning

As we have seen, perception was a primary focus of interest to the Gestalt psychologists, and they took the position that learning plays only a small role in perceptual processes. It is certainly not correct, however, to imply that the topic of learning, considered independently of perception, received no attention from the Gestalt psychologists. Some of the most significant experiments in the history of psychology, experiments still cited in contemporary psychology books, are those Köhler devised to study problem solving in apes. It seems true, however, that learning, although certainly not neglected, played a role subordinate to perception in Gestalt psychology.

From its very beginning, Gestalt psychology opposed the Thorndikian trial-and-error learning and, later, the Watsonian stimulus–response learning. In fact, the members of the Gestalt school felt that one of their most important contributions to psychology was their consistent criticism of associationistic and S–R theories of learning. To illustrate the Gestalt view of learning, we discuss Köhler's work on apes and Wertheimer's work on productive thinking in humans.

The Mentality of Apes: Köhler

Mention was made earlier of Köhler's confinement on the island of Tenerife during World War I, during which time he investigated the intelligence of chimpanzees as shown in their solving of problems. These studies were conducted in and around the animals' cages and involved simple props, such as the bars of the cages themselves (to block access), bananas, sticks for drawing the bananas into the cage, and boxes for climbing.

Congruent with the Gestalt view of perception, Köhler interpreted the results of his animal studies in terms of the whole situation and relations between the various stimuli found therein. He considered problem solving a matter of restructuring the perceptual field. In one of his studies, a banana was placed outside the cage with an attached string leading into the cage. The apes pulled the banana into the cage with little hesitation. Köhler said that in this situation the problem was easily grasped as a whole by the animal. However, if several strings led from the cage in the general direction of the banana, the ape would not clearly recognize at first which string to pull. To Köhler, this indicated that the problem could not be envisioned clearly all at once.

A perhaps more explicit example involved placing an unattached banana just beyond the ape's reach. Now, if a stick were placed near the bars of the cage (facing the banana), the stick and the banana would be seen as parts of the same situation and the ape would readily use the stick to pull in the banana. If the stick were placed at the back of the cage, however, the two objects would be less readily perceived as parts of the same situation. In the latter case, a restructuring of the perceptual field was necessary in order to solve the problem.

Another example involved placing a banana outside the cage, beyond reach, and placing several hollow bamboo sticks, each by itself too short to reach the banana, inside the cage. In order to solve this problem, two sticks would have to be pushed together (the end of one inserted in the end of the other) to produce a stick of sufficient length to reach the banana. Thus, the animal had to perceive an entirely new relationship between the sticks.

Sultan, Köhler's brightest ape, failed when initially confronted with this problem. He first tried to get the banana with one stick; next, he pushed a stick out as far as he could, then pushed it farther with a second stick until the first one touched the banana (an interesting attempt). Sultan did not succeed during a 1-hour trial.

Immediately after this trial, however, while playing with the sticks, Sultan solved the problem, as reported by his keeper:

> Sultan first of all squats indifferently on the box, which has been left standing a little back from the railings; then he gets up, picks up the two sticks, sits down again on the box and plays carelessly with them. While doing this, it happens that he finds himself holding one rod in either hand in such a way that they lie in a straight line; he pushes the thinner one a little way into the opening of the thicker, jumps up and is already on the run towards the railings, to which he has up to now half turned his back, and begins to draw a banana towards him with the double stick. I call the master: meanwhile, one of the animal's rods has fallen out of the other, as he has pushed one of them only a little way into the other; whereupon he connects them again [Köhler, 1927, p. 127].

In later trials, Sultan solved the problem without any difficulty, even when some of the sticks provided would not fit together. Köhler reported that Sultan did not even attempt to join these nonfitting sticks.

Studies such as these were interpreted by Köhler as evidence of insight—the apparently spontaneous seeing of relations.

> The solutions of such problems, when they came, appeared to come suddenly, as though a new "configuration," embracing the whole complicated means to the desired end, had suddenly sprung up in the animal's consciousness; it was exactly as though the appropriate action followed on a "flash of insight," and, as in the case of all insightful behavior, the insight remained a permanent possession, enabling its possessor to act at once appropriately on a subsequent occasion [Flugel & West, 1964, p. 206].

This viewpoint differed dramatically from the trial-and-error learning of Thorndike and others. Köhler became a highly vocal critic of Thorndike's work, arguing that his experimental arrangements were artificial and allowed only blind, random, trial-and-error behavior on the part of the animal. Köhler suggested that the cats in Thorndike's puzzle box, for instance, could not survey the entire release mechanism (all the elements pertaining to the whole), and thus could engage in nothing but trial-and-error behavior. Similarly, an animal in a maze cannot see the overall pattern or design. He sees nothing but each "alley" as he comes to it and so can do nothing but try each of these new paths. In the Gestalt view, the organism must be able to see the relationship among the various parts of the problem before insight can occur.

These famous studies of insight were used to support the Gestalt molar conception of behavior (as opposed to the molecular elementistic view of the associationists and behaviorists) and the Gestalt notion that learning involves a reorganization or restructuring of the psychological environment.

Productive Thinking: Wertheimer

Wertheimer's posthumous *Productive Thinking* (1945) applied the Gestalt learning principles to human creative thinking and suggested that such thinking should be done in terms of wholes. Not only must the learner regard the situation as a whole; the teacher must also present the situation as a whole, not (like Thorndike) hiding the solution and thus, in a sense, requiring the person to make errors.

The case material in this book ranged from the study of children solving geometrical problems to the study of Einstein's thought processes leading to the theory of relativity. (Wertheimer and Einstein were close friends for a number of years.) At all ages and levels of problem difficulty Wertheimer found evidence to support his notion that the whole problem must dominate the parts. He believed that the detailed aspects of the problem should be considered only in relation to the structure of the total situation, and that problem solving should proceed from the whole problem downward to the parts, not the reverse.

Wertheimer believed that if a teacher arranged problems so that elements of classroom exercises were organized into meaningful wholes, then insight would occur. He also demonstrated that once the principle of a problem's solution had been grasped, it readily transferred to other situations.

Wertheimer also attacked the traditional educational practice of mechanical drill and rote learning, which derived from the associationistic theory of learning. Blind repetition is rarely productive, he argued, and cited as evidence the student's inability to solve a variation of a problem when the solution had been learned by rote rather than by insight. He did agree, however, that some material, such as names and dates, should be learned in rote fashion through association strengthened by repetition. Thus, he felt that repetition is useful to a point, but that its habitual use can produce habits of strictly mechanical behavior, resulting in robot-like performance rather than truly creative or productive thinking.

The Principle of Isomorphism

Having established that perceptions are organized wholes, the Gestalt psychologists turned to the problem of the cortical mechanisms involved in perception and attempted to develop a theory of the underlying neurological correlates of perceived *Gestalten*. Brief mention was made earlier of the Gestalt view of the cortex as a dynamic system in which the elements active at a given time interact. This view is in sharp contrast to the so-called "machine" conception of the nervous system, which likens nervous activity to a telephone switchboard that mechanically connects the sensory elements received via associationistic principles. In the latter view, the brain functions passively and is not capable of actively organizing or modifying the sensory elements received. Also, this view of the brain implies a one-to-one correspondence between the perception and its neurological counterpart.

In his original research on apparent movement, Wertheimer suggested that cortical activity is a configural whole process. Since apparent and actual motion are experienced identically, he argued, the cortical processes for actual and apparent motion must be similar. On the assumption that these two kinds of movement are identical, there must be corresponding brain processes. In order to account for the phi phenomenon, there must be a correspondence between the psychological or conscious experience and the underlying "brain experience."

This point of view has been called isomorphism, which says that "*Experienced order in space is always structurally identical with a functional order in the distribution of underlying brain processes* [Köhler, 1947, p. 61]." According to this principle of isomorphism, there is no one-to-one correspondence between the stimulus and the perception. It is the form of the perceptual experience that corresponds to the form of the stimulus. Thus, *Gestalten* are indeed "true" representations of the real world, but are not perfect reproductions of it. A percept is not a literal copy of the stimulus, just as a map is not a literal copy of the terrain it represents.

The percept, however, like the map, is identical (*iso*) in form or shape (*morphic*) to that which it represents, so that it does serve as a reliable guide to the perceived real world. This view has been supported by the three principal Gestaltists and is definitely associated with the Gestalt school.

The position was extended and elaborated upon by Köhler in his book, *Static and Stationary Physical Gestalts*, in 1920. Köhler considered that cortical processes behave in a manner similar to fields of electrical force. He suggested that, like the behavior of an electromagnetic field of force around a magnet, fields of neuronal activity may be established by electro-mechanical processes in the brain in response to sensory impulses. He conducted an extensive research program investigating various aspects of the concept of isomorphism and cortical brain fields. To Köhler, the notion of isomorphism was but one phase of a much more ambitious undertaking to demonstrate that physics, chemistry, biology, as well as psychology, all involve *Gestalten.*

The Reaction in America

The Gestalt movement gained momentum rather quickly in Germany as there were many who were dissatisfied with the artificiality and sterility of the older Wundtian psychology. In the United States, it first met with a less enthusiastic and more varied response. Its progress was comparatively slow, for several excellent reasons. In the first place, American psychology had already advanced beyond structuralism. Behaviorism was the second phase of American opposition to structuralism; hence America was much further removed from Wundtian elementism than Europe was at that time. As far as American psychologists were concerned, the Gestaltists were fighting a dead issue. There was also a language barrier which delayed dissemination of the Gestalt principles. Third, behaviorism was at a peak of popularity in American psychology at that time.

Thus the Gestaltists came to America protesting something that was no longer a vital concern. This was a dangerous situation when we remember that movements need something to oppose—something to push against—in order to survive.

When the Gestaltists became familiar with the trend in America, however, they perceived a new target: behaviorism, with its reductionistic and atomistic tendencies. The Gestaltists argued that behaviorism, like structuralism, dealt with artificial abstractions. It makes little difference, they said, whether analysis is in terms of introspective reduction to elements (Wundt) or objective reduction to conditioned reflexes (Watson): The end result is the same—a molecular instead of a molar approach.

The Gestaltists also took issue with the behaviorists' denial of the validity of introspection and their elimination of consciousness. Although the Gestaltists did not use Wundtian introspection, they favored the study of direct conscious experience.

Post-Founding Developments

The Spread of Gestalt Psychology after the Founding

By the mid-1930s, the Gestalt movement was a strongly united and coherent school, well established primarily in Germany and the United States. Its doctrines and principles were being used in such areas as child psychology, applied psychology, psychiatry, education, anthropology, and sociology. After 1933 and the beginning of the Nazi regime, the three principle proponents of the movement, along with other adherents, brought the message of Gestalt psychology more forcefully to this country, and a good deal of research began within the Gestalt framework. Also, many clinical psychologists began to combine the Gestalt approach with that of psychoanalysis.

By the late 1930s and early 1940s, with the appearance in American journals of Gestalt doctrines and the results of Gestalt-oriented research, Gestalt psychology became a vital part of American psychology. In the country of its birth, it suffered seriously from the departure of its leaders and the effects of the Hitler regime. In addition to the general anti-intellectual orientation of the Nazi era, Gestalt psychology was reduced to a minor position in the German academic system of the day. Some work in the Gestalt tradition went on, but it was of a rather diluted variety. Various areas of applied psychology using theories of wholeness, such as graphology (the study of handwriting), did play a role in clinical assessment. Also, personality testing based on derivatives of Gestalt theory was used extensively in German psychological warfare. On the whole, however, the years of Nazi domination were sterile for German psychology in general. Gestalt psychology has shown a renewed vitality since the 1950s as a part of a vigorous resurgence of interest in psychology in West Germany.

According to Murphy (1949), the general tendency in the United States has been to consider the principles of Gestalt psychology interesting and potentially useful as additions to existing systems, but certainly not the basis of an all-encompassing system in its own right. American psychology has attempted to demonstrate that both elemental and organized responses occur, and that both are useful.

To many psychologists, the Gestalt point of view is still quite an active concern, and it continues to promote substantial research. It no longer enjoys the combative spirit and uniqueness of a school, yet many of its adherents are working to elaborate and refine its basic points. This activity indicates that there has not been a total absorption of Gestalt psychology into the mainstream of American psychology.

Part of the reason for this is the existence of interesting complexities yet unresolved. Also, as recently as 1967, the Gestalt position boasted one of its original founders still living. Köhler provided a living link with the not-so-distant past. Further, Gestalt psychology had an extremely active disciple, Kurt Lewin, who developed a point of view supported by many American psychologists.

Field Theory: Kurt Lewin (1890–1947)

The growing tendency of nineteenth-century science was to think in terms of field relationships, and to move away from an atomistic and elementistic framework. As we have seen, Wertheimer and Gestalt psychology reflected this trend. The concept of field theory arose within psychology as an analogy to the concept of fields of force in physics.

In psychology, the term "field theory" has come to refer almost exclusively to the work of Kurt Lewin.[5] Lewin's position in relation to Gestalt psychology is not clear-cut, for although he is sometimes classed as a member of the Gestalt school, he is equally often regarded as the developer of a separate but related system. He began working independently, but was later closely associated with both Köhler and Wertheimer at the then active center of the Gestalt movement at Berlin. In his productive career as a whole, he went well beyond the framework of the orthodox Gestalt position.

Lewin's work is Gestalt-like in orientation, but it centers on needs, personality, and social factors, whereas the Gestaltists emphasized perception and learning. Where the Gestaltists stressed physiological constructs to attempt to explain behavior, Lewin considered psychology more as a social science. It is simplest to consider Lewin's system as an elaboration or outgrowth of the Gestalt movement for two reasons: (a) he was closely associated with the Gestaltists at Berlin for a time, and (b) his position fits the Gestalt system more readily than any other.

---

[5] Tolman's system, discussed in Chapter 11, is also often considered a field theory. We noted his attempted combination of parts of behaviorism and Gestalt psychology.

Born in Mogilno, Germany, Lewin undertook his university education at Freiburg, Munich, and finally Berlin, where he received his Ph.D. in psychology in 1914. In addition to psychology, he studied mathematics and physics. After a period of military service, for which he was decorated, he returned to the University of Berlin, where he became such a productive and creative member of the Gestalt group that he was considered a colleague of the three senior Gestaltists. At Berlin he performed much important research on association and motivation, and began developing his field theory.

He was already well known in America when, in 1932, he spent 6 months as visiting professor at Stanford. In 1933, he decided to leave Germany permanently because of the Nazi menace. He spent the next 2 years at Cornell and in 1935 he went to the University of Iowa, where he conducted a series of studies in the experimental social psychology of the child. As a result of highly successful research efforts in social psychology, Lewin was invited to develop and head a new research center for group dynamics at the Massachusetts Institute of Technology in 1944. Although he died shortly thereafter (in 1947), his program was so effective that the research center remains active and productive in its new location at the University of Michigan.

Throughout his 30 years of professional activity, Lewin devoted himself consistently to the broadly defined area of human motivation. His research emphasized the study of human behavior in its total physical and social context.

At the outset, Lewin analyzed the basic structure of science, which he believed had evolved through three levels or stages: speculative, descriptive, and constructive. Early Greek science represented the first stage, which was given to large-scale speculative theorizing that attempted to encompass all natural phenomena. At that stage, systems were derived from very few basic concepts and were very general and broad in nature.

The descriptive stage involved the accumulation of the greatest possible number of facts, which were described precisely and objectively. Theorizing was minimized, and attempts at classification were made in terms of very broad abstractions.

The third, or constructive, stage was the one within which Lewin developed his system. He envisaged as its goal the discovery of laws that would permit the prediction of individual phenomena. According to this view, events are lawful and orderly even if they occur in only one case. Taking this constructive stage as his model, Lewin argued that laws of behavior need not be based on statistical averages in order to have value. His psychology thus focuses on the individual, not the mean responses of groups of individuals. He contended that the specific individual and the total situation in which he performs must be understood in order to predict behavior.

The theory of fields in physics led Lewin to consider that the psychological activities of a person occur in a kind of psychological field or "life space." The life space comprises all the events that may possibly influence a person, past, present, and future, since from a psychological standpoint each of these three aspects of life can determine behavior in any single situation. It consists of the needs of the individual as they interact with his psychological environment.

The life space may show varying degrees of differentiation as a function of the amount and kind of experiences the individual has accumulated. Because it lacks experiences, an infant has few, if any, differentiated regions in its life space. A highly educated, sophisticated adult shows complex and well-differentiated life space as a function of his past experiences.

Lewin wanted to use a mathematical model to represent his theoretical concept of psychological processes. Since he was concerned with the single case, statistics were not useful for his purposes. He chose a form of geometry—topology—that he felt was adequate to the task of "maping the life space" so as to show at any given moment all the possible goals of an individual and all the routes to these goals. Topology deals with transformations in space by representing spatial relationships in nonquantitative fashion. It is a conception of space that deals with the order of relationships, but not with their direction or distance. It can show connections among regions within the life space and their spatial relationships to one another. To represent direction, Lewin developed a new form of qualitative geometry called *hodological space,* in which he used vectors to represent directions of movement toward a goal.

To complete the schematic representation of his system, Lewin introduced the notion of valences to refer to the positive or negative value of objects in the life space. Objects that are attractive to the individual or that satisfy his needs have positive valence, while objects that threaten him have negative valence.

Lewin postulated a state of equilibrium between the person and his environment. When this equilibrium is disturbed, a tension (Lewin's concept of motivation or need) arises that leads to locomotion in the attempt to restore the equilibrium. Lewin believed that human behavior involves the continual appearance of tensions, locomotions, and reliefs. This sequence of tension–locomotion–equilibrium is akin to need–activity–relief. Whenever a need is felt, a state of tension exists, and the organism acts in order to release the tension by restoring the equilibrium.

Lewin's "blackboard psychology" included complex diagrams representing all manner of psychological phenomena. In field theory, all forms of behavior can be represented schematically. A simple example of a bit of behavior as it would be represented in Lewin's system is shown in Figure 12.2, which illustrates a situation in which a child wants to go to the movies but is forbidden to do so by his mother. The ellipse represents the life space and C represents the child. The arrow is a vector indicating that C is motivated to go to the movie, which, as indicated, has positive valence. The vertical line is the barrier (the mother) to the goal and is shown to have negative valence. (This is an overly simple example and is not typical of the highly complex psychological phenomena that Lewin was able to represent through his topological and hodological space.)

Lewin's theoretical system generated a great deal of important and influential research. For example, a series of studies were conducted involving his assumption of a *tension-system*. Tension, as we have seen, means motivation or need, and Lewin believed that when a goal is reached, the tension is discharged. The first experimental attempt to test this tension-system proposition was performed, under Lewin's supervision, by Bluma Zeigarnik in 1927. Subjects were given a series of tasks and were allowed to complete some of them, but were interrupted prior to their completion of others. The predictions derived from Lewin's system are that: (*1*) a tension-system develops in a subject when he is given a task to perform, (*2*) if the task is completed, the tension is dissipated, (*3*) if, however, the task is not completed, the persistence of the tension results in greater likelihood of recall of the task. Zeigarnik's results confirmed the predictions in that the subjects recalled the uncompleted tasks more easily than the completed ones. Much subsequent

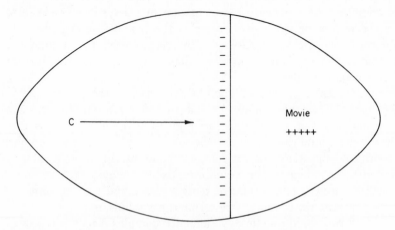

Figure 12.2. Example of a life space.

research has been performed on this phenomenon which has come to be called the *Zeigarnik effect.*

Lewin and Social Psychology

In the early years of his career, Lewin was chiefly concerned with theoretical problems and issues. By the late 1930s, however, he became very interested in social psychology, and his pioneering efforts in this field alone are sufficient to justify his position in the history of psychology.

Perhaps the outstanding feature of Lewin's social psychology, called group dynamics, is the application of concepts dealing with the individual and group behavior. Just as the individual and his environment form a psychological field, the group and its environment form a social field. Social behaviors are seen as occurring in, and resulting from, simultaneously existing social entities, such as subgroups, members, barriers, and channels of communication. Thus, group behavior is a function of the total field situation existing at a given time.

Lewin's early social–psychological research was concerned with behavior in various kinds of social climates. A very famous study involving democratic and authoritarian leadership and its effects on the productiveness and general behavior of groups of boys (Lewin, Lippitt, & White, 1939) is a classic experiment in social psychology. Studies such as this opened up important new areas of social research and contributed greatly to the rapid growth of social psychology.

Lewin stressed the importance of "social action" research—the study of relevant social problems with a view to introducing change. He was much concerned with racial conflicts, and conducted studies in the community on the effects of integrated housing on prejudice, on equalizing opportunity for employment, and on the development and prevention of prejudice in children.

His concern was with the realities of everyday life, and his research transformed real-world problems such as prejudice into controlled experiments so as to benefit from the rigor of the experimental approach without the artificiality and sterility of the academic laboratory.

An important contribution to social psychology is his founding, in 1942, of the Society for the Psychological Study of Social Issues, which fosters research oriented toward the solution of social problems.

A year before his death, Lewin was instrumental in developing what is now called *sensitivity training.* The T-groups (training groups) set up in his National Training Laboratories were the first part of a movement later characterized by encounter groups. Sensitivity training has been applied with great zeal in a wide variety of situations from industry to education, from reducing intergroup conflict to developing individual potential.

In general, Lewin's experimental programs and research findings are more acceptable to many psychologists than his theoretical views. In spite of this, his theoretical influence in social and child psychology and, to some degree, experimental psychology is considerable. Many of his concepts and experimental techniques are also widely accepted in the areas of personality and motivation.

Lewin's considerable influence did not end with his death. His views and concerns are being extended and elaborated very actively in psychology today.

Criticisms of Gestalt Psychology

The following comments refer only to the original Gestalt formulations, not to latter-day derivatives such as Lewinian field theory. Criticisms of the Gestalt position appeared promptly. They included the major criticism that the Gestaltists were trying to solve problems by simply changing them into postulates. For example, organization of conscious perception is not treated as a problem requiring resolution through one means or another, but as a "given"—a phenomenon that exists in its own right. Critics argue that this is tantamount to solving a problem by denying its existence!

Many tough-minded scientists have asserted that the Gestalt position is too vague. These critics charge that some of its basic concepts and many of its terms (organization, for example) are not defined with sufficient rigor to be scientifically meaningful. If it is true that the Gestaltists used vague and ambiguous terms, they may not differ greatly from psychologists of other theoretical persuasions in this respect, including many behaviorists.

The Gestalt psychologists countered these charges by insisting that in a young science, attempts at explanations and definitions must necessarily be incomplete, but that being incomplete is not the same as being vague.

It has also been claimed that the basic tenets of Gestalt psychology are not really new, which is, of course, true since the Gestalt movement, like the others we have discussed, had its historical anticipations. This criticism, however, has no bearing on the relative merits of the Gestalt position.

Some critics allege that Gestalt psychology is too occupied with theory at the expense of adequate experimental research and empirical supporting data. The Gestalt school has been heavily oriented toward theory, but since the time of its founders it has also stressed experimentation and has been both directly and indirectly responsible for a great deal of research.

Related to this criticism is the suggestion that the experimental work of the Gestaltists is inferior to that of S–R theorists in that it lacks adequate control of variables. The same critics argue that the Gestaltists' nonquantified data are not amenable to statistical analysis. The Gestaltists take the position that qualitative results must come first in the investigation of a problem area; therefore, much of their research has deliberately been less quantitative than psychologists of other orientations consider necessary. Much Gestalt research has necessarily been preliminary and exploratory since it often involves investigations of new problem areas (or old areas approached from a completely different point of view). Certain Gestalt psychologists may have conducted inadequately designed and controlled research, but this criticism could be made of some psychologists of any theoretical persuasion. Certainly, no school advocates sloppy experimentation.

A final criticism relates to what some consider the poorly supported and defined physiological assumptions of the system. The Gestaltists readily admit that their theorizing in this area is tentative, but they add that such speculation is recognized as a useful adjunct in any system. In this case, it has generated a great deal of research and the validity of the research results has not been lessened by the speculative framework within which it was conducted.

Contributions of Gestalt Psychology

The Gestalt movement has unquestionably left an indelible imprint on psychology. Like other movements that challenged older traditions, it had a refreshing and stimulating influence on psychology as a whole.

The Gestalt point of view has greatly influenced the area of perception and, to some extent, learning. Its effect on the study of perception is evident in virtually every introductory and experimental psychology textbook. More recent work deriving from the Gestalt school strongly suggests that it is still a vital concern, as discussed earlier.

Unlike its chief temporal competitor, behaviorism, Gestalt psychology remains a separate entity in that its major tenets have not been fully absorbed into the mainstream of psychological thought. It continues to foster interest in conscious experience as a legitimate problem area for at least part of psychology. (Whether this is a fruitful or inhibiting effect is a moot question among psychologists.) Again, this interest in conscious experience is not of the Wundt–Titchener introspective variety, but centers around a modern version of phenomenology. Contemporary adherents of the Gestalt position are convinced that conscious experience does occur and can (indeed must) be studied. They recognize, however, that it cannot be investigated with the same order of precision and objectivity as overt behavior.

Contemporary proponents of a phenomenological psychology are numerous in Europe and the point of view seems to be gaining support in the United States. While not widely accepted in America, psychologists are becoming more familiar with phenomenology, at least to the point of taking issue with it.

Finally, the pointed and consistent criticisms of extant systems offered by Gestalt psychology have had an important influence by demanding a critical reexamination of the opposing positions.

SUGGESTED FURTHER READINGS

Wertheimer
Asch, S. E. Max Wertheimer's contribution to modern psychology. *Social Research,* 1946, **13**, 81–102.
Köhler, W. Max Wertheimer, 1880–1943. *Psychological Review,* 1944, **51**, 143–146.

Koffka
Köhler, W. Kurt Koffka. *Psychological Review,* 1942, **49**, 97–101.

Köhler
Prentice, W. C. H. The systematic psychology of Wolfgang Köhler. In S. Koch (Ed.), *Psychology: A study of a science.* Vol. 1. New York: McGraw-Hill, 1959. Pp. 427–455.
Crannell, C. Wolfgang Köhler. *Journal of the History of the Behavioral Sciences,* 1970, **6**, 267–268.
Henle, M. (Ed.) *The selected papers of Wolfgang Köhler.* New York: Liveright, 1971.
Köhler, W. Gestalt psychology. In D. Krantz, *Schools of psychology.* New York: Appleton, 1969. Pp. 69–85.

Lewin
Lewin, K. *Field theory in social science.* New York: Harper, 1951.
Marrow, A. *The practical theorist: The life and work of Kurt Lewin.* New York: Basic Books, 1969.

General
Ellis, W. D. *A source book of Gestalt psychology.* New York: Humanities Press, 1967. London: Routledge & Kegan Paul, 1938.

Heider, F. Gestalt theory: Early history and reminiscences. *Journal of the History of the Behavioral Sciences*, 1970, **6**, 131–139.

Helson, H. Why did their precursors fail and the Gestalt Psychologists succeed? *American Psychologist*, 1969, **24**, 1006–1011.

Henle, M. (Ed.) *Documents of Gestalt psychology*. Berkeley, California: California Univ. Press, 1961.

Hochberg, J. E. Effects of the Gestalt revolution: The Cornell symposium on perception. *Psychological Review*, 1957, **64**, 73–84.

Katz, D. *Gestalt psychology*. New York: Ronald Press, 1950.

Phenomenology

Combs, A. W., & Snygg, D. *Individual behavior: A perceptual approach to behavior.* (Rev. ed.) New York: Harper, 1959.

Wann, T. W. (Ed.) *Behaviorism and phenomenology: Contrasting bases for modern psychology*. Chicago, Illinois: Univ. of Chicago Press, 1964.

13

Psychoanalysis:
The Beginnings

Introduction

The term *psychoanalysis* and the name Sigmund Freud are familiar to most literate people. While leaders like Fechner, Wundt, or Titchener are seldom known outside professional psychology, Freud enjoys a phenomenal degree of popularity, although his system may be known to the lay public only superficially or inaccurately. It is often a source of disappointment to teachers of psychology to find that so many beginning students think that Freud *is* psychology, and that psychology deals only with the treatment of the mentally disturbed.

Psychoanalysis overlapped to a considerable degree the other schools of psychology with which we have dealt. Consider the situation in 1895, the year in which Freud published his first book, marking the formal beginning of his new movement.

In that year, Wundt was 63 years old and Titchener, just 28, had been at Cornell for only 2 years; structuralism was still a very vital position. The spirit of functionalism was beginning to grow in America, but it had not yet been formalized into a school. Neither behaviorism nor Gestalt psychology had begun. Indeed, Watson was 17 and Wertheimer 15.

At the time of Freud's death in 1939, the entire psychological outlook had changed. Structuralism and functionalism had become history, Gestalt psychology was being vigorously transplanted to the United States, and behaviorism had become the American form of psychology. And, by 1939, Freud had achieved great prominence and his position was already splintered into subschools and derivative movements.

The relationship between psychoanalysis and these schools of psychol-. ogy was, during those years, only temporal. There was no substantive linking, either through assent or dissent, between Freud and the other founders in psychology.

All the other schools with which we have dealt owe their impetus and form to structuralism, either evolving from it, as is the case with functionalism, or revolting against it, as with behaviorism and Gestalt psychology.

In contrast, psychoanalysis was not directly related to these evolutionary and revolutionary trends and movements because psychoanalysis did not originate within psychology. Freud's study of personality and its disturbances was remote from the psychology of the university laboratory. Regardless of their fundamental disagreements, the systems outlined earlier shared an academic heritage; all of these schools formed their basic concepts and approaches in a milieu of laboratories, libraries, and lecture halls. Their traditional areas of concern were perception, sensation, learning, and the like. They were, or strove to be, pure science.

Psychoanalysis, on the other hand, was neither a product of academic halls, nor a pure science. Further, it was not (and still is not) a school or systematic theory of psychology directly comparable to the others. Psychoanalysis has not been greatly concerned with the traditional areas primarily because its goal is to provide therapy for the emotionally disturbed. In aim, subject matter, and methods, psychoanalysis diverged from the mainstream of psychological thought from the very beginning. Its subject matter is abnormal behavior, which had been relatively neglected by the other schools, and its method is clinical observation rather than controlled laboratory experimentation.

Despite the radically different nature of psychoanalysis, it has exerted an undeniable influence on contemporary psychology. In addition, areas outside of psychology—the social sciences, literature, language, religion, philosophy, ethics, and the arts—have felt its impact. We shall see, however, that its acceptance by academic psychology has been, for the most part, less than enthusiastic.

Historical Antecedents

Despite the claims of some of Freud's followers, his insights were not without anticipations. The psychoanalytic movement had very definite intellectual and cultural antecedents. Two major sources of influence led up to the formal founding of psychoanalysis. One was earlier philosophical speculation on the nature of unconscious psychological phenomena, a notion that plays a major role in Freud's thinking. The other was the earlier work in psychopathology.

Early Theories of the Unconscious

We have seen that most of the early history of scientific psychology was concerned with consciousness. The experimental psychology of the late nineteenth century was convinced that the only proper field of study was the content of consciousness. Thus, the main current of work in psychology was directed toward the analysis of conscious experience. There was very little consideration of unconscious determinants of behavior. We saw, too, that the background provided for the new psychology by empirical philosophers was also oriented toward conscious experience.

However, not everyone who pioneered the new psychology or its antecedent philosophy agreed with this exclusive focus on conscious mental content; some believed in the importance of nonconscious processes. Although the influence of the unconscious can indeed be traced to Plato, we will begin by considering more recent antecedents.

Early in the eighteenth century, the great German mathematician and philosopher Gottfried Wilhelm Leibnitz (1646–1716) developed his theory of *monadology*. Monads, which Leibnitz considered the individual elements of all reality, were not physical atoms; they were not even material in the usual sense of the word. Each monad was an unextended psychic entity. Leibnitz went on to insist that although each monad was mental in nature, it had some of the properties of physical matter, and that when enough of them were collected into an aggregate, they created an extension.

Monads were centers of activity and energy. In general terms, they could be likened to perception and are very similar to consciousness. Mental events (the activity of monads) had differing degrees of clearness or consciousness, which could range from the completely unconscious to the most clear or definitely conscious. There were, then, according to Leibnitz, lower degrees of consciousness, which he called *petites perceptions*. The conscious actualization of these he called *apperception*.

For example, the sound of waves breaking on the shore is an apperception. This apperception, however, is made up of all the individual falling drops of water, none of which is conscious by itself. The individual drop of water, like the monad, is the *petite perception* and is not consciously perceived by itself. When sufficient numbers of them congregate, however, they summate to produce an apperception.

A century later, Johann Friedrich Herbart (1776–1841) developed the Leibnitzian notion of the unconscious into the concept of threshold or limen of consciousness. Those ideas below the limen are unconscious. When an idea arises to conscious levels of awareness, Herbart said, it is apperceived (as Leibnitz had said), but Herbart went beyond this. In order for an idea to rise into consciousness, it had to be compatible and congruent with the ideas extant in consciousness. Incongruous ideas could not exist in consciousness at the same time, and ideas that were irrelevant were forced out of consciousness to become what Herbart called inhibited ideas. Inhibited ideas existed below the threshold of consciousness and were akin to Leibnitz's *petites perceptions*. According to Herbart, there is a conflict among ideas in which they actively struggle for realization in consciousness. Boring (1950) suggested that Leibnitz foreshadowed the doctrine of the unconscious, but that Herbart actually began it.

Fechner also contributed to the development of thinking about the unconscious; he used the notion of limen or threshold, but his suggestion that the mind is analogous to an iceberg in that a considerable portion of it is hidden below the surface, where it is influenced by unobservable forces, was a greater influence on Freud.

Shakow (1969) points out that the notion of the unconscious was very much a part of the *Zeitgeist* in the 1880s in Europe. Not only was it of interest to professionals, but it was also considered by laymen to be a fashionable topic of conversation. A book entitled *The Philosophy of the Unconscious* (Von Hartmann) was so popular that it went through nine editions between 1868 and 1882.

Freud, therefore, was not the first to "discover" or even to discuss seriously the unconscious. Although some early thinkers merely mentioned the unconscious, others attributed great importance to it. No one before Freud, however, fully realized the significance of unconscious motivation or found a way to study it. Freud believed that in exploring the unconscious he would be able to explain what had previously been considered inexplicable. He saw unconscious feelings and thoughts as directly or indirectly influencing behavior.

The Influence from Psychopathology

We have seen that a new movement always requires something to revolt against—something to push away from in order to gain momentum.

Since psychoanalysis did not develop within academic psychology, the existing order that it opposed was not Wundtian structuralism nor any other psychological school of thought. To discover what Freud opposed, we must look at the prevailing thought in the area in which he worked— understanding and treating mental disorders.

The history of the treatment of the mentally ill is a fascinating and depressing story in its own right. Much of the earlier history presents a striking picture of man's inhumanity to man. In the Middle Ages, the disturbed individual received almost no understanding and very little treatment. The mind was alleged to be a free agent and hence responsible for its own condition. The "treatment" for the mentally disturbed consisted primarily of blame and punishment, for the causes were considered to be wickedness, witchcraft, and possession by demons.

Nor did conditions improve during the Renaissance; a passage from Boring (1950) recounts events and attitudes characteristic of that period (and presents a message of importance for any time and place).

> The great changes in the social structure at the time of the Renaissance created a general feeling of uncertainty and insecurity . . . . Insecure men, uncertain of the future, frustrated by change, stand ready to exorcise the threat of evil by an uncritical distribution of blame and punishment. Then, as now, they were ready to go witch hunting because they were afraid, and in the fifteenth century the Church did it for them. In 1489 *Jacob Sprenger* and *Heinrich Kraemer*, two Dominican brothers, taking advantage of the recent invention of the printing press, published the *Malleus maleficarum*, a title which perhaps can be best translated as the *Witch Hammer*, since the book was designed to be a tool for hammering at the witches. The *Malleus maleficarum* is a cruel encyclopedia on witchcraft, the detection of witches and the procedures for examining them by torture and for sentencing them. The treatise had the approval of the Pope, of the King of Rome and, after some reluctant resistance, of the Faculty of Theology at the University of Cologne. It identified witchcraft with heresy and for us it identifies witchcraft with the mental disorders, many of whose symptoms it describes with care. For three hundred years in nineteen editions this malevolent compendium remained the authority and guide of the Inquisition as it sought out heresy and demoniacal possession among the people [pp. 694–695].[1]

[1] From Edwin G. Boring, *A History of Experimental Psychology*, 2nd ed., © 1950. Reprinted by permission of Prentice-Hall, Inc., Englewood Cliffs, New Jersey.

The Inquisition continued through the eighteenth century, but in the nineteenth century a more humane and rational attitude toward the mentally ill took hold. In Europe and America, the chains were struck (literally) from the insane as the decline in the influence of religious superstition paved the way for scientific investigation of the causes of mental illness.

During the nineteenth century, there were two main schools of thought in psychiatry, the somatic and the psychic. The somatic school held that organic disturbances of the brain account for abnormalities of behavior, while the psychic school sought causes in the mental or psychological sphere. Physical disturbances of the brain had been found in certain kinds of mental illness but not in others. On the whole, however, nineteenth-century psychiatry was dominated by the somatic school.

Psychoanalysis developed as one facet of a revolt against this somatic orientation. As work with the mentally ill continued, some became convinced that emotional stress was of greater importance than brain lesions in the etiology of abnormal behavior.

Hypnosis played an important role in fostering concern for the psychic causes of abnormal behavior. In the latter part of the eighteenth century, hypnosis was brought to medical attention by Friedrich Anton Mesmer. For a century, *mesmerism* was almost universally rejected by the medical profession, which regarded it as quackery. In England, James Braid (1795–1860) called the phenomena characteristic of the hypnotic state "neurypnology," from which the term hypnosis was later derived. His careful work and disdain for exaggerated claims earned some scientific respectability for hypnosis.

Hypnosis achieved greater prominence with the work of Jean Martin Charcot (1825–1893), who was a physician and head of a neurological clinic at Salpêtrière, the Parisian hospital for insane women. Charcot treated hysterical patients by means of hypnosis with some degree of success. More important, he described the symptoms of both hysteria and hypnosis in medical terms, making the latter phenomenon more readily acceptable to medicine and the French Academy of Science (which had rejected mesmerism three times). Approval by the Academy was vitally important, for it made it "safe" for neurologists to begin investigating the psychological aspects of mental illness.

Charcot's work, however, remained primarily neurological, so that physical disturbances, paralysis, and the like were emphasized in it. Hysteria, therefore, continued to be ascribed to somatic causes until Charcot's pupil and successor, Pierre Janet (1859–1947), accepted Charcot's invitation in 1889 to become director of the psychological laboratory at Salpêtrière. Janet rejected the opinion that hysteria was a physiological disturbance, and saw it instead as a mental disorder. Accordingly, he emphasized mental phenomena, particularly impairments of memory and fixed ideas, and stressed hypnosis as a method of treatment.

The foregoing précis, of course, barely indicates the important work of Charcot and Janet in the treatment of the mentally disturbed. The relevant point here is the change in the concept of the cause of mental illness from the somatic to the psychic or mental. Janet's work appeared shortly before psychoanalysis and was beginning to exert an impact on psychology and psychiatry when it was superseded by Freud's more dramatic ideas.

Other Sources of Influence

Several other influences on Freud deserve mention. The intellectual climate of the eighteenth and nineteenth centuries included the motivational doctrine of hedonism, which stated, in essence, that man strives to gain pleasure and to avoid pain. Associated primarily with Jeremy Bentham and his notion of utilitarianism, hedonism was also supported by some of the British associationists. One of Freud's doctrines, the pleasure principle, was derived from hedonism.

During Freud's university training, he came in contact with the mechanistic school of thought, as represented by the four young physiologists mentioned in Chapter 3: Carl Ludwig, Emil du Bois-Reymond, Ernst Brücke, and Helmholtz. These students of the great Johannes Müller had united to take the position that no forces are to be found in living things that do not exist in inanimate objects. As discussed earlier, they argued that there are no forces active within the organism other than the common physical and chemical ones. Freud was a student of Brücke's, and the latter's mechanistic orientation influenced Freud in formulating his notion of the determined nature of human behavior, a concept he called psychic determinism.

Freud's deterministic orientation was also supported by his interest in Darwinian evolution. Like Darwin, Freud tended to take a biological view of man. (Freud acknowledged that Darwin's work, along with an essay on nature by Goethe, influenced his choice of medicine as a profession.)

Thus, there were many diverse sources of influence on Freud's thinking. It has been said that no small part of Freud's genius was the ability to draw on these various sources to develop his system, a characteristic possessed by all of the founders we have discussed.

Sigmund Freud (1856–1939) and
the Development of Psychoanalysis

The psychoanalytic movement is a highly personal school centered primarily on Freud and secondarily on his disciples. The system Freud developed is much more intimately related to his own life than is the case with other movements that we have discussed. Consequently, the story of his life is of great importance to an understanding of his system.

Freud was born on May 6, 1856, in Freiberg, Moravia (now Pribor, Czechoslovakia). His father was a relatively unsuccessful Jewish wool merchant who, when his business failed in Moravia, moved his family first to Leipzig and then (when Sigmund was 4 years old) to Vienna. Freud remained in Vienna for nearly 80 years.

One of eight children, Freud early demonstrated great intellectual ability, which his family did everything possible to encourage. For instance, his bedroom was the only room in the house to have an oil lamp to provide better light for study; other members of the family had only candles. The other children were not allowed to study music, lest their practice disturb the young scholar. Life for the large Freud family was not easy in Austria, where anti-Semitism was rampant, but at least Jews had been granted citizenship and were able to earn a living in certain occupations.

Freud entered the gymnasium a year early and was a brilliant student, graduating with distinction at the age of 17. During this time he was undecided about his choice of career. His interests included civilization, human culture, human relationships, and even military history. The reading of Darwin's theory of evolution awakened an interest in a scientific approach to an understanding of life and, with some hesitation, Freud decided on medicine. Like others we have met, Freud had no real desire to be a practicing physician but selected medicine in the hope that it would lead to a career in scientific research.

Freud began his studies at the University of Vienna in 1873. Because of his interest in several fields not directly connected with his medical training, he took 8 years to complete his studies. At first he concentrated on biology and dissected over 400 male eels in search of the precise structure of the testes. His results were not very conclusive, but it is of interest that his very first attempt at research concerned sex. He then moved on to physiology and work on the spinal cord of the fish. He apparently enjoyed physiology because he worked for 6 years over a microscope in Brücke's physiological institute. During his medical training, Freud discovered the analgesic properties of cocaine but missed the fame that came to one of his colleagues, who discovered its anesthetic properties. He also took some nonrequired philosophy courses with Franz Brentano.

Freud wanted to remain in scientific work within a university setting, but Brücke discouraged this inclination because of Freud's financial circumstances. Freud became convinced that it would be much too long a time before he could earn a livelihood in the Austrian university world and so he decided to take his medical examinations and enter private practice as a physician. This necessitated working in clinics and hospitals, for he had neglected the clinical aspects of his medical education in order to pursue his research in physiology. During his hospital training, he specialized as much as possible in the anatomy and organic diseases of the nervous system, particularly paralysis, aphasia, the effects of brain injuries in children, and speech psychopathology.

Freud received his M.D. in 1881 and the following year began private practice as a clinical neurologist. It was apparently a difficult step for, although he had become well known for his research in neurology, he was not greatly attracted to private practice in the field. The most compelling reason for his beginning a private practice was his engagement in 1882 to Martha Bernays, who was as poor as he. Their courtship was rather violent at times as Freud evidenced jealousy, depression, and irritability. Their marriage was postponed several times for financial reasons but finally, after a frustrating 4-year engagement, they were married. It is reported that during the first few months of marriage, Freud had to borrow money and even pawn their watches in order to survive. The situation improved, of course, but the early years of poverty were never completely forgotten.

Freud's extremely long working hours prevented his spending a great deal of time with his wife and children (of which there were eventually six). He also vacationed alone, because his wife could not maintain his fast pace.

A friendship of utmost importance to Freud was developed in these difficult years with Josef Breuer (1842–1925), a physician who had gained some renown for his study of respiration and his discovery of the functioning of the semicircular canals. A highly successful and sophisticated general practitioner, Breuer gave the impoverished and younger Freud advice and friendship, and even loaned him money. The two often discussed some of Breuer's patients, one of whom, Anna O.,[2] is of monumental importance in the development of psychoanalysis.

[2] Anna O.'s real name was Bertha Pappenheim, and she later became a social worker in West Germany. See L. Freeman, *The Story of Anna O.* (New York: Walker, 1972).

A very intelligent and extremely attractive 21-year-old, Anna showed a wide range of severe hysterical symptoms—paralysis, memory losses, mental deterioration, nausea, and disturbances of vision and speech. Breuer began treating her by using hypnosis. He found that while under hypnosis she remembered specific experiences that seemed to have given rise to certain symptoms. Moreover, talking about the experiences while in a hypnotic state seemed to relieve the symptoms. For example, Anna went through a period when she could not drink water despite feelings of thirst. Under hypnosis she related that she had had a similar aversion to water in childhood and then recalled that she had seen a dog she disliked drinking from a glass. After telling this incident to Breuer, she found that she could drink water again with no difficulty, and the symptom never recurred.

Breuer saw Anna every day for over a year. During their meetings, Anna would recount the disturbing incidents of the day, after which she often experienced some relief from her symptoms. She referred to her talks with Breuer as "chimney sweeping" and the "talking cure." The procedure was later called "catharsis."

As the treatment continued, Breuer realized (and mentioned to Freud) that the incidents Anna recalled under hypnosis involved some thought or experience that was repulsive to her. When she was able to relive these experiences under hypnosis, her symptoms either became less severe or disappeared altogether.

Breuer's wife grew jealous of the close emotional relationship that arose between Anna and Breuer. Anna exhibited what was later called a positive transference to Breuer, that is, she transferred her feelings toward her father to Breuer. Later in the development of psychoanalysis, transference was seen to be a necessary part of the therapeutic process; however, Breuer saw the situation as a threat to his career and therefore stopped Anna's treatment. A few hours after he told Anna that he could not continue to see her, she experienced the symptoms of hysterical childbirth. Breuer terminated this experience through hypnosis and left with his wife the next day to spend a second honeymoon in Venice (at which time his wife became pregnant)!

In 1885, a small postgraduate grant enabled Freud to spend $4\frac{1}{2}$ months studying in France under Charcot. An important incident took place during this stay in Paris: At a reception one evening, Freud heard Charcot assert vehemently that a certain patient's difficulties had a sexual basis. "But in this sort of case it's always a question of the genitals—always, always, always [Freud, 1914]." To Freud this assessment was an illuminating and exciting insight; thereafter, he was alert to the suggestion of sexual problems in his patients.

In France Freud also had an opportunity to observe Charcot's use of hypnosis in the treatment of hysterics. The French physician had shown that the traditional view of hysteria as an exclusively female malady (the word had derived from the Greek *hystera*, meaning womb) was incorrect by demonstrating the existence of hysterical symptoms in some of his male patients.

On his return from France, Freud presented Charcot's methods and results, including the notion of hysteria in males, to his medical colleagues in Vienna. The poor reception accorded his lecture deeply distressed Freud and intensified his growing animosity toward the medical establishment, which feeling was mutual.

A year after his return from Paris, Freud was once again reminded of the possible sexual basis of a patient's disturbance. A noted gynecologist asked Freud if he would take the case of one of his patients, a woman who suffered strong anxiety attacks that were relieved only if she knew exactly where her doctor was at every moment.

The physician told Freud that the woman's anxieties were due to her impotent husband; the woman was still a virgin after 18 years of marriage. The physician told Freud (Freud, 1914)

> The sole prescription for such a malady . . . is familiar enough to us, but we cannot order it. It runs:

> "R Penis normalis
> *dosim*
> *repetatur!*"

Freud was still associated with Breuer at that time and adopted the methods of hypnosis and catharsis in dealing with his patients. He gradually became less satisfied with hypnosis, however, for although it seemed successful in removing symptoms, it did not seem able to effect a total cure since many patients returned with a different set of symptoms. Furthermore, some neurotic patients could not be easily or deeply hypnotized.

These and other problems induced Freud to abandon the hypnotic portion of the treatment but to retain the so-called talking cure or catharsis. He gradually developed what has been called the most important step in the evolution of the psychoanalytic method: the technique of free association. In this procedure, the patient lies on a couch and is encouraged to talk freely and spontaneously, giving complete expression to every idea, no matter how embarrassing, unimportant, or foolish it might appear. The basic aim of Freud's developing method of psycho-analysis was to bring into conscious awareness memories or thoughts that had been repressed and that were presumably the source of the patient's abnormal behavior. Through the technique of free association, Freud's patients' memories seemed invariably to go further and further back into their childhood experiences. Freud found that many of these repressed memories concerned sexual matters. Already alert to the possible role of sexual factors in the etiology of his patients' illnesses, Freud became more attuned to the occurrence of sexual material in the narratives of his patients.

In 1895, Breuer and Freud published a book, *Studies on Hysteria*, that is often considered the formal starting point of psychoanalysis. It contained a joint paper that had been previously published; five case histories, including that of Anna O.; a theoretical paper by Breuer; and a chapter by Freud on psychotherapy. It was not exactly an overwhelming success. Of the few reviews given the work, most were highly critical, and only 626 copies were sold over the next 13 years. Breuer had been reluctant to publish the book, and this seemed to mark the beginning of the break in his personal friendship with Freud. This split was apparently caused by Freud's emphasis on sex in his theories. By around 1898, the break between the two was complete and apparently never healed.

By the mid-1890s, Freud had become convinced that sex played the dominant role in neurosis. He observed that most of his patients reported traumatic sexual experiences in their childhoods, often involving members of their own families, and he came to believe that neurosis was not possible in a person with a normal sex life.

In an important paper presented to the Society of Psychiatry and Neurology in Vienna in 1896, Freud reported that his patients had revealed experiences resembling seduction in childhood, with the seducer usually being an older relative, most often the father. These seduction traumas, Freud believed, caused the adult neurotic behavior. He further reported that his patients were extremely hesitant in describing the seduction experience in detail and that the entire situation seemed to contain the feeling of unreality. Patients recounted the events in such a manner as to suggest that they actually did not fully remember them—as though they had never really happened. Jones (1953) reported that the paper was given an "icy reception" and that the president of the Society, the noted neurologist, Richard von Krafft-Ebing, commented, "It sounds like a scientific fairy tale [I, p. 263]."

About a year after the presentation of this paper, Freud experienced the sudden revelation of a "great secret": In most cases, these childhood seduction experiences his patients described had never actually occurred.

This realization marked a turning point in the history of psychoanalysis. At first the awareness that his patients were reporting fantasies was a stunning blow to Freud, whose theory of hysteria was based on the reality of these childhood sexual traumas. On reflection, however, he concluded that his patients' fantasies were quite real to them. And since their fantasies centered on sexual matters, sex still had to be the root of their problems. Thus, Freud's basic thesis of sex as a causative factor in neurosis remained intact.

In 1897 Freud began the monumental task of self-analysis. He experienced a number of neurotic difficulties, which were relieved in the course of the analysis, so that he became a more integrated and self-confident person. He undertook self-analysis as a means of understanding himself and his patients better. Our concern here, however, is not his need for self-analysis, but the method he used to conduct it—dream analysis.

In the course of his work Freud had discovered that a patient's dreams could be a rich source of significant emotional material. He discovered that dreams often contain valuable clues to the underlying causes of the disturbance. Because of his positivistic belief that everything had a cause, he felt that events in a dream could not be completely without meaning; that they must result from something in the person's unconscious. (This notion that dream images are symbolic is not unique with Freud, but is actually an ancient theory.)

Realizing that he could not analyze himself by the technique of free association (it is difficult to assume the roles of both patient and therapist at the same time), Freud decided to investigate his dreams. Upon waking each morning, he recorded his dream material of the night before and then free associated to this material.

His self-analysis, which continued for about 2 years, not only benefitted his personality, but also culminated in the publication of the book, *The Interpretation of Dreams* (1900), that was subsequently considered his major work. At the time of its publication, it was either totally ignored or commented on unfavorably. Although it took 8 years to sell the first 600 copies, its importance was eventually recognized and it went through eight editions in Freud's lifetime. He incorporated dream analysis into the body of techniques used in psychoanalysis, and for the remainder of his life devoted the last half hour of each day to self-analysis.

In the very productive years after 1900, Freud developed and expanded his new ideas. In 1901, he published *The Psychopathology of Everyday Life,* which contained the description of the now famous Freudian slip. He suggested that not only in neurotic symptoms, but also in everyday behavior of the normal person, unconscious ideas are struggling for expression and thus are capable of modifying thought and action. What might appear to be casual slips of the tongue or "forgetting," Freud suggested, are actually reflections of real, though unacknowledged, motives. His next book, *Three Essays on the Theory of Sexuality*, appeared in 1905. Earlier, in 1902, some students had urged him to begin a weekly discussion group so that they might learn about his psychoanalysis, as he had begun to call his work. These early disciples, including Alfred Adler and Carl Jung among others, later achieved fame through their opposition to Freud (see Chapter 14), who tolerated no dissent from his emphasis on the key role of sexuality. Anyone who did not accept this tenet was promptly excommunicated, as was the case with several of his major disciples. Later he wrote: "psycho-analysis is my creation; for ten years I was the only person who concerned himself with it . . . no one can know better than I do what psycho-analysis is [Freud, 1914]."

During the first decade of this century, Freud's personal and professional positions improved. His practice increased and a growing number of people took his pronouncements seriously. In 1909, he received the first sign of international recognition when he was invited by G. Stanley Hall to speak at the twentieth anniversary celebration of Clark University. He was awarded an honorary doctorate, which moved him deeply, and he met many other prominent psychologists of the day, including James, Cattell, and Titchener.

The five lectures that he gave at Clark were published the following year in the *American Journal of Psychology* and were later translated into several languages.

Freud was very well received and honored on this visit, yet he left with an unfavorable impression of America, which he harbored for many years. He complained of the quality of American cooking, the scarcity of bathrooms, difficulties with the language, and the informality in manners—shockingly free to a cultured European. He was even offended by a guide at Niagara Falls who referred to him as "the old fellow."

He never returned to America, and once commented to his biographer, Jones, that "America is a mistake; a gigantic mistake, it is true, but none the less a mistake [Jones, 1955, II, p. 60]." In the interest of fairness, it should be noted that Freud also disliked (intensely) Vienna, the city where he lived for so many years (Jones, 1953, I, pp. 293–294).

The official psychoanalytic family came to be torn by discord, dissent, and defections during the first two decades of this century. The break with Adler came in 1911 and that with Jung, whom Freud considered his spiritual son and heir to psychoanalysis, in 1914. By World War I, three rival groups existed, but Freud managed to keep the name "psychoanalysis" for his group. The war years impeded his intellectual advance and reduced the number of his patients and hence his income. With a wife, six children, and a sister-in-law to support, Freud was still greatly concerned over financial matters.

He reached the pinnacle of his fame in the period from 1919 to 1939, the year of his death. He continued to work hard and saw patients for several hours each day, but was able to take 3 months' vacation every summer. During the 1920s psychoanalysis developed as a theoretical system for the understanding of all human motivation and personality, rather than as solely a method of treatment for the disturbed. This conceptual system is discussed later.

In 1923, it was discovered that Freud suffered from cancer of the mouth. (He characteristically smoked 20 cigars a day.) His last 16 years were marked by almost continuous pain (though he continued smoking cigars). He underwent 33 operations, during which portions of his palate and upper jaw were removed. The prosthetic device that this surgery made necessary hampered his speaking so that he became increasingly difficult to understand. Although he continued to see his patients and disciples, he shunned other personal contact. Meanwhile, his fame spread around the world and he met many prominent people, including H. G. Wells and Thomas Mann.

When Hitler came to power, the official Nazi position on psychoanalysis was made clear when Freud's books were burned in May, 1933, in Berlin. As his books were flung onto the fire, a Nazi speaker shouted: "Against the soul-destroying overestimation of the sex life—and on behalf of the nobility of the human soul—I offer to the flames the writings of one Sigmund Freud [Schur, 1972, p. 446]!" Freud's comment on hearing of the book burning was, "What progress we are making. In the Middle Ages they would have burnt me; nowadays they are content with burning my books [Jones, 1957, III, p. 182]." By 1934, the more farsighted psychoanalysts of Jewish descent had left Germany. The vigorous Nazi campaign to eradicate psychoanalysis in Germany was so effective that knowledge of Freud, once so widespread, was almost completely obliterated.

Against the advice of his friends, Freud insisted on remaining in Vienna. In March, 1938, the Nazis invaded Austria and on March 15 his home was overrun by a gang of Nazis. A week later his daughter was arrested and detained for a day. Finally convinced that he should leave, he was not permitted to do so until his unsold books had been brought back from Switzerland to be burned. Partly through the intervention of the American ambassador to France, the Nazis agreed to let Freud go to England. Four of his sisters were later killed in Austria.

A somewhat humorous note attended Freud's departure from Vienna:

In order to secure an exit visa, he had to sign a document attesting to his "respectful and considerate" treatment by the Gestapo, and noting that he had no reason to complain. Having signed the form, he asked if he might add, "I can heartily recommend the Gestapo to anyone [Jones, 1957, III, p. 226]."

Though very well received in England, Freud was unable to enjoy the last year of his life because of his illness. His health failed rapidly but he remained mentally alert and worked almost to the very end.

Years before, when he selected the young Max Schur to be his personal doctor, Freud made him promise that he would not let him suffer unnecessarily when the time came. On September 21, 1939, he reminded the doctor of their earlier talk. "You promised me then not to forsake me when my time comes. Now it's nothing but torture and makes no sense any more [Schur, 1972, p. 529]."

The physician gave him two centigrams of morphine, repeating the dose 12 hours later. Freud went into a coma, his years of suffering finally at an end, and died on September 23, 1939.

Psychoanalysis as a Method of Treatment

Freud found that the "talking-out" method of free association did not always operate so freely, for sooner or later the patient reached a point in his narrative where he was unable, or unwilling, to continue. Freud believed that these *resistances* indicated that the patient had called up a memory or an idea that was too horrible, shameful, or repulsive to be faced. He saw the resistance as a form of protection from emotional pain, and the presence of the pain itself as an indication that the analysis was reaching the source of the difficulty.

Thus, resistance indicated that treatment was proceeding in the right direction and must continue to probe in the same area. Freud placed great stress on helping the patient overcome his resistances. He insisted that the patient face the hidden experience, no matter how disturbing, and see it in the light of reality. In the course of a complete analysis, it was expected that resistance would be encountered and overcome a number of times.

Freud's notion of resistance led to the formulation of a fundamental principle of psychoanalysis: *repression*, which involves the ejecting of painful ideas or memories from conscious awareness. Freud regarded repression as the only adequate explanation for the occurrence of resistance: Unpleasant ideas are not only pushed out of consciousness, they are also forcefully kept out. The therapist had to get the patient to bring this repressed material back into conscious awareness so that he could face it squarely and "learn to live with it." (It is sometimes charged that Freud developed the notions of resistance and repression from Schopenhauer. In 1938, Freud noted that he arrived at these ideas without having read Schopenhauer, to whom, however, he did yield precedence.)

Freud recognized that effective work with neurotic patients depended on the development of a personal intimate relationship between patient and therapist. We noted earlier how the *transference* that Anna O. developed toward Breuer disturbed him so that he had to call a halt to the treatment. Freud viewed the transference of a patient's emotional attitudes from parent to therapist as vital and necessary. The therapist had to wean the patient from childish dependence and help him assume a more adult role in life.

Freud's recognition of the importance of dream material has already been noted. He believed that dreams represent a disguised satisfaction of repressed desires and wishes. Therefore, the dream "story" is much more meaningful and complex than it might otherwise seem.

As an aside, we might note that on Wednesday evening, July 24, 1895, at a table in the northeast corner of the terrace of the Bellevue Restaurant in Vienna, Freud realized that the essence of a dream is wish fulfillment. In accord with Boring's notion that genius often flatters itself by dating its own inspirations, Freud quipped that a tablet should be erected at that spot noting that "Here the secret of dreams was revealed to Dr. Sigm. Freud on July 24, 1895 [Jones, 1953, I, p. 354]."

Dreams, according to Freud, have both a latent and a manifest content. The manifest content is the actual story told in recalling the events that occurred in the dream. The true significance of the dream, however, lies in the latent content, which is its hidden or symbolic meaning. To interpret this hidden meaning, the therapist must proceed from manifest to latent content, that is, interpret the symbolic meaning of the events that are related in the manifest content.

This is a complex task, for Freud felt that the forbidden desires in the latent content were expressed in symbolic form in the manifest content. Although many symbols that crop up in dreams are relevant only to experiences of the particular dreamer, Freud believed that others are common to all men and hence always have the same meaning. These universal symbols include gardens, balconies, and doors, signifying the female body; and church spires, candles, and serpents, signifying the male genitals. Dreams of falling represent the giving in to erotic wishes, while dreams of flying represent a desire for sexual achievement. In spite of their universality, Freud warned against interpreting these common symbols without knowledge of a patient's specific conflicts.

Freud believed a long and intensive course of therapy was required to effect a cure. In dealing with his own patients, he found that no less than five sessions a week, for months or even years, were necessary. With such extensive care, an analyst could handle only a few patients in the course of a year.

Freud also had definite ideas about the training of analysts. He felt that each should be analyzed himself, and then work for 2 years under close supervision before treating patients on his own. He also believed strongly that the practice of psychoanalysis should be a profession independent from medicine.

Freud's Method of Research

Because of the great differences in content and methodology between Freud and the traditional experimental psychology, it is instructive to examine his method of research. It is difficult at times to reconcile some of Freud's theories, particularly the more bizarre, with his thorough training as a scientist, especially his years of physiological research. In spite of his background, Freud did not use the customary experimental methods of research in his work. Although he was undoubtedly familiar with the experimental psychology movement, he did not collect data from controlled experiments, nor did he analyze his results quantitatively. The kind of data he collected and the way in which he collected and interpreted them were thus totally at variance with what was happening in experimental psychology. They had to be different considering the subject matter he chose to study.

Freud derived his theories from his own observations of the narratives and behavior of his patients undergoing analysis. Moreover, since analysis was so lengthy, Freud accumulated great masses of such data, which he then subjected to a critical analysis, using what is called the method of internal consistency.

> Inferences made from one part of the material were checked against evidence appearing in other parts, so that the final conclusions drawn from a case were based upon an interlocking network of facts and inferences. Freud proceeded in his work in much the same way as a detective assembling evidence or a lawyer summing up a case to the jury. Everything had to fit together coherently before Freud was satisfied that he had put his finger upon the correct interpretation [Hall & Lindzey, 1970, p. 54].

Freud saw no inherent obstacles to making relevant and meaningful observations:

> When I set myself the task of bringing to light what human beings keep hidden within them, not by the compelling power of hypnosis, but by observing what they say and what they show, I thought the task was a harder one than it really is. He that has eyes to see and ears to hear may convince himself that no mortal can keep a secret. If the lips are silent, he chatters with his finger-tips; betrayal oozes out of him at every pore. And thus the task of making conscious the most hidden recesses of the mind is one which it is quite possible to accomplish [Freud, 1905b, 77–78].

Freud's theories were formulated, revised, and extended in terms of the evidence as he alone interpreted it. Thus, his own critical abilities were the predominant, indeed the only, guide in his theory building. He seemed to ignore criticism from others, particularly from those not sympathetic to psychoanalysis, and even the wide-ranging criticism from close friends and colleagues that continued throughout his life had little influence on his thinking. Only rarely did he bother to reply to his critics: Psychoanalysis was his system, and his alone.

Psychoanalysis as a System of Personality

As noted, Freud's theoretical system did not cover the topics that were usually included in psychology textbooks of the day. Rather, he explored areas that more traditional psychology had tended to ignore. His theoretical formulations dealt with unconscious motivating forces, the conflicts among these forces, and the effects of these conflicts on a person's behavior.

The Unconscious and Conscious Aspects of Personality

In his earlier work, Freud expressed the belief that man's psychic life consisted of two main parts: the conscious and the unconscious. The conscious part, small and insignificant, presented but a superficial aspect of total personality, whereas the vast and powerful unconscious contained the concealed forces that are the driving power behind all human behavior. Freud also postulated the existence of the preconscious or foreconscious. Unlike the material in the unconscious, that in the preconscious has not been actively repressed; hence it can be easily summoned into conscious awareness.

Freud later revised this simple twofold conscious–unconscious distinction and introduced the famous id, ego, and superego constructs of the mental apparatus. The *id*, corresponding somewhat to Freud's earlier notion of the unconscious, is the most primitive and least accessible part of the personality. The extremely powerful forces of the id include man's instinctive sexual urges and suppressed habit tendencies: "We call it a chaos, a cauldron full of seething excitations." Freud further noted that "The id of course knows no judgements of value: no good and evil, no morality [Freud, 1933, p. 74]." In that the id seeks immediate satisfaction without regard for the circumstances of objective reality, it operates according to what Freud called the pleasure principle, which is concerned with tension reduction.

Man's basic psychic energy or *libido* is contained in the id and is expressed through the notion of tension reduction. Increases in libidinal energy result in increased tension gradients that the organism attempts to reduce to more tolerable levels. To satisfy his needs and maintain a comfortable tension level, an individual must interact with the real world. For example, the person who is hungry must make appropriate movements in his environment to find food in order to discharge the tension induced by hunger. Thus, an effective and appropriate liaison must be effected between the demands of the id and the circumstances of reality. To facilitate this interaction, the *ego* develops out of the id and serves as a mediating agent between the self and the external world. The ego represents what is ordinarily known as reason and sanity, in contrast to the passions of the id.

The id craves blindly, unaware of reality; the ego, on the other hand, is aware of reality, perceives and manipulates it, and regulates the id with reference to it. The ego thus operates in accord with what Freud called the reality principle, holding in abeyance the pleasure-seeking demands of the id until an appropriate object has been found with which to satisfy the need and reduce or·discharge the tension.

The ego does not exist independently of the id; indeed it derives its power from the id. It serves to help, not to hinder, the id, and is constantly striving to bring about id satisfaction.

Freud compared the relation of the ego and the id to a rider on a horse. The horse supplies the energy that the rider directs along the path he wants to travel.

The third part of Freud's structure of personality, the *superego*, develops early in childhood, when rules of conduct taught by parents through a system of rewards and punishments are assimilated. Behaviors that are "wrong" (that bring punishment) become part of the child's conscience, which is one part of the superego. Behaviors that are "good" (that are rewarded) become part of the child's ego-ideal, the other part of the superego. Thus the child's behavior is initially governed by parental control, but once the superego has formed a pattern for conduct, behavior is determined by self-control. That is, the behavior-guiding rewards and punishments are then administered by the individual himself.

Freud said that the superego represents "every moral restriction, the advocate of a striving towards perfection—it is, in short, as much as we have been able to grasp psychologically of what is described as the higher side of human life [1933, p. 67]." It can readily be understood, then, that the superego is in direct conflict with the id. Unlike the ego, the superego does not merely attempt to postpone id satisfaction, but rather to inhibit it completely.

Instincts

Instincts are the propelling or locomotive factors in the dynamics of personality—the biological forces of the individual that release mental energy. Though the word "instinct" has come to be the accepted usage in English, it does not convey the meaning Freud originally intended. Freud's term in German, *Trieb*, is best translated as driving force or urge. The Freudian instincts do not arise from genetic factors but rather from sources of stimulation within the body, and their aim is to remove or reduce the stimulation through some activity such as sexual satisfaction.

While Freud did not attempt to delimit the number of instincts, he believed that they could be classified in two distinct categories: the life instincts and the death instincts. The life instincts, including hunger, sex, and thirst, are concerned with self-preservation and racial survival. The libido is the form of energy through which the life instincts are manifested. The life instincts consist of the creative forces which underlie life itself.

In addition to the creative force of the life instincts, there is also the destructive force of the death instinct. This death instinct can be directed either inward, as in suicide or masochism, or outward, as in aggression and hate. Freud believed that man is irresistably drawn toward death, that "The goal of all life is death [1920, p. 160]."

Thus, Freud gradually acknowledged that aggression and hostility, as well as sex, are important forces in personality. As he grew older, he became more and more convinced that aggression also powerfully motivates human behavior. He even became more conscious of an aggressive tendency within himself. Some of his closest colleagues described him as a "good hater," and some of his writings, as well as the sharpness and finality of his breaks with dissenters suggest a high level of aggressiveness.

Anxiety

An important concept in psychoanalysis, particularly when dealing with neurotic and psychotic behavior, is anxiety, of which Freud noted three kinds: objective, neurotic, and moral. *Objective* anxiety is occasioned by fear of real dangers from the objective world; from it are derived the other two types of anxiety.

Neurotic anxiety arises from the recognition of potential danger inherent in instinctual gratification. It is a fear, not of the instincts per se, but of the punishment likely to follow indiscriminate id-dominated behavior. Thus, neurotic anxiety is a fear of being punished for expressing impulsive desires. *Moral* anxiety arises out of a fear of the conscience. When a person performs (or even thinks of performing) some act that is contrary to the set of moral values comprising his conscience, he may experience guilt or shame. Moral anxiety, then, is a function of how well developed the person's conscience is. The less virtuous individual is less likely to develop moral anxiety.

Regardless of type, anxiety is a tension-inducing force in human behavior, motivating the person to reduce this state of tension. Freud believed that the ego develops a number of protective defenses against anxiety, the so-called *defense mechanisms*. In the mechanism of *identification*, a person identifies himself with (takes on the manner, dress, style of speech, etc., of) another who seems admirable and less vulnerable to the specific danger giving rise to the anxiety. Another defense mechanism, *repression*, is the barring from conscious awareness of an anxiety-provoking stimulus. Its importance in Freud's system was noted earlier. *Sublimation* involves substituting a socially acceptable goal for one that cannot be directly satisfied. In *projection*, the source of anxiety is attributed to someone else, for example, by saying "He hates me" instead of "I hate him." In a further mechanism, *reaction formation*, a person conceals his own disturbing impulse by converting it into its opposite, for instance, replacing hate by love. With the mechanism of *fixation*, a person's development becomes arrested at an early stage because the next stage is too fraught with anxiety. Finally, the mechanism of *regression* involves behavior that indicates a reversion to an earlier developmental stage, one at which there was greater security (where the current source of anxiety was not operative).

Freud believed that anxiety with which an individual could not adequately cope became traumatic, reducing the person to a state of infantile helplessness.

Stages of Personality Development

We noted earlier that Freud was convinced that the neurotic disturbances manifested by his patients had originated in childhood experiences. As a consequence, he became one of the first theorists to place great stress on the development of the child. He believed that the adult personality pattern was established very early in life and was almost completely formed by the age of 5.

In the psychoanalytic theory of development, the child passes through a series of *psychosexual stages of development* from birth to age 5. During these stages, he is considered "autoerotic"; that is, he derives sensual or erotic pleasure by stimulating the various erogenous zones of his body or being stimulated by his mother in her handling of him. Each stage during this period tends to be localized in specific bodily erogenous zones.

The first, or *oral*, stage lasts from birth into the second year. During this stage, stimulation of the mouth, such as sucking, biting, and swallowing, is the primary source of erotic satisfaction. Inadequate satisfaction (too much or too little) at this stage may produce an oral type of personality in which the person is preoccupied with excessive mouth habits, such as smoking, kissing, and eating. Freud believed that a wide range of adult behaviors, from excessive optimism to sarcasm and cynicism, were attributable to incidents occurring during this stage of development.

In the *anal* phase, sexual gratification shifts from the mouth to the anus and the child derives pleasure from the anal zone. R. I. Watson (1971) imagines this situation as a child might see it:

> There is nothing about the odor, texture, of appearance of the feces that are inherently unpleasant. The infant has no innate repulsion. He has created it, and the mother seems to prize it, since she is pleased when he has a movement and concerned when he does not. According to Freudian thinking, defecation is "perceived" by the infant as the giving of a gift. What happens to his gift? The mother flushes it down the toilet! Often he acts out his puzzlement about this strange behavior by toilet play, throwing toys in the toilet, only to retrieve them again [p. 495].

During this stage (which coincides with the period of toilet training) the child may either expel or withhold, and may in either case thereby defy his parents. Strong conflict during this period can result in an anal expulsive adult, who is dirty, wasteful, and extravagant; or an anal retentive adult, who is excessively neat, clean, and compulsive. (Whether or not they agree with the Freudian interpretation of the struggle between parent and child during toilet training, most parents would agree that it is indeed a contentious period, during which the child is often flushed with victory!)

During the *phallic* stage, which occurs at about the end of the third or fourth year, erotic gratification shifts to the genital region. There is much fondling and exhibiting of the genitals, and sexual fantasizing. In addition, Freud posited the development at this stage of an important phenomenon, the Oedipus complex (named after the Greek legend in which Oedipus unknowingly killed his father and married his mother). At this stage the child becomes sexually attached to the parent of the opposite sex and fearful of the parent of the same sex, whom he now perceives as a rival. Ordinarily, the child overcomes this complex, but the attitudes he develops toward the opposite sex during this time persist and influence his relations with members of the opposite sex in adult life.

If, by some stroke of fortune, the child is able to get through the many struggles of these three stages, he enters a period of latency lasting from about his fifth to twelfth years. As the start of adolescence (when puberty strikes) the final *genital* stage begins. During this time, heterosexual behavior is evident and various activities by which the individual prepares for marriage and family are undertaken.

Mechanism and Determinism in Freud's System

As mentioned earlier in this chapter, during Freud's university training he was strongly influenced by the mechanistic school of thought in German physiology. At first glance, the notion of mechanism, which infuses so much of academic psychology, would seem to be irrelevant for Freud's work on the hidden motives of behavior. To the structuralists, and then the behaviorists, man was considered machinelike in his processes and functions. First man's mind, then man's behavior were reduced to their most elemental components, analyzed, and studied in positivistic and materialistic terms.

It is surprising to many readers of Freud to learn that he too was influenced by this same positivistic tradition. No less than experimental psychologists, Freud believed that all mental events were determined—even mistakes and dreams; no bit of behavior could happen by chance or by free will. There is always a cause for each act, a motive, if not conscious, then unconscious.

But there is more to this general mechanistic spirit than determinism. In Chapter 3 we discussed the solemn pledge taken by Brücke, Ludwig, du Bois-Reymond, and Helmholtz: "No other forces than the common physical–chemical ones are active within the organism." Freud—at least early in his career—very much subscribed to this physicalism: the notion that all phenomena of life could be reduced to the principles of physics.

In 1895, Freud worked feverishly on his "Project for a Scientific Psychology" in which he attempted to show that psychology must have a physical base, and that purely mental phenomena exhibit many of the same patterns and characteristics as the neurophysiological processes on which they are based. Psychology, in Freud's view, must be a natural science, the aim of which is "to represent psychical processes as quantitatively determined states of specifiable material particles [Freud, 1895, p. 359]."

His "Project" was never completed, but the physicalistic principles with which he grappled can be found throughout his later writings; he often used terminology from mechanics, electricity, and hydraulics. Even though he found that his subject matter was not amenable to physical and chemical techniques, and consequently modified his intent to model his psychology after physics, he remained true in the large to the overall positivistic philosophy—particularly determinism—which nurtured academic psychology.

It must be said, however, that while he was influenced by this model, he was not constrained or restricted by it. When and where he saw it would not fit, he modified or discarded it altogether. Indeed, in the end, he demonstrated how restricting is the mechanistic conception of man. Freud used this tradition where appropriate, but was also a most effective critic of mechanism where it was not appropriate.

Early Conflicts between Psychology and Psychoanalysis

Psychoanalysis developed, as we pointed out earlier, outside the mainstream of academic psychology. The fact that both the system and its originator were "outsiders" complicated and considerably delayed their acceptance. Indeed, it was even a barrier to serious consideration of psychoanalysis for a time. As Shakow (1969) commented, "Freudian ideas had more obstacles to overcome before being accepted in psychology than had other revolutionary ideas [p. 100]."

There were a number of points of conflict, discussed by Shakow (1969) and Jahoda (1963), that functioned to keep psychoanalysis and psychology apart. The first point has to do with the absence of a sense of continuity in Freud's work, relative to advances in psychology. There were no parallels, no overlapping efforts, because Freud's work had no precedent in the development of psychology. Thus, psychologists could not find a meaningful way of relating Freud's efforts to their own, or to that of their predecessors.

A second point of conflict is that Freud and most of his disciples were trained in medicine, not in psychology (M.D.s not Ph.D.s). Not only did this mean they spoke and thought in different terms, but also it reinforced the psychologists' notions that these people were "outsiders" because they had a different kind of training. According to Barber (1961), one of the sources of resistance in science to a new discovery or theory is any difference in professional specialization between an innovator and the discipline to which he offers his new work.

This difference in training points up a third reason for opposition. Psychology, in its early attempts to become (or remain) a pure science, was method-centered whereas psychoanalysis was problem-centered (Jahoda, 1963). Freud's aim of attempting to help neurotic patients was at sharp variance with psychology's aim of finding laws of human behavior using the methods of natural science.

These different goals and subject matter necessitated different methods of approach. Freud's concern was more molar or global than that of psychology—the total human personality as opposed to specific functions such as perception or learning. Psychology, trying to be a natural science, used the experimental method in which each variable (usually a minute aspect of behavior) was isolated for study. Psychoanalysis was concerned with the total human being, not for a short period in the laboratory, but over a long period of time, and used data covering all aspects of the person's past and present experiences.

Finally, academic psychologists, steeped in the rigors of science, seeking precision and operational definitions of concepts, distrusted and disliked many of the Freudian concepts and terms which could not be quantified or related precisely to concrete empirical variables. Terms such as *ego*, *id*, *repression* were anathema to psychologists who were trying to work with only specific stimulus–response terms.

There were, then, strong reasons for the antipathy shown by psychologists toward psychoanalysis. In spite of these differences, however, we shall see that the barriers between the two disciplines, at first so rigid and absolute, have been breached here and there.

Criticisms of Psychoanalysis

The amount of criticism directed against Freud and his theories, much of which comes from the lay public, is enormous, but we shall restrict our discussion to criticisms from psychology, some of which were noted in the preceding section.

Particularly vulnerable to criticism from experimental psychologists are Freud's methods of data collection. We have seen that he drew his insights and conclusions from his patients' responses while they were undergoing psychoanalysis. Consider some of the deficiencies of such an approach in the light of the experimental method of systematically collecting objective data under controlled conditions of observation.

First, the conditions under which Freud collected his data certainly seem to be unsystematic and uncontrolled. He did not make a verbatim transcript of what each patient said, but preferred to work from notes made several hours after seeing a patient. Some of the original data (the patient's own words) must surely have been lost in the interim as a result of the vagaries of recall with its well-known errors of distortion and omission. Data thus consisted of what Freud remembered. Also, it is possible that in the course of recollection Freud reinterpreted the raw data. In drawing his inferences, he may have been guided by his desire to find material supportive of his hypotheses. In other words, he may have remembered and then recorded only what he wanted to hear. Thus, Freud's reconstruction of the data may not have accurately reflected the actual data as it occurred. Of course, we must consider the possibility that Freud's notes were accurate representations of the raw data but the important point is that it is impossible to know this with any degree of certainty for the original data did not survive.

There is an even more basic criticism of the raw data itself. Even if a complete record had been kept, it would not have been possible to determine the validity or "truth" of what the patients said. Freud made no attempt to determine the accuracy of what his patients reported, and critics argue that he should have tried to verify the patients' reports, for example, by questioning their relatives and friends about the events described. Thus, the distinct possibility exists that the basic step in Freud's theory building—data collection—may be characterized as incomplete, imperfect, and inaccurate.

As for the next step—drawing inferences and generalizations from the data—no one knows exactly how this was done. That Freud never explained the process fully is, of course, another major point of criticism.

As Hall and Lindzey (1970) noted, Freud's writings contain his conclusions but not (*a*) the data from which the conclusions were derived, (*b*) the method by which the data were analyzed, nor (*c*) any systematic account of his empirical findings. Further, since Freud did not attempt to quantify his data, it is impossible to determine the reliability or statistical significance of his findings.

These are serious charges indeed from the standpoint of scientific methodology and theory building. The reader of Freud must, in a sense, accept on faith the validity of his operations and conclusions. Freud wrote, in 1938, that his work was "based on an incalculable number of observations and experiences, and only someone who has repeated those observations on himself and on others is in a position to arrive at a judgement of his own upon it [p. 144]." But of course, as we have seen, Freud's observations cannot be repeated because it is not known for certain exactly what he did in collecting data and in translating observations into generalizations and hypotheses. The language of science is extremely precise and orderly, leaving no room for ambiguities, distortions, and vagaries. It seems that Freud did not speak the same language and it is difficult to translate from one to the other.

Another point of attack concerns the difficulty of deriving empirically-testable propositions from many of Freud's hypotheses. How, for instance, would we empirically test the notion of a death wish? It is used to explain behavior such as suicide, after the fact. How can one use it to empirically predict behavior?

Adherents of operationism argue that Freud's concepts are not operationally defined. (Part of Bridgman's discussion of operationism in Chapter 11 included a description of so-called pseudo-problems, or questions that defy answer by any known experimental test.) By this criterion, many of Freud's concepts cannot be experimentally tested, and some critics feel that they are meaningless, indeed useless, for science.

What of the validity of psychoanalytic theory as a whole? It seems that, except in the broadest sense of the word, there is no such thing as a psychoanalytic theory! There are a large number of generalizations and hypotheses, but there seems to be no orderly framework of theorems, postulates, or precise relationships so necessary to a scientific theory.

Since no overall theory exists, no meaningful overall criticism of it can be attempted (save, perhaps, that psychoanalysis leaves a great deal to be desired from the standpoint of scientific support). It is noted that specific concepts and generalizations have also come under criticism.

In Chapter 14 we shall examine the criticisms from certain of Freud's disciples who broke away to form movements of their own, and from others who, while generally favorable to Freud, nevertheless tried to extend and modify his position.

Contributions of Psychoanalysis

Having noted many important and damaging (indeed, damning, to some) criticisms of psychoanalysis, offered primarily by experimentally oriented psychologists, we must ask why psychoanalysis has not only survived, but also prospered.

All theories of behavior can, unfortunately, be criticized as somewhat lacking in scientific validity. As a result, a psychologist in search of a theory must choose on the basis of criteria other than formal scientific rigidity and precision. One who selects psychoanalysis does not do so in the absence of evidence, however; psychoanalysis does offer evidence, although not the variety traditionally accepted by science (experimental investigations of specific propositions). The psychoanalysts' evidence is based on observation of experience as it occurs.

That psychoanalytic evidence is not the strictly scientific variety does not necessarily mean that the theory is totally incorrect or misleading. Belief in psychoanalysis is based on the intuitive grounds of a perceived appearance of plausibility in Freud's system.

> Any one who accepts or rejects the psychoanalytic theories does so by means of the same kind of reasoning that gives him the thousand and one judgments he is forced to make in everyday life on the basis of insufficient or inadequate evidence—the kind of judgments, in fact, that he is forced to live by, but which have no standing in science. Such estimates, growing out of a multitude of impressions and interpretations, guesses and insights, often result in unshakable convictions, convictions which may be right or wrong but which, from the standpoint of science, cannot be recognized as either proved or disproved [Heidbreder, 1933, pp. 403–404].

Freud's influence on psychiatry and clinical psychology is profound, and his theories are of considerable significance in the more academic and, in the broad sense of the term, experimental psychology. Certain Freudian concepts have gained rather wide acceptance and been assimilated into American academic psychology. These include the role of unconscious motivation, the importance of childhood experiences in shaping adult behavior, and the operation of the defense mechanisms. Interest in these areas has generated much research. It is a tribute to Freud, moreover, that many of his ardent opponents recognize the value of his contributions.

Freud's influence on the general culture has, of course, also been profound. And the impact of his system was felt immediately after his visit to Clark University. Bakan (1966) noted that newspapers in America were full of articles on Freud after 1910 and that over 200 books had been written on Freudian analysis in this country by 1920.

Thus, his acceptance by the lay public came much earlier and with greater force than his acceptance by academic psychology.

One general source of influence is Freud's contribution to the radical change that has taken place in sexual mores. This century has seen a gradual loosening of sexual restraint in behavior as well as in art, literature, and the various media of entertainment. Also, it seems that his emphasis on sex helped to popularize his views. Even when discussed in scientific writings, sex has definite sensational appeal (witness the sales of the Kinsey reports and, more recently, the highly technical Masters and Johnson work). Also of interest is Freud's exciting and colorful style of writing, rare in scientific work.

Despite criticisms of his lack of scientific rigor and methodology, Freud's psychoanalysis has become an important force in contemporary psychology. Boring, in the 1929 edition of his *History of Experimental Psychology*, expressed regret that psychology had no truly great man of the stature of a Darwin or a Helmholtz. Yet, only 21 years later, in the second edition of his text, Boring changed his opinion. Reflecting the development in psychology during those two decades, Boring spoke of Freud as being psychology's great man: "Now he is seen as the greatest originator of all, the agent of the *Zeitgeist* who accomplished the invasion of psychology by the principle of the unconscious process [Boring, 1950, p. 743]."

It must be stressed, however, that despite Freud's recognized genius and the acceptance—or at least the more receptive consideration—of some parts of his system, psychoanalysis still retains a separate identity and, for the most part, has not been absorbed by the mainstream of current psychological thought.

However, no matter what one's evaluation of psychoanalysis, and whatever the eventual status of the system, there is no denying that Freud himself possessed the attributes of greatness.

> He was a pioneer in a field of thought, in a new technique for the understanding of human nature. He was also an originator, even though he picked his conceptions out of the stream of the culture—an originator who remained true to his fundamental intent for fifty years of hard work, while he altered and brought to maturity the system of ideas that was his contribution to knowledge. . . . It is not likely that the history of psychology can be written in the

next three centuries without mention of Freud's name and still claim to be a general history of psychology. And there you have the best criterion of greatness: posthumous fame [Boring, 1950, pp. 706–707].

SUGGESTED FURTHER READINGS

Hypnotism
Shor, R. E., & Orne, M. T. (Eds.) *The nature of hypnosis: Selected basic writings.* New York: Holt, 1965.

Freud
Choisy, M. *Sigmund Freud: A new appraisal.* New York: Philosophical Library, 1963.
Freud, S. *An autobiographical study.* Translated by J. Strachey. New York: Norton, 1963. (First published in 1925.)
Hale, N. *Freud and the Americans: The beginnings of psychoanalysis in the United States, 1876–1917.* New York: Oxford Univ. Press, 1971.
Hall, C. S. *A primer of Freudian psychology.* Cleveland, Ohio: World Publishing Co., 1954.
Jones, E. *The life and works of Sigmund Freud.* New York: Basic Books, 1953–1957. 3 vols.
Nelson, B. (Ed.) *Freud and the 20th century.* New York: Meridian, 1957.
Schur, M. *Freud: Living and dying.* New York: International Universities Press, 1972.
Whyte, L. *The unconscious before Freud.* Garden City, New York: Doubleday, 1962.
Wollheim, R. *Sigmund Freud.* New York: Viking Press, 1971.

General
Freeman, L. *The story of Anna O.* New York: Walker, 1972.
Jahoda, M. Some notes on the influence of psychoanalytic ideas on American psychology. *Human Relations,* 1963, **16,** 111–129.
Shakow, D., & Rapaport, D. *The influence of Freud on American psychology.* New York: International Universities Press, 1964.
Skinner, B. F. Critique of psychoanalytic concepts and theories. *Scientific Monthly,* 1954, **79,** 300–305.

14

Psychoanalysis:
After the Founding

After its formal founding, psychoanalysis proceeded in two different directions. On the one hand, there was a group of analysts who more or less adhered to the central tenets of Freudian thought, although they modified and elaborated certain concepts after Freud's death. A second group, however, disagreed completely with some of Freud's major points. While refusing to disavow their psychoanalytic orientation, these dissenters devised new theories meant to correct what they considered the deficiencies and inadequacies in Freud's thinking. We have seen that Freud did not tolerate dissension, and that those who espoused different positions "left the movement not at all with the tacit agreement to differ but rather in an aura of heavy disapproval and the sort of invective that was once heaped upon the heads of heretics . . . [Brown, 1963, p. 37]."

Carl Gustav Jung (1875–1961)

Once regarded by Freud as heir apparent of the psychoanalytic movement—the "Crown Prince," as Freud called him—Jung's close friendship with Freud disintegrated in 1914, and he began what he called analytical psychology.

The Life of Jung

Born in a Swiss village on Lake Constance, of a quite scholarly family, Jung initially wanted to become an archeologist. Unfortunately, his family was poor so he could only afford to study at the University of Basel which, at the time, did not offer courses in archeology. He chose medicine instead and completed his medical degree in 1900. Attracted to psychiatry, his first professional appointment was at the psychiatric clinic at the University of Zurich, which was directed by Eugen Bleuler, the well-known psychiatrist noted for his influential work on schizophrenia. In 1905, Jung was appointed a lecturer in psychiatry at the university, but after several years resigned these appointments to devote his efforts to private practice, research, and writing.

Jung became interested in Freud in 1900 after reading *Interpretation of Dreams*, which he described as a "masterpiece." By 1906, the two men had begun to correspond, and a year later Jung went to Vienna to meet Freud. At their initial meeting, the two men talked with great animation for 13 hours, an exciting beginning for their close but short-lived friendship. In 1909, Jung accompanied Freud to America for the Clark University commemorative ceremonies at which they both lectured.

It is important to note that, unlike some of Freud's other disciples, Jung made a number of field expeditions to Africa, Arizona, and New his own, and at least the beginnings of some unique ideas at the time of their first meeting. Thus, he was possibly less malleable, less suggestible, than a younger man still a student and unsure of his own professional identity.

Though he did become a disciple of Freud's, Jung was never—even in the beginning of the relationship—a totally uncritical one, although he did suppress his criticisms early in their affiliation. Later, while writing *The Psychology of the Unconscious* (1912), he was much troubled for he realized that this public statement of his position (at variance with Freud's) would probably damage their relationship. For 2 months he was unable to proceed with the book, so disturbed was he at Freud's potential reaction. Of course, he did publish it, and the inevitable occurred.

In 1911, largely through Freud's efforts and in spite of strong opposition from its Viennese members, Jung became the first president of the International Psychoanalytic Association. Freud apparently believed that anti-Semitism might impede the movement if a Jew headed the group; the Viennese members, almost all of whom were Jewish, presumably resented Jung, a younger man, because they had seniority in the movement and because of Jung's alleged anti-Semitism.

Shortly after Jung was elected, the friendship between him and Freud showed signs of strain. Jung had begun to deemphasize the role of sex and was expressing a different concept of the libido in his book in 1912 and in a series of lectures at Fordham University. Friction grew, and in 1912 the two men agreed to terminate their personal correspondence. Relations were completely severed in 1914, when Jung resigned his presidency and withdrew from the association. Although they never saw one another again, Jung retained his admiration for Freud.

In line with an interest in the relevance of myths for the individual, Jung made a number of field expeditions to Africa, Arizona, and New Mexico in the 1920s to study the mental processes of preliterate people. In 1932, he was appointed a professor at the Federal Polytechnical University in Zurich, a position he occupied until poor health obliged him to resign in 1942. In 1944, a chair of medical psychology was founded for him at the University of Basel, but again his poor health prevented his keeping the position for more than a year.

He remained actively productive in research and writing for most of his 86 years, publishing an astonishing array of books. His many awards included honorary degrees from Harvard and Oxford. He was read and respected throughout the world, and was known to people in all walks of life.

Jung's System: Analytical Psychology

Perhaps the most basic point of difference between Jung and Freud concerns the nature of the libido. Whereas Freud defined libido in predominantly sexual terms, Jung regarded it as a generalized life energy, of which sex was only one part. For Jung, this libidinal life energy expressed itself in growth and reproduction as well as other kinds of activity, depending on what was most important for an individual at a given point in time.

Jung's refusal to regard the basic life energy as exclusively sexual left him free to give different interpretations to behavior that Freud could define only in sexual terms. For instance, during the first 3 to 5 years of life (which Jung called the presexual phase), the Jungian view is that libidinal energy serves the functions of nutrition and growth, with none of the sexual overtones of Freud's conception of these years. Jung rejected the notion of the Oedipus complex (in Freudian terms) and explained the child's attachment to his mother in terms of a dependency need with satisfactions and rivalries associated with the mother's food-providing function. As the child matures and develops in his sexual functioning, Jung maintained, these nutritive functions become overlaid and combined with sexual feelings. To Jung, libidinal energy took a hetero-sexual form only after puberty.

It is important to note that Jung did not altogether deny the existence of sexual factors. Instead, he reduced the role of sex to only one of a whole range of drives comprising the libido.

The Structure of Personality

Jung used the term *psyche* to refer to the mind, which he said consisted of three levels: the conscious, the personal unconscious, and the collective unconscious. At the center of consciousness is the ego, which is generally akin to a person's conception of himself. Consciousness comprises perceptions, memories, and the like, and is the avenue of contact with reality that enables a person to adapt to his environment.

Jung believed that too much emphasis had been given to consciousness, which he considered second in importance to the unconscious. The conscious aspect of the psyche is like the visible portion of an island. A larger unknown part exists beneath the (small) part that can be seen above the water, and Jung stressed this mysterious hidden base.

He believed there are two levels or parts of the unconscious. Just beneath consciousness there exists the *personal unconscious*, which belongs to the individual. It consists of all the impulses and wishes, the faint perceptions, and numerous other experiences that have been either suppressed or forgotten. Incidents from the personal unconscious, however, can be easily recalled to conscious awareness, which indicates that it is not a very deep level of unconsciousness.

Below the personal unconscious is the third psychic level, the *collective unconscious*. This deepest level of all contains, unknown to the individual, the influence of the cumulative experiences of all past generations, including primitive ancestors.

> The collective unconscious is the storehouse of latent memory traces inherited from man's ancestral past, a past that includes not only the racial history of man as a separate species, but his prehuman or animal ancestry as well. The collective unconscious is the psychic residue of man's evolutionary development, a residue that accumulates as a consequence of repeated experiences over many generations [Hall & Lindzey, 1970, p. 83].

Jung felt that evolutionary theory, by demonstrating a similarity in brain structure in all races of man, could account for the universality of the collective unconscious.

In terms of our island analogy, a number of small islands rising above the surface of the water represent the individual conscious awareness of a number of people. Land areas just beneath the water, which are exposed to view by the action of the tides, represent the individual's personal unconscious. The ocean floor, on which all the islands ultimately rest, is the collective unconscious.

Jung emphasized the powerful forces preserved in the collective unconscious because he felt that they contributed most to psychic development. He called the inherited tendencies in the collective unconscious *archetypes,* and saw them as preexisting determinants of mental experience that dispose an individual to behave in a manner similar to that manifested by his racial ancestors when confronted with an analogous situation.

Jung believed archetypes are experienced as emotions and mental images, and that they are typically associated with such significant human experiences as birth and death, or with particular stages of life (adolescence, for example) and reactions to extreme dangers. His intensive investigation of the mythical and artistic products of different civilizations resulted in the discovery of certain symbols that are common to all, even cultures so widely separated that there was no possibility of direct influence. In his work with patients, Jung found what he considered definite traces of mythological images in their dreams.

Four of the many archetypes Jung found seemed to recur more often than others, to be laden with emotional significance for man, and to be traceable to ancient historical myths of diverse origins. These four principal archetypes, which Jung considered separate personality systems, are the persona, the anima, the animus, and the shadow.

The *persona,* or outermost aspect of personality, conceals the true self. It is the mask donned by an individual when he comes in contact with others, and it represents him as he wants to appear to society; thus it may not correspond to his "real" personality. The notion of persona is apparently akin to the sociological concept of role playing, which posits that a person acts the way he thinks others expect him to.

The archetypes *anima* and *animus* reflect the notion that men and women exhibit both masculine and feminine tendencies. The anima refers to feminine characteristics in man, whereas the animus denotes masculine characteristics in woman. As with the other archetypes, these arise out of the primitive past of the species, in which men and women took on some of the behavioral and emotional tendencies of the opposite sex.

The *shadow* archetype (the darker self) is the inferior, animal-like part of the personality, man's racial heritage from the lower forms of life. As such, it contains all immoral, passionate, and objectionable desires and activities. Jung said that the shadow urges us to do those things that we ordinarily would not allow ourselves to do. Having performed such actions, we usually insist that something "came over us": Jung claimed that the "something" is the primitive part of our nature.

A final part of Jung's system is his notion of *self*, which he considered the most important archetype of all. Comprising all aspects of the unconscious, the self provides unity and stability to the entire structure of personality. As a representation of the "whole man," it attempts to achieve complete personal integration, and can be considered a drive or urge toward self-realization, which Jung felt could not occur until middle age. One symbol that Jung found repeatedly in various cultures was the *mandala*, or magic circle. He considered it symbolic of the total unity and wholeness toward which all men strive.

Personality Development

One of the unique features of Jung's approach—and another point on which he differed radically from Freud—was his conception of the development of the individual's personality. Freud looked "backwards" to determine what factors in earlier life shaped the personality of the adult. Personality was, to him, determined by these past events.

Jung, too, agreed that past events in the history of the individual, his race, and his species affect and shape personality, but he went beyond this. Not only is man shaped by the past, he argued, but by the future as well, by his goals and aspirations.

Man is always developing, striving, reaching for something in the future, an ultimate goal that Jung called *self-actualization*. By that term he meant a harmony and fullness or completeness of every aspect of the personality, the fullest development of the self.

Introversion–Extraversion

Jung is probably best known for his discussion of introversion and extraversion, which are defined in terms of the direction of libidinal energy. He regarded them as two attitudes or modes of reacting to specific situations.

The *extravert* directs the libido outside the self to external events, people, and situations. A person of this type is strongly influenced by forces in his environment and is very sociable and self-confident in a wide range of situations.

The libido of the *introvert* is directed inward: The individual is more contemplative, introspective, and resistant to external influence. He is less confident in his relations with other people and the external world, and tends to be relatively unsociable and shy.

Jung believed that these opposing attitudes exist in every person in varying degrees, but that one is generally more pronounced than the other. He did suggest, however, that no one is a total introvert or extravert, but rather that the dominant attitude at a given moment can be influenced by the situation. For example, a normally introverted person might become quite sociable and unreserved in a situation in which he is vitally interested.

According to Jung, personality differences are also reflected via the *functions*, which are used to orient ourselves to both the external objective world and the internal subjective world. Functions include sensation, thinking, feeling, and intuition. Sensation is the conscious perception of physical objects; thinking is a conceptual process that provides meaning and understanding; feeling is a subjective process of weighing and valuing; and intuition involves perceiving in an unconscious manner.

Jung considered thinking and feeling to be rational modes of responding in that they involve reason and judgment, whereas sensation and intuition he considered irrational because they depend on the concrete and specific stimulus world. Within each pair, only one mode can be dominant at a given time. This dominance of function can be combined with the dominance of either introversion or extraversion to produce a number of possible personality types.

Word Association

Jung developed the now famous word association test as a therapeutic tool. In this test, a list of words is read to a patient, who responds to each with the first word that comes to mind. In addition to measuring the time taken to respond to each word, Jung measured changes in breathing and, using a psychogalvanometer, in the electrical conductivity of the skin. These two physiological measures provided additional evidence of emotional reactions to specific words. If a particular word produced a long response time, irregularity in breathing, and a change in skin conductivity, Jung deduced the existence of an unconscious emotional problem connected with the stimulus word or with the reply.

Comment

Jung has influenced not only psychology and psychiatry, but also religion, history, art, and literature. Arnold Toynbee, Philip Wylie, and Lewis Mumford, among many others, have acknowledged him as a source of inspiration (Hall & Lindzey, 1970). Scientific psychology has for the most part ignored Jung's analytical psychology. Aside from the fact that not all of his books were translated into English until 1966, his less than lucid writing style impedes understanding. Further, his disdain for traditional scientific methods repels experimentally oriented psychologists, to whom Jung appeals even less than Freud, for Jung's writings contain a great deal of mysticism and religion.

The same kinds of criticisms noted in relation to Freud's supporting evidence are applicable to Jung, as he too relied on clinical observation and interpretation rather than controlled laboratory investigation. Analytical psychology has received less searching criticism than Freudianism, probably because Freud's overpowering stature in psychoanalysis relegates Jung (and others) to second place in terms of professional attention.

This is not to deny Jung's eminence and importance: His ideas are thought-provoking and novel, and he presents an optimistic concept of man that many find a welcome change from Freud. Jung was a scholarly, vital personality who inspired great loyalty in his adherents. There have been signs of a growing Jungian influence in recent years, particularly among youth. Jung's attention to such areas as occultism, mysticism, consciousness expanding, and self-fulfillment appears compatible with the interests of many young people in the Western world.

Social–Psychological Theories in Psychoanalysis: The *Zeitgeist* Strikes Again

As we have seen, Freud was strongly influenced by the mechanistic and positivistic outlook that pervaded nineteenth-century science. Around the end of the nineteenth century, there appeared new disciplines that suggested the possibility of viewing man in other than a biological and physical frame of reference. Anthropology, sociology, and social psychology were finding evidence to support the proposition that man is the product of the various social forces and institutions that comprise his environment. These new ideas suggested that man should be studied as a social animal rather than as a strictly biological one.

As varied cultures were studied by anthropologists, it became clear that the neurotic symptoms and taboos hypothesized by Freud were not found universally, as he had suggested. To give just one example, taboos against incest do not exist in all societies. Further, sociologists and social psychologists found that much human behavior is a result of social conditioning rather than instinctive biological factors.

Thus, the intellectual spirit of the times revised man's concept of himself, but Freud, to the dismay of some of his followers, continued to stress instinctual, biological determinants of personality. As a result, some theorists, usually younger and hence less constrained by tradition, began to move away from orthodox Freudian psychoanalysis and to reshape psychoanalytic theory along lines congruent with the orientation provided by the social sciences. Three of these socially oriented dissenters, Adler, Horney, and Fromm, are discussed here.

Alfred Adler (1870–1937): Individual Psychology

Adler is usually considered the earliest figure in the social–psychological brand of psychoanalysis because he broke with Freud in 1911. He later developed a theory in which social interest plays a major role.

The Life of Adler

Born of rather wealthy parents in a suburb of Vienna, Adler said that he led an unhappy childhood. The apparent reason was his conviction that he could never live up to the achievements of his eldest brother, who seemed a model child in every way and was his mother's favorite. (Alfred was his father's favorite.) A sickly youngster who did not walk until the age of 4, he was watched over with great care. In spite of his poor health and the feeling of being both ugly and too small, he was a friendly and sociable child.

At 4, while recovering from a near-fatal illness, Adler decided to become a physician. This he eventually did, receiving his degree from the University of Vienna in 1895. After first specializing in ophthalmology and then practicing general medicine, Adler went into psychiatry. About 1902, he began meeting with Freud's weekly discussion group, of which he became a highly esteemed leading member.

Over the course of the next several years, Adler developed a theory of personality that differed in important respects from Freud's. By 1911, he had become openly critical of Freud's emphasis on sexual factors. A year earlier, Freud had named Adler president of the Viennese Analytic Society, apparently in an effort to reconcile the growing differences between them. The inevitable split was made complete in 1911, when Adler resigned his presidency and officially broke with the Freudian position.

Adler served as a physician in the Austrian Army during World War I, and later organized child guidance clinics in the Vienna school system. During the 1920s, his individual psychology attracted much favorable attention throughout the world, and many followers came to study under him in Vienna. He lectured in several countries, and, in 1926, came to the United States, where he was warmly welcomed. After a number of visits to this country, he made it his home in 1934 and became Professor of Medical Psychology at the Long Island College of Medicine. In 1937, while on a strenuous lecture tour, he died in Aberdeen, Scotland.

Freud, in replying to a friend who was greatly saddened by Adler's death, wrote: "I don't understand your sympathy for Adler. For a Jewish boy out of a Viennese suburb a death in Aberdeen is an unheard-of career in itself and a proof of how far he had got on. The world really rewarded him richly for his service in having contradicted psychoanalysis [Scarf, 1971, p. 47]."

Adler wrote numerous books and articles, many of them addressed to the lay public. Adlerian theories continue to be promoted and expounded today in the *American Journal of Individual Psychology* and by the American Society of Individual Psychology.

Adler's Systematic Position

Adler and Freud were quite sharply opposed to one another in their theoretical positions. Whereas Freud's theories emphasized the role of the past in influencing behavior, Adler's orientation was toward the future. The division of personality into separate parts or aspects is an essential part of Freudian theory, whereas the Adlerian approach emphasizes the unity of personality.

Adler developed his system of individual psychology along social lines, another departure from Freud. Adler saw human behavior as determined not by the biological forces of instinct, but by social forces. He believed that we can understand an individual's personality only through investigation of his social relationships and his attitude toward others. He held that social interest develops very early in infancy:

> The first social situation that confronts a child is its relation to its mother, from the very first day. By her educational skill the child's interest in another person is first awakened. If she understands how to train this interest in the direction of cooperation, all the congenital and acquired capacities of the child will converge in the direction of social sense [Adler, 1930, p. 403].

Social attitude and interest, then, are developed through learning experiences. Adler, like Freud, recognized the importance of the early formative years of childhood, but Adler's focus was on social and not biological forces.

Another point of difference between the theories of Freud and Adler concerns the importance of consciousness. Whereas Freud stressed unconscious determinants of behavior, Adler emphasized the conscious. He considered man first and foremost a conscious being who is aware of his motivations. To Freud, man's behavior is determined by his past experiences. In contrast, Adler believed that man is more strongly influenced by what he thinks the future holds in store. Strivings for future goals can modify and influence what a person does at a given moment. For example, a person living in fear of eternal damnation after death behaves in accordance with this expectation. Thus, anticipations of future events can strongly affect present behavior.

Striving for Superiority

Mention was made earlier of Adler's emphasis on the essential unity and consistency of personality. This outlook posits a dynamic driving force that channels the various resources of personality toward one overriding goal. This final goal, toward which all men strive, is superiority, which comprises more complete and perfect development, accomplishment, fulfillment, and realization of the self. In this view, sex is not the dominant drive, but rather one of a number of means to the end of superiority.

Adler saw this striving in every aspect of personality:

> It runs parallel to physical growth. It is an intrinsic necessity of life itself. . . . All our functions follow its direction; rightly or wrongly they strive for conquest, surety, increase. The impetus from minus to plus is never-ending. The urge from "below" to "above" never ceases. Whatever premises all our philosophers and psychologists dream of—self-preservation, pleasure principle, equalization—all these are but vague representations, attempts to express the great upward drive. . . . a fundamental category of thought, the structure of our reason, . . . *the fundamental fact of our life* [Adler, 1930, pp. 398–399].

This striving for superiority is innate, according to Adler, and is responsible for all progress, not only at the level of the individual, but in all the history of civilization. It carries person and race ever upward from one stage of progress to the next.

Inferiority Feelings and Compensation

As we have seen, Adler did not agree with Freud that the primary basis of motivation centers on sexual factors. He believed instead that a general feeling of inferiority is the prime determining force in behavior. At first he related this feeling of inferiority to defective parts of the body. The child with a hereditary organic weakness will develop an inferiority complex and, as a result, will direct his efforts at compensating, and overcompensating, for this defect. He will overemphasize the deficient function, so that just as Demosthenes forcefully overcame his stuttering to become a great speaker, a child with a weak body may, through intensive exercise, excel as an athlete.

Adler later broadened the scope of this concept to include any physical, mental, or social handicap, real or imagined. He believed that the extreme helplessness and smallness of the infant produces a general feeling of inferiority that is experienced by everyone, since all children are totally dependent on their environments. The child, consciously aware of his inferiority, is at the same time driven by his innate striving for superiority. Thus, he is goaded on by the need to overcome his inferiority and insecurity. Adler believed that this "pushing and pulling" process continues throughout life, impelling an individual toward greater accomplishments.

Inferiority feelings, therefore, function to the advantage of both individual and society, since they lead to continuous improvement. However, childhood inferiority feelings that are met with excessive pampering or rejection by the parents can bring about abnormally expressed compensatory behaviors.

Style of Life

As noted in the foregoing, man's overriding goal, superiority, is universal, according to Adler. However, he recognized the existence of a wide variety of behaviors that could be used to reach this goal. Thus, different people manifest their striving for superiority in different ways, and each develops his characteristic mode of responding—his own style of life.

> it appears that after the fourth or fifth year of life the style of life has been fashioned as a prototype, with its particular way of seizing upon life, its strategy for conquering it, its degree of ability to cooperate [Adler, 1930, p. 403].

The style of life involves the set of behaviors by means of which a person compensates for his real or imagined inferiority. In our example of the child with a weak body, his style of life involves all those activities (exercise, practice at games, etc.) that will result in an increased physical strength. This early formed life style becomes firmly fixed and difficult to change, and provides the framework within which all later experiences are handled.

Thus, Adler emphasized the importance of the early years of life in forming an individual's personality as much as Freud did. He also greatly stressed the family as a factor in personality development. A child with a handicap, therefore, might consider himself a failure but, through compensation and with the help of understanding parents, might transform his inferiorities to strengths.

On the other hand, a child who is overly indulged by his parents may become self-centered, have no social interest, and expect others always to accede to his wishes; and a neglected child may develop a style of life that involves seeking revenge against society. Both pampering and neglect undermine a person's confidence in his ability to cope with the demands of life.

The Creative Self

Considered the pinnacle of his theory, Adler's concept of the creative self posits an individual's capacity to determine his personality in accord with his unique style of life. The creative self represents an active principle of human existence that may be likened to the older concept of soul. Certain abilities and raw experiences, Adler maintained, are available to man from his heredity and environment, but these are only

> the bricks which he uses in his own "creative" way in building up his attitude toward life. It is his individual way of using these bricks—or in other words, it is his attitude toward life—which determines his relationship to the outside world [1935, p. 5].

The concept of the creative self stresses the idea that man is a consciously active force in shaping his own personality and destiny. Thus, Adler saw man as capable of directly participating in his own fate rather than having it passively determined by past experiences, as Freud had claimed.

Order of Birth

In examining the childhood backgrounds of his patients, Adler placed great emphasis on the relation between personality and order of birth.

He felt that the oldest, middle, and youngest children have quite different social experiences resulting in the formation of different personalities. Adler noted that the oldest child, for example, receives a great deal of attention until he is dethroned by the birth of a second child. As a result, he theorized, the first-born may feel insecure and hostile toward people. Adler said that criminals, neurotics, and alcoholics are often first-born children. He found the second child to be intensely ambitious, rebellious, and jealous, constantly trying to surpass the first-born. Nevertheless, Adler considered him better adjusted than either the first-born or the youngest child. He saw the latter as spoiled and the most likely to be a behavior problem as a child and as an adult.

Comment

Adler's theories were warmly received by many people who were dissatisfied, and often repelled, by Freud's picture of man dominated by sexual forces and determined by childhood experiences. It is, after all, more pleasing to consider man as consciously directing his own development and destiny. Adler presented a much more satisfying and optimistic concept of man. His stress on the importance of social factors, to the relative exclusion of biological determinants, is usually considered a positive contribution. This attitude reinforced an already growing interest in the social sciences and the beginnings of a reorientation by the more traditional psychoanalysis in order to render its principles more applicable to the diverse behaviors found in different cultures.

Of course, Adler's system does not lack critics. Many claim his theories are superficial because they rely on a large number of "common-sense" observations from everyday life. Whether this is a valid criticism, however, is debatable, since a large number of his observations, regardless of origin, appear to many to be shrewd and insightful.

It is also argued that Adler was not a very consistent systematic theorist in that his position leaves too many questions unanswered. What, precisely, is this creative force by which an individual directs his behavior? Why do people not become reconciled to their inferiority? What are the relative roles of heredity and environment in this process? Of course, it must be remembered that Adler's is not the only system with questions yet to be answered.

The criticisms that more experimentally oriented psychologists directed at Freud and Jung apply to Adler as well.

Finally, it has been said that Adler's influence is much greater than generally recognized because other theorists (Horney and Fromm, for example) have been influenced by his work.

Karen Horney (1885–1952)

Trained as a Freudian psychoanalyst in Berlin, Horney considered her work to involve modifying and extending Freud's work rather than being distinctly non-Freudian.

Horney was born in Hamburg, Germany, but little is known of her childhood years. She entered medical school at the University of Berlin, receiving her M.D. in 1913. From 1914 to 1918 she undertook psycho-analytic training at the Berlin Psychoanalytic Institute. She began private practice in 1919 and became a faculty member at the institute.

Over the next 15 years, Horney wrote a number of journal articles, most of them concerned with problems of the feminine personality and demonstrating her disagreement with certain of Freud's concepts. In 1932, she came to the United States as associate director of the Chicago Institute for Psychoanalysis. In 1934, she established a private practice and taught at the New York Psychoanalytic Institute; but a growing disaffection for orthodox Freudian theories led her to break with the latter, where-upon she founded the American Institute of Psychoanalysis and remained its head until her death in 1952.

Before discussing Horney's system, let us consider her points of dis-agreement with Freud. Actually, Horney considered herself a disciple of Freud and accepted several of his basic principles. "Though retaining what I considered the fundamentals of Freud's teaching, I realized . . . that my search for a better understanding had led me in directions that were at variance with Freud [Horney, 1945, p. 13]." Indeed, parts of her system are so strongly at variance with Freud's that it occasionally becomes difficult to recognize her ideas as falling within the Freudian framework.

Horney felt, correctly, that some of Freud's basic assumptions were influenced by the spirit of the times in which he worked, and that times had changed drastically by the 1930s and 1940s when she set about formu-lating her system. The intellectual and cultural mores had altered, for instance, attitudes toward sex and the relative roles of the sexes had shifted about, so that many of Freud's theories were no longer in line with the spirit of the times.

Horney did not agree with Freud that personality development depends on unchangeable instinctive forces. She denied the preeminent position of sexual factors, challenged the validity of the Oedipus theory, discarded the libido concept and the Freudian structure of personality. She said that these concepts were a burden on psychoanalysis rather than its cornerstone.

Freud and Horney also differ basically in their conceptions of human nature:

> Freud's pessimism as regards neuroses and their treatment arose from the depths of his disbelief in human goodness and human growth. Man, he postulated, is doomed to suffer or to destroy. . . . My own belief is that man has the capacity as well as the desire to develop his potentialities and become a decent human being . . . I believe that man can change and go on changing as long as he lives [Horney, 1945, p. 19].

There are other differences, but the important point is that Horney rejected much of what Freud had said. She did accept, however, certain of Freud's tenets, including the belief in absolute determinism, the notion of unconscious motivation, and the existence of emotional, nonrational motives.

Horney's System

The fundamental concept in Horney's theory is basic anxiety, defined as "the feeling a child has of being isolated and helpless in a potentially hostile world [Horney, 1945, p. 41]." This basic anxiety can result from many different expressions of parental attitudes and behavior toward the child, including dominance, lack of protection, lack of warmth, erratic behavior, etc. In short, anything that disturbs the secure relations between the child and his parents is capable of producing anxiety. It must be remembered that this anxiety is not innate but rather results from environmental factors; it is socially created.

In the place of Freud's life and death instincts as major motivating forces, Horney considered the helpless infant to be seeking security in a world that is hostile and threatening. She claimed that the decisive driving power for man is the need for safety, security, and freedom from fear and threat.

Horney shared with Freud the belief that personality develops in early childhood but, whereas Freud detailed psychosexual stages of development, Horney focused on the way the growing child is treated by his parents, denying any such universal instinctual phases as an oral stage or Oedipus complex. She said that a child's possible development of anal or oral or phallic tendencies resulted from parental behaviors. She saw nothing in a child's development as universal. Rather, everything was considered dependent on culture and social–environmental factors. She attempted to show how all the developmental conflicts that Freud had ascribed to instinctual sources could be attributed to social forces.

Thus, Horney stressed the importance of early childhood experiences and parents' relations with their child, since the latter could either satisfy or frustrate his need for safety and security. The environment provided to the child and the way he reacts to it, she said, form the structure of personality.

Horney's Theory of Neurosis

As noted, Horney's main concept is basic anxiety developing out of a child's relations with his parents. When this socially or environmentally produced anxiety arises in a child, he develops a number of behavioral strategies in an attempt to deal with his feelings of insecurity and helplessness. He thus structures his personality in response to the demands of his specific environment.

When one of these behavioral strategies becomes a fixed part of the personality, it then becomes one of the so-called *neurotic needs* (or modes of defense against anxiety) of which Horney posited 10. Some of these include the need for affection and approval, prestige, personal achievement, perfection, and independence. All these neurotic needs can be reduced to one or another of three directional categories: (*1*) movement toward people, as in the need for love; (*2*) movement away from people, as in the need for independence; and (*3*) movement against people, as in the need for power.

Movement toward people involves acceptance of helplessness and an attempt to win the affection of others and be dependent on them. This is the only way in which the individual can feel secure with others. The movement away from people involves staying apart from others, avoiding any situation of dependence. Movement against people involves an acceptance of hostility, rebellion, and aggression against others.

Horney felt that none of these needs are realistic ways to deal with anxiety and that they themselves can give rise to basic conflicts because of their incompatibility. Once a person firmly establishes his method of coping with anxiety, his behavior ceases to be flexible enough to permit alternative modes of expression. For instance, if his fixed behavior is inappropriate in a particular situation, he is unable to change it to meet that situation's demands. This entrenched behavior intensifies the individual's difficulties because

> the attitudes do not remain restricted to the area of human relationships but gradually pervade the entire personality, as a malignant tumor pervades the whole organic tissue. They end by encompassing

not only the person's relation to others but also his relation to himself and to life in general [Horney, 1945, p. 46].

Horney also invoked the concept of the neurotic's *idealized self-image*, which provides him with a false picture of his personality. This self-image is an imperfect and totally misleading mask that prevents the neurotic from understanding and accepting his "true" self. In donning it, the neurotic denies the existence of his inner conflicts. The image, which to the neurotic is genuine, enables him to believe that he is far superior to the man he actually is.

Horney believed the neurotic's basic conflicts are neither innate nor inevitable, but arise out of undesirable social situations in childhood and can be prevented if the child's homelife is characterized by understanding, security, love, and warmth.

Comment

Horney's optimism about the possibility of avoiding neurotic conflicts was welcomed by many as a relief from the pessimism of Freudian theory. Wolman (1960) suggested that Horney's contribution to psychological theory is considerable in that she has introduced a model of personality that stresses social factors, attributing little, if anything, to innate factors.

Horney's theory of personality may be weaker than Freud's in clarity, internal consistency, and level of formal development. Many feel that it is easier to simply accept or reject Freud's theory than to attempt to reshape it as Horney did. So radical is her departure from basic Freudian concepts that her system is frowned on by more orthodox psychoanalysts. Her evidence, like that of Jung, Adler, and Freud, is taken from clinical observations and is thus subject to the same questions regarding its scientific legitimacy noted earlier.

Erich Fromm (1900–   )

Unlike Jung, Adler, and Horney, Fromm studied sociology and psychology before training in psychoanalysis and becoming a therapist. Because of these early interests, Fromm's theories have been described as social philosophy rather than as strictly psychological theories (Cofer & Appley, 1964).

Born in Frankfurt, Germany, in 1900, Fromm studied psychology and sociology at Heidelberg, Frankfurt, and Munich, receiving his Ph.D. from Heidelberg in 1922. He took his psychoanalytic training in Munich and at the Berlin Psychoanalytic Institute, and came to the United States in 1933. He lectured at the Chicago Psychoanalytic Institute before moving to New York, where he engaged in private practice. He has taught at a number of universities and institutes in the United States and more recently at the National University in Mexico City.

One of Fromm's basic interests is the effect of large aspects of society on the individual. He believes, for instance, that political organizations no longer provide the firm guidance and secure structure they once did. He suggests that contemporary man has succeeded in freeing himself from dependence on nature, only to find himself isolated from his fellow man. Consider the feeling of belonging, dependence, and security a child has in his relations with his parents. When he reaches adulthood, he achieves independence but at the expense of his earlier security. Similarly, in the evolution of society toward greater mobility, complexity, and impersonality, man has lost his once secure relationship with smaller, more primary groups, such as the tribe or village, as well as with nature itself.

Fromm suggests that man is motivated to escape his ever-growing freedom and return to a more secure existence. He believes that the prime motivating force in human existence is not the satisfaction of instinctual drives, but the desire to revert to a condition of dependence. In his book *Escape from Freedom* (1941) which was written during the Nazi regime, Fromm suggested that Nazism attracted people because it offered an escape from intolerable freedom and a return to secure dependency. In short, Fromm views man's nature as culturally or socially, and not biologically, determined.

The two most common systems through which man can regain security, according to Fromm, are humanism and authoritarianism. Authoritarianism involves the external imposition on a society of a highly rigid set of guiding principles, producing a state of bondage or slavery. Fromm rejects this system as an effective solution to man's problem of isolation because he believes that a society that prevents the individual from realizing his full potential thereby generates hostility against itself.

A far more effective solution, Fromm claims, is humanism, in which man unites with his fellow man in the spirit of love and shared work, or mutual cooperation. Fromm envisages a society, called Humanistic Communitarian Socialism, in which each person is a brother to every man and hence does not feel alone.

According to Fromm, man has five specific needs that arise from the conditions of his lonely existence: the need for a sense of individual identity; the need to feel that he belongs to society (rootedness); the need to transcend his base animal nature as a creative human being; the need to relate satisfactorily to his fellows; and the need for a stable and consistent orientation or frame of reference.

Fromm notes that society, unfortunately, does not provide adequate means for satisfying these needs. Further, social and political institutions often produce conflicts by satisfying certain needs at the expense of others; for example, a strong identification with an industrial or national symbol frustrates the need for personal identity.

Fromm's system offers several ways to escape the isolation and insecurity he believes predominate in modern society. In his *Man for Himself* (1947) and *The Heart of Man* (1964), he identifies them as dynamic orientations of character: receptive, exploitative, hoarding, marketing, and productive. Although no one exhibits only one such orientation, Fromm believes that one may be dominant in a given person.

> In the receptive orientation a person feels "the source of all good" to be outside, and he believes that the only way to get what he wants—be it something material, be it affection, love, knowledge, pleasure—is to receive it from that outside source. In this orientation the problem of love is almost exclusively that of "being loved" and not that of loving [Fromm, 1947, p. 62].

The person becomes submissive and dependent on others, needing someone (or some system) to take care of him. Such individuals will go to great lengths to maintain strong identification with others. (In Horney's terms, this orientation involves a movement toward people.)

The exploitative orientation is manifested as very aggressive behavior and corresponds to Horney's movement against people. People thus oriented do not expect to receive from others, but rather take from or exploit others, by force or cunning, according to the philosophy "might makes right."

The hoarding orientation involves the perception of the outside world as threatening, which leads to distrust of and rigidity toward people. The hoarding person tends to save and possess, becoming frugal, miserly, and letting as little as possible (material things or emotions) out; he evaluates his security in terms of tangible possessions and wealth.

The fourth orientation—marketing—reflects the advent of capitalism, according to which personal success is adjudged by one's acceptability to those who use his services or employ him. The person therefore plays a variety of socially approved roles and concentrates on selling himself rather than on fulfilling his potential. Since a person's value depends more on his success in the market place and less on his personal qualities, the situation does not lead to a feeling of security. In this kind of orientation, a man says to others, in essence, "I am as you want me to be."

All four of these orientations Fromm considered to be pathological.

The truly healthy person manifests the productive orientation in which he is able to realize his full potential and achieve his goals without misusing or abusing others. This is apparently accomplished by making a creative contribution to one's family, occupation, or society at large. More recently, Fromm has introduced a pair of new orientations: necrophilious, describing a person who is attracted to death; and biophilious, a person attracted to life.

Comment

The overall theme in Fromm's writings is man's relations to society. He remains optimistic about man's ability to shape a society that will allow him to develop into a fully human creature. This point of view is highly acceptable to many in that it offers the hope that man can introduce constructive forces into his society to render the human condition more distinctly human. It has been suggested, however, that Fromm's philosophy of life does not really justify such a high degree of optimism. He sees man in a never-ending conflict with nature; since man knows "too much, he is unable to accept his fate naïvely. . . . there is never peace of mind, never harmony between man and universe, but only a continuous struggle and search for new solutions, none of them ever a final one. This is, to quote Fromm, man's tragic fate: 'to be part of nature, and yet to transcend it' [Wolman, 1960, p. 368]."

Critique of the Social–Psychological Theories

The theorists discussed in this section share an obvious point of similarity in that their work may be labeled "social–psychological." They all place considerable emphasis on the role of social variables in the development of the individual personality. Although they do acknowledge varying degrees of intellectual debt to the work of Freud, each constitutes a vigorous protest against the Freudian notion of the primacy of instinct in personality formation.

Thus, they see man's behavior as determined not exclusively by instinctual, biological forces, but rather by the types of interpersonal relationships to which the individual is exposed, particularly in childhood. Sexual forces in personality development are minimized by these theorists, who believe that it is not sexual experiences that determine personality, but rather that the socially developed personality determines the nature of sexual responses.

Just as the role of instinct is minimized, so too is the role of the libido and its manifestations, such as the Oedipus complex and psychosexual stages of development. Anxiety and expressions of abnormal behavior do not originate in instinct, libido, and sex, but instead develop from early social relationships experienced. To these theorists, man is not irrevocably doomed to anxiety, as in Freud's deterministic theory, since anxiety can be avoided by the proper kinds of childhood social experiences.

According to Freud, man's behavior is universally static; the social–psychological theorists, on the other hand, consider man's behavior quite flexible and capable of being consciously and continuously changed by the individual. Man's social organizations, too, are flexible and liable to alteration by man. While recognizing that social mores can be modified only gradually and with difficulty, these theorists optimistically agree that man is able to develop the kind of social system most appropriate to his requirements.

Hall and Lindzey (1970) discuss two points of criticism that have been directed against the social–psychological theorists. First, it is argued that their conception of man as a rational, conscious, and socialized being is unconvincing in the light of his all-too-frequently disappointing and irrational behavior. One rejoinder to this charge is to blame man's past and present displays of violence, injustice, etc., on a particular social system. As noted earlier, however, these theorists argue that man shapes society to best suit his needs. We are left with the paradox of man, an eminently rational, perfectible, socialized being, who has nevertheless developed an abundance of social systems inadequate, indeed in many cases injurious, to his needs.

The second criticism accuses these theorists of neglecting the social processes through which a person is shaped, that is, of leaving unanswered the question of how a person learns to be a properly functioning member of society. The social–psychological theories draw on the general concept of learning to explain personality formation, but neglect the specific mechanisms of the learning process. This neglect, moreover, seems more serious since learning has been a topic of paramount importance in American psychology for many years.

The Mainstream after Freud

We have noted that Freud alone fashioned and shaped the development of psychoanalysis. When he died, his loyal followers were left the difficult problem of what to do with Freud's system now that he could no longer determine its direction. The course they chose involved: (1) elaborating and extending certain less well-developed aspects of his system, (2) making more explicit some of his postulates, (3) attempting more precise definitions of certain basic concepts, (4) extending the range of behavior covered by psychoanalytic interpretations, and (5) employing research methods other than the psychoanalytic interview (Hall & Lindzey, 1970, pp. 61–62).

These neo-Freudians used Freud's system as a base; his pronouncements are not radically changed so much as they are extended and amplified. A very strong allegiance and intellectual debt to Freud is obvious in their writings, where Freud's works are continually used as the most important authority to support newer positions. Nevertheless, a number of important trends have appeared in psychoanalysis since Freud's death.

Hall and Lindzey (1970) discuss several recent modifications in psychoanalysis, the first of which concerns the emergence of the ego as a more independent part of personality. Although Freud attributed important functions to the ego, he considered it subservient to the id, which was the center of attention in his system. The neo-Freudians have accorded greater status and autonomy to the ego, which they consider independent of the id in both function and origin. This newer concept proposes that the ego and id are formed early in life and have distinct origins in inherited predispositions and separate courses of development. Thus, the ego is looked on as a rational guiding system responsible for intellectual and social development, independent of the id, with its own sources of energy as well as its own motives and goals.

A second modification is a diminished emphasis on instinctual determinants of personality. Though perhaps not departing so radically from Freud's system as the social–psychological theorists, these more recent psychoanalysts have recognized the influence on personality of psychological and social variables. In more contemporary psychoanalytic literature, there is less use of the term "instinct" and more of the term "drive." Personality development is more often explained in terms of the individual's life history rather than innate forces. Biological factors tend to be de-emphasized in favor of an approach wherein personality formation is accounted for through primarily psychological structures arising from early experiences.

The third important modification in Freud's system of psychoanalysis arises from the change in emphasis just discussed. Increased interest in early experiences of the individual has brought about more studies of infants and children. Freud, as we have seen, was also interested in early experiences, but he worked with inferences drawn from the remembered childhood experiences of his patients. The new approach, in contrast, observes developmental processes directly, as they take place in childhood. In recent years, psychoanalytically oriented investigators have conducted much research on development, using this method of direct observation. Much of this work has been reported in the annual volumes of *The Psychoanalytic Study of the Child,* of which Anna Freud has been co-editor since its beginning in 1945.

A fourth change in the direction of psychoanalysis has to do with increased interest in the experimental testing of psychoanalytic propositions. There has been more frequent use of nonanalytical methods, such as the observational studies of children just mentioned. Patients' reports are no longer the sole means of verifying psychoanalytic hypotheses. A growing body of experimental literature, reporting research with both human and animal subjects, has drawn heavily on psychoanalytic concepts, for which it has in turn provided some measure of experimental support.

Finally, there is evidence of a steadily growing rapprochement between psychoanalysis and academic experimental psychology. Prominent representatives from both camps have, through their research and writing activities, helped to bring about some degree of reconciliation, particularly since World War II. Both psychoanalysis and experimental psychology have tended to investigate some problems of common interest, such as factors in motivation. The rapid growth of clinical psychology in the years since World War II has led many psychologists to recognize the possible value of psychoanalysis as a therapeutic device. There is also the undeniable fact that psychoanalysis has strongly influenced the entire Western culture; this has not gone unrecognized by psychologists.

Nevertheless, profound differences between psychology and psychoanalysis remain. A great deal of mutual disaffection, indeed, hostility, still separates the two approaches, and many psychologists continue to reject the validity and utility of psychoanalytic theory, regardless of the extent of its modifications.

SUGGESTED FURTHER READINGS

Jung
Evans, R. I. *Conversations with Carl Jung.* Princeton, New Jersey: Van Nostrand, 1964.
Fordham, F. *An introduction to Jung's psychology.* Baltimore, Maryland: Penguin, 1959.
Jacobi, J. *The psychology of C. G. Jung.* (Rev. ed.) New Haven, Connecticut: Yale Univ. Press, 1951.
Storr, A. *C. G. Jung.* New York: Viking Press, 1973.

Adler

Ansbacher, H. L., & Ansbacher, R. R. (Eds.) *The individual psychology of Alfred Adler.* New York: Basic Books, 1956.

Orgler, H. *Alfred Adler: The man and his work.* New York: Putnam, 1965.

Horney

Horney, K. *The collected works of Karen Horney.* New York: Norton, 1963. 2 vols.

General

Brown, J. A. C. *Freud and the post-Freudians.* London: Cassell & Co. Ltd., 1963.

Hartmann, H. *Essays on ego psychology: Selected problems in psychoanalytic theory.* New York: International Universities Press, 1964.

Rapaport, D. Structure of psychoanalytic theory. In S. Koch (Ed.), *Psychology: A study of a science.* Vol. 3. New York: McGraw-Hill, 1959. Pp. 55–183.

15

Epilogue:
More Recent Developments

We have seen how the various systems of psychological thought came into being, prospered for a time, and then, with the exception of psycho-analysis, were absorbed by the mainstream of contemporary psychology. We also saw that each movement grew strong through opposition to another system. When there was no longer any need for strong and vociferous protest, the schools, as such, died a gradual death. Yet each of these protests died a successful death because it made substantial contributions to psychological thought. Thus, each was a fruitful protest—each accomplished its mission.

Such a conclusion seems warranted even in the case of structuralism which left little, if any, direct mark on the contemporary scene. Yet we cannot deny the substantial influence of the structuralist position on the subsequent course of psychology's development. It gained psychology its independence and served as a formidable and well-defined starting point—a substantial base to inspire opposition. Even this rather thoroughly destroyed system, then, served a valuable purpose.

For a time, primarily in the 1920s and 1930s, when the era of schools was at its peak, the psychology of the day made a rather sorry showing. Heidbreder noted in 1933 that:

> System after system announces its principles, each imposes its order
> on the facts that arrest its attention, and each puts its case with
> a degree of plausibility. The difficulty is that they all do so and
> that they are all more or less at odds with each other. . . . this
> is the situation after more than half a century of effort: systems
> in plenty, but no one interpretation of the facts of psychology to
> which all psychologists, or even a majority, agree [p. 413].

Thus, the leaders of each school attempted to establish psychology in
their own image. There was disagreement over the problems of definition,
subject matter, and methodology. The intensity of the debates among
the various schools reached a peak in the 1920s. Psychologists as well
as outside observers witnessing these controversies viewed the future of
psychology pessimistically. Many felt that psychology could never realize
its ambition of becoming a science on a par with the natural sciences.
The division of psychology into separate camps was spoken of as "one
of the scandals of contemporary science" at the Ninth International Congress of Psychology in 1929.

   In retrospect, however, a more optimistic picture of the role of the
schools emerges. It now can be seen that the period of the schools represented a phase of normal development and served as an important milestone in the development of psychological thought. It is recognized that
each school made contributions, some presenting new empirical data,
some offering new insights and generalizations, and others correcting
or destroying the propositions of a rival school.

The Dissolution of the Schools

   With the exception of psychoanalysis, the distinctiveness of the various
schools began to fade around 1930, and controversy began to subside.
One of the many factors that helped to bring about this change in the
psychological scene was the death, or at least withdrawal from active
and open debate, of each of the leaders of the schools. This was particularly evident in the case of Titchener, who died in 1927. No one of
his stature and ability remained to carry the banner of structuralism
and do battle with its opponents. The effect of Titchener's death was
noted by Boring (1927):

> The death of no other psychologist could so alter the psychological
> picture in America. . . . The clear-cut opposition between behavior-
> ism and its allies, on the one hand, and something else, on the other,

remains clear only when the opposition is between behaviorism and Titchener, mental tests and Titchener, or applied psychology and Titchener. His death thus, in a sense, creates a classificatory chaos in American systematic psychology [p. 489].

Another factor involved the differences of opinion that arose within the schools themselves and weakened their solidarity. Within the behaviorist camp, for instance, we discussed the emergence of theorists who adhered to the basic behavioristic emphasis on increased objectivity, yet differed from strict Watsonian behaviorism. The same kind of divisive emphasis within psychoanalysis was also noted.

Finally, it became apparent to many psychologists that the various approaches were not as irreconcilable as had been thought. A mutual recognition and acceptance of contributions, both conceptual and methodological, by the rival systems developed. The various lines of theory and research began to converge. Even Titchener remarked, as early as 1921, that the terms and concepts of "functional" and "structural" as descriptive qualifications in psychology were becoming obsolete. Woodworth noted in 1930 that the schools actually had more in common than had first appeared.

Individual psychologists became more and more suspicious of the schools' claims that the growing body of psychological data could be ordered within the framework of one system. By the 1930s and 1940s, more and more psychologists declined to align themselves with a particular school (and even to theorize at all) because of the division and controversy. The schools came to be viewed as too restrictive and dogmatic, and many felt that the development of final systems and global theories that attempted to encompass all behavior was premature at a time when many facts were still undetermined and many relationships not yet investigated.

And so the schools passed into history, although their heritage lingers on. We have discussed some of the more current efforts in psychology that grew out of the schools, and will now consider the mainstream of contemporary American psychology. Psychologists today no longer exclusively rally around a Gestalt, behaviorist, or functionalist flag. There is a greater tendency toward eclecticism with regard to theories, methods, and concepts.

However, as Woodworth and Sheehan (1964) note, in spite of the dissolution of the schools, if you ask a contemporary psychologist, "What do you think of psychoanalysis?" or "Are you a behaviorist?" his reply will not be one of total indifference. Major points of difference still exist between contemporary objective (neo-behavioristic) psychology and psychoanalysis, which still stands as an orientation not integrated into the mainstream of psychology. This situation will no doubt persist until psychoanalysis achieves scientific status—and many question whether this will ever occur.

Contemporary American Psychology

Before we discuss the nature of contemporary psychology in America, let us consider its phenomenal growth. Only a few psychologists constituted the charter membership of the American Psychological Association in 1892. By the time of the demise of the schools in 1930, membership had risen to 1100. By 1973, the membership had grown to over 35,000 members and is increasing rapidly. Watson (1971) estimated that over half of the world's psychologists live and work in the United States, and Chaplin and Krawiec (1968) noted that at least 90% of the world's work in psychology is American in origin.

Psychology is growing not only in numbers, but also in degree of specialization. The size of the APA has necessitated the formation of separate divisions: Those representing scientific interests include experimental psychology, evaluation and measurement, developmental psychology, and physiological and comparative psychology, among others; professional divisions include industrial, school, clinical, military, and consumer psychology. The annual national meeting and various regional meetings are well supported, often to the extent that several hotels are needed to accommodate all those attending.

This "population explosion" is paralleled by an "information explosion" of journal articles, books, and other publications, making it increasingly difficult for a psychologist to keep up with all the developments outside of his own specialty areas and, in many cases, even within his major area of interest.

To give an example of the sharp rate of increase in psychological publications, let us note the number of articles included in the *Psychological Abstracts*. In 1961, over 7000 articles were summarized. In just 6 years, the number increased to 17,000, and in 1972 more than 24,000 articles were abstracted.

There is nothing to indicate that this increase will not continue. To keep abreast of all published works in psychology would require reading at least 66 books and journal articles each and every day of the year!

As to the dominant nature or theme of contemporary American psychology, R. I. Watson (1965) describes the prevailing trends as encompassing determinism, naturalism, physicalism, functionalism, operationalism, quantification, hypothetico-deductivism, and environmentalism.

Chaplin and Krawiec (1968) describe contemporary American psychology as a functionalistic behaviorism, noting that psychology has become even more behavioristic in definition than it was during the 1930s, while retaining the strong functionalistic spirit from that earlier time.

There are several consequences of this behavioristic and functionalistic dominance of contemporary psychology, according to Chaplin and Krawiec (1968, pp. 605, 608).

First, experiments are arranged or designed so as to uncover the nature of the intervening variables linking stimulus and response, and the laws and principles that determine their relationship. Thus, psychology takes a more inferential approach to the study of human behavior because of its strong interest in the functional processes in the individual which give meaning to the objective behavioral events being observed.

Second, psychologists have become more concerned with the processes of motivation due, in part, to the greater interest in intervening variables and to the functionalistic cast pervading psychology.

Finally, and not surprisingly, American psychology is characterized by the wide-scale application of its findings and principles to problems of a very practical nature. As we have seen, American psychology from its very beginnings had a much stronger applied orientation than its European counterparts. Cattell and J. B. Watson, among others, were strongly concerned with applying psychology to real-world problems, and this aspect of the discipline comprises an important part of contemporary American psychology, as we shall see in more detail in a later section.

Another characteristic of American psychology in recent decades is a renewal of interest in theoretical issues. This began in the late 1940s and 1950s and differs considerably from that of the 1920s and 1930s. During the era of the schools, theories or systems existed on a grand scale and attempted to encompass all of psychology within a single framework. John B. Watson, for example, attempted to explain all aspects of behavior—thinking, emotion, learning, etc.—within one behavioristic system. The newer attempts at theorizing are considerably more circumscribed and restricted, so much so that the term "miniature theory" has come to describe, aptly, today's theories. Some of these theories deal with a single area, such as learning, motivation, or personality. Most, however, are concerned with even more restricted functions or processes; that is, they attempt to explain a very small portion of behavior, such as performance in a very specific learning situation, such as conditioning or verbal learning.

The foregoing comments do not mean to imply that all contemporary psychologists are conducting research in the light of a particular miniature theory. A substantial portion of current research is conducted in the absence of *any* formally stated theoretical structure. Very often, the results of a particular study suggest further research on that topic. For example, it is common for a study to be replicated, with a change in the subject population (from children to adults, for example). Research to determine the effect of a laboratory stress situation on performance on a particular kind of test is likely to be followed by research using tests that measure other functions. Thus, we have a distinct trend toward specificity in theory construction, and research problems concerned with quite limited areas of behavior.

Methods

It was noted earlier that contemporary American psychology is primarily behavioristic in nature and definition. From this statement it follows that the methods of psychology are characterized by operationism and objectivity. The experimental method remains fundamental; indeed, its use as well as its rigor has increased.

In fact, so rigorous has been the application of the experimental method to the subject matter of psychology that it has even been turned upon itself. One of the most exciting and important areas of research in recent years is the so-called research on research, that ·is, the investigation by experimental means of the experimental method. A growing number of articles and books deal with the effects of various attributes of the experimenter (including the hypothesis he holds), and of the human subject, on the outcome of research (Friedman, 1967; Rosenthal, 1966; Rosenthal & Rosnow, 1969; Schultz, 1969, 1970). These investigations warn us of a wide variety of unintended factors that can influence research results, and are certainly in the best scientific tradition of self-criticism and correction. Far from weakening the value of the experimental method, such research can only result in improving it, if researchers take heed of the impact of these unintended biasing factors.

Progress in electronics and engineering has led to the development of very sophisticated and elaborate laboratory apparatus and measuring devices. These advances have also greatly increased both the objectivity and precision of data collection in psychology.

Not only the techniques of data collection, but also the methods of analyzing data have improved. A development of major importance is the widespread use of computers, which are able to analyze vast amounts of data in very short periods of time. Their use has intensified the already prominent trend toward greater quantification in psychology.

Thus, we can see that the methods of modern psychology closely emulate those of the natural sciences—a direction in which psychology has been moving since the days of Wundt. Developments in computers and in sophisticated electromechanical apparatus and measuring techniques have perhaps complicated the training requirements of modern psychologists. An experimental psychologist today must be part engineer, electrician, and mathematician if he is to use adequately the tools at his disposal. This trend is evidenced by the publication in recent years of books dealing with electrical circuits, computers, and aspects of instrumentation written for behavioral scientists (Sidowski, 1966; Uttal, 1968; Hetzel & Hetzel, 1969, for example).

In addition to these methodological changes in experimental psychology, there have also been changes in the scope or range of application of these methods. The term "experimental psychology" no longer refers exclusively to basic research, nor is it restricted to the once traditional areas of sensation, perception, and learning. Today, social, child, industrial, and educational psychologists as well as "pure" research psychologists use the experimental method. Further, in keeping with America's functional orientation, experimental psychology is no longer exclusively academic; laboratory research is being conducted in industrial and military situations.

Major Research Areas

Although research today covers a wide field, four areas—learning, perception, motivation, and personality—comprise the major areas of interest among academic psychologists. The following comments on these areas are not intended to be comprehensive, rather to highlight the current scene.

Learning

Research on learning continues to attract a major share of attention in the United States, and perhaps reflects the environmentalistic cast of American psychology. In our discussions of the schools, we noted the great interest in learning on the part of Pavlov, Watson, Thorndike, and others that has presaged the work of a great many modern-day psychologists. We have already mentioned the more recent developments in learning of Hull, Skinner, Guthrie, and Tolman, and the continuing work of their followers.

Learning behavior has been studied over the entire range of the phylo-genetic scale, from the flatworm to the college sophomore. For the most part, contemporary American learning research and theory is based on animal research and is behavioristically oriented. In learning theory, as in all psychology, the day of the large-scale global theory is past, and modern miniature theories and more specific and restricted types of learning are being tested and studied.

The current focus is on such areas as human verbal learning, instru-mental learning, animal learning (also, in specific species), and human motor learning. Many workers in these areas see them as fundamental to the understanding of all other aspects of human functioning. While not denying the importance of perception, emotion, personality, and the like, many believe that these areas are studied more fruitfully when con-sidered as problems in learning.

Although the most striking development in the history of learning theory is the domination of behavioristic conditioning oriented systems based on animal studies, contemporary learning theory and research also emphasize the study of intervening variables. Though retaining a strong behavioristic cast, theorists are evidencing great interest in the covert aspects of learning, such as the role of reinforcement, retroactive inter-ference, and so on. Indeed, the most important variable investigated in the last 25 years or so is the nature of reinforcement and its function in learning. This trend strongly suggests that the strict S–R brand of behaviorism has proven less than adequate in understanding the nature of the learning process.

Perhaps the most exciting recent development in learning research is the investigation of the neurochemical bases of learning. The discovery of ribonucleic acid (RNA) suggests the possibility that learning may be explained in chemical as well as psychological terms. Briefly, experi-ments have shown that learning may cause changes in RNA. When RNA from a trained animal is then injected into an untrained animal, the latter demonstrates the learned behavior, thus suggesting a chemical transfer of learning. The evidence is controversial and inconsistent, but it has generated a great deal of continuing research.

Published studies on learning theory and research constitute a substan-tial part of the extensive literature in psychology as a whole. Many com-prehensive textbooks and professional monographs have appeared, and much learning research is published in journals whose scope extends be-yond learning per se, such as the *Journal of Experimental Psychology* and the *Journal of Personality and Social Psychology*. In addition, special-ized journals concentrating on specific problems in learning have ap-peared, such as the *Journal of Verbal Learning and Verbal Behavior*.

Research findings in learning have been applied to the field of education in the form of programmed instruction and teaching machines. Learning is an area that continues to receive much attention in contemporary American psychology.

Perception

Perception, a traditional research area in psychology, continues to attract substantial attention, but is not as frequent a subject of study as learning. The approach to the study of perception has altered drastically in recent years. Under the aegis of the so-called "new look" in perception, there has been a pronounced tendency since World War II to emphasize certain inner determinants of perception, such as needs, values, attitudes, and personality factors. Prior to that, the traditional emphasis was centered almost solely on various aspects of the stimulus situation.

The process of perception is no longer regarded merely as the combination of sensory impressions deriving their meaning from stimulus organization or past experience. Motivational, emotional, and social factors are now recognized as influential in determining not only what an individual perceives, but also the manner in which he perceives it. This does not mean that the role of stimulus factors has been neglected or ignored in contemporary research, but interest in inner determinants of perception reflects one of the major emphases of the contemporary scene.

Current theoretical work in the area of perception has developed within Gestalt, behaviorist, and functionalist frameworks. As noted in the discussion of the Gestalt point of view, that school's most significant contribution has been in the area of perception. The Gestaltists' emphasis on the innate factors of organization and their tendency to minimize the role of experience and stimulus factors have received considerable support from the research work of Lewin, Gordon Allport, Postman, and others.

Working within a behaviorist framework, the Canadian psychologist Hebb developed a neurological theory of perceptual functioning that stresses the importance of learning in perception. Hebb postulates a cell assembly conceived of as a group of cortical neurons that, through learning, become associated with one another. This associationistic theory, with its neurological foundation, has revitalized the role of learning in perception, a role that had declined because of the strong influence of Gestalt psychology.

Regardless of systematic position, contemporary psychologists seem to take a functionalistic approach to perception. Perception is increasingly being treated as a fundamentally important process in man's interactions with his experiential world. As a result of this trend, applied psychologists as well as academic researchers have been compelled to recognize and study perceptual processes.

Motivation

Motivation, perhaps the most central of all aspects of human functioning, remains one of the less fully developed areas of contemporary psychology. In the early years of psychology's development, it received little direct attention. (Perhaps the "determining tendencies" of the Würzburg group were a prelude to later study.) More direct interest was provided by the evolutionary emphasis on adaptation and biological drives, and by Freud's concern with unconscious motivation.

In spite of these few early efforts and the practical importance of the area, theories of motivation remain much less well formulated than those of learning and perception. There has been much research of value in recent times, but a general theory of motivation is lacking.

Progress in the area has been deterred by the many opposing points of view, differing experimental approaches, and disagreements over proper terminology and problems of definition. A fundamental dichotomy exists between the behavioristic–comparative theorists working with animal subjects, who are concerned with the physiological basis of motivation, and the often nonexperimental theorists of an analytic persuasion, concerned with the more psychological basis of motivation.

As in other areas of psychology, miniature theories devoted to a single motive or a small group of motives have been developed. For example, McClelland (1953) has conducted exciting research on the need for achievement. Others have successfully assessed need for affiliation and need for power. Great progress has also been made in investigating the neurological bases of motivation. Researchers have isolated centers in the brain which seem to control hunger and thirst, and others concerned with pleasure and pain. Thus, a great deal of research is being undertaken but progress in motivational theory has been slow.

There are signs, however, of increasing recognition of and concern over this unsatisfactory state of affairs. There is, further, a growing awareness that the area of motivation is a central problem for psychology. A final source of encouragement is that many learning theorists have become interested in motivation as an integral aspect of learning, and those working in perception and personality are also recognizing the role of motivational determinants in their areas of study.

Personality

As noted earlier, concern with personality theory was not evidenced in the initial school of psychology and was but little developed in the

American schools. Psychoanalysis, more than any other orientation, has generated an interest in the study of personality. As a consequence of the development and spread of psychoanalysis, theories of personality have proliferated both in Europe and America, as noted in Chapter 14. In addition to the psychoanalytic-nurtured personality theories, other systems of personality have developed since the 1930s. Consequently, there now exist in American psychology several theoretical and methodological orientations. This diversity is partly the result of the extremely broad nature of the subject matter of personality, which has attracted psychologists with sharply different theoretical orientations. It is hard to imagine a conceptual or methodological orientation that could not include the study of personality.

Some current theoretical efforts stress a biological approach to personality study, whereas others use a social or cultural approach. Some emphasize conscious aspects of personality, others the unconscious; some are highly objective and rely heavily on empirical research, whereas others are very subjective and rely on uncontrolled observation, primarily of patients' behavior. American psychologists on the whole seem to prefer experimental–learning approaches, in keeping with the general objective, behavioristic, environmentalistic flavor of contemporary American psychology.

Other Developments

An outstanding feature of contemporary psychology is the intensive research interest in the area of physiological psychology. As we have seen, psychology was very closely related to physiology in the beginning. Prompted by quite recent advances in physiology and endocrinology, physiological psychologists have studied the physiological functioning of the organism and biochemical factors in behavior. Recent years have seen rapid advances in the development of more precise physiological measuring apparatus, largely of the electronic variety.

Particularly impressive is the research in brain physiology. With the development of new techniques for implanting electrodes in the brain has come exciting research involving self-stimulation of the organism and mapping of functional areas of the cortex. The combination of physiological methods of investigation with operant conditioning techniques has opened up several new research areas emphasizing both overt behavior and neurophysiology, as well as their interaction. Recent research on the reticular activating system of the brain and its relation to the amount and kind of stimulation to which the organism is exposed has led to other new research areas (such as sensory deprivation) and theoretical considerations.

Major breakthroughs have been made in tracing cortical activities during periods of sleep and dreams. Also, biofeedback research has attracted a great deal of public as well as professional attention. Through biofeedback research it has been found that a person can control various aspects of his physiological functioning (brain waves, heart rate, etc.) through feedback on bodily responses. Biochemists and psychologists are working together to investigate how the chemical composition of the brain might be affected by purely psychological variables such as new learning. Mention was made earlier of studies to determine the chemical bases of learning.

It is small wonder that some psychologists see the mushrooming activities in physiological psychology as the most potentially productive in the understanding of behavior.

The area of social psychology has flourished with great vitality since its modest beginnings in the early years of this century. Its research methods have become increasingly sophisticated, and the range of behavior it encompasses is enormous. It has made substantial contributions to the traditional areas of learning, perception, motivation, and personality by drawing attention to the influence of social and cultural forces on these basic processes. Concerned with group behavior and the effects of group membership on individual behavior, social psychology is working effectively in such areas as group problem-solving ability, mass behavior, leadership, conformity, communication, attitude formation and change, and prejudice. Social psychology has been applied to so-called "real world" problems in the areas of propaganda and public opinion, the national concern over racial prejudice, effects of televised violence on children, and so on. Findings from social psychological research were cited in the 1954 Supreme Court decision against racial segregation in the public schools and are increasingly used by a variety of presidential commissions on aspects of American life. This rapidly growing area enjoys enormous research productivity.

The initial impetus provided by Galton, Cattell, and Binet has carried the field of psychological testing to a prominent position in contemporary American psychology. Literally millions of psychological tests are given each year to school children, college students, military personnel, and people in government, business, and industry. It is almost impossible to reach maturity in the United States today without having taken at least one psychological test. No matter what an individual's plans, there seems to be a psychological test to be taken first.

Many psychologists in academic settings have conducted a great deal of research on the development and use of psychological tests. Others in business, government, or the military have been administering, scoring, and interpreting these tests, thereby influencing the lives and careers of millions of people. The widespread use of these tests has evoked some concern in recent years. The United States Congress has held hearings to determine whether and to what degree psychological testing constitutes an invasion of privacy, with the result that at least one well-known personality test has been barred from use by government agencies. Despite the reaction against testing, the advantages gained from the use of well-constructed tests by competent and conscientious testers seem to outweigh any possible disadvantages—at least thus far.

The area of clinical psychology has also expanded rapidly since its beginnings in the work of Freud and others. In America, thousands of clinical psychologists are involved in the diagnosis and treatment of the emotionally disturbed. Some nonclinical psychologists express concern and dismay at the relative lack of well-controlled research in this area and the fact that psychotherapy remains more art than science. The number of psychologists working in clinical settings in mental institutions or in private practice is increasing, but a shortage of trained personnel still exists.

One major development in clinical psychology in recent years has been the very widespread use of the behavior-modification technique of treatment. Using relatively simple conditioning procedures, behavior modification apparently has a high rate of "cures" for a variety of disorders, and is becoming increasingly popular.

An area of study from physiological research is fraught with implications for the future of clinical psychology. Much research has been performed on the chemical bases of mental illness (particularly schizophrenia) which could lead to chemical rather than psychological therapy.

Finally, group techniques of therapy, as opposed to individual analysis, are being used with greater frequency.

Another area of more professional than scientific orientation includes the complex of activities subsumed under the label "industrial or organizational psychology," which has grown considerably since its beginnings around the time of World War I. Industrial psychologists work in industrial, governmental, and military settings, and are primarily concerned with selecting the right man for the right job, training workers to do their jobs more efficiently, and solving problems of supervision and other factors (such as fatigue and morale) that affect job performance. A number of clinical psychologists also work on the industrial scene and claim success in reducing accidents, absenteeism, sickness, etc., by their concern with various social and emotional factors relevant to the work environment.

A recently developed branch of industrial psychology is concerned with the design of highly technical and sophisticated military equipment such as is found in aircraft, missile and space systems, submarines, and the like. Called engineering psychology (or human engineering), it strives to design equipment to fit the man, that is, to make the best possible use of man's capabilities in operating the equipment quickly and efficiently.

Finally, some industrial psychologists are concerned with areas of marketing and motivation research, such as advertising, packaging, and creating consumer demand.

While many industrial psychologists apply their knowledge of psychology to practical problems, others conduct relevant research in academic settings. Some research is carried out by those working in industry, but it is less in quantity than the academic research.

Professionalization

As we have seen, psychology began as an almost exclusively academic enterprise. With the exception of the psychoanalysts, virtually all psychologists were employed at universities or colleges, a situation that remained true as late as 1930. We also know that several of the important founders or pioneers of psychology were strongly opposed to any professionalization or application of psychology.

No such climate of thought exists today, nor has psychology remained a discipline allied only to the academic world. Indeed, no more than 40% of the psychologists in the United States are employed by universities. The majority work for government agencies of all levels, industry and business, clinics and hospitals, public schools, and the military services.

Psychology has found its way into virtually every aspect of American life. It would be difficult to find a segment of contemporary society that has not been influenced in some way, however tangential, by psychology.

The differences between the purely scientific and the applied aspects of psychology have come into sharp focus since World War II, when the major growth in applied psychology occurred. Relations between science and practice, between "pure" and applied, have shown evidence of considerable strain. Some consider that those who apply psychology have sacrificed their scientific integrity and have not contributed sufficiently or effectively to the advancement of knowledge in the field. The practitioners of psychology counter by accusing the academic psychologists of leading an "ivory tower" existence and showing no concern about problems in the real world to which they might be able to offer solutions.

A major source of contention between the two groups is that not all attempts at application of psychology have been supported by adequate scientific evidence. This situation comes about for several reasons: Very often there is simply no time to conduct full-scale well-controlled research into real problems that require quick action. Then, too, many industrial organizations balk at the cost of such adequate research programs.

Also, the practitioner may be pressed for a quick answer, possibly to permit the meeting of a contract deadline. He is forced to make a decision within a period that does not allow him to wait for research findings. He therefore presents an "educated guess" based on available evidence, no matter how fragmentary or inconclusive. Many feel such a guess is better than no answer at all.

Since the answers the applied psychologist is called on to provide rest in large measure on the availability of the findings of the academic research psychologist, perhaps a closer working relationship between the two groups is in order. In this way, the practitioner would be able to suggest, for the attention of the academician, urgent problem areas in which a paucity of research data exists.

Contemporary Psychology in Other Countries

There seems to be little question that the United States leads in the vigorous promotion of both research and application of psychology and in its acceptance and use by society at large. (Wundt's comment, *ganz Amerikanisch*, comes to mind.) It would be a mistake, however, to ignore or minimize the growth, importance, and increasing vigor of psychology in other parts of the world, particularly in Western Europe and Japan. American psychology can no longer afford to take an attitude of smug provincialism. We shall discuss briefly some of the current developments.

Germany

Psychology in Germany suffered a calamitous setback during the Nazi era and World War II. Since the war, however, the task of rebuilding psychology has been actively pursued to the point where a number of branches of the discipline—particularly social, industrial, and educational psychology, as well as the study of personality and guidance—are now flourishing.

In the years immediately after the war, experimental research was not widely practiced, nor was there much acceptance of quantitative methods. That seems to have changed in more recent years. While interest in a phenomenological approach is still strong in Germany (as it is in much of Western Europe), growing numbers of psychologists are accepting increased objectivity and methodological rigor in their research. Indeed, in many research areas, experimental work in Germany is the epitome of elaborate and precise experimental design and quantitative analysis.

German psychologists show a strong interest in personality and its measurement, and in perception, motivation, and social psychology, particularly group dynamics. Applied psychologists are also very active, notably in the areas of education, industry, vocational and child guidance, and intelligence and achievement testing.

England

Psychology developed rather slowly in English universities, but the field has grown rapidly since World War II with the opening of new universities and greater opportunities for graduate study. It bears some resemblance to psychology in the United States, though there is perhaps a bit less of an objective emphasis, and learning is not a primary topic (despite the origins of associationism in England). In recent years, psychology in England has gained considerable prestige, and public and government support.

English psychology evidences a strong bent toward practical application, as reflected in the very rapid growth of clinical psychology in recent years. While experimental psychology has progressed slowly, albeit substantially, the most important contributions of English psychologists have been in the areas of statistics, psychometrics, and educational psychology.

The tradition of Galton has been carried on most effectively in the emphasis on individual differences and the statistical techniques with which to measure them. The field of mental testing has been prominent, not only in research, but also in application to the educational system.

Soviet Union

Direct extensive political influence has rendered the development of psychology in the Soviet Union entirely different from that in other countries. After 1936, all Western psychological influences—such as testing and industrial psychology—were eliminated. A turning point in the history of Soviet psychology occurred in 1950, when Pavlovian theory was given the sanction of official state doctrine. Since this change, Soviet psychology has become much more active and productive.

Recent years have seen a marked increase of interest in the areas of personality, social psychology, and information theory. Psychophysiological research, conducted primarily by physiologists, has included studies of conditioning and physiological psychology, and has produced important research on brain processes.

A great deal of attention has been focused on problems of education, and in more recent years there has developed a keen interest in engineering psychology. Indeed, according to Brozek (1973), human engineering is now a very important part of Soviet psychology. Further, an industrial social psychology is being fostered to deal with such practical problems as worker motivation and alienation. Very little work is reported in clinical psychology or psychological testing, and Freud is not in favor.

A greater exchange of ideas is occurring among Russian psychologists and those of the Western world. Soviet works have been translated into other languages, and Russian translations have been made of major American books. A significant event was the 1966 meeting in Moscow of the Eighteenth International Congress of Psychology.

Japan

Psychology in Japan is flourishing; the very active Japanese Psychological Association has three journals and a membership of more than 3000.

Research in the empirical tradition is strong and characterized by a high degree of rigor and methodological sophistication. The primary area of research attention is perception—particularly visual perception—and much work has been done on perceptual constancy, illusions, and depth perception.

Second in research emphasis is learning, with a great interest in animal behavior utilizing mazes, Skinner boxes, and other electronic apparatus. Much learning research is also conducted on human subjects.

Recent years have seen bursts of research in physiological psychology, sleep, sensory deprivation, and sensory overload. There is also great interest in educational, clinical, and social psychology.

There has been a widespread exchange of ideas among Japanese and Western psychologists. Japanese publications are translated into English, and the Twentieth International Congress of Psychology was held in Japan in 1972.

Other Countries

Generally speaking, psychology in Canada bears a close resemblance to that in the United States, although the derivatives of the work of Hebb speak to a distinctly Canadian origin. Research on sensory deprivation, though also practiced elsewhere, originated under Hebb's aegis and continues there today.

There is a widespread interest in motivation; two authoritative texts have been written by Canadian psychologists and are widely used in this country. Verbal learning and memory also claim a major share of Canadian research attention.

There has been a vigorous spirit of growth in psychology in Australia. Articles and books from that country are appearing with greater frequency here. There is a strong interest in research on animal learning, conducted within a behavioristic framework. Research on perception, a modified form of social psychology, and physiological psychology are also important areas of interest.

The Netherlands shares a number of the psychological interests of the Scandinavian countries. Important work on perception is being carried out, and applied psychology is widely practiced and well received.

These brief comments cannot, of course, do justice to the importance and scope of the psychological activities in these countries and others. The point to be remembered is that these developments have become increasingly important—too much so to be ignored by American psychologists.

The Future:
Humanistic Psychology?

What will psychology's future be? Many believe it will continue within the same behavioristic framework, with the experimental method remaining the *sine qua non* of psychological research. Indeed, the experimental method may become even more precise and objective as more sophisticated equipment and apparatus become available (as they surely will), and as more advanced electronic computers for data analysis are developed. As a result, psychology may become all the more empirical, and the future may see even greater specialization as the storehouse of data grows in both depth and detail.

It must be noted, however, that all is not calm within contemporary American psychology. Since the 1950s, voices of dissent have been heard, largely from without the behavioristic camp, although of late some behaviorists themselves have joined in the call for a new movement, a *humanistic psychology.* This approach is still too new and tenuous to be considered an integral part of the history of psychology, but we cannot ignore its growing strength.

The members of this new force feel that behaviorism is a narrow, artificial, and relatively sterile approach to the understanding of man. The emphasis on studying only overt behavior tends, they suggest, to dehumanize man and reduce him "to a larger white rat or a slower computer [Bugental, 1967, p. vii]." They argue that the image of man provided by the S–R orientation presents, at best, an incomplete picture of human nature and, at worst, one that may be totally inaccurate. Behaviorism, in other words, does not "come to grips" with what is unique about man: those highly subjective qualities and capacities that set him apart from the laboratory animal. A psychology based on separate and discrete conditioned responses makes of man a mechanized computer-like organism responding deterministically to the stimuli presented to him. The humanists argue that man is much more than an Orwellian robot, and cannot be objectified, quantified, and reduced to S–R units. Man is not such an "empty organism."

The humanistic psychologists argue that the vast amounts of research on overt behavior have added little to our understanding of man. As one of the leading proponents of a humanistic psychology, Abraham Maslow (1908–1970), put it: "We are offered beautifully executed, precise, elegant experiments which, in at least half the cases, have nothing to do with enduring human problems . . . [Maslow, 1965, p. 21]."

The members of this movement of protest are thus highly critical of continued reliance on the behavioristic approach to the study of man with its mechanistic, reductionistic, elementistic, and simplistic tendencies. However, they are also highly critical of the psychoanalytic approach. Specifically, Maslow has criticized Freud for studying only disturbed individuals—the neurotics and psychotics. By focusing only on mental illness, Maslow asked, how can psychology ever know anything of man's positive qualities and characteristics. He argued that psychology has disregarded such attributes as joy, satisfaction, contentment, ecstasy, kindness, and generosity because it has focused only on the dark side, the "sick" side of man. It has ignored man's great strengths and positive virtues and concentrated instead on his weaknesses. As Maslow noted: "The study of crippled, stunted, immature, and unhealthy specimens can yield only a cripple psychology and a cripple philosophy [1954, p. 234]."

It is against this "cripple psychology"—the narrow, ahuman, and sterile psychology put forth by both behaviorism and psychoanalysis—that Maslow and others propose an alternative—a new force in psychology, a third force.

Humanistic psychology is, or at least hopes to be, a fresh orientation—a new framework or attitude toward psychology, rather than a new psychology per se. Its protagonists state that they do not wish it to be a new school of thought or a specific content area, but rather an attempt to reshape and supplement the existing form of psychology. James F. T. Bugental, the first president of the American Association for Humanistic Psychology (1962–1963), describes the movement:

> Humanistic psychology has as its ultimate goal the preparation of a complete description of what it means to be alive as a human being. . . . Such a complete description would necessarily include an inventory of man's native endowment; his potentialities of feeling, thought, and action; his growth, evolution, and decline; his interaction with various environing conditions . . . the range and variety of experience possible to him; and his meaningful place in the universe [1967, p. 7].

All aspects of uniquely human experience thus come under the purview of the humanistic psychologist: love, hate, fear, hope, happiness, humor, affection, responsibility, the meaning of life, etc. Most of these aspects of human existence are not found in any form in current textbooks of psychology, for they are not amenable to operational definition, precise quantification, and laboratory manipulation.

It is easier to state with clarity what humanistic psychologists are against than to describe what they are for and how they hope to achieve their goals. In part, this is because the movement is young and lacks a single leader or founder who can authoritatively state (or dictate) its position—as Watson or Freud did for their movements.

Nevertheless, there are similarities and parallels among the various workers in the field, as indicated in what follows.

The Association for Humanistic Psychology published a four-part statement of theme or purpose (while noting that there is not unanimous agreement on these points).

> 1. A centering of attention on the experiencing *person*, and thus a focus on experience as the primary phenomenon in the study of man. Both theoretical explanations and overt behavior are considered secondary to experience itself and to its meaning to the person.
> 2. An emphasis on such distinctively human qualities as choice, creativity, valuation, and self-realization, as opposed to thinking about human beings in mechanistic and reductionistic terms.
> 3. An allegiance to meaningfulness in the selection of problems for study and of research procedures, and an opposition to a primary emphasis on objectivity at the expense of significance.

4. An ultimate concern with and valuing of the dignity and worth of man and an interest in the development of the potential inherent in every person [Bühler & Allen, 1972, pp. 1–2].

In another position statement, Bugental (1967) noted six fundamental points of emphasis that distinguish humanistic psychology from behaviorism.

1. Adequate understanding of human nature cannot be based exclusively (or even in large part) on research findings from animal studies. Again, man is not "a larger white rat," and a psychology based on animal data obviously excludes distinctly human processes and experiences.
2. The research topics chosen for investigation must be meaningful in terms of human existence and not selected solely on the basis of their suitability for laboratory investigation and quantification. Currently, topics not amenable to experimental treatment tend to be ignored.
3. Primary attention should be focused on man's subjective internal experiences, not on elements of overt behavior. This is not to suggest that overt behavior be discarded as a subject of study, but rather that it should not be the only subject of investigation.
4. The continuing mutual influence of the so-called pure psychology and applied psychology should be recognized. The attempt to sharply divorce them is detrimental to both.
5. Psychology should be concerned with the unique individual case instead of the average performance of groups. The current group emphasis ignores the atypical, the exception, the person who deviates from the average.
6. Psychology should seek "that which may expand or enrich man's experience . . . [Bugental, 1967, p. 9]."

There are two aspects of the *Zeitgeist* which seem to favor the humanistic psychology movement and may well speed its progress. One comes from the general culture and the other from physics, psychology's omnipresent model.

Humanistic psychology seems to be reflecting the kind of unrest and disaffection currently being voiced against the mechanistic aspects of contemporary Western culture. Humanistic psychologists imply that behaviorism is, if not antihuman, then ahuman, and they resist the conception of man as an animal functioning mechanically and deterministically in response to his environment or his early years of experience.

Many current social critics suggest that Western, and particularly

American, culture has also dehumanized, depersonalized, and de-individ-
ualized man to the extent that he is regarded as an infinitesimal part
of an immense societal machine. It has been suggested that people are
no longer viewed as humans, but as personnel, statistics, and averages.
As individuals, we have a reduced sense of personal identity and a lessened
ability to actively shape our own lives. Society, through the giant bureau-
cracies, molds our destinies for us to a greater extent. "In an acceleratingly
rationalized, pervasively systematized society, we are numbered—quite
literally. Count the numbers through which your existence is proved—by
machines [Hentoff, 1966, p. 277]." Even our names have less importance;
if we lose our numbers, soon we may have difficulty in proving that
we exist!

The critics tell us we grow increasingly estranged from society and
from ourselves: regimented, controlled, computerized, manipulated, alien-
ated, alone, numbered, and helpless, all of which seems ideal for a behavioristic view of man as a nicely functioning well-ordered machine. Indeed,
it has been suggested that modern psychology has reinforced this dehumanizing influence of contemporary society. Koch (1964) commented:

> That modern psychology has projected an image of man which
> is as demeaning as it is simplistic, few intelligent and sensitive non-
> psychologists would deny. . . . Of all fields in the community of
> scholarship, it should be psychology which combats this trend. In-
> stead, we have played no small role in augmenting and supporting
> it [pp. 37–38].

But, like the humanistic movement in psychology, there are voices
of dissent speaking out against the dehumanizing forces of modern
society. They are few in number (so far) and often have trouble being
heard as they speak against the prevailing wind, but they are speaking,
warning us against the dangers of an overly objective and numbered
society. This *Zeitgeist* of social criticism, then, may be reflected in the
humanistic psychologists' plea for the study of man as a distinctly human
being.

The second part of the *Zeitgeist* stems from the rejection, in the early
years of this century, of the Galilean–Newtonian world view of the
universe as a machine, which, as we have seen, served as the model
for psychology from its beginnings as a science. The framework of
physics has changed, as well as man's outlook on science and the physical
world.

The important point for our purposes is the suggestion, derived from
this new look in physics, that the previously held scientific ideal of a

totally objective reality is not attainable. Physics now recognizes that what we call objective knowledge is, in the final analysis, subjective—that is, dependent on the observer. All knowledge is therefore "personal knowledge" (Polanyi, 1958).

The rejection of a totally objective machine-like subject matter and the admission of subjectivity into science are congruent with the humanistic psychologists' objection to the image of man as a machine and their plea for the admission of subjective experience (consciousness) as a legitimate part of the subject matter of psychology.

It is important to note that the humanists are not arguing for the rejection of science as the framework within which to study man, but rather for an expansion and enlargement of science. Science, they argue, does not refer exclusively to laboratory manipulative research in which the subject (rat or man) is viewed as a stimulus–response machine that can be programmed as can a computer.

As Maslow noted: "Scientific methods . . . are our only ultimate ways of being sure that we *do* have truth . . . . Only science can overcome characterological differences in seeing and believing. Only science can progress [1968, p. viii]."

It is, of course, too early to attempt any evaluative commentary on humanistic psychology. The extent of its impact remains to be seen, but it certainly warrants watchful and critical attention.

It is also too early to know if the movement can resist becoming formalized into a school of thought (as it seems to want to resist doing). However, there are several reasons for suspecting that it will not be able to resist this stage of development. Its members are highly vocal in pointing out the weaknesses of the older positions; behaviorism and psychoanalysis are both well-developed bases against which to push. Also, many humanistic psychologists are young and filled with a revolutionary zeal and sense of righteousness as they do battle with the evils of the establishment.

Some of the trappings of formalization are already present: The *Journal of Humanistic Psychology* was established in 1961, the American Association for Humanistic Psychology in 1962, and the Division of Humanistic Psychology of the American Psychological Association in 1971.

If the history of psychology as portrayed in these chapters tells us anything at all, it is that when a movement becomes formalized into a school, it gains a momentum that can be stopped only by its own success in overthrowing the established position. And, as we have seen, when that happens, the free-flowing arteries of the vigorous youthful movement begin to harden. Flexibility turns to rigidity, revolutionary passion to protection of position, and eyes and minds close to new ideas;

in short, a new establishment is born. And so it is in the ever-changing progress of any science: an evolutionary building to ever higher levels of development; not a final culmination, but continuing growth.

SUGGESTED FURTHER READINGS

Contemporary American Psychology
Annual Review of Psychology, Vol. 25. Palo Alto, California: Annual Reviews, 1974.
Hebb, D. O. What psychology is about. *American Psychologist*, 1974, **29**, 71–79.
Murphy, G. The psychology of 1975: An extrapolation. *American Psychologist*, 1963, **18**, 689–695.
Smith, M. B. Is psychology relevant to new priorities? *American Psychologist*, 1973, **28**, 463–471.
Tyler, L. Design for a hopeful psychology. *American Psychologist*, 1973, **28**, 1021–1029.

Psychology in Other Countries
Brebner, J., & Drever, J. Psychology in Europe, Australia, and Canada. In M Marx & W. Hillix, *Systems and theories in psychology* (2nd ed.). New York: McGraw-Hill, 1973. Pp. 489–519.
Brozek, J. Soviet psychology. In M. Marx & W. Hillix, *Systems and theories in psychology* (2nd ed.). New York: McGraw-Hill, 1973. Pp. 521–548.
Iwahara, S. Oriental psychology. In M. Marx & W. Hillix, *Systems and theories in psychology* (2nd ed.). New York: McGraw-Hill, 1973. Pp. 549–568.
Reavis, L. Psychology in the emerging nations: Latin America, Africa, and the Middle East. In M. Marx & W. Hillix, *Systems and theories in psychology* (2nd ed.). New York: McGraw-Hill, 1973. Pp. 569–588.

Humanistic Psychology
Bühler, C., & Allen, M. *Introduction to humanistic psychology*. Monterey, California: Brooks/Cole, 1972.
Maslow, A. *The farther reaches of human nature*. New York: Viking Press, 1971.
Severin, F. T. (Ed.) *Discovering man in psychology: A humanistic approach.* New York: McGraw-Hill, 1973.

References

The classic reference work in the history of psychology is *A History of Experimental Psychology* by E. G. Boring (New York: Appleton, 1950). Several sourcebooks are available which contain selections of original works by the great psychologists and articles on theoretical issues. These include:

Dennis, W. *Readings in the history of psychology.* New York: Appleton, 1948.

Diamond, S. *The roots of psychology.* New York: Basic Books, 1974.

Drever, J. *Sourcebook in psychology.* New York: Philosophical Library, 1960.

Henle, M., Jaynes, J., & Sullivan, J. *Historical conceptions of psychology.* New York: Springer, 1973.

Herrnstein, R. J., & Boring, E. G. *A source book in the history of psychology.* Cambridge, Massachusetts: Harvard Univ. Press, 1965.

Rand, B. *The classical psychologists.* Boston, Massachusetts: Houghton, 1912.

Sahakian, W. S. *History of psychology: A source book in systematic psychology.* Itasca, Illinois: F. E. Peacock, 1968.

Shipley, T. *Classics in psychology.* New York: Philosophical Library, 1961.

In addition, the *Journal of the History of the Behavioral Sciences,* begun in 1965, contains scholarly articles on a wide variety of topics. Also of interest are the autobiographical sketches of the major figures in the history of psychology in the following:

Murchison, C. *A history of psychology in autobiography,* Vols. 1, 2, 3. Worcester, Massachusetts: Clark Univ. Press, 1930–1936.

Boring, E. G., Langfeld, H. S., Werner, H., & Yerkes, R. *A history of psychology in autobiography*, Vol. 4. Worcester, Massachusetts: Clark Univ. Press, 1952.

Boring, E. G., & Lindzey, G. *A history of psychology in autobiography*, Vol. 5. New York: Appleton, 1967.

Lindzey, G. *A history of psychology in autobiography*, Vol. 6. Englewood Cliffs, New Jersey: Prentice-Hall, 1974.

Adler, A. Individual psychology. In C. Murchison (Ed.), *Psychologies of 1930*. Worcester, Massachusetts: Clark Univ. Press, 1930. Pp. 395–405.

Adler, A. The fundamental views of Individual Psychology. *International Journal of Individual Psychology*, 1935, **1**, 5–8.

Allen, G. *William James*. New York: Viking Press, 1967.

American Psychological Association, Committee on the Role of Psychology in Small and Large Institutions, Subcommittee of Curriculum Differences. Undergraduate training for psychologists. *American Psychologist*, 1958, **13**, 585–588. (a)

American Psychological Association, Committee on Distinguished Scientific Contribution Awards. The American Psychological Association Distinguished Scientific Contribution Award for 1958. *American Psychologist*, 1958, **13**, 729–738. (b)

American Psychological Foundation. Presentation of the first Gold Medal Award. *American Psychologist*, 1956, **11**, 587–589.

Angell, J. R. *Psychology*. New York: Holt, 1904.

Angell, J. R. The province of functional psychology. *Psychological Review*, 1907, **14**, 61–91.

Bakan, D. Behaviorism and American urbanization. *Journal of the History of the Behavioral Sciences*, 1966, **2**, 5–28.

Barber, B. Resistance by scientists to scientific discovery. *Science*, 1961, **134**(3479), 596–602.

Bekhterev, V. M. *Objective psychology*. Leipzig: B. G. Teubner, 1907. Published in English as *General principles of human reflexology*. New York: International Publishers, 1932.

Bergmann, G. The contribution of John B. Watson. *Psychological Review*, 1956, **63**, 265–276.

Berkeley, G. *An essay towards a new theory of vision*. In M. W. Calkins (Ed.), *Berkeley: Essay, Principles, Dialogues*. New York: Scribners, 1957. Pp. 1–98. First published in 1709.

Berkeley, G. *A treatise concerning the principles of human knowledge*. In M. W. Calkins (Ed.), *Berkeley: Essay, Principles, Dialogues*. New York: Scribners, 1957. Pp. 99–216. First published in 1710.

Boas, M. *The scientific renaissance: 1450–1630*. London: Collins, 1962.

Boring, E. G. Edward Bradford Titchener, 1867–1927. *American Journal of Psychology*, 1927, **38**, 489–506.

Boring, E. G. *A history of experimental psychology*. New York: Appleton, 1929.

Boring, E. G. *A history of experimental psychology*. (2nd ed.) New York: Appleton, 1950.

Boring, E. G. A history of introspection. *Psychological Bulletin*, 1953, **50**, 169–189.

Boring, E. G. *History, psychology, and science: Selected papers*. New York: Wiley, 1963.

Brentano, F. *Psychology from an empirical standpoint*. Leipzig: Duncker & Humblot, 1874.

Breuer, J., & Freud, S. *Studies on hysteria*. Leipzig: Franz Deuticke, 1895. [Vol. 2, *Standard Edition*. See Freud.]

Bridgman, P. W. *The logic of modern physics*. New York: Macmillan, 1927.

Bridgman, P. W. Remarks on the present state of operationism. *Scientific Monthly*, 1954, **79**, 224–226.

Brown, J. A. C. *Freud and the post-Freudians*. London: Cassell, 1963.

Brozek, J. Soviet psychology. In M. Marx & W. Hillix, *Systems and theories in psychology*. (2nd ed.) New York: McGraw–Hill, 1973. Pp. 521–548.

Bugental, J. *Challenges of humanistic psychology*. New York: McGraw–Hill, 1967.

Bühler, C., & Allen, M. *Introduction to humanistic psychology*. Monterey, California: Brooks/Cole, 1972.

Burnham, J. On the origins of behaviorism. *Journal of the History of the Behavioral Sciences*, 1968, **4**, 143–151.

Burt, C. The concept of consciousness. *British Journal of Psychology*, 1962, **53**, 229–242.

Carr, H. *Psychology*. New York: Longmans, Green, 1925.

Carr, H. Functionalism. In C. Murchison (Ed.), *Psychologies of 1930*. Worcester, Massachusetts: Clark Univ. Press, 1930. Pp. 59–78.

Cattell, J. McK. The conceptions and methods of psychology. *Popular Science Monthly*, 1904, **46**, 176–186.

Cattell, J. McK. Early psychological laboratories. *Science*, June 1, 1928, 543–548.

Chaplin, J., & Krawiec, T. *Systems and theories of psychology*. (2nd ed.) New York: Holt, 1968.

Cofer, C., & Appley, M. *Motivation: Theory and research*. New York: Wiley, 1964.

Comte, A. *The positive philosophy of Comte*. London: G. Bell, 1896.

Cuny, H. *Ivan Pavlov: The man and his theories*. New York: Paul S. Eriksson, 1965.

Dallenbach, K. Autobiography. In E. G. Boring & G. Lindzey (Eds.), *A history of psychology in autobiography* (Vol. 5). New York: Appleton, 1967. Pp. 57–93.

Darwin, C. *On the origin of species by means of natural selection*. London: Murray, 1859.

Darwin, C. *The descent of man*. New York: Appleton, 1871.

Darwin, C. *The expression of the emotions in man and animals*. London: Murray, 1872.

Darwin, C. *Biographical sketch of an infant*. 1877.

De la Mettrie, J. *L'homme machine*. Translated by M. Calkins. Chicago, Illinois: Open Court, 1912. First published in 1748.

Dewey, J. *Psychology*. New York: Harper, 1886.

Dewey, J. The reflex arc concept in psychology. *Psychological Review*, 1896, 3, 357–370.

Dewey, J. Psychology and social change. 1900. Published as *Psychology and social practice*. Chicago, Illinois: Univ. of Chicago Press, 1901.

Durant, W., & Durant, A. *The lessons of history*. New York: Simon & Schuster, 1968.

Ebbinghaus, H. *On memory*. Leipzig: Duncker & Humblot, 1885.

Ebbinghaus, H. *The principles of psychology*. Leipzig: Veit & Co., 1902.

Ebbinghaus, H. *A summary of psychology*. Leipzig: Veit & Co., 1908.

Esper, E. *A history of psychology*. Philadelphia, Pennsylvania: Saunders, 1964.

Evans, R. *B. F. Skinner: The man and his ideas.* New York: Dutton, 1968.

Fechner, G. *Elements of psychophysics.* Leipzig: Brietkopf & Härtel, 1860. Translated by H. Adler. New York: Holt, 1966.

Ferster, C. B., & Skinner, B. F. *Schedules of reinforcement.* New York: Appleton, 1957.

Flugel, J., & West, D. *A hundred years of psychology.* New York: Basic Books, 1964.

Freeman, L. *The story of Anna O.* New York: Walker, 1972.

Freud, S. *The standard edition of the complete psychological works of Sigmund Freud.* Translated from the German under the general editorship of J. Strachey, in collaboration with Anna Freud. London: Hogarth Press.
On the origins of psycho-analysis. 1895. Vol. 1.
The interpretation of dreams. 1900. Vols. 4–5.
The psychopathology of everyday life. 1901. Vol. 6.
Three essays on the theory of sexuality. 1905 (a). Vol. 7.
Fragment of an analysis of a case of hysteria. 1905 (b). Vol. 7.
Five lectures on psycho-analysis. 1910. Vol. 11.
On the history of the psycho-analytic movement. 1914. Vol. 14.
Beyond the pleasure principle. 1920. Vol. 18.
New introductory lectures on psycho-analysis. 1933. Vol. 22.
Outline of psycho-analysis. 1938. Vol. 23.

Friedman, N. *The social nature of psychological research.* New York: Basic Books, 1967.

Fromm, E. *Escape from freedom.* New York: Holt, 1941.

Fromm, E. *Man for himself.* New York: Holt, 1947.

Fromm, E. *The heart of man.* New York: Holt, 1964.

Galton, F. *Hereditary genius.* London: Macmillan, 1869.

Galton, F. *English men of science: Their nature and nurture.* London: Macmillan, 1874.

Galton, F. *Natural inheritance.* London: Macmillan, 1889.

Gruber, C. Academic freedom at Columbia University, 1917–1918: The case of James McKeen Cattell. *American Association of University Professors Bulletin,* 1972, **58**(3), 297–305.

Guthrie, E. R. *The psychology of learning.* New York: Harper, 1935. Revised edition, 1952.

Hall, C., & Lindzey, G. *Theories of personality.* (2nd ed.) New York: Wiley, 1970.

Hall, G. S. *Adolescence.* New York: Appleton, 1904.

Hall, G. S. *Jesus, the Christ, in the light of psychology.* Garden City, New York: Doubleday, 1917.

Hall, G. S. *Recreations of a psychologist.* New York: Appleton, 1920.

Hall, G. S. *Senescence.* New York: Appleton, 1922.

Hall, G. S. *The life and confessions of a psychologist.* New York: Appleton, 1923.

Hall, M. H. An interview with "Mr. Behaviorist" B. F. Skinner. *Psychology Today,* 1967, **1**(5), 21–23, 68–71.

Harrison, R. Functionalism and its historical significance. *Genetic Psychology Monographs,* 1963, **68**, 387–423.

Hartley, D. *Observations on man. His frame, his duty, and his expectations.* London: J. Leake & W. Frederick, 1749.

Heidbreder, E. *Seven psychologies.* New York: Appleton, 1933.

Helmholtz, H. *Physiological optics.* Leipzig: Voss, 1856–1866.

Helmholtz, H. *On the sensations of tone.* 1863.

Hentoff, N. The cold society. *Playboy Magazine,* September, 1966, 133ff.

Herrnstein, R. J., & Boring, E. G. (Eds.) *A source book in the history of psychology.* Cambridge, Massachusetts: Harvard Univ. Press, 1965.

Hetzel, M., & Hetzel, C. *Relay circuits for psychology.* New York: Appleton, 1969.

Hilgard, E. *Theories of learning.* (2nd ed.) New York: Appleton, 1956.

Holt, E. B. *The Freudian wish and its place in ethics.* New York: Holt, 1915.

Horney, K. *Our inner conflicts.* New York: Norton, 1945.

Hull, C. L. *Hypnosis and suggestibility.* New York: Appleton, 1933.

Hull, C. L., Hovland, C. I., Ross, R. T., Hall, M., Perkins, D. T., & Fitch, F. B. *Mathematico-deductive theory of rote learning: A study in scientific methodology.* New Haven, Connecticut: Yale Univ. Press, 1940.

Hull, C. L. *Principles of behavior.* New York: Appleton, 1943.

Hull, C. L. *Essentials of behavior.* New Haven, Connecticut: Yale Univ. Press, 1951.

Hull, C. L. *A behavior system.* New Haven, Connecticut: Yale Univ. Press, 1952.

Hume, D. *A treatise of human nature.* London: J. Noon, 1739.

Jahoda, M. Some notes on the influence of psycho-analytic ideas on American psychology. *Human Relations,* 1963, **16**, 111–129.

James, W. *The principles of psychology.* New York: Holt, 1890.

James, W. *Talks to teachers.* New York: Holt, 1899.

James, W. *Varieties of religious experience.* New York: Longmans, Green, 1902.

James, W. *Pragmatism.* New York: Longmans, Green, 1907.

Joncich, G. *The sane positivist: A biography of Edward L. Thorndike.* Middletown, Connecticut: Wesleyan Univ. Press, 1968.

Jones, E. *The life and work of Sigmund Freud, 1856–1900.* New York: Basic Books, 1953 (Vol. I), 1955 (Vol. II), 1957 (Vol. III).

Jung, C. *The psychology of the unconscious.* Leipzig: Franz Deuticke, 1912.

Kinkade, K. *A Walden Two experiment: The first five years of Twin Oaks Community.* New York: Morrow, 1973.

Kinsey, A. *Sexual behavior in the human male.* Philadelphia, Pennsylvania: Saunders, 1948.

Kinsey, A. *Sexual behavior in the human female.* Philadelphia, Pennsylvania: Saunders, 1953.

Koch, S. Psychology and emerging conceptions of knowledge as unitary. In T. Wann (Ed.), *Behaviorism and phenomenology.* Chicago, Illinois: Univ. of Chicago Press, 1964. Pp. 1–41.

Koestler, A. *The case of the midwife toad.* New York: Random House, 1971.

Koffka, K. *The growth of the mind.* New York: Harcourt, 1921.

Koffka, K. Perception: An introduction to Gestalt-theorie. *Psychological Bulletin,* 1922, **19**, 531–585.

Koffka, K. *Principles of Gestalt psychology.* New York: Harcourt, 1935.

Köhler, W. *The mentality of apes.* Berlin: Royal Academy of Sciences, 1917. English edition, 1927.

Köhler, W. *Static and stationary physical Gestalts.* Braunschweig: Vieweg, 1920.

Köhler, W. *Gestalt psychology.* New York: Liveright, 1929.

Köhler, W. *The place of value in a world of facts.* New York: Liveright, 1938.

Köhler, W. *Dynamics in psychology.* New York: Liveright, 1940.

Köhler, W. *Gestalt psychology: An introduction to new concepts in modern psychology.* New York: Liveright, 1947.

Köhler, W., & Wallach, H. Figural after-effects. *Proceedings of the American Philosophical Society,* 1944, 88(4), 269–357.

Kuhn, T. S. *The structure of scientific revolutions.* (2nd ed.) Chicago, Illinois: Univ. of Chicago Press, 1970.

Külpe, O. *Outline of psychology.* Leipzig: Englemann, 1893.

Larson, C., & Sullivan, J. Watson's relation to Titchener. *Journal of the History of the Behavioral Sciences,* 1965, 1, 338–354.

Lashley, K. *Brain mechanisms and intelligence.* Chicago, Illinois: Univ. of Chicago Press, 1929.

Lewin, K., Lippitt, R., & White, R. Patterns of aggressive behavior in experimentally created social climates. *Journal of Social Psychology,* 1939, 10, 271–299.

Locke, J. *An essay concerning human understanding.* New York: Dover, 1959. First published in 1690.

Lowry, R. *The evolution of psychological theory.* Chicago, Illinois: Aldine–Atherton, 1971.

McClelland, D., Atkinson, J., Clark, R., & Lowell, E. *The achievement motive.* New York: Appleton, 1953.

McDougall, W. *Introduction to social psychology.* London: Methuen, 1908.

Mach, E. *The analysis of sensations.* 1885.

MacLeod, R. B. Review of *Cumulative record* by B. F. Skinner. *Science,* 1959, 130, 34–35.

Malthus, T. *Essay on the principle of population.* 1789.

Marx, M., & Hillix, W. *Systems and theories in psychology.* (2nd ed.) New York: McGraw-Hill, 1973.

Maslow, A. *Motivation and personality.* New York: Harper, 1954.

Maslow, A. A philosophy of psychology: The need for a mature science of human nature. In F. Severin (Ed.), *Humanistic viewpoints in psychology.* New York: McGraw–Hill, 1965. Pp. 17–33.

Maslow, A. *Toward a psychology of being.* (2nd ed.) Princeton, New Jersey: Van Nostrand-Reinhold, 1968.

Masters, W., & Johnson, V. *Human sexual response.* Boston, Massachusetts: Little, Brown, 1966.

Masters, W., & Johnson, V. *Human sexual response.* Boston, Massachusetts: Little, Brown, 1970.

Matson, F. W. *The broken image.* New York: George Braziller, 1964.

May, R. *Psychology and the human dilemma.* Princeton, New Jersey: Van Nostrand-Reinhold, 1967.

Merton, R. Priorities in scientific discovery. *American Sociological Review,* 1957, 22(6), 635–659.

Mill, James. *Analysis of the phenomena of the human mind.* London: Baldwin & Cradock, 1829.

Miller, G. *Psychology: The science of mental life.* New York: Harper, 1962.

Miller, G., & Buckhout, R. *Psychology: The science of mental life.* (2nd ed.) New York: Harper, 1973.

Morgan, N. *The California syndrome.* Englewood Cliffs, New Jersey: Prentice-Hall, 1969.

Mueller, C. G., Jr., & Schoenfeld, W. N. Edwin R. Guthrie. In W. Estes, S. Koch, K. MacCorquodale, P. Meehl, C. G. Mueller, Jr., W. N. Schoenfeld, & W. Verplank, *Modern learning theory*. New York: Appleton, 1954. Pp. 345–379.

Müller, J. *Handbook of physiology*. 1833–1840.

Müller-Freienfels, R. *The evolution of modern psychology*. New Haven, Connecticut: Yale Univ. Press, 1935.

Murphy, G. *Historical introduction to modern psychology*. (Rev. ed.) New York: Harcourt, 1949.

Murphy, G., & Kovach, J. *Historical introduction to modern psychology*. (3rd ed.) New York: Harcourt, 1972.

Nance, R. Current practices in teaching history of psychology. *American Psychologist*, 1962, **17**, 250–252.

Pavlov, I. P. *Lectures on conditioned reflexes*. Petrograd, 1928.

Pavlov, I. P. *Selected works*. Moscow: Foreign Languages Publishing House, 1955.

Perry, R. B. *The thought and character of William James*. Boston, Massachusetts: Little, Brown, 1935.

Peters, R. S. (Ed.) *Brett's history of psychology*. Cambridge, Massachusetts: Massachusetts Institute of Technology Press, 1965.

Pillsbury, W. Essentials of psychology. 1911.

Planck, M. *Scientific autobiography*. New York: Philosophical Library, 1949.

Polanyi, M. *Personal knowledge*. Chicago, Illinois: Univ. of Chicago Press, 1958.

Postman, L. *Psychology in the making*. New York: Knopf, 1962.

Rice, B. Skinner agrees he is the most important influence in psychology. *New York Times Magazine*, March 17, 1968, pp. 27ff.

Roback, A. A. *History of American psychology*. New York: Library Publishers, 1952.

Romanes, G. J. *Animal intelligence*. London: Routledge & Kegan Paul, 1883.

Rosenthal, R. *Experimenter effects in behavioral research*. New York: Appleton, 1966.

Rosenthal, R., & Rosnow, R. (Eds.) *Artifact in behavioral research*. New York: Academic Press, 1969.

Ross, D. *Granville Stanley Hall: The psychologist as prophet*. Chicago, Illinois: Univ. of Chicago Press, 1972.

Ruckmick, C. A. The use of the term *function* in English textbooks of psychology. *American Journal of Psychology*, 1913, **24**, 99–123.

Sarton, G. *The study of the history of science*. New York: Dover, 1936.

Scarf, M. The man who gave us "Inferiority Complex," "Compensation," "Aggressive Drive" and "Style of Life." *New York Times Magazine*, February 28, 1971, pp. 10ff.

Schultz, D. The human subject in psychological research. *Psychological Bulletin*, 1969, **72**, 214–228.

Schultz, D. (Ed.) *The science of psychology: Critical reflections*. New York: Appleton, 1970.

Schur, M. *Freud: Living and dying*. New York: International Universities Press, 1972.

Shakow, D. Psychoanalysis. In D. Krantz (Ed.), *Schools of psychology*. New York: Appleton, 1969. Pp. 87–122.

Sidowski, J. *Experimental methods and instrumentation in psychology*. New York: McGraw-Hill, 1966.

Skinner, B. F. *The behavior of organisms: An experimental analysis.* New York: Appleton, 1938.

Skinner, B. F. *Walden Two.* New York: Macmillan, 1948.

Skinner, B. F. *Science and human behavior.* New York: Macmillan, 1953.

Skinner, B. F. A case history of scientific method. *American Psychologist,* 1956, **11,** 221–233.

Skinner, B. F. *Verbal behavior.* New York: Appleton, 1957.

Skinner, B. F. John B. Watson, behaviorist. *Science,* 1959, **129,** 197–198.

Skinner, B. F. Behaviorism at fifty. *Science,* 1963, **140,** 951–958.

Skinner, B. F. Autobiography. In E. G. Boring & G. Lindzey (Eds.), *A history of psychology in autobiography* (Vol. 5). New York: Appleton, 1967. Pp. 387–413.

Skinner, B. F. *The technology of teaching.* New York: Appleton, 1968.

Skinner, B. F. *Contingencies of reinforcement.* New York: Appleton, 1969.

Skinner, B. F. *Beyond freedom and dignity.* New York: Knopf, 1971.

Solso, R. Recommended readings in psychology during the past 17 years. *American Psychologist,* 1971, **26,** 1083–1084.

Stumpf, C. *Psychology of tone.* Leipzig: Hirzel, 1883 & 1890.

Thorndike, E. L. Animal intelligence. *Psychological Review Monograph Supplement,* 1898, **2.**

Thorndike, E. L. *The elements of psychology.* New York: Seiler, 1905.

Thorndike, E. L. *Human learning.* New York: Appleton, 1931.

Titchener, E. B. *An outline of psychology.* New York: Macmillan, 1896.

Titchener, E. B. *A primer of psychology.* New York: Macmillan, 1898. (a)

Titchener, E. B. The postulates of a structural psychology. *Philosophical Review,* 1898, **7,** 449–465. (b)

Titchener, E. B. *Experimental psychology.* New York: Macmillan, 1901–1905.

Titchener, E. B. *A text-book of psychology.* New York: Macmillan, 1909–1910.

Titchener, E. B. The schema of introspection. *American Journal of Psychology,* 1912, **23,** 485–508.

Titchener, E. B. Wilhelm Wundt. *American Journal of Psychology,* 1921, **32,** 161–178, 575–580.

Tolman, E. C. *Purposive behavior in animals and men.* New York: Appleton, 1932.

Tolman, E. C. A stimulus-expectancy need-cathexis psychology. *Science,* 1945, **101,** 160–166.

Tolman, E. C. Autobiography. In E. G. Boring, H. S. Langfeld, H. Werner, & R. Yerkes (Eds.), *A history of psychology in autobiography* (Vol. 4). Worcester, Massachusetts: Clark Univ. Press, 1952. Pp. 323–339.

Turner, F. J. *The significance of the frontier in American history.* New York: Holt, 1947.

Turner, M. *Philosophy and the science of behavior.* New York: Appleton, 1967.

Uttal, W. *Real-time computers: Technique and applications in the psychological sciences.* New York: Harper, 1968.

Watson, J. B. Psychology as the behaviorist views it. *Psychological Review,* 1913, **20,** 158–177.

Watson, J. B. *Behavior: An introduction to comparative psychology.* New York: Holt, 1914.

Watson, J. B. *Psychology from the standpoint of a behaviorist.* Philadelphia, Pennsylvania: Lippincott, 1919.

Watson, J. B. *Behaviorism.* New York: Norton, 1925.

Watson, J. B. *Psychological care of the infant and child.* New York: Norton, 1928.

Watson, J. B. Behaviorism. *Encyclopedia Britannica,* 1929, **3,** 327–329.

Watson, J. B. *Behaviorism.* (Rev. ed.) New York: Norton, 1930.

Watson, J. B. Autobiography. In C. Murchison (Ed.), *A history of psychology in autobiography* (Vol. 3). Worcester, Massachusetts: Clark Univ. Press, 1936. Pp. 271–281.

Watson, J. B., & McDougall, W. *The battle of behaviorism.* New York: Norton, 1929.

Watson, R. I. The historical background for national trends in psychology: United States. *Journal of the History of the Behavioral Sciences,* 1965, **1,** 130–138.

Watson, R. I. *The great psychologists.* (3rd ed.) Philadelphia, Pennsylvania: Lippincott, 1971.

Weiss, A. *A theoretical basis of human behavior.* 1925.

Wertheimer, Max. Experimental studies of the perception of movement. *Zeitschrift für Psychologie,* 1912, **61,** 161–265.

Wertheimer, Max. Gestalt theory. In W. Ellis (Ed.), *A source book of Gestalt psychology.* London: Routledge & Kegan Paul, 1938. Pp. 1–11.

Wertheimer, Max. *Productive thinking.* New York: Harper, 1945.

Wertheimer, Michael. *A brief history of psychology.* New York: Holt, 1970.

White, A. D. *A history of the warfare of science with theology in Christendom.* New York: Free Press, 1965.

Wolman, B. *Contemporary theories and systems in psychology.* New York: Harper, 1960.

Woodworth, R. S. *Dynamic psychology.* New York: Columbia Univ. Press, 1918.

Woodworth, R. S. *Psychology.* New York: Holt, 1921.

Woodworth, R. S. Dynamic psychology. In C. Murchison (Ed.), *Psychologies of 1930.* Worcester, Massachusetts: Clark Univ. Press, 1930. Pp. 327–336.

Woodworth, R. S. *Contemporary schools of psychology.* New York: Ronald Press, 1931.

Woodworth, R. S. *Experimental psychology.* New York: Holt, 1938.

Woodworth, R. S. *Contemporary schools of psychology.* (2nd ed.) New York: Ronald Press, 1948.

Woodworth, R. S. *Dynamics of behavior.* New York: Holt, 1958.

Woodworth, R. S., & Schlosberg, H. *Experimental psychology.* (Rev. ed.) New York: Holt, 1954.

Woodworth, R. S., & Sheehan, M. *Contemporary schools of psychology.* (3rd ed.) New York: Ronald Press, 1964.

Wundt, W. *Contributions to the theory of sensory perception.* 1858–1862.

Wundt, W. *Lectures on the minds of men and animals.* Leipzig: Voss, 1863.

Wundt, W. *Principles of physiological psychology.* Leipzig: Engelmann, 1874.

Wundt, W. *Zur Erinnerung an Gustav Theodor Fechner. Philosophische Studien,* 1888, **4,** 471–478.

Wundt, W. *Outline of psychology.* Leipzig: Engelmann, 1896.

Wundt, W. *Folk psychology.* Leipzig: Engelmann, 1900–1920.

Yerkes, R., & Morgulis, S. The method of Pavlov in animal psychology. *Psychological Bulletin,* 1909, **6,** 257–273.

Index

A

Aaron, R., 35
Acquisition, law, 250
Act psychology (Brentano), 74–75
Adler, A., 11, 308, 335–340, 344, 350, 378
Allen, G., 129–132, 151, 378
Allen, M., 373, 376, 379
Allport, G., 151, 361
American Psychological Association, 2, 4, 86, 139, 142, 147, 156, 157, 197, 198, 212, 256, 268, 356, 375, 378
American Psychological Foundation, 169, 237, 256, 378
Analytical psychology (Jung), 328–334
Anecdotal method, 124, 125
Angell, J. R., 11, 77, 126, 154, 157–159, 168, 173, 176, 178, 192, 196, 197, 378
Animal intelligence, 180, 183
Animal psychology, 104, 105, 108, 109, 115, 124–126, 173, 176–192, 197, 207, 259, see also Comparative psychology
Ansbacher, H., 351
Ansbacher, R., 351
Anthropometric Laboratory, 120–121
Anxiety, 316–317, 342, 343, 348

Apperception, 62–63, 297–298
Appley, M., 242, 344, 379
Applied psychology, 108, 153, 172, 203, 284, 355, 357, 364, 366–367
Archetypes, 331–332
Asch, S., 292
Associated reflex, 190
Association, 26, 29–34, 65, 70, 72, 78, 121–122, 148, 182, 183, 186, 188, 190, 204, 235, 260, 286
Associationism, 23, 180–181, 183, 266, 273, 277, 279, 281, 282, 361, see also British empiricists and associationists
Atkinson, J., 382
Atomism, 34, 209, 264, 283, 285
Australia, current psychology, 370

B

Babkin, B., 192
Bakan, D., 106, 195, 222, 324, 378
Baldwin, J. M., 146
Balz, A., 34
Barber, B., 320, 378
Beach, F., 257
Behaviorism, 11, 33, 106, 159, 160, 175–260, 262, 269, 270, 281, 283–285, 290, 291,

Behaviorism (*cont.*)
    295, 296, 318, 354, 355, 357, 358,
      360–362, 370, 371
  definition, 199, 207
Bekhterev, V. M., 189–190, 209, 378
Bentley, M., 106
Bergmann, G., 221, 222, 257, 378
Berkeley, G., 28–30, 35, 378
Binet, A., 148, 364
Birth order, 339–340
Bixenstine, V., 258
Blanshard, B., 258
Bleuler, E., 328
Boas, M., 27, 378
Boring, E. G., 2, 4, 5, 8, 13, 14, 17, 21,
    46, 52–54, 56, 59–61, 67, 69, 71, 72,
    80, 81, 85, 102, 106, 113, 126, 127,
    133, 139, 140, 151, 169, 173, 221,
    224, 229, 258, 267, 268, 270, 298,
    299, 311, 324–325, 354–355, 377, 378,
    381
Bower, G., 258
Braid, J., 300
Brain, role in learning, 226–227
Brazier, M., 54
Brebner, J., 376
Brentano, F., 11, 73–75, 80, 81, 262–263,
    303, 378
Breuer, J., 303–306, 311, 379
Bridgman, P. W., 227–229, 257, 322, 379
British empiricists and associationists,
    23–34, 40, 52, 55, 69, 209, 228, 254,
    262, 301
Broca, P., 38
Brown, J. A. C., 327, 351, 379
Brozek, J., 369, 376, 379
Brücke, E., 301–303, 319
Buckhout, R., 2, 58, 130, 382
Bugental, J., 371–373, 379
Bühler, C., 373, 376, 379
Bühler, K., 79
Burnham, J., 191–193, 195, 379
Burnham, W., 151
Burt, C., 209, 379
Butterfield, H., 34

C

Canada, current psychology, 370
Carmichael, L., 257

Carr, H., 11, 159–168, 171–173, 379
Catharsis, 304, 305
Cattell, J. McK., 2, 11, 59, 65, 81, 141,
    144–151, 153, 168, 180, 191, 192, 197,
    226, 308, 357, 364, 379
Chaplin, J., 2, 356, 357, 379
Charcot, J., 11, 300, 301, 304, 305
Chicago, University, 160, 171, 178, 196,
    225, 230
Childhood, influence on adult behavior,
    306, 307, 314–315, 317–318, 323,
    336–337, 339, 340, 342–344, 347–349
Child psychology, 105, 143, 267, 284, 286,
    290, 359
Choisy, M., 325
Clark, R., 382
Classical conditioning, *see* Conditioning
Clinical observation, 296, 312–313,
    321–322, 334, 344, 350
Clinical psychology, 350, 365
Cofer, C., 242, 344, 379
Cognitive map, 233, 234
Cognitive theory of learning (Tolman),
    233–234, 243
Collective unconscious, 330–331
Columbia University, 146–149, 168–170,
    180
Combs, A., 293
Comparative psychology, 125, 137, 178,
    179, 204–205, 230, 356, 362, *see also*
    Animal psychology
Compensation, 338
Comte, A., 11, 24, 102, 177, 379
Conditioned reflex, 186–188, 191, 207, 209,
    212, 227, 238, 260, 284
Conditioning, 186, 188–190, 208–210,
    212–215, 217, 226, 235, 238, 242, 243
Connectionism, 180–182
Conscience, 314
Consciousness, 87, 94–95, 109, 114, 133,
    135–136, 156–160, 164, 176–179,
    190–192, 200, 204, 206, 207, 218, 219,
    224, 225, 228, 230, 231, 239, 260,
    275–276, 284, 297, 298, 310, 311,
    313–315, 319, 330, 331, 337
  elements, 56, 60–62, 78–80, 89–91,
    98–100, 105, 108, 115, 260, 264, 265
Contiguity, 73, 213, 235, 243
Crannell, C., 292
Creative self, 339

Creative synthesis, 63, 262
Crovitz, H., 126
Crutchfield, R., 14
Cuny, H., 187, 192, 379

D

Dallenbach, K., 86, 379
Darwin, C., 10, 11, 68, 108–115, 117,
    124–127, 153, 181, 301, 324, 379
Darwin, E., 109, 111
Deese, J., 258
Defense mechanisms, 316, 323
De la Mettrie, J., 17, 379
Dennis, W., 151, 377
Descartes, R., 11, 17–24, 32, 34, 39, 115,
    124, 177
Determining tendency, 79, 80, 362
Determinism, 220, 254, 301, 318–319, 342,
    348, 357
Dewey, J., 11, 139, 141, 150, 154–157, 170,
    173, 196, 379
Diamond, S., 377
Diserens, C., 192
Dollard, J., 245
Donders, J., 64
Dreams, 307, 311, 331
Drever, J., 376, 377
Drive, 170, 224, 241–243, 250, 349, 362
    primary, 242, 243
    secondary, 242, 243
Drive reduction, 224, 250
du Bois-Reymond, E., 301, 319
Durant, A., 14, 379
Durant, W., 14, 379
Dynamic psychology (Woodworth), 170

E

Ebbinghaus, H., 68–73, 77, 80, 81, 379
Educational psychology, 143, 359
Effect, law, 179, 182, 213, 233, 236, 242
Ego, 314, 315, 320, 330, 349
Elementism, 155, 158, 262–265, 281, 283,
    285, 371
Ego-ideal, 315
Ellis, W., 292
Emotion, 134, 137–138, 199, 211, 213–214,
    360, 361
Empiricism, 17, 30, 34, 40, 235, 257

Empty-organism approach, 248, 371
Engineering psychology, 366
England, current psychology, 368
English empiricists and associationists, *see*
    British empiricists and association-
    ists
Environmentalism, 198, 212, 216, 257, 357,
    359
Eponymy, 13
Equipotentiality, law, 226
Esper, E., 5, 379
Eugenics, 118, 123
Evans, R., 248, 258, 350, 380
Evolution, 68, 109–115, 117, 123–125, 128,
    140, 142–143, 145, 149, 151, 156, 158,
    239, 301, 331, 362
Exercise, law, 182, 213
Extinction, 188, 249–251
Extirpation, 38, 39, 226
Extraversion, 332–333

F

Fearing, F., 54
Fechner, G., 40, 42, 46–54, 57, 69, 73,
    116, 295, 298, 380
Feigl, H., 34
Ferster, C. B., 252, 380
Field theory (Lewin), 285–290
Fitch, F. B., 381
Fixation, 316
Flourens, P., 38
Flugel, J., 2, 123–124, 280, 380
Folk psychology, *see* Social psychology
Fordham, F., 350
Franz, S., 226
Free association, 305–307, 310
Freeman, L., 303, 325, 380
Frequency, law, 213, 236, 242
Freud, A., 350
Freud, S., 10, 11, 74, 80, 142, 217, 295–299,
    301–325, 327–329, 332, 334–342, 344,
    347–349, 362, 365, 371, 372, 379, 380
Friedman, N., 358, 380
Fritsch, G., 39
Fromm, E., 11, 335, 340, 344–347, 380
Functionalism, 11, 77, 106–173, 175–179,
    191–192, 201, 259, 262, 269, 270, 295,
    296, 355, 357, 359, 361
    definition, 158–160

G

Galileo, 16, 27, 51, 254
Galton, F., 11, 65, 68, 108, 109, 115–124, 126, 127, 143, 146, 148, 149, 153, 246, 364, 368, 380
Ganz Amerikanisch, 145, 149–150, 367
Genetic psychology, 143
Germany, current psychology, 367–368
Gestalt psychology, 11, 23, 63, 74, 76, 80, 105, 106, 135, 159, 229, 230, 233, 259–293, 295–296, 355, 361
Gestalt qualitäten, 263, 272
Goldstein, K., 267
Goodfield, J., 35
Great man theory, *see* Personalistic theory of history
Group dynamics, 286, 289–290
Gruber, C., 147, 380
Gruhle, H., 267
Guthrie, E. R., 11, 235–237, 243, 258, 359, 380

H

Habit, 134, 138, 159, 202, 205–206
Habit formation, 205, 210
Habit strength, 243
Hale, N., 325
Hall, A. R., 34, 35
Hall, C., 312, 322, 325, 330, 334, 348, 349, 380
Hall, G. S., 2, 11, 139–144, 146, 150, 151, 153, 308, 380
Hall, M., 381
Hall, Marshall, 38
Hall, M. H., 245, 253, 380
Harper, R., 151
Harrison, R., 154, 173, 380
Hartley, D., 31–32, 39, 380
Hartmann, H., 351
Hebb, D., 257, 258, 361, 370, 376
Hedonism, 301
Heidbreder, E., 9, 49, 80–81, 105, 106, 133, 137, 154–155, 169, 171, 269–270, 323, 353–354, 381
Heider, F., 293
Helmholtz, H., 23, 40, 42–44, 46, 54, 57, 64, 75, 116, 301, 319, 324; 381
Helson, H., 293

Henle, M., 292, 293, 377
Henri, V., 148
Hentoff, N., 374, 381
Herbart, J., 11, 48, 298
Herrnstein, R. J., 13, 17, 113, 377, 381
Hetzel, C., 359, 381
Hetzel, M., 359, 381
Hilgard, E., 244, 258, 381
Hillix, W., 245, 382
Hitzig, E., 39
Hochberg, J., 293
Hodological space, 287, 288
Holt, E. B., 11, 223–224, 229, 381
Hooker, J., 111, 112
Horney, K., 11, 335, 340–344, 346, 350, 381
Hovland, C. I., 245, 381
Hull, C. L., 11, 224, 237–245, 247, 248, 250, 258, 359, 381
Hulse, S., 258
Humanism, 345
Humanistic psychology, 257, 370–376
Human subject, 88–89, 209, 358
Hume, D., 30–31, 381
Hypnosis, 238, 300, 301, 304, 305, 313, 325
Hypothetico–deductive method, 241
Hysteria, 300–301, 304–306

I

Id, 314, 315, 320, 349
Ideas, 23–26, 29–33, 298
Identification, 316
Imageless thought, 78
Individual differences, 68, 109, 115–124, 145, 146, 148–150
Individual psychology (Adler), 335–340
Industrial psychology, 356, 359, 365–366
Inferiority, 338–340
Insight, 280–282
Instinct, 211, 212, 219, 315–316, 342, 345, 347–349
death, 315, 342
life, 315, 342
Instinct theory (McDougall), 219
Instrumental conditioning, *see* Operant conditioning
Intervening variable, 231–234, 239, 241, 360

Introspection, 60–61, 66, 67, 73–80, 88,
　　89, 96–98, 101–106, 108, 133,
　　135–137, 145, 160, 164–165, 170, 173,
　　175–177, 191, 199, 200, 203–209, 212,
　　216, 219, 225, 229, 230, 263, 266, 269,
　　283, 284, 292
Introversion, 332–333
Irvine, W., 126
Isomorphism, 282–283
Iwahara, S., 376

J

Jacobi, J., 350
Jaensch, E., 264
Jahoda, M., 320, 325, 381
James, W., 2, 11, 67, 124, 128–141, 144,
　　150, 151, 153, 155, 157, 170, 173,
　　179, 180, 213, 261, 263–264, 308, 381
Janet, P., 11, 300–301
Japan, current psychology, 369
Jastrow, J., 150, 151
Jaynes, J., 377
Johnson, V., 324, 382
Joncich, G., 150, 180, 182, 183, 193, 381
Jones, E., 306, 308–311, 325, 381
Jung, C., 11, 142, 308, 327–334, 340, 344,
　　350, 381
Just noticeable difference, 45–46, 49, 51,
　　148

K

Kant, I., 11, 51, 102, 262
Katz, D., 264, 293
Kimble, G., 245
Kinkade, K., 254, 381
Kinsey, A., 324, 381
Koch, S., 258, 374, 381
Koenigsberger, L., 54
Koestler, A., 84, 381
Koffka, K., 11, 229, 265–268, 292, 381
Köhler, W., 11, 265–268, 270, 279–283,
　　285, 292, 381, 382
König, A., 71
Kovach, J., 2, 383
Krafft-Ebing, R., 306
Krawiec, T., 2, 356, 357, 379
Krech, D., 14
Kuhn, T. S., 8, 14, 382
Külpe, O., 11, 76–81, 85, 266, 382

L

Lachman, S., 54
Ladd, G., 54, 169
Lamarck, C. de, 110, 113
Lange, C., 138
Langfeld, H. S., 81, 378
Larson, C., 197, 198, 382
Lashley, K., 11, 225–227, 257, 382
Learning, 162, 179–183, 188, 206, 207,
　　211–213, 224–227, 231, 233–239,
　　242–243, 250, 277, 279, 281, 285, 291,
　　296, 320, 336, 348, 364
　current status, 109, 258, 359–362
　Gestalt principles, 278–282
　one-trial, 236–237
Leibnitz, G., 11, 297–298
Leipzig Laboratory, 58, 59, 61, 64–66,
　　71, 72, 74, 75, 77, 108, 109, 122,
　　127, 141, 144, 145
Lewin, K., 11, 285–290, 292, 361, 382
Libido, 314, 315, 329, 330, 332, 341, 348
Life space, 287, 288
Lindzey, G., 312, 322, 330, 334, 348, 349,
　　378, 380
Lippitt, R., 289, 382
Lockard, R., 126
Locke, J., 25–28, 30, 32, 35, 382
Loeb, J., 11, 178, 196
Lowell, E., 382
Lowry, R., 20, 27, 35, 39, 245, 382
Luce, A., 35
Ludwig, C., 301, 319
Lyell, C., 110–112

M

McClelland, D., 362, 382
MacCorquodale, K., 258
McDougall, W., 2, 34, 219–222, 382, 385
Mach, E., 11, 263, 382
McKellar, P., 106
MacLeod, R. B., 247, 382
Malthus, T., 113, 382
Marbe, K., 78
Margenau, H., 257
Marrow, A., 292
Marx, M., 245, 382
Maslow, A., 371, 375, 376, 382
Mass action, law, 226

Masters, W., 324, 382
Materialism, 24, 39, 40, 177, 178, 318
Matson, F. W., 35, 258, 382
Maudsley, H., 102
May, R., 5, 382
Maze, 179, 231, 233, 234, 281
Mechanism, 15–17, 26, 27, 31–35, 39, 40,
    88, 89, 177–179, 181, 209, 239, 240,
    254, 257, 264, 301, 318–319, 334, 371,
    374
Meehl, P., 258
Mental chemistry, 26
Mental illness, early treatment, 299–301
Mental imagery, 122
Mentalism, 29, 177, 190, 207, 210, 211,
    230, 234, 239, 257
Mental tests, 120–121, 123, 148, 149, 173,
    180, 355
Merton, R., 112, 382
Mesmer, F., 300
Mesmerism, 300
Miles, W., 173
Mill, James, 33, 382
Miller, G., 2, 58, 130, 183–184, 260–261,
    382
Miller, N., 245
Mind–body problem, 19–23, 34, 46–49,
    177
Miniature theory, 244, 357, 358, 360, 362
Monads, 297
Moorehead, A., 126
Morgan, C. L., 11, 125, 126, 178, 179, 190
Morgan, C. T., 257
Morgan, N., 28, 382
Morgulis, S., 179, 385
Motivation, 80, 170, 224, 242, 286, 357,
    359, 361, 362, 364
  current status, 362
  unconscious, 309, 318, 337, 338, 342,
    345, 350
Motivology, see Dynamic psychology
Mowrer, O., 245
Mueller, C. G., 237, 258, 383
Müller, G. E., 72–73, 81, 264
Müller, J., 37–38, 40, 57, 301, 383
Müller–Freienfels, R., 51, 383
Münsterberg, H., 132, 150
Murchison, C., 377
Murphy, G., 2, 66, 284, 376, 383

N

Nance, R., 3, 383
Naturalistic theory of history, 10–14
Nazi regime, 267, 268, 284, 286, 309–310,
    345, 367
Need-reduction theory, 243
Nelson, B., 325
Nerve–muscle preparation, 43
Netherlands, current psychology, 370
Nerve–muscle preparation, 43
Neurotic needs (Horney), 343–344
Newton, I., 16, 27, 254
Nissen, H., 257
Nonsense syllables, 70, 73, 205

O

Oedipus complex, 318, 329, 341, 342, 348
Ogden, R., 81
Operant conditioning, 249–250, 253–256,
    360, 363
Operationism, 227–229, 257, 320, 322, 357,
    358
Order of birth, see Birth order
Orgler, H., 351
Orne, M., 325
Orth, J., 78

P

Pavlov, I. P., 11, 12, 179, 183–190, 192,
    209, 213, 236, 238, 242, 249, 259,
    260, 359, 369, 383
Pearson, K., 119, 126
Perception, current status, 109, 359–362,
    364
Perceptual constancies, 269
Perceptual organization principles,
    277–278, 361
Perkins, D. T., 381
Perry, R. B., 67, 151, 383
Personalistic theory of history, 10–14
Personality, 285, 296, 309, 313–318, 320,
    330–333, 335–337, 339–344, 347–349,
    359–364
  current status, 362–363
Personal unconscious, 330–331
Peters, R. S., 2, 383
Phenomenology, 264, 292, 293

Phi phenomenon, 265, 266, 269, 282
Physiological psychology, 356, 363–364
Physiology, influence on psychology, 3, 21, 24, 37–54
Pillsbury, W., 192, 201, 383
Pirenne, M., 34
Planck, M., 8, 268, 383
Pleasure principle, 301, 314
Poffenberger, A., 151, 173
Polanyi, M., 375, 383
Positivism, 24, 102, 177, 178, 247, 255, 257, 307, 318, 334
Postman, L., 12, 193, 361, 383
Pragmatism, 137, 150, 156
Prentice, W. C. H., 292
Primary qualities, 27–28
Productive thinking (Wertheimer), 279, 281–282
Programmed learning, see Teaching machine
Projection, 316
Pseudo-problem, 227, 228, 322
Psychiatry, 19th century, 300–301
Psychic determinism, 301
Psychic reflex, see Conditioned reflex
Psychoanalysis, 11, 104, 160, 224, 260, 284, 295–351, 354–356, 363, 371
  conflicts with psychology, 319–320, 350, 356
  definition, 296
Psychological testing, current, 364–365
Psychopathology, 297–301
Psychophysics, 50–51, 64, 65, 73, 75, 105, 148, 159, 161, 163–164, 208, 210
Psychosexual stages of development, 317–318, 342, 347
Puglisi, M., 81
Punishment, 182, 250
Purposive behaviorism (Tolman), 230–234
Puzzle box, 181, 226, 231, 236, 237, 281

Q

Questionnaires, 122, 123, 143, 173
Quetelet, A., 119

R

Rachlin, H., 258
Rancurello, A., 81

Rand, B., 377
Rapaport, D., 325, 351
Reaction formation, 316
Reaction time, 64–65, 145, 148
Reality principle, 314
Reavis, L., 376
Recency, 213, 242
Reductionism, 155, 225, 240, 257, 283, 371
Reeves, W., 34
Reflex arc, 155–156, 227
Regression, 316
Reinforcement, 179, 188, 213, 233, 234, 236, 241–243, 249–252, 254, 360
  schedules, 250–252
Repression, 306, 310, 311, 316, 320
Resistance, 310, 311
Reward, 182, 233, 243
Rice, B., 253, 255, 383
Roback, A. A., 85, 383
Romanes, G. J., 11, 124–126, 178, 179, 190, 383
Rosenthal, R., 358, 383
Rosnow, R., 358, 383
Ross, D., 140, 142, 151, 383
Ross, R. T., 381
Rubin, E., 264
Ruckmick, C. A., 171, 383

S

Sahakian, W. S., 377
Sarton, G., 35, 177, 383
Scandinavian countries, current psychology, 370
Scarf, M., 336, 383
Scher, J., 34
Schizophrenia, 328, 365
Schlosberg, H., 169, 385
Schoenfeld, W. N., 237, 258, 383
Schools of thought
  definition, 7–10
  dissolution, 353–356
Schultz, D., 222, 358, 383
Schumann, F., 73
Schur, M., 309, 310, 325, 383
Secondary qualities, 27–28
Self-actualization, 332
Sensitivity training, 289–290
Set, see Determining tendency
Severin, F., 376

Sex, 304–308, 314, 315, 317–318, 324, 329, 330, 335, 337, 338, 340–342, 347, 348

Shakow, D., 81, 298, 319, 320, 325, 383

Sheehan, M., 169, 259, 355, 385

Shipley, T., 377

Shor, R., 325

Sidowski, J., 359, 383

Sign Gestalts, 233

Simon, T., 148

Simultaneous conditioning, 236

Skinner, B. F., 11, 198, 218, 221, 222, 245–259, 325, 359, 369, 380, 384

Skinner box, 249, 250, 253

Small, W., 179

Smith, M. B., 376

Snygg, D., 293

Social psychology, 59, 289–290, 334, 359, 364

Social–psychological theories in psychoanalysis, 334–349

Solso, R., 4, 384

Soviet Union, current psychology, 368–369

Spence, K., 245

Spirit of the times, 7, 10, 12, 41, 52, 56, 66, 72, 133, 256–257, 334, 341, *see also Zeitgeist*

Spontaneous recovery, 188

Statistical methods, 118–120, 123, 146, 238

Stevens, S., 54, 257

Stimulus error, 87, 103

Stimulus generalization, 188

Stimulus–response (S–R) connection, 155, 169, 180–182, 186–188, 190, 191, 209, 210, 224–226, 230, 232, 236, 239, 242–243, 249, 291, 320, 360, 371

Storr, A., 350

Stream of consciousness, 136

Striving for superiority (Adler), 337, 338

Stroboscope, 265, 268

Structuralism, 11, 52, 55–109, 115, 135, 150, 154, 158, 160, 170, 172, 173, 175, 176, 201, 230, 259, 260, 265, 266, 269, 277, 283, 295, 296, 299, 318, 353–355

Stumpf, C., 11, 74–76, 80, 81, 268, 384

Style of life, 338–339

Sublimation, 316

Sullivan, J., 197, 198, 377, 382

Superego, 314, 315

T

Teaching machine, 246, 253–254, 361

Tension reduction, 314

Tension-system, 288

Terman, L., 142

Thorndike, E. L., 11, 149, 168, 178–183, 193, 213, 226, 236, 242, 243, 250, 259, 279, 281, 359, 384

Titchener, E. B., 11, 55, 58, 67, 72, 79, 81, 83–107, 109, 116, 135, 136, 148, 153, 154, 158, 171, 172, 175, 191, 197, 209, 223, 229, 292, 295, 308, 354–355, 384

Tolman, E. C., 11, 224, 229–235, 243, 258, 285, 359, 384

Topology, 287, 288

Toulmin, S., 35

Transference, 304, 311

Tridimensional theory of feeling, 62, 63, 65, 78

Tropism, 178, 233

Turner, F. J., 128, 384

Turner, M., 102, 228, 229, 384

Two-point threshold, 44–45, 148

Tyler, L., 376

U

Unconscious, 297–298, 307, 313–315, 319, 323, 324, 330–333, 337, 342

Utilitarianism, 301

Uttal, W., 359, 384

V

Valence, 287, 288

Verbal behavior (Skinner), 252–253

Verbal report, 207–209, 219, 221

Vierordt, 50

Volkmann, A., 50

Von Ehrenfels, C., 11, 74, 263, 266, 272

Vorzimmer, P., 126

W

Wallace, A. R., 111, 112

Wallach, H., 268, 382

Wann, T., 258, 293

Warden, C., 126, 192

Warner, L. H., 192

Warren, R. M., 54

Warren, R. P., 54

Watson, J. B., 10, 11, 176–179, 183, 189, 191, 192, 195–227, 229–231, 235, 239, 244, 247, 254, 256, 257, 279, 284, 295, 355, 357, 359, 372, 384, 385

Watson, R. I., 2, 4, 52, 122, 207, 317, 356, 385

Watt, H., 78, 79

Weber, E., 40, 44–46, 48, 49, 52, 116, 205

Weber–Fechner law, 49

Weiss, A., 224–225, 385

Werner, H., 378

Wertheimer, Max, 11, 265–268, 271–279, 281–282, 285, 292, 295, 385

Wertheimer, Michael, 5–6, 385

West, D., 2, 123–124, 280, 380

White, A. D., 19, 113, 385

White, R., 289, 382

Whitehead, A., 35

Whyte, L., 325

Wish fulfillment, 311

Wollheim, R., 325

Wolman, B., 65, 237–238, 244–245, 344, 347, 385

Woodworth, R. S., 11, 54, 149, 151, 168–170, 173, 189, 211, 216, 222, 231, 259, 355, 385

Word association, 65, 122, 333

Wundt, W., 2, 7–8, 11, 23, 40, 42, 51–69, 71–81, 83–85, 88–91, 102–104, 107, 109, 116, 122, 127, 128, 131–133, 135, 136, 139–142, 144, 145, 150, 153, 154, 158, 173, 175, 177, 188, 191, 195, 209, 229, 254, 259–262, 264–266, 269, 271, 283, 284, 292, 295, 299, 359, 367, 385

Würzburg school, 73, 77–81, 91, 362

Y

Yerkes, R., 178, 179, 206, 225, 378, 385

Young, T., 43

Z

Zeigarnik, B., 288–289

Zeitgeist, 12–14, 16, 17, 54, 55, 110, 127, 192, 218, 264, 298, 324, 334, 373, 374, *see also* Spirit of the times